A HISTORIAN FOR ALL SEASONS

A HISTORIAN FOR ALL SEASONS

Essays for Geoffrey Bolton

Edited by
Stuart Macintyre,
Lenore Layman and
Jenny Gregory

© Copyright 2017
© Copyright of this collection in its entirety is held by the editors, Stuart Macintyre, Lenore Layman and Jenny Gregory.
© Copyright of the individual chapters is held by the respective authors.
All rights reserved. Apart from any uses permitted by Australia's Copyright Act 1968, no part of this book may be reproduced by any process without prior written permission from the copyright owners. Inquiries should be directed to the publisher.

Monash University Publishing
Matheson Library and Information Services Building
40 Exhibition Walk
Monash University
Clayton, Victoria 3800, Australia
www.publishing.monash.edu

Monash University Publishing brings to the world publications which advance the best traditions of humane and enlightened thought.

Monash University Publishing titles pass through a rigorous process of independent peer review.

www.publishing.monash.edu/books/has-9781925495607.html

Series: Australian History
Series Editor: Sean Scalmer

Design: Les Thomas

Cover image: Brian Richards

National Library of Australia Cataloguing-in-Publication entry:

Title:	A historian for all seasons : essays for Geoffrey Bolton / edited by Stuart Macintyre, Lenore Layman, Jenny Gregory.
ISBN:	9781925495607 (paperback)
Subjects:	Bolton, G. C. (Geoffrey Curgenven), 1931-2015
	Festschriften--Australia.
	Essays.
	Australia--History.
Other Creators/Contributors:	
	Macintyre, Stuart, 1947- editor.
	Layman, Lenore, editor.
	Gregory, Jenny, editor.

Printed in Australia by Griffin Press an Accredited ISO AS/NZS 14001:2004 Environmental Management System printer.

The paper this book is printed on is certified against the Forest Stewardship Council ® Standards. Griffin Press holds FSC chain of custody certification SGS-COC-005088. FSC promotes environmentally responsible, socially beneficial and economically viable management of the world's forests.

CONTENTS

Notes on Contributors.. vii

Abbreviations x

Introduction xi

Chapter 1   Geoffrey Bolton: A Lifetime of History................. 1
Stuart Macintyre

Chapter 2   History at Home, or How Do You Know That's True? 40
Carol Bolton

Chapter 3   'The Character Business': Biographical Political Writing in Australia....................................... 48
Mark McKenna

Chapter 4   'Yarning in the Street': The Evolution of Australian Public History...................................... 71
Graeme Davison

Chapter 5   Geoffrey Bolton and the British World 97
Carl Bridge

Chapter 6   'Do unto others': Australia and the Anglican Conscience, 1840–56 and Afterwards 113
Alan Atkinson

Chapter 7   *Spoils and Spoilers:* Geoffrey Bolton's Environmental History 141
Andrea Gaynor and Tom Griffiths

Chapter 8   The Peripatetic Professor and a Sense of Place 171
             Jenny Gregory

Chapter 9   'The North': Colonial Hegemony and Indigenous
             Stratification 204
             Tim Rowse and Elizabeth Watt

Chapter 10   Fear, Affection and *Wurnan*: Reframing Station History
             in the Kimberley through Jack Wherra's Art 236
             Mary Anne Jebb

Chapter 11   The Challenges of Family Ageing 1920–64: Nettie and
             Vance Palmer 270
             Pat Jalland

Chapter 12   Western Australian Entrepreneurism: The Life of
             Deborah Hackett 295
             Lenore Layman

Works by Geoffrey Bolton 332

NOTES ON CONTRIBUTORS

Alan Atkinson completed his Ph.D. at the Australian National University in 1976, and Geoff Bolton gave him his first academic job in the following year, as a tutor at Murdoch University, an appointment that shaped his life. He has just completed the third and final volume of *The Europeans in Australia*, and moved back to Western Australia.

Carol Bolton knew Geoffrey Bolton for fifty-nine years and was married to him for fifty-seven. She read English at Oxford and tutored at Monash and the University of Western Australia before retraining as a clinical psychologist and analytic psychotherapist. She had a private practice. She still does a little teaching and supervision.

Carl Bridge as a spotty undergraduate first heard Geoffrey Bolton give a superlative seminar paper at the University of Sydney in 1970, and he took over the reins of the Menzies Centre for Australian Studies at the University of London in 1997, fifteen years after Geoffrey had been its inspirational first head. Carl's *Australia in Peace and War, 1914–18*, a documentary collection co-edited and co-written with David Lee and Jatinder Mann, will appear in 2018.

Graeme Davison first encountered Geoff in 1961 when he came as a guest lecturer to Allan Martin's Australian History class at Melbourne University. Forty years later they became historical advisors to the National Museum of Australia. Davison's latest books are *Lost Relations: Fortunes of My Family in Australia's Golden Age* (2015) and *City Dreamers: The Urban Imagination in Australia* (2016).

A HISTORIAN FOR ALL SEASONS

Andrea Gaynor enjoyed Geoff's avuncular leadership on several committees and remembers *Spoils and Spoilers* as a formative text in her career as an environmental historian. Her forthcoming book, *Big Skies: Land, People and History in Australia's Mallee Country*, co-authored with Katie Holmes, Richard Broome and Charles Fahey, will be published by Monash University Publishing.

Jenny Gregory co-authored *Claremont: A History* with Geoff and remains grateful for his generosity towards a junior colleague who had criticised his view of Western Australia's interwar years. Her research focuses on urban history and heritage, but her most recent book is *Seeking Wisdom: A Centenary History of the University of Western Australia*.

Tom Griffiths first met Geoff Bolton at his lecture on regional history ('The Belly and the Limbs') at the Royal Historical Society of Victoria in 1982, and worked with him for almost two decades on the Editorial Board of the *Australian Dictionary of Biography*. His most recent book is *The Art of Time Travel: Historians and Their Craft*.

Pat Jalland was inspired by Geoff Bolton as a colleague at Murdoch University. Her most recent publication is *Old Age in Australia: A History*, which Geoff was delighted to see included west coast history. Her recent research has focused on the history of old age, death and bereavement.

Mary Anne Jebb was a member of Geoffrey's late Friday afternoon honours group at Murdoch University in 1986, which combined the best of Oxbridge traditions with the Murdoch University ethos: rigorous, voluble debate, and sherry. She creates multi-media histories from oral history recordings and recently co-edited *Long History, Deep Time: Deepening Histories of Place*.

NOTES ON CONTRIBUTORS

Lenore Layman enjoyed being a colleague of Geoff Bolton at Murdoch University. She has most recently published *Blood Nose Politics: A Centenary History of the WA National Party*, worked on the Australian Asbestos Network website on the health disaster of asbestos use in Australia, and is currently busy on a variety of community history projects.

Stuart Macintyre was recruited to Murdoch University by Geoffrey Bolton in 1976 and worked with him on the *Oxford History of Australia*. His most recent publication is *Australia's Boldest Experiment: War and Reconstruction in the 1940s*, and he is completing a study of what has happened to Australia's universities.

Mark McKenna is Professor of History at the University of Sydney. He has published widely in Australian political history, biography and Indigenous history. His most recent book is *From the Edge: Australia's Lost Histories*.

Tim Rowse is an Emeritus Professor at Western Sydney University. He has researched Aboriginal history since the early 1980s – focusing at first on colonial authority in central Australia, before moving on to deal with the national political story. He has recently finished a book about Australia's dealings with Indigenous Australians since Federation.

Elizabeth Watt is a Research Fellow at Deakin University. She has recently completed a Ph.D. in anthropology at the Australian National University. Her thesis, which began as a study of the reception of the Cape York Welfare Reform Trial in Hope Vale, explores class-based differences that have emerged within Aboriginal society since colonisation.

ABBREVIATIONS

ABC	Australian Broadcasting Commission
ADB	*Australian Dictionary of Biography*
AIATSIS	Australian Institute of Aboriginal and Torres Strait Islander Studies
AMP	Australian Mutual Provident Society
ANU	Australian National University
BDC	Barracks Defence Council
CYWRT	Cape York Welfare Reform Trials
CHOGM	Commonwealth Heads of Government Meeting
KLC	Kimberley Land Council
NLA	National Library of Australia
PD	Police Department
PHA	Professional Historians Association
R & I Bank	Rural and Industries Bank of Western Australia
SLWA	State Library of Western Australia
SROWA	State Records Office of Western Australia
UTS	University of Technology, Sydney
UWA	University of Western Australia

INTRODUCTION

Geoffrey Bolton was the most versatile and widely travelled of his generation of Australian historians. After completing an undergraduate degree at the University of Western Australia he undertook research on the pastoral industry in the State's Kimberley region for a Master of Arts. A scholarship allowed him to study overseas, and he followed many before in choosing Balliol College in Oxford. Keith Hancock recruited him to the burgeoning Institute of Advanced Studies at the Australian National University in 1958 and after that he was an early appointment to Monash University, one of the first of new universities created in an era of growth and experiment. He returned in 1966, at the age of thirty-five, to a chair at the University of Western Australia, but in 1973 was attracted once more to pioneering in a new university, Murdoch. The stint there lasted nearly two decades, punctuated by three years establishing the Australian Studies Centre in London, and in 1989 he accepted a chair at the University of Queensland. His final academic post was back in Perth at Edith Cowan University, though following retirement he became the Chancellor of Murdoch University.

Geoffrey had a deep attachment to his native Western Australia. It gave him early opportunities: as a student he was recruited to the council of the State's historical society, helped edit the principal literary journal and contributed scripts to the ABC's local radio station. From his return in the late 1960s he was in constant demand for all manner of tasks, and in retirement he wrote and spoke of Western Australia's heritage with an authority and public recognition unparalleled in any other part of the country. Yet his ambitions required him to travel and his interests were always far wider than one State, so throughout his academic career he continued to look elsewhere. He eagerly accepted invitations to sit on national committees, and applied repeatedly (although selectively) for chairs in the east. 'I have practised history largely as a provincial', he declared, seeing that location as allowing an independent perspective at the cost of greater recognition.[1]

His career exemplifies the dynamics of the history profession. He commenced studies in one of the six tiny departments in Australia's foundational universities; by the 1970s there were more than five hundred tenured historians working in large departments that supported a rich variety of teaching and research; and then, with the reworking of universities at the end of the 1980s, the place of history as an integral part of a liberal education could no longer be assumed. He began as 'young Geoffrey' in an enclosed masculine hierarchy practising a tightly prescribed discipline. He experienced the student radicalism of the late 1960s with discomfort, welcomed the broadening of access to higher education, encountered resistance from colleagues in his attempts to enlarge the curriculum, remained ill at ease with theoretical incursions, was drawn into university administration, and was angered by the philistinism of the corporate university. Despite all the distractions, he continued to perform those supernumerary tasks that sustain the discipline – thesis examination, manuscript assessment, book reviews – and as contemporaries became more protective of their time he kept up attendance at conferences and workshops, invariably interested and supportive. He continued to introduce himself as Geoffrey, though happily accepted

---

1   Geoffrey Bolton, 'A Provincial Viewpoint', in Bruce Bennett (ed.), *Australia In Between Cultures: Specialist Session Papers from the 1998 Australian Academy of the Humanities Symposium* (Canberra: Australian Academy of Humanities, 1999), p. 79.

INTRODUCTION

the common contraction to Geoff. For a younger generation he was a father figure of a particularly sympathetic kind.

Over sixty years Geoffrey produced a remarkable body of work. His first book was an expanded version of the B.A. honours thesis on Alexander Forrest (1958), and later biographies of Richard Boyer (1967), Edmund Barton (2000) and Paul Hasluck (2014), as well as his volume in the *Oxford History of Australia* (1990), testify to a sustained interest in politics and public life.[2] The influence of Lewis Namier was apparent in close attention to networks of patronage and influence in his study of *The Passing of the Irish Act of Union* (1966), and his fascination with the intricate pedigrees of landed society found expression in an essay on 'The Idea of a Colonial Gentry' (1968). A survey of *Britain's Legacy Overseas* (1973) anticipated a later vogue for 'the British World'. He was an early exponent of oral history, especially in his Depression study *A Fine Country to Starve In*, and applied it to his own childhood in *Daphne Street* (1997). The early study of the Kimberley (1954) was followed by a regional history of North Queensland (1963), and an appreciation of the consequences of indiscriminate economic development yielded his pioneering environmental history, *Spoils and Spoilers* (1981). This is to say nothing of the commissioned institutional histories, edited works, articles, chapters, the ninety-one contributions to the *Australian Dictionary of Biography*, occasional works and many other pieces produced to meet the requests he so seldom refused.

This volume of essays testifies to the breadth of Geoffrey's scholarship, the influence that he exerted across a number of fields and the warm affection in which he was held. It was conceived when the

---

2   Details of all these publications are given in the list of 'Works by Geoffrey Bolton' at the end of this volume.

three editors gathered for his funeral in Perth in 2015, and from sharing memories we turned to the goal of producing a collection that would explore his legacy. We invited contributions from scholars who shared his interests and encouraged each to take his work as a starting-point for a broader essay on that branch of history. Our purpose was not so much a detailed examination of Geoffrey's own work, though there is plenty of that, as to follow how lines of inquiry that he pursued have been extended. Most of the contributors were longstanding friends and colleagues of Geoffrey, while some had only limited contact. It is indicative of the warm regard for him that all we approached were keen to participate. We think he would have enjoyed the collection, which is offered as a tribute.

The volume opens with a biographical essay that considers Geoffrey's intellectual formation and extended career. He was one of a distinguished generation of historians who began their education during the 1930s in the shadow of the Depression. Scholarships enabled them to attend university after World War II and complete training overseas. They established their careers in the 1950s and in doing so put Australian history at the forefront of the academic profession. Geoffrey was a leader of this transformation, notable for his versatility and readiness to take up new opportunities. Stuart Macintyre's essay considers the advantages and disadvantages of an academic life lived for long periods on the geographic periphery of the national conversation, though also one that allowed him to mark out an independent perspective of 'the middle way'. The biographical account draws attention to highs and lows as Geoffrey undertook so many activities beyond the university, always wanting to increase the understanding and appreciation of the past. History, for him, was more than an academic pursuit.

INTRODUCTION

In the following essay Carol Bolton recalls conversations with her husband on how we make sense of the past. He was, as she testifies, a man with an all-consuming vocation: among overtures to a prospective wife, an inquiry about her family's papers is uncommon. She relates also how, when she was collecting stories of her family, his instinct was to document them and hers to ponder why the stories had been passed on. Geoffrey found his vocation through archival research and his inclination was to gather information as the basis of historical explanation. By his own admission, he was mistrustful of theory. 'How could you generalise', he asked, 'until you gathered all the data?'[3] But the conversations between them, especially after Carol retrained as a psychotherapist and he worked on his later biographies, suggest a growing understanding that the archives raise as many questions as they answer. Carol's original discipline was literature and Geoffrey's history writing was enriched by his own study of English (he taught it before going to Oxford) and literary imagination. An easy conversationalist and an attentive listener, he excelled in characterisation of all manner of historical actors.

After these opening essays, the remainder take up areas of Geoffrey's research, writing and public activity. Mark McKenna introduces his examination of the current vogue among politicians for publishing memoirs and diaries by recalling a conversation with Geoffrey at the last conference he attended in 2015, one organised by the National Centre of Biography at the ANU, the home of the *Australian Dictionary of Biography*. Geoff had been present at the *ADB*'s creation in the 1950s; he chaired its Western Australian working party and provided entries for every one of the nineteen volumes that have appeared so far. Characteristically, Geoffrey expressed

---

3   'A Provincial Viewpoint', p. 81.

enthusiasm for Mark's project and criticism of the self-serving nature of so many political testaments. His own scepticism about politicians' use of history was evident in a deft essay of 'Two Pauline Versions' of the Menzies era (1995), one by Paul Hasluck and the other by Paul Keating. Mark draws our attention to the way the rash of publications by politicians marks a withdrawal of politics from policy to personality.

Graeme Davison considers Geoffrey as a public historian, a title he did not claim but an activity he practised alongside the turn by academically trained historians to employment outside the university. This essay considers the impulses for such activity, its rewards and the disputes that can arise between public historians and those wanting to promulgate a different understanding of the past. Davison also draws attention to history's public purpose, and the way it can provide understanding and enable better choices about the future.

Like many other Australian history graduates of his generation, Geoffrey pursued further study in Oxford. Most intended to return and pursue careers here and most did. Apart from his teachers John Legge and Frank Crowley, they included Geoffrey Serle, Hugh Stretton and Ken Inglis. Geoffrey did not see his return as final and for some time pursued British as well as Australian history. Study leave at the University of Kent enabled him to write a revisionist account of *Britain's Legacy Overseas* (1972), which Carl Bridge sees as anticipating the reorientation of imperial history from the metropolitan centre to an appreciation of the patterns of movement and exchange across 'the British World'. Bridge also explains Geoffrey's foundational role in reciprocating the intellectual traffic as head of the Australian Studies Centre in London from its establishment in 1982 until 1985.

INTRODUCTION

Alan Atkinson takes his point of departure from Geoffrey's work on the journals of an Anglican archdeacon, John Ramsden Wollaston, ministering in the infant colony of Western Australia. His efforts to provide spiritual and social leadership there had limited success, but Atkinson draws our attention to the activities of wealthy landed Anglican laymen in New South Wales in the years between the suspension of convict transportation in 1840 and the levelling effects of the gold rush in the 1850s. He traces their ideas of an orderly, improved and caring social order back to the theological currents of the Oxford Movement in England and new ideas of conscience and mutuality. The impulse for improvement found particular expression in the creation of the University of Sydney.

Andrea Gaynor and Tom Griffiths put Geoffrey at the centre of their essay on environmental history. They suggest that his book *Spoils and Spoilers* (1981) was the first attempt to synthesise a growing body of work on different aspects of the subject and also rode the wave of an increasing concern for the consequences of human habitation of Australia. Geoffrey made good use of the findings of scientists, historical geographers and archaeologists, though he added his own appreciation of nature writing. He attested to the destructive consequences of greed and ignorance, while affirming the capacity of Australians to learn from their mistakes. As Gaynor and Griffiths explain, he also brought an historical intelligence to the subject, giving his book a keen awareness of local and regional difference as well as a temporal dimension and attention to changing sensibilities.

Jenny Gregory's subsequent essay on the history of place illustrates the potency of public history. She writes of the deep attachment to suburbs, streets, neighbourhoods and buildings as sites of memory and the conflicts that can arise when they are threatened.

In examining three instances of the concern for place in Perth, she demonstrates the variety of public history practice and brings out Geoffrey as a particular kind of public historian, first in defending the heritage of Perth and then, after much soul-searching, accepting the attachment of his name to its redevelopment at Elizabeth Quay.

Geoffrey's Western Australian location led him early into one of the most fruitful of his subjects – the history of northern Australia and its people – to which he returned numerous times throughout his career. Across half a century he became increasingly aware that the historical conventions in which he was trained disabled him from exploring and understanding Aboriginal peoples' history, and late in life he planned further work on the north to pursue his shift in thinking and approach. Two essays in this volume make Aboriginal experience their central subject and show how northern history is transformed by this shift.

Tim Rowse and Lizzie Watt observe that Geoffrey wrote two regional histories, first of the north of Western Australia and then of North Queensland. He treated them separately, seeing them as shaped by the relationship with the more populous south of their respective States, and discerned different outcomes for their Indigenous peoples – though together they suggested that the history written from Melbourne and Sydney did not hold for the top half of the country. Rowse and Watt use this as a point of departure for their historical account of race-based status difference among Indigenous Australians, analysing the languages of unity and distinction that were central to colonial practices and have continued resonance to this day.

Their essay is complemented by one from Mary Anne Jebb, who worked with Geoffrey in the 1990s on an unpublished study of the

INTRODUCTION

Kimberley cattle industry. Geoffrey reflected in an essay at that time, 'Portrait of the Historian as a Young Learner' (1994), on the limits of his understanding of race relations in the industry. If he discerned the reliance on Aboriginal labour, especially among the battling smallholders who lived with Aboriginal women, he had been too reliant on the official record and the testimony of the station owners. Here Jebb uses the remarkable pictures carved onto boab nuts by Jack Wherra, a Ngarinyin man, that document the turbulent relations between white men and Aboriginals, the ways they regulated their relationships and above all the way that his people drew the white men into their system of personal and social obligations.

The final two essays take up a form of history that Geoffrey practised so assiduously. Ill at ease with generalisations about structure and agency, he was drawn to study how individuals worked out their lives in specific circumstances. So too Pat Jalland's books on ageing and death go beyond policies and institutions to explore the lived experience of old age and bereavement. In this essay she takes up the common practice whereby women took responsibility for elderly relatives. First she shows the writer and critic Nettie Palmer caring for her mother and aunts, and then the strains on her ailing husband Vance and troubled daughter Aileen as her own condition deteriorated. This study sheds light on the sacrifices that women were expected to make even as institutional provision began.

While Geoffrey turned his hand with success to a wide variety of historical topics, it was in biographical mode that he seems to have been most at home. He enjoyed his contributions to the *Australian Dictionary of Biography*, delighted in uncovering snippets to add to the narratives he was piecing together and remained committed to the importance of the *ADB* enterprise over the decades. Lenore Layman has taken up one biographical project that Geoffrey very much looked forward to tackling in retirement but did not live to realise – a study of Deborah Drake-Brockman, aka Lady Hackett, Lady Moulden and Dr Deborah Buller Murphy. Layman situates this enterprising woman in her Western Australian colonial context, examining how Geoffrey and fellow historians have interpreted that State history. A woman and mining entrepreneur, Deborah was not a typical subject for Geoffrey's pen, yet her biography illuminates some key themes in Western Australian history.

The editors are most grateful for the encouragement and assistance of Geoffrey's family in undertaking this publication – Carol, Patrick and Matthew. We also acknowledge Brian Richards, who took the photograph that appears on the cover and has given his permission to reproduce it.

Chapter 1

GEOFFREY BOLTON

A Lifetime of History

Stuart Macintyre

Why did a boy growing up in suburban Perth in the 1930s and 1940s become a historian? Many years after he had done so, Geoffrey identified a number of influences. 'My interest in history began with my father', he stated in the last of his reminiscences, and recalled books of history and biography in the family home. Then there was his mother's fondness for the historical romances of Georgette Heyer, Jeffrey Farnol and the Baroness Orczy, which supplemented his reading of R.M. Ballantyne, Arthur Conan Doyle, John Buchan and soon Walter Scott. At secondary school there was the teacher who informed him: 'You know, there are people called university lecturers who do nothing except teach and write history'.[1]

Thanks for information and insights to Patrick Bolton, Bill Bunbury, Graeme Davison, Brian de Garis, Jenny Gregory, Lenore Layman, Ged Martin, Clive Moore, Doug Munro, and, above all, Carol Bolton.

1 Diary, 21, 23 December 2014. In a series of entries at this time, probably prompted by a premonition of failing health, he set down a fuller account of his early life than given in earlier memoirs and oral histories. The diaries are held by Carol Bolton.

That prospect excited an exceptionally able pupil who would win the State exhibitions in English and History in the Leaving examinations of 1947 and was already known among classmates as 'the professor'. His talent was evident at a very young age. 'Six-year-old North Perth Boy Knows All the Answers', a popular weekly newspaper proclaimed during his first year at the local primary school. This prodigy had the uncanny ability to give the day of the week for any date, knew the years of battles and treaties, and took an informed interest in international affairs. After a psychology lecturer at the university confirmed Geoffrey's precocious intelligence, his parents allowed him to demonstrate it to the newspaper providing he was not named. The precaution failed. A 'lightly built blue-eyed boy' living in North Perth with encyclopaedias as his favourite reading was readily identifiable, and Geoffrey was already marked out by a lack of physical coordination that handicapped him at sport. Having been put up a year and already top of the class, he was mocked as 'Nuts and Bolts' and bullied. He learned how to deal with this by clowning and 'being a bit of a wag'.[2]

Geoffrey's parents had come as children from England. His father, Frank Bolton, was born in an outlying suburb of London, Walton-on-Thames, and migrated with his parents to New Zealand. After lack of means thwarted an aspiration to become a teacher, he travelled after World War I to Australia to look up another family from Walton-on-Thames, the Ransleys. They had farmed at Pingelly but were now living in Perth and there Frank Bolton married his childhood friend Winifred Ransley. Geoffrey, born on Guy Fawkes Day 1931, was their first child after a stillbirth; another son, Roger,

---

2   Perth *Mirror*, 24 September 1938; Geoffrey Bolton, interviewed by Stuart Reid, July 1994 – March 1995, State Library of Western Australia OH2618, transcript, p. 5.

CHAPTER 1

followed six years later. Frank worked as senior clerk for a motorcycle firm. Initially the family rented in North Perth and in 1939 they were able to put down the deposit on a modest cottage in nearby Daphne Street. Winifred's widowed father, Fred Ransley, who lived with them, also worked as a clerk.

They lived plainly, on good terms with their neighbours and without close involvement in local affairs. Grandfather Ransley was a Tory whose reminiscences went back to England in the 1890s and in family lore to his grandfathers and grand-uncles who were smugglers on the Romney Marsh in the 1820s, one of them transported to Van Diemen's Land. Frank Bolton became active in the Anglican church during the 1940s and his interest in history was oriented to the establishment: according to Geoffrey, he was a great authority on the numerous progeny of Queen Victoria, and Geoffrey himself by the age of eight could recite the regnal dates of English monarchs – as throughout his life he could passages from Charles Dickens's *A Child's History of England.* His mother identified strongly with England. At school there were stories of Australian explorers and excerpts from Lawson and Paterson in the class readers; at home he listened to the radio serial 'Dad and Dave'. These made much less of an impression.

Geoffrey finished primary school a year early, in 1942, and won a scholarship to Wesley College. A year later he was eligible to sit for one of the State's secondary scholarships, and succeeded. These were usually tenable at Perth Modern School but his mother favoured him staying on at the private school, so the government scholarship was transferred there. Wesley College, near the banks of the Swan River in South Perth, was a late addition to the leading Anglican, Presbyterian and Catholic secondary schools, with a strong Methodist ethos and a clientele wealthier than the Boltons. Geoffrey took three languages, French, German and Latin, in addition to History, English and Mathematics. The study of Latin sharpened his prose with the quality of 'vivid succinctness', while from his own reading of Gibbon he picked up a 'lifelong interest in the versatility of the semi-colon and a feel for the anticlimactic adjective'. Already he wanted to write history: while still fourteen he began a series of biographies of Australian prime ministers – the one on Barton would be completed more than half a century later. It was the history teacher, Roy ('Boxer') Collins, who told him that there were academic careers and also put him in charge of cataloguing the school library. He completed his schooling in 1947 with distinctions in History, English, Latin and German.[3]

When Geoff began at the University of Western Australia in 1948 he was one of just under 2000 students; the number fell as ex-servicemen and women studying under the Commonwealth Reconstruction Training Scheme completed their courses, and even when he left for Oxford in 1954 the enrolment had not recovered. At school, as 'a gawky adolescent, troubled with pimples', he had lacked social confidence. Now, thrown into the company of those who suffered no such inhibition – his contemporaries included Bob Hawke, Max Newton, Peter Durack and Billy Snedden – he found his feet. Midway through his first year he became assistant editor of the student newspaper, *Pelican*, and in the following year he was the editor with John Stone as business manager and Rolf Harris drawing cartoons.[4]

---

[3] 'Scholarships', *The West Australian*, 23–24 September 1943; Diary, 23 December 2014; Reid interview, p. 14; Student Record, University of Western Australia.

[4] David S. Macmillan, *Australian Universities: A Descriptive Sketch* (Sydney: Sydney University Press, 1968), p. 77, Appendix 4; Geoffrey Bolton, 'The History of the Historian', in Rae Frances and Bruce Scates (eds), *The Murdoch Ethos: Essays in Australian History in Honour of Foundation Professor Geoffrey Bolton* (Perth: Murdoch University, 1989), p. 271.

CHAPTER 1

The Arts degree involved nine subjects, including two three-year disciplinary sequences (or majors), and an optional fourth honours year. He chose History and English as his majors, with Philosophy, German and Economics the supplementary subjects. The head of the History Department was Fred Alexander, an energetic generalist who had run the show since the 1920s but attained professorial status only in the year Geoffrey arrived. Paul Hasluck held a readership to work on the official war history, but did no teaching and went into parliament at the end of 1949. John Legge was a tough-minded young Melbourne graduate with interests in historical theory and the Asia-Pacific, more rigorous than Josh Reynolds, senior tutor at a residential college and a part-time lecturer who taught the first-year course in Tudor and Stuart history – Geoffrey recalled how this 'picturesque old don' was able to scratch both his head and his backside and give a lecture at the same time. That was the only subject in which he failed to achieve an A but in his second year he had a clean sweep of Bs and Fred Alexander suggested he shed the extracurricular distractions.[5]

It was presumably for this reason that he dropped out of a national quiz in 1950. He had won a Perth radio competition on historical knowledge in his last year at school, pipping John Wheeldon, but the one conducted in 1950 tested general knowledge and was open to all-comers. Geoffrey finished well ahead of the field in the State final, when the press was astounded by him knowing the name of a trawler stolen from its berth in Hull in 1936 and navigated with the aid of a school atlas as it wandered the Atlantic; the crew printed

---

5   Diary, 25 December 2014, 2 January 2015; see Brian de Garis, 'The Department of History in the University of Western Australia, 1913–1965', *Studies in Western Australian History*, 8 (1988), esp. pp. 12–16.

postage stamps when they reached Guyana and Geoffrey remembered the *Girl Pat* from his stamp-collecting childhood. But the national final was conducted by radio hook-up in the first week of the academic year without him.[6] He resigned his editorship of *Pelican* in May of that year, though not before attending a conference of university student newspapers in Melbourne. He had his friend David Hutchison, president of the Student Guild, propose such a meeting to the National Union of Australian University Students, nominating Perth as the venue in the calculated expectation it would prefer Melbourne. His counterpart there, Geoffrey Blainey, wrote to say he saw no need for such a conference and, in an unlikely anticipation of their debate over the tyranny of distance, Geoffrey Bolton replied that he would if he lived in Perth.

The meeting of editors was Geoff's first trip outside Western Australia and made a strong impression. Melbourne, in a grey late autumn, had the ambience of a large city with intellectual amenities absent from Perth, and he was already conscious of the History Department that Max Crawford had created. Looking back, he came to feel that the intellectual stimulation it provided, not to mention 'that enormous self-confidence that Melbourne people have about their own city', put him five years behind contemporaries such as Geoff Blainey and Ken Inglis. While we should not take too seriously his profession of a 'fierce jealousy' of their advantages, the feeling that reputations were established and judgments determined in the southeast corner of the continent would oppress him in later years.[7]

---

6   Diary, 24 December 2014; 'Stamps Helped Him To Win Quiz', *The West Australian*, 27 February 1950; 'Inter-State Men in Quiz Team', *The Age*, 7 March 1950.

7   Bolton, 'A Provincial Viewpoint', p. 81; Reid interview, p. 34.

CHAPTER 1

He achieved an A in both History III and English III, and his fourth-year honours thesis secured a first-class degree. Since the thesis was to be based on archival sources, the topic was restricted to Western Australian history and Geoffrey chose Alexander Forrest because he wondered why his statue was more prominently situated than that of his more famous brother, John. It was the young historian's first venture into Australian history and one in which he set out to apply the same rigour as in well-established fields of scholarship. The rewards of archival research perhaps confirmed his resistance to more analytical forms of interpretation. He admitted that John Legge, whose course in Asian history he enjoyed and who supervised his thesis, 'sometimes lost me' on the philosophy of history. 'I don't make the leaps of insight or generalisation', he would declare; 'I'm a tortoise rather than hare'. Besides, 'how could you generalise until you gathered all the data?' When a student put him onto Huizinga's *Waning of the Middle Ages*, it came as a revelation. He tried to read Marx but was repelled by the 'hectoring style of argument'.[8]

He wondered why intelligent students a few years ahead of him such as Dorothy Hewett could be so committed to communism; indeed a *Pelican* editorial supported Menzies' legislation to outlaw the Communist Party. His reason for opposing the subsequent referendum to allow that ban is revealing: it was in reaction to the Young Liberals who shouted down their opponents.[9] Similarly, the High Church views of the local vicar caused him to veer towards agnosticism. His liberalism recoiled from dogma and for some time he took

---

8   Geoffrey Bolton interviewed by Neville Meaney, 11 September 1986, NLA TRC 2053/6, pp. 9-10; Reid interview, pp. 21, 35, 42; Diary, 24 December 2014; 'A Provincial Viewpoint', p. 81.
9   *Pelican*, 5 May 1950; Reid interview, p. 20. He also criticised intolerance during the referendum campaign in a letter to *The West Australian*, 26 September 1951.

refuge in his writing as well as personal interactions in irony – a practice abandoned in mid-life when he realised it was not always understood.

How did these attitudes form? Looking back, he thought he imbibed an aversion to the abuse of power from his parents. They came from that frugal and cautious section of the lower middle classes that Menzies invoked in his celebrated radio broadcast to 'The Forgotten People' (they voted Labor only twice, in 1943 and 1972), acutely conscious that whether business or unions held the whip hand it was 'the people in the middle' who were likely to get hurt. One of the works he read in first year was Lord Halifax's *The Character of a Trimmer* (1684), upholding moderation and compromise against extremism and intolerance. Halifax's insistence that his trimming was not opportunism, that statecraft required holding the centre and pursuing the middle way, made a lasting impression.[10]

* * *

Frank Crowley, another Melbourne historian, returned to Perth in 1952 after completing a second doctorate at Oxford. In 1949 Crowley had used a research fellowship to begin compiling a comprehensive bibliography of Western Australian history and he now became the supervisor of Geoffrey's Masters thesis on the Kimberley pastoral industry. In these informal days of grace and favour, Fred Alexander found £100 for Geoffrey to head up north and handed the money over with instructions to make it last. So in June 1952 he took the train to Meekatharra, found a lift on the mail-truck to Marble Bar

---

10 Meaney interview, pp. 5-6, 13.

CHAPTER 1

and sat on the back of a utility with drunken shearers on the road to Port Hedland, though the Pardoo Sands forced him to complete the journey to Broome by air. He had the good fortune to fall in with Don McLeod and Donald Stuart, who were camped at Marble Bar with the Aboriginal co-operative Pindan group, and he carried an introduction to Mary Durack, who was wintering in Broome and beginning to write the story of her pioneering grandfather, *Kings in Grass Castles*. She gave him entrée to other pastoral families and he established a life-long ability to converse easily with people from all walks of life. These were encounters that stimulated his historical imagination: the relations between the pastoralists and their Aboriginal workers put him in mind of the circumstances of slaves in the Roman villa and the Norman feudal system. If he came to feel that he had missed much he should have seen, he intended until the end of his life to return north and fill in the gaps.[11]

The £100 exhausted, Geoffrey returned to Perth in September to spend the next year in research and writing, completing the thesis late in 1953. He found Crowley, 'a wild man' out of hours, to be an excellent supervisor who taught him a lot about working in archives. Still living with his family, Geoffrey supported himself with payments from the ABC and punting on horse races. Though that enthusiasm would pass, he had a betting system that yielded modest yet generally reliable returns and after attending a yearling sale mused in the diary begun at this time that he might 'go in for horses if I ever become really wealthy'. On Christmas Eve he learned of the award of a Hackett Fellowship that provided £1200 for two

---

11   Geoffrey Bolton, 'Portrait of the Historian as a Young Learner', in Duncan Graham (ed.), *Being Whitefella* (Perth: Fremantle Arts Centre Press, 1994), pp. 119-25; Geoffrey Bolton interviewed by Bill Bunbury, ABC Hindsight, 29 April 2001, CD.

years of international study. He would leave for England in August 1954 and meanwhile expanded his Honours thesis on Alexander Forrest to book length, boiled down the Masters one into a 20,000 word article, undertook various tasks in the History Department (over the hot summer he laboriously collated 500 copies of the 1200 roneoed pages of Crowley's bibliography) and taught in the English Department.[12]

It was almost inevitable that Geoffrey Bolton would go to Balliol, as Alexander, Reynolds, Legge, Crowley and so many others had. Upon hearing of the Hackett award, he wrote to another former Balliol man, Keith Hancock, and soon he was in correspondence with Hugh Stretton, who was a Fellow there. The predecessors had generally pursued an undergraduate course of studies, more demanding and prestigious than was available here, though some with an eye to changing academic expectations urged him to begin a research higher degree. 'This uncertainty is most provoking', he stated, and compromised by doing both. Oxford admitted him, as a graduate, to undertake a shortened two-year B.A. in Modern History. The medievalist Richard Southern was his moral tutor, while the history tutors included Christopher Hill, 'Marxist but civilised', and E.H. Carr, who lay on a sofa as the undergraduate read his essay; if it was good he would sit up and if it was very good he took to his feet while taking it apart.[13]

Geoffrey's first year at Oxford was not unlike that at the University of Western Australia, the many distractions compounded by a trip to Italy, and Hill awarded him a B+ in Tudor and Stuart history,

---

12 Diary, 7 March 1954, 2 January 2015; 'Eight Students Win University Awards'. *The West Australian*, 24 December 1953.

13 Diary, 14 March 1954, 2 January 2015.

CHAPTER 1

'which is what I deserved but not good enough'. When he took off for Vienna in the summer of 1955, the Master – Sir David Keir, another historian – asked the Dean whether the Australian was doing enough reading. 'Rest assured, Master, Mr Bolton has a sufficiency of ambition.' There was certainly ambition. Geoffrey had told the Dean that six of the ten professors of history in Australia came from Balliol and he intended to be the seventh. There was also a dash of audacity. Upon arriving in England he converted the first instalment of his Hackett allowance into shares in the recently de-nationalised steel industry, and sold them at a profit following Anthony Eden's electoral victory in May 1955 (when Geoffrey voted Tory) to finance the excursion to Austria. After that it was head down and he completed the degree in 1956 with a first.[14]

During his undergraduate studies Geoffrey also attended the seminars of Vincent Harlow, the Oxford professor of imperial history, on 'The Founding of the Second British Empire' as well as a summer school in Trinity College Dublin. Attracted to Ireland, he decided to write his doctoral thesis on its incorporation into the United Kingdom following the 1798 rebellion, a measure that required the Irish parliament to vote itself out of existence. Although the Boltons had no Irish ancestry, he was intrigued with the way its Protestant Ascendancy formed a settler culture similar to that in Rhodesia and Kenya, or indeed the Kimberley pastoralists. Another parallel became more apparent to him subsequently: the Anglo-Irish were marginal to the British establishment as Western Australians were marginal to the Commonwealth.[15]

---

14   Diary, 17 January 1955, 2 January 2015; Meaney interview, pp. 20, 22.
15   Bolton, 'A Provincial Viewpoint', p. 81; Deborah Gare, 'Images from a Life in Australian History: An Interview with Geoffrey Bolton', *Limina*, 4 (1998), p. 92.

A HISTORIAN FOR ALL SEASONS

The Irish parliament's passage of the Act of Union in 1801 had commonly been attributed to Crown patronage and corruption. Geoffrey was not satisfied by this Whig interpretation. Partly influenced by Lewis Namier's influential recasting of late eighteenth century British political history, he did not see the parliamentarians as place-hungry oligarchs but rather responding to an interplay of economic, social and religious influences mediated by local and regional considerations. Accordingly, he approached Namier and arranged to meet him at the tearoom of the Institute of Historical Research in London, where the great man held court. Namier, who was impressed, suggested Geoffrey tackle the 1774 British parliament but the novice was conscious that Namier's retinue of doctoral students was doomed to remain in his shadow, commonly ending up as assistant lecturers in universities such as 'Hull or Southampton', and demurred. With the complaint that 'Balliol never sends me any young men', Namier dismissed him.[16]

Balliol provided Geoffrey with a Beit Senior Research Fellowship to pursue his doctorate, grandly named but worth only £300 and supplemented with odds and sods. The cost of living was cheaper in Dublin, but his depleted wardrobe was apparent to friends when he returned to Oxford. Among them was Carol Grattan, who read English at Lady Margaret Hall and stayed on to qualify as a teacher. Their friendship blossomed into romance so that when Keith Hancock offered a fellowship at the ANU, they married two weeks before leaving for Australia in mid-1958.[17]

Hancock's offer allowed Geoffrey a year to write up the thesis, which was finally accepted in 1961 and revised for publication in

---

16   Reid interview, pp. 50-51; Bolton, 'A Provincial Viewpoint', p. 81.
17   Reid interview, pp. 52-53.

CHAPTER 1

1966. It is a noticeably more assured work than *Alexander Forrest* (which Frank Crowley saw through the press in his absence), partly because the sources were so much richer, the scholarship deeper. The Irish study has a stronger and more delineated interpretation, a command of detail and felicity of expression that became his hallmark. There is also an errata slip that asks the reader to disregard a footnote reference to an appendix (analysing the composition of the Irish parliament) that he decided to omit. Perhaps most revealing is the annotated bibliography. He describes the 1913 edition of *Burke's Landed Irish Gentry* as 'despite imprecisions, improbabilities and misprints, a mine of information'; a secondary account is damned for a 'treatment marred by cocksure judgements and inadequate research'; his terms of commendation are 'intelligent', 'unbiased', 'moderate'.[18] More than thirty years later, when Geoffrey attended a conference in Belfast to mark the bicentenary of the Act of Union, the Irish historians showered him with praise. 'There is no point in covering the same ground as Professor Bolton did in his admirable (and for 1966 precociously perceptive) book'; it remained 'an essential guide to the subject' and its conclusions were taken as 'axiomatic'.[19]

* * *

Keith Hancock would support Geoffrey's career as Fred Alexander did. The two mentors had been fellow students at Melbourne and Oxford, but one could provide only local patronage (and was amply

---

18   G.C. Bolton, *The Passing of the Irish Act of Union: A Study in Parliamentary Politics* (London: Oxford University Press, 1966), pp. 31, 228-30.

19   Peter Jupp, 'Britain and the Union, 1797–1801', A.P.W. Malcolmson, 'The Irish Peerage and the Act of Union, 1800–1971'; S.J. Connolly, 'Reconsidering the Irish Act of Union', *Transactions of the Royal Historical Society*, 6th series, 10 (2000), pp. 197, 230, 399.

repaid by Geoffrey's solicitude in later years) whereas the other was a potentate of the profession. It was in Alexander's class that Geoffrey read Hancock's magisterial *Survey of British Commonwealth Affairs* (1937–42) and Bruce Hunt, a leading Perth doctor who had been Hancock's close friend in Melbourne, encouraged Geoffrey to contact the great man in London, where he was director of the Institute of Commonwealth Studies. Geoffrey admired Keith Hancock for his span, his prose style and his liberalism. Hancock knew and approved of Geoffrey's early venture into regional history, and in late 1956 discussed the possibility of an appointment at the Research School of Social Sciences at the ANU, where he was about to become director. So in 1957, when the older man had returned to Australia and was approached by the North Queensland Local Government Association to write a history of their district, his mind turned immediately to the penniless younger man completing his doctorate in Oxford.[20]

The young couple adapted to life in a bush capital with 30,000 residents that was still to acquire a lake, gardens and urban amenities. They established a circle of friends and their first son, Patrick, was born there in 1961. Geoffrey was drawn into the work of the Research School of Social Sciences. Keith Hancock had him organise a conference on medieval studies and he collaborated with Ann Moyal, then laying the foundations of the *Australian Dictionary of Biography* while its nominal editors feuded, in compiling a biographical register of the Western Australian parliament – she noticed 'a touch of Britain' in the lanky West Australian's voice.[21] The historian Jim Davidson and

---

20   Bolton, 'A Provincial Viewpoint', p. 82; Meaney interview, p. 29.
21   G.C. Bolton and Ann Mozley, *The Western Australian Legislature, 1870–1933* (Canberra: Australian National University, 1961); see Ann Moyal, *Breakfast with Beaverbrook: Memoirs of an Independent Woman* (Sydney: Hale & Iremonger, 1995),

CHAPTER 1

the geographer Oskar Spate of the neighbouring Research School of Pacific Studies provided guidance on North Queensland's multiracial character. Participation in Hancock's interdisciplinary Wool Seminar broadened Geoffrey's intellectual horizons.[22]

The ANU supported research with a plenitude that startled the indigent newcomer: there were funds for four trips to North Queensland and a vehicle, as well as typists, a cartographer and reference librarians. Geoffrey made his first visit in the summer of 1959 and returned with Carol for a longer stint in the winter.[23] As in the Kimberley, he drew on stories that were told to him, 'fossicked out' records in regional towns, and made extensive use of local newspapers then stored in the stables of Parliament House in Brisbane. *A Thousand Miles Away* takes its title from a song of the Cooktown gold rush, and a delegate to the North Queensland New State Convention had used the same phrase as recently as 1955. The book opens with the statement: 'North Queensland is undoubtedly the most successful example in the British Commonwealth of settlement in the tropics by Europeans'. That theme was pursued through studies of prospectors, pastoralists and planters applying practices brought from further south in search of quick rewards and only later learning how to adapt to their environment. With the quelling of Aboriginal resistance and the displacement of Chinese and Melanesian communities, Geoffrey suggested, North Queensland was assimilated into the rest

---

pp. 118, 137-49, and 'Sir Keith Hancock: Laying the Foundations, 1959–62', in Melanie Nolan and Christine Fernon (eds), *The ADB's Story* (Canberra: ANU E Press, 2013), pp. 49-77.

22 Geoffrey Bolton, 'Rediscovering Australia: Hancock and the Wool Seminar', in D.A. Low (ed.), *Keith Hancock: The Legacy of an Historian* (Melbourne: Melbourne University Press, 2001), pp. 180-200.

23 Reid interview, p. 69; Jim Davidson, *A Three-Cornered Life: The Historian W.K. Hancock* (Sydney: UNSW Press, 2010), p. 416.

of Australia. At Jacaranda Press, a young Brian Clouston proved 'a very effective larrikin'. The book was well received and passed through three subsequent impressions.[24]

Hancock made it clear from the outset that the fellowship would run for just three years, after which Geoffrey would have to find a teaching job elsewhere. Having tutored for Manning Clark while in Canberra, he gave a series of lectures in Australian history for the University of Melbourne in the last term of 1961.[25] Among those who observed their success was John Legge, the foundation professor of history at the new Monash University, who recruited him to a senior lectureship there. Since Geoffrey Serle was teaching Australian history at Monash, Geoffrey Bolton took responsibility for a course on European history from 1600 to 1815. Working up his lectures, he developed a style of presentation that would intrigue generations of students. To enable him to judge their reactions, he dispensed with a script in favour of a few brief notes and soon they too were abandoned. Thereafter he lectured in a measured tempo, sometimes examining the floor and sometimes the ceiling as he searched for the best order of exposition, but never for a name, date or correct syntax. He found from experience it was best to cover the important points early, then maintain interest with illustrative examples before returning at the end to reinforce the exposition. It was at Monash, also, that he grew the beard by which generations of students remembered him.[26]

---

24   G.C. Bolton, *A Thousand Miles Away: A History of North Queensland to 1920* (Canberra: Jacaranda in association with the Australian National University, 1963), pp. vii, 321, 331; Meaney interview, p. 31; Reid interview, p. 74; see Lyndon Megarrity, 'Geoffrey Bolton's *A Thousand Miles Away*: Origins, Influence and Impact', *History Australia*, 12, 3 (2015), pp. 7-29.

25   'Notes and News', *Historical Studies Australia and New Zealand*, 10, 37 (1961), p. 127.

26   Reid interview, pp. 83-85.

CHAPTER 1

Although the appearance of *A Thousand Miles Away* in 1963 increased Geoffrey's standing as an Australian historian, it was by no means clear that he would pursue a career in that field. There was an understanding with Carol that they would return to England within a few years, and as he revised his book on the Irish Act of Union he published two articles in the prestigious *Economic History Review*, then embarked on a biography of William Eden, an influential diplomat, administrator and member of Pitt's Cabinet.[27] The Monash appointment brought a reconsideration of these plans. Should he consolidate his research in Australian history or eighteenth-century Britain? Hancock had put him onto the North Queensland project, but Hancock's major works (the *Survey of British Commonwealth Affairs*, the civil history of Britain in World War II and the biography of Smuts) were written by invitation and he had not regarded it as necessary to encourage his protégés to 'cut out their own themes'.[28]

In an attempt to do so, Geoffrey approached an Australian friend from his Oxford days with the suggestion of writing a biography of his father, Sir Richard Boyer, who had died recently after sixteen years as chair of the ABC. Boyer was a high-minded and widely admired figure whose life spanned the Methodist ministry, war service, pastoralism and public office, and Geoffrey conceived the biography as illuminating 'the basic problems of expressing Australian liberalism (small l) through the machinery of government'.[29] The book that

---

27 Successive drafts yielded six chapters, amounting to nearly 200 pages, but left the latter half of Eden's career to be written; Bolton Papers, NLA Acc.16.016, Box 8, Folder 50.

28 G.C. Bolton, 'Some British Reactions to the Irish Act of Union', *Economic History Review*, 18, 2 (1965), pp. 367-75; 'The Founding of the Second British Empire', *Economic History Review*, 19, 1 (1966), pp. 195-200; Reid interview, p. 79.

29 Geoffrey Bolton to 'Dick' [Boyer's son], 10 August 1961, Bolton papers, NLA Acc.05/139, Box 3, Folder 'Sir R. Boyer'.

resulted carried admiration to the verge of identification. It portrayed Boyer as a 'classic example' of the liberal tradition that affirmed the autonomy of the individual and the duty of service, a strong believer in liberty of conscience with a hatred of censorship and a zeal for education and understanding. If Boyer was perhaps 'too ready to avoid unpleasantness', he treated everyone he met with 'a warm and unforced attention'. The work suffered from the unavailability of ABC records (though when Ken Inglis used them, they did not greatly alter Geoffrey's judgments) and he came to think that his subject's lack of cunning weakened his own treatment of the political dimension.[30]

Then, as Fred Alexander approached retirement, the University of Western Australia decided to replace him with two professors. Bert Hallam, an English medievalist, gained one of them and Richard Southern suggested that Geoffrey was a far stronger historian and ought to apply for the other. With appointment to the second chair in 1966, Geoffrey and Carol were able to buy a house in Claremont. Their second son, Matthew, was born in the following year and Carol, who had tutored in English at Monash, found similar work at the University of Western Australia. Yet there was no intention to settle down in Perth, for Geoffrey's career hopes and Carol's separation from family and friends pointed elsewhere; there was also that disconcerting feeling of returning to a place left behind.

His old university had grown and a substantial History Department had recently moved into a new building, but Geoffrey was struck by the continuation of practices discarded at the ANU and

---

30 G.C. Bolton, *Dick Boyer: An Australian Humanist* (Canberra: Australian National University Press, 1967), pp. 141, 234, 283; Reid interview, p. 92; see K.S. Inglis, *This Is the ABC: The Australian Broadcasting Commission 1932–1983* (Melbourne: Melbourne University Press, 1983), chs 3–5.

CHAPTER 1

Monash: lecturers still wore gowns, the professors suits.[31] He was keen to innovate in teaching and research, and had some success with new appointments in Asian and maritime history, though Bert Hallam did not welcome change. The two men rotated the headship and Geoffrey served a term as Dean of the Arts Faculty. He believed that professors carried an obligation to provide leadership and found satisfaction in doing so, though the duties of office ate into his time for research. There were also a number of other commitments. He chaired the Western Australian working party of the *Australian Dictionary of Biography*, was involved in the State museum and library, played an increasingly important role in preserving and promoting the Dutch shipwrecks discovered on the State's coast, and was active in the formation of the Australian Historical Association.[32]

Apart from desultory pursuit of the Eden biography, he was occupied at this time with two major projects. The first was a study of Western Australia during the Depression, for he was conscious that this had been a landmark in the lives of his parents' generation and wanted to record their memories before it was too late. With the assistance of Terry Owen, he conducted interviews and wove the testimony into the narrative. Perhaps unconsciously, he was also comparing the place in which he was born with the one to which he returned as a mining boom swept away the landmarks of the past. He took his title, *A Fine Country to Starve In*, from a sceptical remark made by the economist Edward Shann about the State's self-congratulatory centenary celebrations in 1929, and opened with a superb evocation of the old order before relating the misery and despair that followed.

---

31 The growth of the department is recorded in de Garis, 'The Department of History in the University of Western Australia, 1913-1965', pp. 17-20.
32 Harris interview, pp. 95-97. I draw here on the diary, which was resumed at this time, and information from Carol Bolton.

Although the book records the protests of ruined farmers and unemployed wage-earners, it departs from other Australian work done at this time in the assertion the Depression did little lasting damage to the social fabric.[33] Perth was 'the most isolated city in the world, its inhabitants incurious about events beyond their shores and almost as incurious about their neighbours to landward', so their resentment was directed against the distant federal government more than their own. Besides, this society was still close to its pioneering roots, free of class or sectarian rancour, moderate in its politics and with a 'tradition of togetherness'. Here was an early version of what would come to be criticised as 'the gentry myth' of Western Australia, though Geoffrey preferred to call it 'the consensus myth' – and while he thought he was merely distilling the way that earlier Western Australians believed themselves to be different, the sympathetic eloquence of *A Fine Country* allowed readers to think that its author shared the same consensual values. The book concludes with the observation that Western Australia was unlikely to experience again the adversity that allowed it to be called a fine country to starve in – 'but had it the wisdom and adaptability to be a fine place in which to prosper?'[34]

The other book written at this time was a short interpretive account of British imperial history, enabled by a year of study leave at the University of Kent in 1971. The original working title was 'The British Empire', but since it combined an overview of acquisition

---

33 See, for example, Robert Cooksey (ed.), *The Great Depression in Australia* (Canberra: Australian Society for the Study of Labour History), to which he contributed an essay on 'Unemployment and Politics in Western Australia'.

34 G.C. Bolton, *A Fine Country to Starve In* (Perth: University of Western Australia Press, 1972), pp. 1-2, 267-69; 'A Provincial Viewpoint', pp. 82-83. Criticism began with C.T. Stannage, *Western Australia's Heritage: The Pioneer Myth*, University Extension Monograph Series no. 1 (Perth: University of Western Australia, 1985) and Geoffrey replied in the introduction to a new edition of the book in 1994.

CHAPTER 1

and administration with a more extended consideration of the consequences, it became *Britain's Legacy Overseas* – and for the first time the author dropped the more formal G.C. for Geoffrey. A point of departure was the argument of the American historian Louis Hartz that every colonial society was a fragment of its European origins, defined and confined by the ideology implanted at its moment of foundation. Laying emphasis on the successive waves of immigrants and ideas that washed the British colonies of settlement, the book compared their political institutions and government practices, ethnicity, religion, education and the creative arts. 'The British Empire', Geoffrey stated, 'was founded under Elizabeth I and dispersed under Elizabeth II'. Its lasting legacy was bringing Western culture into contact with a large number of different cultures throughout the world.[35]

Neither book had the success Geoffrey hoped for. *A Fine Country* was taken as a contribution to Western Australian history of limited relevance to national historiography, while *Britain's Legacy Overseas* suffered from its publication in a paperback format aimed at a dwindling student market in imperial history. In the early 1970s Geoffrey entered a period of self-doubt. While he had achieved his ambition of a chair, the recognition he craved was more elusive. He began to feel his career might begin to resemble those of older historians such as Fred Alexander in Perth or Gordon Greenwood in Brisbane, 'destined to pursue a fruitful career as teacher, administrator and minor public figure in a middle-sized state capital, but not quite equal to the writing of first-rate Australian history'.[36]

---

35 Geoffrey Bolton, *Britain's Legacy Overseas* (London: Oxford University Press, 1973), pp. 5, 155; see also 'Louis Hartz', *Australian Economic History Review*, 13, 2 (1973), pp. 168-76.
36 Bolton, 'A Provincial Viewpoint', p. 83; Gare, 'Images from a Life in Australian History', p. 92.

He compared his situation to that of Geoffrey Blainey, who had returned to an academic career after working as a freelance historian and won celebrity with the bold and imaginative *Tyranny of Distance* in 1966. Bolton took issue with the book's reinterpretation of the reasons for creating a penal colony in New South Wales and was discomfited by an ensuing exchange of journal articles, his own expertise in the period and knowledge of the British archives brushed aside by the Melbournian's irreverent iconoclasm.[37] He also began to feel stultified in Perth and applied unsuccessfully for chairs in Melbourne and Canberra. That he was passed over was a further blow to his self-esteem.

For the most part the History Department was a congenial workplace, its members (in those innocent days before academics crouched alone over their networked computers) spending much of the day in each other's company and periodically exchanging domestic hospitality. The atmosphere grew strained in 1972, partly because of a colleague who was a bully and an intriguer; it is a measure of his destructiveness that Geoffrey described him as 'the only academic I've ever truly hated'. Although Geoffrey resumed the headship following study leave in 1971, he seemed incapable of bringing this troublemaker to heel and his diary recorded snide comments from others as well as disagreeable departmental meetings.[38] He felt a lack of encouragement and was discouraged by the Arts Faculty's rejection of his efforts to create a Sociology department, which were in part

---

37 Their polemical exchange in the pages of the *Australian Economic History Review* during 1968 and 1969 is reprinted in Ged Martin (ed.), *The Founding of Australia: The Argument About Australia's Origins* (Sydney: Hale & Iremonger, 1978), pp. 91-121; see also the letter from Blainey to Bolton, 10 January 1968, Bolton Papers, NLA Acc.13/139, Box 3, Folder 'Botany Bay'.

38 Reid interview, p. 9; Diary, 9, 13, 20 March, 23 June, 14 July 1972.

CHAPTER 1

stimulated by a younger generation's challenge to empirical forms of history and his desire to find a sharper cutting-edge for his research.

In these circumstances he was attracted to throwing in his lot with the new Murdoch University that he was helping to design. He was a member of its planning board, attracted to the innovative character of the venture and by this time under what must have been flattering pressure to become a foundation professor. Should he do so? Carol was not enthusiastic; those who had supported his application for the ANU chair advised him he needed to consolidate his publication record; and he was not sure it was the right move but felt he could not 'decently recede'. Brian de Garis, a friend with whom Geoffrey discussed the matter, observed that he 'had a great deal of difficulty in saying no'.[39]

The die was cast when Murdoch's foundation vice-chancellor let it be known that Geoffrey would join, occasioning further unpleasantness to which he responded in a public lecture on 'Why I am leaving the University of Western Australia to go to Murdoch'. He explained that while the older university was set in its 'academically respectable' ways, the decision was personal. 'I felt I might too easily find myself sublimating the desire to work by a little scholarly conversation in the tea-room, a little light commentary, a little wistful grumbling about the great ideas I might have if only I were in a position to innovate. Murdoch looks like a good cure for any tendency towards premature ossification.'[40]

* * *

---

39   Diary, 20, 31 October 1972; email from Brian de Garis, 23 October 2015.
40   'Why I am leaving the University of Western Australia to go to Murdoch', 15 June 1973, Bolton, Papers, NLA Acc.05/139, Box 3, Folder 'Minor Publications and Speeches'.

The hopes for Murdoch were not fulfilled. A handsome open court of vernacular design was erected in a pine plantation on the southern edge of Perth, the covered walkways with their exposed jarrah beams combining the feel of a pastoral homestead veranda with the atmosphere of an academic cloister. But teaching began in 1975, just as the Commonwealth responded to mounting economic difficulties by reducing outlays. The expansion of higher education that made Murdoch possible was over and university funding remained frozen for the next decade. The new university's enrolments were below expectations and a national review in 1979 proposed that it be merged with the old one – a threat averted only because the premier, Sir Charles Court, stood firm. Geoffrey was able to make just a handful of appointments to the History program within a School of Social Inquiry that yoked Economics, Psychology, Women's Studies and Peace and Conflict Studies in an uneasy relationship. He designed and taught an imaginative Introduction to History to first-year students whose choice thereafter was limited. Many were attracted to the exotic counter-culture proclaimed by academics recruited from the American West Coast; Geoffrey accepted these enthusiasms, even if he showed little interest in the orgone box that sat in the corner of the School meeting room. Other academics had different expectations and both as foundation Pro Vice-Chancellor and later as Dean he found it difficult to resolve their competing demands.[41]

Murdoch did provide an opportunity to work with scientific colleagues interested in environmental studies and his own course on environmental history provided the basis for the next book, *Spoils and*

---

41   Geoffrey Bolton, 'Attempting History at Murdoch', *Australian Historical Association Bulletin*, 13 (December 1977), pp. 6-13; his *It Had Better Be a Good One: Murdoch University's First Ten Years* (Perth: Murdoch University, 1985) underplays the difficulties.

CHAPTER 1

Spoilers. Drawing on a wide range of primary and secondary sources, it provided a succinct account of how Australians had made their environment, often in reckless ignorance but with a growing awareness of the consequences. The book was suggested by Heather Radi for her successful Allen & Unwin series on 'The Australian Experience' and its success helped restore Geoffrey's confidence.[42] Almost immediately, Oxford University Press invited him to edit a history of Australia. A mammoth team of the country's leading historians was already at work on a Bicentennial History, its novel design of five reference volumes and five 'slices' of a single year of the Australian past encountering scepticism, so Geoffrey decided the Oxford History would consist of five narrative volumes, each one (apart from his own) written by a younger member of the profession.[43]

A fellowship at St John's College, Cambridge, in 1979 had helped him to complete *Spoils and Spoilers*. He now looked for relief from Murdoch to tackle the Oxford History and sounded out the possibility of a year in the chair of Australian Studies at Harvard.[44] The next vacancy there was some years off but an alternative suddenly appeared. After protracted negotiation, the Australian government created an Australian Studies Centre that would be attached to the Institute of Commonwealth Studies at the University of London. The announcement in early 1982 of Geoffrey's appointment as foundation professor for a term of three years was widely publicised.[45]

---

42 Geoffrey Bolton, *Spoils and Spoilers: Australians Make Their Environment 1788–1980* (Sydney: Allen & Unwin, 1981); 'A Provincial Viewpoint', p. 84.
43 David Cunningham to Geoffrey Bolton, 6 June 1979, Bolton to Cunningham, 1 August, 26 September 1979, Bolton Papers, NLA Acc.05/139, Box 3, File 'Oxford History'.
44 Geoffrey Bolton to Noel Butlin, 20 October 1981, Butlin to Bolton, 25 August 1982, Bolton Papers, NLA Acc.05/139, Box 1, Folder 'Correspondence 1980–82'.
45 Bolton Papers, NLA Acc.05/139, Box 1, Folder 'London 1982–85'.

Apart from this welcome recognition and the attractions of living in England (and seeing more of his brother and sister-in-law, who lived there), he expected the appointment to provide respite from the problems of Murdoch and his many other commitments. He badly underestimated the demands the Centre would impose on him and the difficulties of living alone, for Matthew, the younger son, was still at school and did not want to leave Perth, so Carol did not accompany him. Geoffrey flew back from London several times a year but after each visit had to plunge into an administrative backlog. He was expected to develop a teaching program, create an academic network in Australian studies, build scholarly resources to support it, promote intellectual traffic between the two countries, conduct seminars and provide a base for various endeavours. He had the assistance of a lecturer, the political scientist John Warhurst, and an economist on secondment from the Department of Trade, Bob Lim, whose contacts with Australia House proved valuable – as did his Chinese ancestry in rebutting criticism of White Australia.[46]

Geoffrey was anxious to correct British misapprehensions. In an interview given to *The Australian* on the eve of taking up the post, he said that one of his tasks would be to dispel the impression of brash vulgarity given by Rolf Harris and Barry Humphries. Harris took no offence. Humphries did and appeared on the doorstep of the Centre in Russell Square as Professor Les Patterson to record a television interview with David Frost that was predictably venomous in its caricature.[47] That was just one of Geoffrey's tribulations. Although the Centre was part of the Institute of Commonwealth Studies, it had its

---

46 Geoffrey Bolton, 'The Empire Strikes Back at Russell Square', *Australian Historical Association Bulletin*, 39 (June 1984), pp. 6-8.
47 *The Australian*, 21 August 1982; Barry Humphries, 'Professor Patterson's Christmas Package for the Poms', *Quadrant*, 27, 1–2 (1983), pp. 36-37; Diary, 29, 30 June 1983.

CHAPTER 1

own committee of management chaired by Zelman Cowen, who had recently retired as Governor-General and maintained a vice-regal expectation of being fully consulted, so frequent trips to the Master's Lodge of Oriel College in Oxford were required. Relations between the administrative staff of the Institute and Centre were strained, and the constituent colleges of the University of London were loath to accredit the Centre's teaching. There were visiting vice-chancellors to entertain and receptions at Australia House to attend. Above all, there was a stream of Australian scholars, all of whom seemed to think their host had no other calls on his time.

Meanwhile Geoffrey resumed work on the Eden biography, to little effect. It was his habit to rise early in order to write undisturbed before attending to other business, but diary entries record a lack of progress: 'Fiddle around for two hours with Oxford History but writing blocked'; 'At my desk at 6 a.m. slogging without inspiration'; 'Time continues to go quickly without achievement'.[48] The award of an Officer of Australia in 1984 cheered him but soon the wanderlust returned. There was a succession of inquiries about pending vice-chancellorships, a tilt at the directorship of the Research School of Social Sciences at the ANU, and in early 1985 a disconcerting interview for the post of vice-chancellor of the University of Western Australia, to which he was invited to apply. The selection committee pressed him at length on his administrative bent and one member asked if he was perhaps 'too balanced to take decisions'. He answered that was a fair criticism 'but I think I've changed'.[49]

Geoffrey consoled himself that he would be quite happy 'soldiering on at Murdoch and writing'; a new vice-chancellor there spoke of

---

48 Diary, 29 February, 5 March, 17 August 1984.
49 Diary, 15 January 1985.

him becoming an elder statesmen with more time for writing, but in the meantime persuaded him to undertake an additional task, a short history of the university.[50] The Oxford History was becoming another torment. It was meant to appear well before the Bicentennial History but Geoffrey had no sooner persuaded the director of the Press to set back the publication date than he assured one of the contributors 'it would be silly to adhere too vigorously to David Cunningham's rescheduled guidelines'. Although there were unavoidable setbacks – one author dropped out early and had to be replaced, another died suddenly with nothing written – Geoffrey's absence made it hard to monitor progress. To make matters worse, Stuart Macintyre completed his volume on time and was impatient for it to appear. When Geoffrey returned from London in the second half of 1985, he had over 100,000 words to write. Two years later he had completed just four chapters and confessed to a new director of Oxford University Press that he was 'as anxious as you to extricate myself from this ridiculous situation'. The volume finally appeared in 1990 with an acknowledgment that Carol had lived too long with what was known in the family as 'the bloody book'.[51]

This was the low point. Upon returning to Perth in 1985, he was drawn back into the problems at Murdoch. He would drive out there during non-instruction periods to attend to an accumulation of correspondence (personal letters were handwritten, others dictated to his secretary) and 'soon find myself involved in therapy sessions' with

---

50 Diary, 10, 30 August 1984, 15 January 1985; letter, Geoffrey Bolton to Peter Boyce, 5 September 1984, Bolton Papers, NLA Acc.16.016, Box 22, Folder 112.

51 Diary, 18 June 1983, Geoffrey Bolton to Sandra McComb, 12 August 1987, Bolton Papers, NLA Acc. 05/139, Box 4, Folder 'Oxford History General 1983–1988'; Geoffrey Bolton, *The Oxford History of Australia. Volume 5, 1942–1988: The Middle Way* (Melbourne: Oxford University Press, 1990), p. x.

CHAPTER 1

unhappy colleagues. Once more he agreed to all manner of requests. 'Fear I am lapsing back into habits inimical to composition', he confessed. He became a member of the interim council of the National Maritime Museum and a committee of the Australian Bicentennial Authority chaired by Beryl Beaurepaire and charged with choosing the two-hundred people 'who made Australia great'. Both required regular trips east but neither the disputes over the Maritime Museum nor argument over the respective merits of Ned Kelly and Nettie and Vance Palmer advanced the Oxford History and meanwhile his biography of Eden as well as a long overdue history of Claremont 'lurked reproachfully in the background'.[52]

He was Dean until the middle of 1988 and set out a program of writing for the second half of the year that allowed a fortnight for each of his overdue manuscripts, only to take off for six weeks in London. Under these impossible pressures he seized the opportunity presented to him when he was helping the University of Queensland to select a professor of Australian history and was asked if he would take the post. That in doing so he dashed the hopes of a Perth applicant he knew wanted it keenly attests to his desperation. 'Queensland I hope will be a new start, both for Carol and me and also professionally. It is a nice thing to have a new opportunity at 57.'[53]

* * *

Queensland did not turn out quite like that. There were difficulties in arranging a hospital appointment offered to Carol, so once more he was making regular trips back to Perth. He lived in one

---

52 Diary, 23 May 1987, 16 February 1988.
53 Diary, 29 October 1988.

of the university colleges, suggesting he did not intend to stay, and left within five years – indeed he was negotiating a return to Perth within months of delivering an admittedly delayed inaugural lecture.[54] Efforts to regenerate a somewhat tired and divided department had limited success, but then he no longer felt the same need to carry colleagues with him. He was sufficiently in demand to feel wanted without the burden of expectations left behind. Queensland gave him a respite from distraction and a chance to consolidate at a time when things started to go his way.

The overdue volume of the *Oxford History of Australia* proved a success; published in 1990, it passed through several impressions, went to a second edition in 1996 and still sells steadily. Covering the period 1942 to 1988, the book provided a wide-ranging, deftly constructed narrative of the country's fortunes from wartime emergency to Bicentenary celebrations. It was responsive to the new currents of historiography, especially gender, ethnicity, Indigenous and environmental history, which are woven into a narrative of government, economy and society. The actors are drawn deftly: Chifley, 'whose calm and adroit managerial skills hid a hard core of anger against privilege'; Menzies, 'a politician of consummate professionalism who places a low value on ideology'; Whitlam ('on the fourteenth day Gough rested'); Joh Bjelke-Petersen, 'as usual going to extremes'. For his title Geoffrey chose *The Middle Way*, and reminded readers that it was a guiding precept of Chinese classical civilisation as well as ancient Greece. Australians also eschewed extremes. If they were slow to apply native intelligence to their own needs and opportunities, leisure and pleasure kept them out of trouble.[55]

---

54 Geoffrey Bolton, *Who Owns Australia's Past?* Inaugural Lecture Delivered at the University of Queensland, 18 March 1992 (Brisbane: University of Queensland Press, 1993).
55 Bolton, *The Oxford History of Australia*, vol. 5, pp. 8, 161, 215 281, 290, 291.

CHAPTER 1

Almost immediately, Geoffrey was invited to deliver the ABC's Boyer Lectures for 1992, the name of this prestigious annual event as gratifying as the national audience it delivered. He drew his title, *A View from the Edge*, from 'working experience' in two cities in the southwest and northeast corners of the country, using the ABC's acronym for its outlying studios, BAPH (Brisbane, Adelaide, Perth and Hobart) to remonstrate against the aggrandisement of Sydney, Canberra and Melbourne. His resentment of the neglect of history written outside this 'golden triangle' was longstanding, and in 1982 the absence of any attention beyond Western Australia to the large and important new State history edited by Tom Stannage provoked him to protest, in a public lecture entitled 'The Belly and the Limbs' fittingly given in Melbourne, the centre of solipsism.[56] He employed the same metaphor of the belly and the limbs (taken from Shakespeare's *Coriolanus*) in the Boyer Lectures, though now defended the inland capital of Canberra against its critics and laid the blame for short-changing the outer States on Sydney and Melbourne.

Although Geoffrey had long offered public commentary (he was a regular contributor of 'Notes on the News' for the ABC), he had done so as an observer rather than a controversialist, more circumspect and less prominent than historians such as Manning Clark and Geoffrey Blainey. In projecting a historical perspective onto current predicaments, his Boyer Lectures signalled greater public engagement. He blamed the excesses of the 1980s for the painful recession and reminded listeners that earlier generations showed resilience in adversity. He regretted the short-sighted pursuit of economic growth,

---

56   G.C. Bolton, 'The Belly and the Limbs', *Victorian Historical Journal*, 53, 1 (1982), p. 6; see C.T. Stannage (ed.), *A New History of Western Australia* (Perth: University of Western Australia Press, 1981). He used 'The Belly and the Limbs' as the provisional title of the lectures; see David Hill to Geoffrey Bolton, 17 February 1992, Bolton Papers, NLA Acc.16.016, Box 21, Folder 108.

the adversarial rancour in public life and weakness for symbols at the expense of substance, insistent that Australians were capable of learning from their mistakes. Just as they had succeeded in making 'the difficult change from an ethnically monochrome society to a pluralist society', so they could find the wisdom to care for their country and make 'satisfactory reparation to the Aboriginal Australians for the deprivations they have suffered' – provided they listened and learned. 'A nation gains confidence to shape its destiny from an improved understanding of its past experience.' This was an exhortation to restore the middle way.[57]

By now Geoffrey was negotiating a return to Perth. The head of Edith Cowan University, recently formed from Western Australia's metropolitan network of teachers colleges, sought him to help lift its academic standing and Carol was keen to end the commuting. Negotiations were protracted. Geoffrey was not willing to share an office, needed secretarial support and wanted reassurance on the teaching load – at the University of Queensland he lectured to first-years (leaving tutorials and assessment to younger staff), taught honours classes and supervised postgraduates, amounting to just half the contact hours that were the norm at Edith Cowan.[58] These matters were eventually arranged to his satisfaction, though not the expectation of playing a university leadership role and rightly so, for he was singularly ill-suited to the exacting regimen of institutional management that was displacing earlier collegial practices. He would guide and encourage junior colleagues, use his contacts to assist Edith Cowan, eventually write its history, but his energies were directed

---

57 Geoffrey Bolton, *A View from the Edge: An Australian Stocktaking*, the 1992 Boyer Lectures (Sydney: ABC Books, 1992), pp. 11, 58, 69.
58 Geoffrey Bolton to Doug Jecks, n.d. [June 1992], 30 June 1992; and to Roy Lourens, 7 February 1993, Bolton Papers, NLA Acc.05/139, Box 1, Folder 'Edith Cowan'.

CHAPTER 1

more and more to outside activity. He worked there happily enough, with a visiting fellowship at All Souls in Oxford in the second half of 1995, until retirement in the following year.

That did not end his academic involvement. Murdoch offered an attachment that led to him becoming Chancellor in 2002, and he was no stranger to the other Western Australian universities, but they were now points of reference for a seemingly endless round of public activities – speaking, chairing, launching books and attending ceremonies, mentoring, counselling, lobbying and troubleshooting. He still found it hard to say no and many who requested his assistance would accept no other. The only refuge from these constant demands was the rural retreat he and Carol had acquired at Ballingup, 250 kilometres south of Perth, and the increased freedom after 1996 to head down there enabled him to enter a period of renewed creativity.

While in Brisbane, he had been drawn into a network of academics anticipating the Commonwealth centenary with a series of conferences that revisited the landmark events of the federal movement, from Henry Parkes' Tenterfield speech in 1889 through to Commonwealth Inauguration Day in 1901. Geoffrey began by recalling the contribution of Samuel Griffiths in drafting a properly federal constitution for the Convention of 1891, and then decided to undertake a biography of Edmund Barton.[59] A grant from the Australian Research Council and a Harold White Fellowship at the National Library assisted progress, though by this time all his major books had a long gestation and this one only just made the centenary.

His purpose was to rescue Barton from neglect ('What country would forget the name of its first prime minister?' was the somewhat

---

59   Geoffrey Bolton, 'Samuel Griffith: The Great Provincial', in *Papers on Parliament* 13 (1991), pp. 19-33.

earnest question the government's Council for the Centenary of Federation asked Australians in its 2001 advertising blitz) and also to rehabilitate his reputation. 'Toss Pot Toby' was commonly regarded as sybaritic and indolent; he turned up late for the first meeting of the Commonwealth Cabinet. Despite a paucity of personal papers, Geoffrey was able to build a convincing picture of a man of sweet temper who lived beyond his means and probably suffered from a bipolar condition – so that periods of intense effort were followed by lapses into torpor – compounded by loneliness when prime ministerial duties in Melbourne separated him from his family. The biography established Barton as a genuine statesman who exemplified the constructive qualities of mediation and consensus. Geoffrey suggested that Melbourne historians, in their veneration of Deakin, were responsible for the underestimation of Barton, and argued that the Sydneysider was alone able to mobilise the popular movement that brought less populous States and their fractious representatives into a national settlement. As a young historian who had written two biographies, Geoffrey was conscious of John La Nauze's injunction that the genre should be reserved for mature scholars; this exercise, with its assured exposition and insight, was undoubtedly a work of maturity. The book won literary awards and the Council for the Centenary of Federation arranged for a copy to be distributed to every school in the country.[60]

Transition to retirement also enabled Geoffrey to complete a number of delayed projects, including a history of Claremont that he took on in the 1970s and carried forward in collaboration with Jenny Gregory – upon its appearance in 1999 he confessed that 'there

---

60   Geoffrey Bolton, *Edmund Barton: The One Man for the Job* (Sydney: Allen & Unwin, 2000), pp. viii-ix, 59, 230, 341-44.

CHAPTER 1

were other distractions'.⁶¹ He collaborated more expeditiously with Geraldine Byrne in commissioned histories of Edith Cowan University and the Supreme Court of Western Australia. She was used to his ways and adept in hunting down references that he could still recall but no longer attribute.⁶²

Geoffrey's aversion to conflict was evident in another centennial project, the National Museum. This had been established twenty years earlier but had no permanent home until a new building, possibly excessive in its symbolic design, was opened on Canberra's Action Peninsula in March 2001. Given Geoffrey's earlier service on the Council of the National Maritime Museum, it was hardly surprising that he, along with Graeme Davison and John Mulvaney, was asked to advise the Museum as it prepared the first exhibitions. Simmering tensions between the curators and conservative members of the Museum Council erupted into controversy before the Museum opened in 2001. Here Geoffrey's effort to resolve the differences was ill judged; the invigilators of 'black armband' history had no interest in a middle way.⁶³

But as he grew in eminence (he was declared Western Australian of the Year in 2006), he became more willing to speak out. In 2009 he condemned the neglect of Western Australia's cultural institutions at

---

61 Preface, Geoffrey Bolton and Jenny Gregory, *A History of Claremont* (Perth: University of Western Australia Press, 1999), p. vii; 'Profile', *Perth Weekly*, 1 June 1999 in Bolton Papers, NLA Acc.06.16, Box 22, Folder 112.

62 Geoffrey Bolton and Geraldine Byrne, *The Campus That Never Stood Still: Edith Cowan University, 1902–2002* (Perth: Edith Cowan University, 2002), and *May It Please Your Honour: A History of the Supreme Court of Western Australia 1861–2005* (Perth: Supreme Court, 2005).

63 Geoffrey Bolton, Submission to NMA Review', 3 March 2003, Bolton Papers, NLA Acc.16.106, Box 21, Folder 110; see Graeme Davison, 'Conflict in the Museum', in Bain Attwood and Stephen Foster (eds), *Frontier Conflict: The Australian Experience* (Canberra: National Museum of Australia, 2003), pp. 201-14.

a public forum. Those who led the State during the previous mineral booms of the 1890s and 1970s, he said, had the vision to make provision for a library, museum, art gallery and concert hall. This time there was just the Maritime Museum in Fremantle (he chaired its archaeology advisory committee), while the earlier history museum in Fremantle had closed and both the State Record Office and State Museum (he was a member of its governing body) awaited appropriate facilities. Future generations might regard this one, he warned, as 'provincial pygmies'.[64]

Vision and posterity were in the forefront of his mind as he undertook a history of Western Australia. This was commissioned before Cambridge University Press embarked on a series of State histories, though it appeared after those for New South Wales, Queensland and Victoria appeared, and followed a similar design: a concise depiction of a distinctive course of events. The working title was 'Land of Mirages', the final *Land of Vision and Mirage* more balanced and expressive of his theme that this isolated society was given to big projects 'hastily planned and executed' that never fulfilled their promoters' grand visions but usually left a residue of modest growth. The episodes of 'tunnel vision' and slapdash execution were interwoven with political, economic, social and cultural developments, drawing on Geoffrey's remarkable knowledge of Western Australian history; he excelled in the characterisation of both notable and little-known figures.[65]

---

64 Geoffrey Bolton, 'Town Hall Forum', 19 October 2009, www.historycouncilwa.org.au/wp-content/11.2009/1019

65 Geoffrey Bolton to Terri Anne White, 30 April, 2005, Bolton Papers, NLA Acc.16.016, Box 21, Folder 108; Geoffrey Bolton, *Land of Vision and Mirage: Western Australia since 1826* (Perth: University of Western Australia Press, 2008), pp. 1, 125, 204.

CHAPTER 1

The nearest equivalent to *Land of Vision and Mirage*'s wealth of local detail and thematic unity is the history of Victoria that Geoffrey Blainey published in the Cambridge series two years earlier (it had an earlier outing in 1984 as *Our Side of the Country*). The two Geoffreys kept up an association, not always without tension. Geoffrey Blainey's histories of mining and industry were success stories, whereas from his earliest writing on the Kimberley and North Queensland Geoffrey Bolton gave a more qualified assessment. The two men differed temperamentally, the Victorian sure in his judgments and unyielding in controversy, the Western Australian less outspoken; it did not help that Bolton so often measured his standing against Blainey. With a touch of irony, he wrote in his diary when he was made an Officer of the Order of Australia that he was 'very pleased to be on the same status as Geoffrey Blainey, J.M. Ward and Alan Bond'. A few months later, when back in Perth, he spoke at the invitation of the Murdoch History Society on the public furore that followed Geoffrey Blainey's 1984 statement on Asian immigration and was reported as saying that since the controversialist had no scholarly authority on the subject his views 'were of no more value than the man in the street'. This drew Blainey into public protest: 'How long do I have to live, what else do I have to do, to become qualified?' Again in his diary, Bolton confessed that the incident left him depressed and intensely agitated.[66]

Characteristically, it was Bolton who wrote to Blainey to patch up this skirmish and Bolton again who in 2000 helped initiate a conference in Melbourne devoted to Blainey's work. This occasion, part tribute and part appraisal, had awkward moments that were eased by the warmth and respect between the two Geoffreys. A decade later,

---

66   Diary, 2 May, 5 September 1984; *The West Australian*, 21 September 1984.

Geoffrey Blainey returned the compliment by travelling to Perth for a public forum on the question 'Is Australia Going West?' By then Geoffrey Bolton's eminence had softened the preoccupation with the advantages of his Melbourne contemporaries (he called it 'one of his neuroses') and the mutual regard of the two men was clear.[67]

In 2015 Geoffrey told his friend Ged Martin to cherish his seventies; 'the eighties are less fun but better than the alternative'.[68] He suffered a serious illness in 2003 and subsequently felt the onset of emphysema, a family weakness. There was still a project to complete and this one too was long overdue. It was the biography of Paul Hasluck, whom he had known for much of his life and with whom he shared both an appreciation of their provincial place of opportunity and a need to go beyond it. The book was completed in 2014. It pays close attention to Hasluck's career as a diplomat, his ministerial direction of Aboriginal policy, Papua New Guinea and foreign affairs, and finally his execution of the office of Governor-General; but above all it explores with penetrating empathy the character of an intensely private man of public affairs, often disappointed but steadfast to his standards.[69]

Geoffrey was also a man of probity; when invited to contribute an essay to a collection on the deadly sins he chose hypocrisy as perhaps the most common. But he pointed out that hypocrisy arose from the exercise of power and 'outside power relationships there is little

---

67   Blainey acknowledged Bolton's conciliatory letter in his own, 6 December 1984, Bolton Papers, NLA Acc.05/1239, Box 1, Folder '1984'; Deborah Gare, Geoffrey Bolton, Stuart Macintyre and Tom Stannage (eds), *The Fuss That Never Ended: The Life and Work of Geoffrey Blainey* (Melbourne: Melbourne University Press, 2003); Gare, 'Images from a Life', p. 94; 'Is Australia Going West?' www.abc.net.au/tv/bigideas/stories/2012/11/12/3629116.htm

68   Ged Martin, 'Geoffrey Bolton 1931–2015: A Tribute', http://www.gedmartin.net/martinalia-mainmenu-3/234-geoffrey-bolton-1931-2015-a-tribute

69   Geoffrey Bolton, *Paul Hasluck: A Life* (Perth: UWA Publishing, 2014).

need for dissembling'.[70] He was not good at power relationships and perhaps his greatest disappointments were caused by the way they operated in universities and the academic profession. But he bore his disappointments with fortitude, kept resentments to himself and never allowed them to affect personal dealings. He was also a singularly kind and supportive man who found comfort in his family, kept his friendships in good repair, was unfailingly supportive of colleagues, set all manner of strangers at ease and always tried to help. As his health declined and he was diagnosed in 2015 with an inoperable cancer, he continued to participate to the last.

Geoffrey had unusual gifts: erudition, prodigious memory and literary grace. If he was uneasy with abstract systems of thought, he applied a subtle and independent intelligence to a wide range of historical subjects. He was not alone in yearning for success but never preened himself or put others down. Nor did he parade his learning. He drew from a remarkable stock of knowledge with a grasp of context and command of detail employed with a dexterity that gave his writing such lucidity. He worked across specialist fields, his interests capacious and his sympathies responsive to contemporary concerns. Above all, he was happy in his vocation and to the very last put himself at the service of history.

---

70 Geoffrey Bolton, 'Hypocrisy', in Ross Fitzgerald (ed.), *The Eleven Deadly Sins* (Melbourne: William Heinemann, 1993), p. 54.

Chapter 2

HISTORY AT HOME, OR HOW DO YOU KNOW THAT'S TRUE?

Carol Bolton

In the spring of 1957 a group of young people from Oxford are gathering at a country house for a dance. One young woman has been upstairs leaving her outdoor clothes and is now about to find her way down to the ballroom. There is a very imposing staircase and she starts to walk down. At the bottom is a small group of young men whom she knows, but not well. She does her best to make a striking entrance and she thinks she has succeeded when one of the young men detaches himself from the group and moves towards her. 'Perhaps he will ask me to dance', she thinks. He looks at her very intensely and says 'Carol, have you any family papers?'

To understand this interaction the reader needs to know that the young woman's surname was one which figured quite prominently in the history of the Irish Act of Union of 1800 on which the young man was planning to write his doctoral thesis.

I had no family papers of the right kind, but reader I married him a year later. History was to be an important part of our life together.

CHAPTER 2

When we first met Geoffrey was already a deeply committed historian and an ambitious student. He told one of his tutors at Oxford that he was going to be a professor at a university in Australia. This at a time when there were only ten chairs in history in the whole country. He had a lifetime of plans ahead of him and no shortage of ideas for research and writing. At this point in our relationship I probably did not know very much about how and why history mattered so much to him beyond the obvious delight and fascination it held for him. I would learn more about its meaning and will return to this topic later. My background was in English literature. Later I retrained as a clinical psychologist and psychotherapist. All these disciplines have one thing in common: they are concerned to use narrative to make sense of human experience. However, they differ in where they position themselves in relation to subjectivity and objectivity.

This was a matter for discussion between us. It was well illustrated when I was attempting to write about what I called my family myths. That was not an attempt at a family history; what I wanted to do was to collect stories which had been passed down from my grandparents about some of their early experiences. I did not hear them from my grandparents but from their children. The stories must have had a certain significance to be passed on; I thought of them as myth because they illustrated what the family thought was important, something about how the family understood itself. I was writing about a profound experience my grandfather had one late afternoon as he, the virtuous apprentice, was left to shut up the shop in which he worked in Belfast. Along came a Salvation Army group who held an open-air service just as he was putting up the shutters and locking the door. He listened, was drawn to their message, became a convert and so changed his life and the future of the family. As I wrote I remarked to Geoffrey that I wondered where the shop had been. 'We could probably find out', said Geoffrey. He was horrified when I replied that I didn't want to undertake that kind of research; what was important was the way that the story had been passed on. After we had discussed the matter he understood where I was coming from and how different it was from what he did as a historian.

I told this tale to a psychoanalyst friend who remarked that it very well illustrated the difference between the two disciplines. The historian is looking for the most objective position from which to tell his story and backs it up with research. The psychotherapist looks at the significance of what is given in the narrative and the significance of what is left out. This distinction allowed us to play with these ideas and to look at links between our two disciplines.

Another area for discussion, sometimes playful, occasionally very serious, was the matter of theory. Geoffrey was hesitant about theory-driven history because he thought that theory could get in the way of seeing what was there. He worked without a theory, he would say. I insisted that this was impossible: if you say that theory is to be avoided then that in itself is a theory. Also presumably a theory is present in the decisions about what to put in and what to leave out.

A third area which came to have some prominence as he wrote more biographies and as I became immersed in psychotherapy was the question of how the biographer might make sense of his subject's inner world. Both of us had reservations about biographies which relied in a rather formulaic way on some psychological theory, Erikson for instance, or some part of Freudian theory. Amateur psychoanalysis seemed distasteful. What might be appropriate?

CHAPTER 2

This discussion was an ongoing subject for us. What inferences could/should the biographer make, what evidence could be used? When I was feeling mischievous I would put forward the proposition (not original to me; Freud said it first) that novels can be more 'true' to human nature than biographies. For instance, George Eliot can give us a more accurate and detailed picture of the movement of the human heart in following the workings of Dorothea's mind in *Middlemarch* than any biographer can hope to do with his subject because he does not have access to the mind of his subject in the way a novelist, a gifted one, has. Nevertheless, for us the question of what could be understood, what could be described and what could be inferred from the material available to the biographer remained a very lively subject for discussion. In particular, we discussed over the last few years various aspects of Paul Hasluck's life. He appealed to Geoffrey as a subject for many reasons. Both of them were scholarship boys from Western Australia with ambitions to move onto the national stage. I sometimes think that the relationship between biographer and subject has some similarity to the relationship between therapist and patient. In each case two minds are joining to make sense of a story. Hasluck's mind was partly accessible through the very extensive collection of papers available to Geoffrey. We discussed many aspects of his documented thinking. This included wondering about Hasluck's view of himself as 'a model prisoner' (his own description), his Salvation Army background from which he escaped and the vicissitudes of a marriage which often entailed long periods of separation. Sometimes I offered thoughts which were clearly related to my professional expertise but, as the daughter of Salvation Army officers myself, I was also able to offer some ideas based on my own experience.

Geoffrey, despite his caution about theory-based history, found some of the theoretical material coming fairly recently from psychoanalysis valuable. One writer whose work has become prominent in much recent psychoanalytic thinking is Wilfred Bion. Despite some very complex theoretical writing, Bion came to a position where he affirmed the importance of not knowing. By this he didn't mean ignorance but a capacity to put aside preconceptions and attend to what is happening in the moment. Bion quoted Keats' thinking about what he called negative capability: *'that is when man is capable of being in uncertainties, mysteries, doubts without any irritable reaching after facts'*; in other words in a receptive frame of mind not coloured by expectations. This has obvious relevance for the therapist and patient in a psychotherapy session. I think it also has relevance for the historian and his relationship with his material. I think it is how Geoffrey approached his research. He greatly enjoyed the writing of his books but perhaps he enjoyed even more the research which preceded that. He seldom wanted research assistants, he had such a good time among the source material himself.

Our discussions were often about the balance between the openness and not knowing which precedes the creative process and the questions that the writer might bring to their search of the material. The balance between these two positions I think is where the writer creates meaning.

I want to think briefly about what Geoffrey didn't write. Next on the, still long, list of books he would like to have written was to have been an exploration of his life as a historian. He would have started with his Masters dissertation about the Kimberley cattle industry, reflected on why he chose that topic and how he worked at the time and then explored how he might go about it with the advantage of his

CHAPTER 2

current experience and wisdom. This would have gone on through all his various research projects. He hoped, and I hoped too, that he would be able to interrogate the younger Geoffrey and perhaps have some dialogue with his earlier self. I think that this would have been a rich and valuable book for him and for his readers.

On a lighter note I am sad that we did not collect his stories for children. His character, Cocky Feathers, was a white cockatoo who, with a goat called Billy the Kid, had many adventures set in the historical past. I remember for instance one about Julius Caesar and Pompey which introduced his listeners, successively his younger brother, his children and his grandchildren, to life in ancient Rome. I think such a collection might have been a best-seller.

Also unwritten but lovingly remembered are the narratives he told me about various places we visited. His knowledge and understanding enriched all my experience. Not long before he died we went to an exhibition of Chinese painting at the National Gallery of Victoria. Before we went I asked him to put that period of Chinese history into context for me. There followed a fascinating survey of Chinese history from about 600BCE to the present day, placing the paintings perfectly in context. Our travels to places such as Rome, Istanbul and North Queensland were similarly enriched. I know that the capacity for lively narrative was one of the things that made his undergraduate lectures so attractive to students.

Geoffrey's enthusiasm for history and his generous nature meant that he was very supportive to others working in the discipline. Many students and colleagues benefited from his support, his willingness to discuss, to guide and to appreciate their work. It gave him particular pleasure when someone who had been a student of his told him how important and memorable some of his lectures had been.

A HISTORIAN FOR ALL SEASONS

Living with history brought much meaning and colour into my life. Our different professional trainings and skills allowed us to explore some aspects of narrative and point of view in ways from which we both benefited. As I reflect now on what history might have meant to Geoffrey and how that affected his work and his view of the world, I think in particular of two things. In watching him at work and hearing him talk about history one encountered the sheer pleasure for him of the immersion in his subject. He was like a child playing on the beach, expressing intense pleasure in exploring what is there. But as any psychotherapist knows, play is a serious and meaningful affair, a way of making sense of the world. So a greater understanding of the past leads to a greater understanding of the present. That aspect of history was very important to Geoffrey. Since his death I have often been part of discussions about current political issues. A question has arisen about some of the antecedent events which are relevant to understanding the present issue but none of us in the discussion is quite sure of the facts. 'Geoffrey would know' is a common refrain.

I have sometimes thought that, in his concern to show us the past in order to illuminate the present, he was in the role of the minstrel who narrated epic tales with significance for his community of listeners. Certainly such epics were part of his internal world. When, before he died, we discussed what might be said at his memorial service about his view of the world he asked me to quote from the Old English poem 'The Battle of Maldon': 'Mind must be harder, heart must be stouter, the spirit grow stronger as our strength grows less'. These words are put into the mouth of an elderly knight surveying a very powerful enemy force. The poet is surveying the knight and giving his audience an insight into the historical situation and the

CHAPTER 2

man's philosophy for life. I like to think that Geoffrey did something similar in his writing of history. Human beings tell stories to make sense of experience. History holds up both a light to illuminate what has happened and a mirror to help people see themselves and their past in a way that Geoffrey hoped would encourage his audience to be more reflective about the present.

Chapter 3

'THE CHARACTER BUSINESS'

Biographical Political Writing in Australia

Mark McKenna

In July 2015 I was a participant in a workshop ('Historians as Autobiographers') held at the ANU in Canberra, which Geoffrey Bolton also attended. Over lunch, we talked about our respective papers, mine on Manning Clark and Geoffrey's on historians and their 'networks'. I mentioned that I had been toying with the idea of writing an essay on the spate of political memoirs, diaries, autobiographies and biographies published over the last decade or more, to which Geoffrey responded with typical enthusiasm. I recall that he was distinctly unimpressed by many of the examples we discussed.

Working on the history of the Pilbara at the time, I was also keen to tap Geoffrey's prodigious knowledge. Generous as always, he scribbled down his contact details and insisted that we meet for lunch when I came to Perth later that year. The essay that follows would undoubtedly have benefited from that conversation. Geoffrey had a

CHAPTER 3

lifelong passion for political biography. His biographies of Edmund Barton and Paul Hasluck, both written in the latter part of his career, are exemplary not only for their scholarship but also for their wit, insight and compassion. Recalling the moment in 1952 when Barton entered his life during a hotel conversation with a 73-year-old station hand who had observed Barton at close quarters in the 1890s, Geoff captured both his own enthusiasm and his companion's thirst: 'We talked while I sipped my beer and he drained his crème de menthe from five-ounce glasses'.

Geoffrey was acutely conscious that his chronological biographical narratives were seen as unfashionable within academic circles. 'So it is', he observed in 2006:

> that the practitioner of political biography may be compared to an old-fashioned craftsman in an Alpine village laboriously carving cuckoo clocks by time-honoured methods, while in the big town in the valley below the Swatch factory is turning out bright new up-to-the-minute products replete with every new device fresh from the laboratories of culture studies and post-modernism.

He need not have worried. As with his ninety-one *Australian Dictionary of Biography* entries, his biographies of Barton and Hasluck will remain the standard reference works for decades to come. As a political biographer, Geoffrey grappled with two challenges in particular: 'the self-consciousness with which political figures concern themselves with their reputation in the eyes of posterity' and the 'interface between private and public character'. Both these challenges lie at the heart of any attempt to understand the recent profusion of biographical political writing in Australia. The essay that follows is the belated result of the conversation that I shared with Geoffrey in Canberra in 2015.[1]

***

In October 1964, Richard Crossman, Minister for Housing and Local Government in Harold Wilson's newly elected Labour government, was struggling to adjust to his life in Whitehall: 'my room is like a padded cell, and in certain ways I am like a person who is suddenly certified a lunatic and put safely into this great vast room, cut off from real life and surrounded by [the civil service]'. Crossman's *The Diaries of a Cabinet Minister* – acerbic, penetrating and alarmingly frank from the perspective of the British Labour Party, which tried to stop their publication when they appeared posthumously in three volumes more than a decade later – exposed 'the secret operations of government concealed by the thick masses of foliage' otherwise known as democracy. Given his devastatingly comic depiction of the

---

[1] Geoffrey Bolton, *Barton: The One Man for the Job* (Sydney: Allen & Unwin, 2000), p. vii; Geoffrey Bolton, 'The Art of Australian Political Biography', in Tracey Arklay, John Nethercote and John Wanna (eds), *Australian Political Lives: Chronicling Political Careers and Administrative Histories* (Canberra: ANU Press, 2006). Sean Scalmer's work provides the most recent and comprehensive examination of political memoirs in Australia; see Sean Scalmer, 'The Rise of the Insider: Memoirs and Diaries in Recent Australian Political History', Trevor Reese Memorial Lecture, Australian Studies Centre, King's College London, 2009; Sean Scalmer and Nathan Hollier, 'I, Diarist: Examining Australian Politics from the "Inside"', *Australian Journal of Politics and History*, 55, 2 (2009), pp. 170-189; the latter provides a comprehensive historical overview of political diaries and memoirs and draws on Max Weber's strategy of the 'ideal type', to classify Australian political diaries under three categories, 'the *patrician*, the *radical* and the *professional*'. Finally, one of the best recent examinations of Australian political biography is Christine Wallace, 'The Silken Cord: Contemporaneous Australian 20th-Century Prime Ministerial Biography and its Meaning', Ph.D. thesis, ANU 2015; Wallace presents a convincing case for seeing biographies of prime ministers as a form of political intervention, one that is capable of changing perceptions of prime ministers and directly impacting on what Wallace calls their 'reputational capital'. She also shows that ghost-written political hagiography began with biographies of Billy Hughes.

CHAPTER 3

civil service, it was little surprise that Crossman's diaries inspired the 1980s television comedy *Yes Minister*. As Clive James saw when he reviewed the diaries in the *New York Review of Books* in 1977, 'they purport to be about men governing institutions, but they are just as much about institutions governing men'.[2]

Nothing quite like Crossman's diaries had appeared in print before in Britain. His eye for the everyday and his intuitive grasp of human relationships — Harold Wilson 'lying in bed eating kippers, with one kipper thrown on the carpet for his Siamese cat to finish', and on Wilson's marriage to the poet Mary Baldwin: 'I am sure they are deeply together but they are now pretty separate in their togetherness' — stripped away the façade of respectability that had for so long veiled the workings of Britain's political institutions. Such an unvarnished account, Crossman believed, could only be written 'by someone who knew party politics from the inside'. As both an 'observer' and a 'doer', a political scientist and a 'journalist M.P.', he was ideally suited to the task.[3]

Crossman knew himself as well as he knew others. Determined not to hide his 'own worst failings' and remarks that made him 'look

---

[2] Clive James reviewing Crossman's *Diaries*, *New York Review of Books*, 31 March 1977; www.clivejames.com/pieces/hercules/crossman; on his motivations, Richard Crossman, *The Diaries of a Cabinet Minister, Volume One* (London: Hamish Hamilton and Jonathan Cape, 1975), p. 11.

[3] Crossman on Wilson, 17 March 1966, quoted in Alan and Irene Taylor (eds), *The Assassin's Cloak* (Edinburgh: Canongate Books, 2000), pp. 149-50; his self-description is in Crossman, *The Diaries of a Cabinet Minister, Volume One*, p. 11. Crossman's diaries were preceded by those of the Welsh civil servant, Thomas Jones. His three-volume *Whitehall Diaries* (1916–1930) were published posthumously between 1969 and 1971, and provoked considerable controversy regarding Cabinet confidentiality. Jones was Cabinet secretary to four prime ministers (George, Law, Baldwin and MacDonald). While his diaries lacked Crossman's vivid and frank descriptions of politicians, 'no other source for the period' conveyed in so 'convincing a manner how things really were and how the members of the cabinet actually behaved'; Keith Middlemas (ed.), *Thomas Jones: Whitehall Diary*, Volume I, 1916–1925 (London: Oxford University Press, 1969), p. xv.

silly in print', he saw his diary both as an attempt to 'avoid self-deception' and 'a continuous record' of his 'whole ministerial life'. Dictated religiously every weekend while his memory was 'still hot', he was well aware that his observations would one day become of 'quite special historical value'. He would not be disappointed. By the standards of today's unshockable media culture, Crossman's revelations might appear tame, but his ambition to reveal the hitherto unseen practice of day-to-day government caught the imagination of a generation of politicians throughout the English-speaking world.[4]

In 1999, when former Labor minister Neal Blewett published *A Cabinet Diary: A Personal Record of the First Keating Government*, he acknowledged Crossman's impact: 'This is the first time a Cabinet diary of this nature has been published in Australia', he wrote, 'although Richard Crossman in *The Diaries of a Cabinet Minister* began the practice in the United Kingdom a quarter of a century ago'.[5] As it turned out, Crossman's diaries were in the back of more than one Labor Cabinet minister's mind at the time. In 1985, when Gareth Evans visited England as Bob Hawke's Minister for Resources and Energy, he paid homage at Crossman's manor house in Oxfordshire. Already emulating his literary role model by keeping a diary, Evans was determined to do for Australian politics what Crossman had done for Britain. Almost three decades later, when he finally published *Inside the Hawke–Keating Government: A Cabinet Diary*, Evans explained how he had been inspired by Crossman's attempt to show how 'government actually works in practice' and to paint 'a complete, rather than selective, picture of the events ... which filled [his]

---

4   Crossman, *The Diaries of a Cabinet Minister, Volume One*, pp. 12-13.
5   Neal Blewett, *A Cabinet Diary: A Personal Record of the First Keating Government* (Adelaide: Wakefield Press, 1999), p. 2.

ministerial days'.[6] Shortly after its publication, Laura Tingle noted that all the 'young things' in Caucus were 'hoovering up' Evans' *Cabinet Diary* to gain an understanding of how government worked.[7]

Like Crossman, Evans and Blewett came from academic backgrounds and were more conscious of the historical precedents and limitations of the genre. They also displayed far more patience than the surfeit of today's political diarists and memoirists. Years of cooling off before publication is now the exception rather than the rule. Contracts are signed not only when politicians are still in parliament, but in some cases politicians are diary-wired before they have even taken their seat. In 2013 the Australian Motoring Enthusiasts' Party's Ricky Muir closed his first press conference as Senator, quipping that he had to race back to his office to write up his diary. Perhaps Muir was spruiking. If so, he failed to secure a publisher's contract. Yet his remark caught the zeitgeist flawlessly.[8] What began nearly half a century ago as the finely-honed participant's view of politics has since become a tidal rush of everything from crude apologia, thinly veiled political intervention, prurient gossip, narcissistic self-promotion, and a handful of genuinely revelatory accounts of executive government in which Richard Crossman's ghost still hovers.

Since the publication of *The Latham Diaries* in 2005 and the period of leadership instability that ensued soon afterwards, the sharp

---

6   Gareth Evans, *Inside the Hawke Keating Government: A Cabinet Diary* (Melbourne: Melbourne University Press, 2014), p. xiii.

7   Tingle quoted in Jane Messer, 'Australia is Awash with Political Memoir', *The Conversation*, 9 September 2015; http://theconversation.com/australia-is-awash-with-political-memoir-but-only-some-will-survive-the-flood-46386

8   In a memorable footnote in his article, 'The Idea of a Colonial Gentry', *Historical Studies*, 13, 51 (1968), p. 321, n. 38, Geoff Bolton confessed: 'I remember having read, though I cannot at the moment trace, an obituary notice'. Like Geoff, I remember having heard Muir's quip that he had to get back and write up his diary for the day, though I cannot at the moment trace it.

increase in the number of political books – everything from biography, diary, memoir and autobiography – has been much remarked on. Sales have been healthy. John Howard's *Lazarus Rising* has shifted well over 100,000 copies, Julia Gillard's *My Story* more than 70,000 and Mark Latham's *Diaries* in excess of 60,000. In a country where book sales of more than 4000 units are considered extremely successful, other political books have exceeded sales of 20,000 (*The Costello Memoirs*, Kerry O'Brien's *Keating*, Nikki Sava's *The Road to Ruin* and Peter Garrett's *Big Blue Sky*) while many others have easily sold more than 5000 copies. Recording the recent trending of political books is one thing, understanding the deluge quite another.[9]

In an ever expanding market, the crucial determinants of popularity have remained largely constant: the status of the author and subject (descending from prime ministers and Opposition leaders to Cabinet ministers and insider accounts); voice (first-person insider accounts appeal more than political analysis); immediacy (wait more than eighteen months in a 24/7 media culture and the subject risks being forgotten); and finally, the level of intimate or scandalous detail that is revealed (all of which becomes more potent as it touches on the office of prime minister). The vast array of such books defies tidy categorisation just as publishers, booksellers and critics hold widely differing views regarding their cultural significance.[10]

---

9   Sales figures quoted in Jane Messer, 'Australia Is Awash with Political Memoir', and Jason Steger, 'Have Australian Readers Had Enough of Books about Politics?', *The Sydney Morning Herald*, 9 January 2016.

10 Neal Blewett is one of the few recent political diarists who is aware of what is sacrificed as well as gained in the genre. Introducing his *Cabinet Diary* (p. 1), he writes: 'It is not a personal memoir, in which a political career is vindicated in retrospect. Unlike a memoir, this account sacrifices reflection for the first-hand response, hindsight for immediacy, and perspective for hasty judgement'. Aside from the books referred to elsewhere in this chapter, recent examples of political memoir published by Melbourne University Publishing include *Windsor's Way* by Tony Windsor (2015), *Black Dog Daze: Public Life, Private Demons* by Andrew Robb (2011), *Living Politics* by Margaret

CHAPTER 3

Nearly all of this tide falls under the rubric of life writing. The politician tells his or her 'own story' (often with assistance) or someone tells it for them (with or without their cooperation). Within these two broad categories there is myriad variety – scholarly political biography (its broader, long-term understandings of political culture increasingly marginalised), popular political biography (usually written by journalists and published when the subject is within the leadership circle), political memoir, diary and autobiography, 'personalised policy essay', 'sharp little biographies of political players' (as described by their most effective exponent, David Marr), and analyses of political leadership crises with a strong biographical element, some of which fly unapologetically under titles borrowed from TV crime

---

Reynolds (2007), *The Independent Member for Lyne* by Rob Oakeshott (2014), *Machine Rules: A Political Primer* by Stephen Loosley (2015), Greg Combet, *The Fights of My Life* (with Mark Davis) (2014), and Maxine McKew, *Tales from the Political Trenches* (2013). See also Bob Brown, *Optimism: Reflections on a Life in Action* (Melbourne: Hardie Grant, 2014); Wayne Swan, *The Good Fight: Six Years, Two Prime Ministers and Staring Down the Great Recession* (Sydney: Allen & Unwin, 2014); Peter Garrett, *Big Blue Sky: A* Memoir (Sydney: Allen & Unwin, 2015); and Pauline Hanson, *Untamed & Unashamed: The Autobiography* (Melbourne: Jo Jo Publishing, 2007). Important earlier examples include Graham Richardson, *Whatever it Takes* (Sydney: Bantam Books, 1994); Bob Hawke, *The Hawke Memoirs* (Melbourne: Mandarin Heinemann, 1994); Don Watson, *Recollections of a Bleeding Heart* (Sydney: Random House, 2002); and Graham Freudenberg, *A Figure of Speech: A Political Memoir* (Brisbane: John Wiley, 2005). Significantly, Freudenberg points out (p. vii) that his retirement coincided with a renewed interest in political speeches, which has occurred contemporaneously with the boom in political memoirs and diaries.For another example of what will likely become an increasingly prominent category, the journalist's memoir, see Greg Sheridan's *When We Were Young and Foolish: A Memoir of My Misguided Youth with Tony Abbott, Bob Carr, Malcolm Turnbull, Kevin Rudd & Other Reprobates* (Sydney: Allen & Unwin, 2015), which like Chris Mitchell's *Making Headlines*, also includes revelations of private conversations with Abbott and Rudd. See also Chris Bowen, *Hearts and Minds: A Blueprint for Modern Labor* (Melbourne: Melbourne University Press, 2013). Finally, both Tony Abbott's *Battlelines* (Melbourne: Melbourne University Press, 2009, updated 2013) and Bill Shorten's *For the Common Good: Reflections on Australia's Future* (Melbourne: Melbourne University Press, 2016) were timed to bolster their political careers at crucial times and ground their political philosophy and policies in their personal experience. Shorten, for example, claims (p. 5) that although it's not autobiography, this book 'gathers up my political story-from my earliest days in suburban Melbourne to what I now advocate as Labor leader'.

drama (*The Killing Season*, *The Stalking of Julia Gillard*) and luridly epitomise Alan Clark's dictum: 'There are no true friends in politics. We are all sharks circling, and waiting, for traces of blood to appear in the water'.[11] Amidst this cacophony little is stable, least of all the author, as Louise Adler, Executive Director of Melbourne University Publishing, and the person who has led the publication of political diaries and memoirs in Australia, recently pointed out:

> Contemporary political memoirs are rarely produced without editorial support – the unacknowledged ghostwriter, the credited co-author, advisers, researchers, fact checkers and a legion of loyal staff. The 'author' is what semioticians might call an 'unstable' category, an unusually capacious term that permits a looser definition than other genres.[12]

---

11 Alan Clark, Diary, 30 November 1990, https://books.google.com.au/books?id=eWycAQAAQBAJ&pg=PA372&dq=alan+clark+sharks+circling&hl=en&sa=X&redir_esc=y#v=onepage&q=alan%20clark%20sharks%20circling&f=false. For David Marr on the *Quarterly Essay* political biographies, see his Seymour Lecture, National Library of Australia, 8 September 2016 (not yet available online); 'personalised policy essay' is taken from Neal Blewett's helpful typology of biographical political writing; (1) personalised policy essay; (2) political autobiography; (3) political memoir; (4) politician's autobiography; and (5) political diary; see Neal Blewett, 'The Personal Writings of Politicians', in Arklay, Nethercote and Wanna (eds), *Australian Political Lives*, p. 91. For another example of participant eyewitness history, see Sarah Ferguson, *The Killing Season Uncut* (Melbourne: Melbourne University Press, 2016); Ferguson explains on p. 23 why her interviews with Tanner were cut from the program – 'The author of *Sideshow: Dumbing Down Democracy*, a trenchant critique of the media, wasn't inclined to provide answers that suited the tempo of the program'. This was also mentioned by Neal Blewett in his review of *The Killing Season*; 'He Said, She Said: The Book of a Commanding Documentary', *Australian Book Review*, August 2016, pp. 12-13. The explicitly biographical focus of *The Killing Season* differs from Lenore Taylor and David Uren's *Shitstorm: Inside Labor's Darkest Days* (Melbourne: Melbourne University Press, 2010); lastly, see Niki Savva, *The Road to Ruin: How Tony Abbott and Peta Credlin Destroyed Their Own Government* (Melbourne: Scribe, 2016); Savva's introduction is a telling example of the increasingly close relationship between politicians and journalists, each trying to out-manoeuvre the other.

12 Louise Adler, 'Political Memoirs', *Meanjin*, 74, 3 (Spring 2015), pp. 237-39; Adler's role in shaping the publishing culture of biographical political books can be gauged by noting how many Melbourne University Publishing political authors thank Adler in their acknowledgments for suggesting the idea of their book in the first place. http://mupublishing.tumblr.com/post/127448927933/louise-adler-on-political-memoirs

CHAPTER 3

If 'loose definition' is one hallmark of the recent wave of biographical political writing, 'loose reliability' is its natural bedfellow. The methods employed by authors and their collaborators to arrive at a 'truthful account' are as varied as recollections of meetings in Canberra. There are no agreed rules, only those imposed by the author. Like Howard and Hawke, most make no attempt to reflect on their methodology. Rather, they simply ask the reader to believe that they will 'deal objectively' with the material and 'tell it as it was'. Very few write their memoir or autobiography with the same aim as former Labor minister Barry Jones – 'to explain my life to myself' – while the handful of authors who do contemplate their means of arriving at the truth do little more than reveal the spectacularly improvised nature of the genre.[13]

Collaborating with Malcolm Fraser to produce his *Political Memoirs*, Margaret Simons described her role as the 'curator' of Fraser's life story, imagining wishfully that she could 'disappear behind the material'. In compiling *Keating*, Kerry O'Brien claimed that he was 'neither Paul Keating's biographer nor his ghostwriter'. Rather, O'Brien, who relied partly on conversations 'paraphrased from memory', saw the book as an 'amalgam' of Keating's 'authentic voice' and his own 'robust challenges to [Keating's] account of the political history he lived through and his part in it'.[14] As co-author of *The Costello Memoirs*, Peter Coleman 'discussed, edited and improved on each draft' with Peter Costello yet insisted nonetheless: 'these are his memoirs, not

---

13 Barry Jones, *A Thinking Reed* (Sydney: Allen & Unwin, 2006), p. 1; John Howard, *Lazarus Rising: A Personal and Political Autobiography* (Sydney: Harper Collins, 2010); Howard writes on p. 4 that 'I endeavour to deal objectively with the key relationships of my years in politics'.

14 Kerry O'Brien, *Keating* (Sydney: Allen & Unwin, 2015), p. x; Malcolm Fraser and Margaret Simons, *The Political Memoirs* (Melbourne: Miegunyah Press, 2010); Simons describes the book as 'part memoir and part authorised biography' on p. 1.

mine'.¹⁵ Composing *The Reith Papers*, Peter Reith relied on an unusual hybrid of diary and memoir, selectively quoting diary entries as catalysts for personal recollection. *The Latham Diaries* were initially written up from notes by Mark Latham a week or so after the event, then later transcribed into the computer preserving the original entries. For the reader to trust any of these idiosyncratic means of truth-telling requires an act of faith. 'Trust me', the author purrs, 'I will tell you what actually happened'.¹⁶

Leaving aside the more obvious potential for after-the-event embellishment, softening of initial judgments, omission of essential data and editorial pruning and clarification for the purposes of readability, the vast gap between what 'actually happened' (which ideally requires more than one perspective) and the book that finally emerges as 'my story' is undeniable. Yet perhaps this is given. As Doris Lessing remarked, 'we make up our pasts'. All forms of biographical writing are notoriously unreliable: the biographer struggles to capture the lives of others, forever chasing the phantom of the life 'as lived'; the autobiographer is inevitably Janus-faced – the self of the narrative a 'stranger to the self who writes'; while the memoirist is reliant upon the most unreliable instrument of all.¹⁷ The much more vexing question is what the surge in biographical political writing reveals about the lives of the governing class and the state of Australia's political culture.

---

15   Peter Costello with Peter Coleman, *The Costello Memoirs: The Age of Prosperity* (Melbourne: Melbourne University Press, 2008), p. 6.
16   Peter Reith, *The Reith Papers* (Melbourne: Melbourne University Press, 2015), p. 6; curiously, Reith's book contains a final chapter entitled 'The Back Story', which is essentially a potted political autobiography; Mark Latham, *The Latham Diaries* (Melbourne: Melbourne University Press, 2005), p. 2.
17   Lessing quoted in Mark McKenna, '"National Awakening", Autobiography, and the Invention of Manning Clark', *Life Writing*, 13, 2 (2016), pp. 207-20.

CHAPTER 3

In 2007, when James Walter lamented the 'sheer prevalence of mediocre campaign style biographies of virtually every party luminary ... too numerous, and mostly too lacking in usable insight to cite', he asked imploringly 'but why are they deemed necessary?'[18] Even those who have lived inside the Canberra bubble, such as former Labor minister, Lindsay Tanner, decry the current obsession with 'personal dramas' rather than policy and 'ideas': 'Since I left federal parliament in 2010', Tanner writes in his introduction to *Politics without Purpose*, 'I have been asked many times when I am going to write my political memoirs. My answer is always "Never". With Australian political debate drowning in vacuous narcissism, I have no wish to impose my inevitably self-serving recollection of mostly forgettable events on the reading public.'[19] Tanner's palpable cynicism points to one of the glaring paradoxes of the recent outpouring of political memoir and biography. At a time when electorates in liberal democracies are frequently diagnosed as 'alienated' or 'disengaged', and 'mistrust' of the political class is endemic, our culture is saturated with political talk and political books are widely read, and not only by the cognoscenti. Rather than 'distorting' the political process, the inundation of political books is a mirror; so many of them instantly redundant on the one hand, yet cumulatively, a telling portrait of contemporary politics on the other.[20]

---

18   James Walter, 'Political Biography', in *The Oxford Companion to Australian Politics* (Melbourne: Oxford University Press, 2007), p. 415.

19   Lindsay Tanner, *Politics with Purpose: Occasional Observations on Public and Private Life* (Melbourne, Scribe, 2012), p. 1.

20   In his 2009 Trevor Reese Lecture, Sean Scalmer argued that political memoirs and diaries were 'increasingly confessional, immediate, ambitious, interventionist and cynical' and that their popularity 'threatens to distort popular understandings of both the past and the political process'.

A HISTORIAN FOR ALL SEASONS

Politicians have long sought to shape the historical record. Self-consciousness comes with the territory. Dilettante or old hand, every MP chisels their place in history, hoping that even if no one appears to be listening now, someone might in the future. Yet when it comes to history, there's much faux humility from our political masters. Positioning political memoir as an act of community service, the politician pleads that they are motivated by little more than a desire to provide the 'raw materials' for historians.[21] Robert Menzies, for example, claimed that he had written his memoirs 'for the assistance of tomorrow's historians'.[22] Whether future historians will play the dutiful scribes they are so often imagined to be is doubtful. Among the current crop of political books, claims to provide the reader with a 'ringside seat when history is being made' (Bruce Hawker on Kevin Rudd's 2013 election campaign) are legion, as is naked indulgence in 'legacy building': 'aside from not being prepared to let ideologues rewrite history, as a patriot I can't resist the urge to tell a proud story of Australia' (Wayne Swan introducing his memoir of his time as federal Treasurer). Only a minority of politicians aspire to perform the highwire act of being both observer and participant.[23]

Bob Carr's *Diary of a Foreign Minister* begins with an epigraph from David Hare's 1993 play *The Absence of War*, which is based on British Labour leader Neil Kinnock's time as Opposition leader. 'I found myself asking a question which will always haunt us and to

---

21 Gareth Evans quotes 'raw materials' for historians from Bob Carr's review of Neil Blewett's Cabinet Diaries, in Gareth Evans, *Inside the Hawke Keating Government*, p. xii.

22 Robert Menzies, *Afternoon Light: Some Memories of Men and Events* (Melbourne: Cassell, 1967), p. 1.

23 Wayne Swan, *The Good Fight: Six Years, Two Prime Ministers and Staring Down the Great Recession* (Sydney: Allen & Unwin, 2014), p. xii; Bruce Hawker, *The Rudd Rebellion: The Campaign to Save Labor* (Melbourne: Melbourne University Press, 2013), p. 1.

which no easy answer appears', Hare's lead character muses after his election loss. 'Is this history? Is everything history? Could we have done more? Was it possible? And how shall we know?' Like Hare's Kinnock, Carr is haunted by the question of whether his eighteen-month stint as foreign minister will matter: 'Had this been history? ... was it all history?' In Russia, his tenure as foreign minister all but over, Carr gazes out a train window on his way from Saint Petersburg to Moscow to 'more clusters of derelict dachas, clumps of pine and birch and marshes' and finally reassures himself: 'Yes, it was history ... But speeding fast, and already fading like an illusion.'[24] The history to which Carr appeals has vanished before it arrives. In today's media environment – best described by the *Guardian*'s Katherine Murphy as 'a cycle of constant cross-current, contention and disruption' – history is now.[25] The din of ceaseless news obliterates the past. The only memory is of constant change. This mania for immediacy, which Gareth Evans has sardonically compared to 'Dante's ninth circle of hell', sacrifices reflection for the 'authentic' eyewitness account.[26] Participants' political history is valued far more than after-the-event analysis. Nowhere were these trends more obvious than in the *Latham Diaries*, in which Latham, bizarrely, seemed determined to gazump journalists:

---

24   Bob Carr, *Diary of Foreign Minister* (Sydney: NewSouth Publishing, 2014), pp. vii, 475, 477; see also Carr's 'Diary Keeping: A Personal Perspective', in David Clune and Ken Turner (eds), *Writing Party History: Papers from a Seminar Held at Parliament House, Sydney, May 2006* (Sydney: New South Wales Parliament, 2006), pp. 5-10.
25   Katherine Murphy, 'How to Be a Political Reporter: Know Your Beat, Respect the Reader, Hold Your Nerve', *Guardian Australia*, 1 February 2016; www.theguardian.com/media/2016/feb/01/how-to-be-a-political-reporter-know-your-beat-respect-the-reader-hold-your-nerve
26   Launch by Professor the Hon. Gareth Evans, Chancellor of the ANU, 14 April 2014, www.gevans.org/speeches/speech547.html

> In understanding political events, the Australian public depends heavily on journalists, people who can never go behind the scenes and provide a first-hand account of the political process. By its nature, their work is derivative, relying on second- and third-hand interpretations. This has weakened the reliability of the public record. The electorate has had little exposure to the other side of public life, to what happens behind the newspaper headlines, behind the political spin and manipulation of the news cycle ... This book aims to overcome that deficiency ... a diary can go places that the media or historians can never see, and it does so with a striking immediacy, free from revisionism and party political censorship.[27]

Latham's contempt for journalists (who he later describes as 'animals') blinds him to the fact that he uncritically accepts the rationale of the very media he derides: elevating the 'fly-on-the wall' account above considered reflection. It fails to occur to him that many of the historians and journalists he elbows aside in his eagerness to narrate 'politics in the raw' actually have the capacity to provide a far less 'jaundiced account' of his time as Labor leader than the one he provides in his diaries, which are blatantly self-serving and constantly undermined by bitterness ('My commitment to the cause was destroyed by the bastardy of others'). Taunting journalists – they 'only ever see a small fraction of what happens in politics' – Latham unwittingly pointed to one of the forces that would drive the publication of so many political books: the ever-intensifying struggle between politicians and journalists to claim authorship of political history and assert their story over those of others.[28]

---

27 p. vii.
28 Latham, *The Latham Diaries*, pp. 3-5, and the 'bastardry of others', p. 414; see also p. 411, where Latham describes his resignation and refers to the media as 'animals': 'Freedom day. It's done. I felt calm and determined at my press conference. Organised it for Ingleburn mid-afternoon to make the animals scurry away from the

CHAPTER 3

In Canberra everyone is an insider. Cheek-by-jowl in the same ruthlessly competitive environment and surrounded by so much 'media noise', politicians and journalists are both desperate to puncture the clamour with a line that their audience will buy and follow: a narrative which might last more than a nanosecond and on which the pack will feed. Each side needs the other. Neither side trusts the other. Like Latham, many of today's political authors claim to be both players and analysts; insisting that the only legitimate and *authentic* interpreter of politics is the person who was 'there' – the (allegedly) unfiltered and untainted voice of the eyewitness. This struggle for political authority, credibility, trust and ultimately power is partly a by-product of the merging of what was once two separate worlds: the journalist and the politician. No longer content with their traditional roles, journalists seek to become players: shock-jocks become Senators or share equal billing on the *Q&A* stage with Cabinet ministers; reporters who once interviewed prime ministers stand against prime ministers in their own seat, and retiring newspaper editors write memoirs which divulge their private conversations with the rich and powerful. At the same time, politicians and their staff regularly cross over to the other side: one-time prime-ministerial advisors become hired snipers on Sky News, former Opposition leaders star in their own FM radio program (*Lathamland*), and, like old footballers

---

front of our home ... enjoyed watching the media reaction: falling over themselves, rolling around on the ground, wetting themselves with excitement, little boys and girls at play.' Latham's criticisms of the media echoed those of Graham Richardson in *Whatever it Takes*. Richardson argued, p. x, that those in the press gallery 'have never taken part in the battles, never risked their present, let alone their future ... no matter how hard their noses are pressed against the window pane, those outside the process find difficulty in understanding the personal dilemmas of so many players who have had to reconcile personal and factional loyalties ...' For another discussion of Latham's *Diaries*, see Scalmer and Hollier, 'I, Diarist: Examining Australian Politics from the "Inside", especially pp. 174-75.

retiring from the sporting arena to the commentator's box, former MPs regularly take up the op-ed pen, dispensing gratuitous political advice to their former teammates. The representation of parliamentary democracy is now akin to the stock exchange floor: a crowd of undifferentiated brokers trading in ideas, opinion, policy bubbles, misinformation and shady promises. Trapped in the Canberra bearpit, their hands raised high, each shrill voice shouts down the other. For those tasked with framing, advancing and legislating policy, the task of rising above the fray and governing the country becomes harder daily.[29]

Reviewing Chris Mitchell's recently published memoir *Making Headlines* in *The Australian*, Nicolas Rothwell offered one of the more cogent diagnoses of this malaise: 'the key message of Mitchell's memoir', argued Rothwell, 'is how strong the campaign to manage and marginalise the media has become. Politicians build their own narratives and promote them. The media knows this and fights back. A kind of shadow arms race has developed as a result: a contest with threats, blandishments, feints and confidences as its stock in trade.'[30] Biographical political books are unquestionably one of the major

---

[29] After Abbott's removal, Peta Credlin took up a position as commentator with Sky News. One-time shock jock Derryn Hinch entered the Senate after the 2016 election while Alan Jones regularly appears on ABC TV'S *Q&A* to provide 'balance'. The former editor of *The Australian*, Chris Mitchell, published his memoir *Making Headlines* (Melbourne: Melbourne University Press, 2016), in which he divulged conversations with former prime ministers, particularly Abbott and Rudd; Mark Latham's FM radio program 'Lathamland' followed on the heels of his implosion at the Melbourne Writers Festival in August 2015; see both www.triplem.com.au/sydney/shows/lathamland/blog/listen-and-download-the-new-lathamland-podcast/ and www.abc.net.au/news/2015-08-22/mark-latham-appearance-disappointing-melbourne-writers-festival/6717484. Finally, on the increasing difficulty of governing in Australia, see Andrew Markus, 'Trust in the Australian Political System', *Papers on Parliament*, 62 (October 2014) www.aph.gov.au/senate/~/~/link.aspx?_id=1713CA0133C845D8B54945046F5C7B8B&_z=z

[30] Nicolas Rothwell, reviewing Mitchell's *Making Headlines*, *Weekend Australian Review*, 1–2 October 2016, pp. 16-17, 20.

CHAPTER 3

sources of political 'narrative' to which Rothwell alludes, many of them standing as little more than an extended arm of the politician's media arsenal. Their publication – so often extracted and immediately condensed into bite-size sized morsels such as the ubiquitous bio-feature published in weekend magazines – is much more than news.

In an era when trust in politicians has evaporated, the only way to make the public figure credible is through the selective exhibition of the politician's private world. Political philosophy and policy reform are not sold intellectually: rather, they are embroidered in carefully scripted narratives that ground politics in the personal life-story of the leader. Nor is the leader's political conviction found in Cabinet meetings or party machinations. Instead, the principles that will guide the nation's future apparently lie in the dimly lit hallways of the leader's childhood memories. In 2010, barely two weeks after she had taken the leadership from Kevin Rudd, Julia Gillard asked 'for the Australian people's trust to move Australia forward'. Revealing herself as a 'shy child' transformed through the sacrifices of her Welsh immigrant parents, Gillard recalled her mother 'cooking and scrubbing pots in a Salvation Army aged care home', and her father's shiftwork as a nurse in a psychiatric hospital; stories of hardship that stood not only as a metaphor for the success of Australia's postwar immigration program, but also, as she explained, had shaped her political 'values'.[31] The man Gillard deposed had spoken of his childhood too: a young boy who grew up on a dairy farm in the Gold Coast hinterland, left fatherless at eleven after a fatal car accident, his mother and family evicted and forced to sleep in their car before

---

31   Julia Gillard's speech, 12 July 2010, www.theaustralian.com.au/archive/politics/julia-gillard-tells-in-a-speech-of-her-childhood-her-family-and-their-values/story-e6frgczf-1225890891763

they found temporary accommodation. Kevin Rudd's 'struggle-town to the Lodge' was an all too familiar refrain.[32]

Posting a Liberal campaign advertisement on his Facebook page earlier this year that included childhood photos, Malcolm Turnbull told the story of his single-parent father's unconditional love – 'I was the main object of everything he wanted to achieve' – and his family's adversity: 'we didn't have much money, he was a hotel broker and for most of that time he was battling like a lot of people are, a lot of single parents are'.[33] In order to vote for our political leaders, it seems that we have to see our own life experience mirrored in theirs. They have to become 'family', which is probably one reason why our relationship with them is so fraught. Political autobiographies and memoirs are a natural extension of the same phenomenon. Publishers crave more intimate detail from their political authors, while politicians strategically deploy their life stories as allegories of national experience. In a culture in which the electorate has become increasingly sceptical of all kinds of political communication – from press releases to doorstop grabs, tweet-bombs, Facebook walls that are little more than thinly veiled propaganda, and set-piece parliamentary performances designed for television news – 'character' and personal biographies have become the last islands of 'genuine' information, their origins forged in a pre-political time and their telling responsible for establishing trust and political credibility. And not only in Australia. The 2016 Presidential election campaign in the United States was

---

32   On Kevin Rudd's background, see '20 Things You Need to Know About Kevin Rudd', *The Age*, 3 December 2006.
33   Tom McIlroy, 'Federal Election 2016: Malcolm Turnbull Remembers His Dad in New Campaign Ad', *The Sydney Morning Herald*, 6 June 2016.

CHAPTER 3

largely understood by political commentators as a battle of 'character' between Hillary Clinton and Donald Trump.[34]

Character came most dramatically to the fore in Australian politics in the winter of 2010. David Marr's *Quarterly Essay* 'Power Trip' was widely credited with 'undermining' Rudd before he was removed by his Labor colleagues in June that year.[35] At the very end of the essay, Marr described his dinner with Rudd at a waterfront pub in Mackay. When Rudd asked what line he'd take in the essay, Marr answered him bluntly: he was an 'orator of skill' who could also be 'a bore'. He was also a prime minister 'unloved by his own caucus' whose 'government might well fall'. Unsurprisingly, Rudd was furious. Marr vividly described the 'dressing down' that followed:

> I have hurt him and he is angry ... He doesn't scream and bang the table as he does behind closed doors. We're in the open. The voice is low. He is perfectly composed ... In his anger Rudd becomes astonishingly eloquent. This is the most vivid version of himself I've encountered. At last he is speaking from the heart, an angry heart. Face to face it's so clear. Rudd is driven by anger. It's the juice in the machine ... Who is the real Kevin Rudd? He is the man you see when the anger vents. He's a politician with rage at his core, impatient rage.[36]

---

34   There are countless examples (googling 'Hillary Clinton This Election Is About Character' brings them up). See, for example, Todd S. Purdum, 'The 2016 Race Isn't About Issues. It's About Character', *Politico*, 8 August 2016, www.politico.com/magazine/story/2016/08/does-anyone-care-about-issues-anymore-or-only-whether-trump-is-crazy-214150
35   John Warhurst suggested that Marr's essay had played a role in Rudd's downfall; see his 'Much Ado Abbott Nothing: David Marr's Quarterly Essay Misses the Mark', *The Conversation*, 18 September 2012, https://theconversationhttps://theconversation.com/much-ado-abbott-nothing-marrs-quarterly-essay-misses-the-mark-9627
36   David Marr, *Rudd v Abbott: Two Classic Quarterly Essays* (Melbourne: Black Inc., 2013), pp. 138-39.

Shortly after the essay's publication, Marr was confronted on ABC TV's *Q&A* by Professor Jayashri Kulkarni, a psychiatrist from Monash University, who argued vehemently that he wasn't qualified to make such a diagnosis, least of all in regard to someone in public life such as Rudd. Stunned, Marr tried to hold his ground, defending his right to interpret Rudd's character. 'You do medical treatment,' he replied, 'I'm a biographer, a reporter. I [ask] what's that person like and how does he operate? You cannot bar people from doing that.' Other commentators such as *Crikey*'s Mark Bahnisch chimed in, accusing Marr of 'amateur psychology' and arguing that he had reduced Rudd's complex personality to one primal emotion 'putatively the result of childhood trauma'. 'Rudd', Bahnisch insisted, 'should be judged on the public benefits of his actions, not on a whole bunch of inferences from his biography'. Reflecting on the encounter five years later, Marr refused to back down. 'What ... I should have said to the angry professor was this: "Biographers are in the character business too".'[37]

Marr has naturally denied that his *Quarterly Essay* had anything to do with Rudd's downfall. And his defence that biographers have long sought to understand what motivates their subjects has many eminent supporters. As Judith Brett explains, the first question she seeks to answer as a political biographer is 'what is the deep source of political energy for that person. What drives the subject?' More significant than the biographer's qualifications in psychology or the largely unanswerable question of the political impact of Marr's essay is the fact that, more than any other recent example of political

---

37 David Marr, The Hazel Rowley Memorial Lecture, Adelaide Festival, 4 March 2015, www.hazelrowley.com/memorial_speech_david_marr.pdf
and Mark Bahnisch, www.crikey.com.au/2010/06/09/david-marr%E2%80%99s-anger-hypothesis-is-torturously-argued/

biography, Marr's essay dramatically signalled the rise of 'character' in contemporary politics, or as he put it, our growing willingness 'to make sense of the country through biography'. As one of the few serious writers on 'character', Marr's work stands apart from the recent wash of biographical political writing that brazenly seeks to deploy character for political advantage, drawing his inspiration, as he has explained, from an earlier generation of journalists – Mungo MacCallum, Alan Ramsay, Craig McGregor and Bob Ellis – who 'never lost sight of the role of character in public life'. Yet whether political biography, 'if it's out in time', can actually help us 'decide the fate of the country' as Marr has claimed, is less certain. What is undeniable, however, is the dramatic nature of the shift.[38]

The flood of biographical political writing published in the last decade is symptomatic of the fact that we are increasingly being asked to judge the actions and policies of our political leaders on the basis of their character alone. The deliberate attempts by politicians to massage their biographies only make them fair game for journalists, their potential fall from grace ever greater. We are asking more of our political leaders and giving them less time to deliver. We want to know them intimately, not only as politicians but as 'one of us'. And we are as quick to worship them as we are to revile them. Again and again, personality prevails over policy, intimacy and immediacy over analysis. The political class draws ever inwards, daily losing its capacity to stand outside itself because so many of its roles have become interchangeable, a situation that only makes it easier for populists to cast its members indiscriminately as 'elites'. Nostalgic for

---

[38] Judith Brett, 'Recording Non-Labor Politics through Biography', in Arklay, Nethercote and Wanna (eds), *Australian Political Lives*, p. 25. Also see Marr, Hazel Rowley Lecture, Adelaide Festival, 4 March 2015.

a time when prime ministers were bold enough to advance a program for national renewal, we scan the horizon for a leader who will take the opportunity to use power creatively.

The success of political biography and the continuing interest of publishers and readers alike also points to more profound changes in how Australia is governed. For a country that has never sought to define its identity through its political institutions, politics today occupies an even more central position. Despite regional and State divergence, the political conversation emanating from Canberra holds the nation together more than we might be willing to acknowledge. As the overwhelming public response to the death of former Labor Prime Minister Gough Whitlam on 21 October 2014 demonstrated – surely a watershed in the history of public commemoration in Australia – Australians now possess a greater readiness to remember figures of intellectual, political and creative vision. The mirror that we hold up to ourselves is becoming larger, the patterns of our self-understanding, attachment and remembrance at once more diverse and less tangible.

Chapter 4

'YARNING IN THE STREET'

The Evolution of Australian Public History

Graeme Davison

Geoffrey Bolton never called himself a public historian. From his perspective, there was no other sort. 'These were my people and it is right that I should be their chronicler', he writes in *Daphne Street*, his delightful history of the lower-middle-class street in which he grew up.[1] Whether he was writing about his home, his city, his State or his nation, Geoffrey was speaking about, and for, his people. He perceived no conflict between his academic and public roles. 'He very much liked to hear non-historians say that they had enjoyed some book of his and his work was to a large extent aimed at a non-historian audience', Carol Bolton observes. He moved easily between local, regional, State, national and international spheres of activity. His innate generosity of spirit embraced all levels of

---

1   As a 't'othersider' with scant local knowledge of Geoffrey's public activity in Western Australia, I have relied heavily on the help of Carol Bolton, Bill Bunbury, Lenore Layman and Stuart Macintyre, which I gratefully acknowledge here. Geoffrey Bolton, *Daphne Street* (Fremantle: Fremantle Arts Centre Press, 1997), p. 1.

society, making him, as others have noted, very much a historian of the middle ground.

From the nineteenth century we historians inherited two contrasting role models. Leopold von Ranke exemplified the German ideal of academic precision and specialisation, critical documentary study, and scientific detachment. 'Ranke was the representative of the age which instituted the modern study of history', his English admirer Lord Acton claimed. 'He taught it to be critical, to be colourless, and to be new'. Geoffrey Bolton was well schooled in that tradition in Perth and Oxford. Judicious, scholarly, respectful of his academic peers, he was a consummate professional, critical and alert to the new, though never colourless.

Ranke's alter ego was the romantic nationalist historian, exemplified in their age by Jules Michelet and Thomas Carlyle. The historian's task, according to Michelet, was to be the voice of the people. He held up a mirror to the nation, offering his fellow citizens an affirmative, if not entirely uncritical, sense of who they were, where they had come from, and where they were heading. Writing history was the highest form of citizenship. 'God has given me in History the means of participating in everything', he declared.[2] Geoffrey Bolton offered Western Australians a positive sense of their identity. If he became their Mr History, it was not just for what he said and wrote, but because he participated in everything: launching books, giving broadcasts, serving on boards and committees, encouraging his students and colleagues, hardly ever declining an invitation to speak.

Geoffrey enjoyed and valued an unusual breadth of social acquaintance and acceptance. Convivial, witty, and an accomplished

---

[2] John Burrow, *A History of Histories* (London: Allen Lane, 2007, Penguin 2009), p. 392.

CHAPTER 4

raconteur, he was at home in almost any company. He liked people and they liked him. Bill Bunbury, who often interviewed him for his ABC programs *Talking History* and *Hindsight*, recalls how 'Geoffrey would often swing his long legs down from a table and regale his audience with stories'. Often hilarious, these stories revealed his prodigious memory, his intimate local knowledge of Western Australian society as well as his grasp of the bigger Australian picture. A good listener as well as a good talker, he was among the first senior Australian historians to use interviews as well as written sources in his 1972 book on the impact of the Great Depression in Western Australia, *A Fine Country to Starve In*.

So much at home in any company, Geoffrey may have underestimated – or, I suspect, knowingly ignored – the divisions and conflicts that others took to heart. As an undergraduate, he invited friends from Peppermint Grove to his parents' humbler home in North Perth. In the Kimberley he had mixed with Aborigines and pastoralists. At Balliol his friends included aristocrats and scholarship boys. If he viewed Western Australian society as intimate and harmonious it was because that is how he experienced it. 'Good Western Australians disliked extremes in politics, kept on friendly terms with their rivals, and never rocked the boat', he observed in his masterly introduction to *A Fine Country to Starve In*. 'Controversies occurred, of course, but they were kept within limits: they were family rows.' Politicians were not VIPs but 'affable, accessible men who lived in suburban bungalows, and could be met for a yarn in the street'.[3]

Yarning in the street is a nice image, not just of Geoffrey's Perth but also of his preferred style of public engagement. 'Unashamedly a

---

3   G.C. Bolton, *A Fine Country to Starve In* (Perth: University of Western Australia Press, 1972), pp. 4-5.

creature of the Anglican tradition of the *via media*', he looked instinctively for the sensible middle ground, confident that men and women of goodwill could usually agree, or at least agree to differ.[4] He was a public historian in the same way that he was a public man. His wit, affability and generosity of spirit opened doors and diffused conflict. As a student of eighteenth-century English history, he understood the arts of patronage and diplomacy. Among his unfinished projects was a biography of a great conciliator, William Eden, Lord Auckland.

Some of Bolton's UWA predecessors, more angular characters like Edward Shann and Frank Crowley, had challenged the local consensus before retreating to academic fortresses in the east. Fred Alexander, who Bolton succeeded as professor in 1966, was at home in Perth and played a pivotal public role in adult education and the Western Australian Public Library, but took little part in local historical debates. As Stuart Macintyre shows, Bolton was ambivalent about the role he had inherited from Alexander. He chafed against the isolation and provincialism of Perth and deplored what he saw as the 'Hume Highway hegemony' of ideas and power in Australia.[5] He yearned for the prestige and influence he associated, perhaps mistakenly, with a chair in one of the east coast universities. Yet he also knew that distance could be emancipating, and celebrated the insights that came from looking at Australia 'from the edge'.[6]

Gradually and reluctantly, Bolton came to acknowledge that the society of his youth, where public men yarned in the street, was

---

4 Geoffrey Bolton, '*The Tyranny of Distance* Revisited', in Deborah Gare, Geoffrey Bolton, Stuart Macintyre and Tom Stannage (eds), *The Fuss that Never Ended: The Life and Work of Geoffrey Blainey* (Melbourne: Melbourne University Press, 2003), p. 30.

5 Geoffrey Bolton, *Land of Vision and Mirage: Western Australia since 1826* (Perth: University of Western Australia Press, 2008), p. 2.

6 Geoffrey Bolton, 'The Opportunities of Distance', *Distance Education*, 7, 1 (1988), pp. 5-22. Bolton, *A View from the Edge: An Australian Stocktaking*, Boyer Lectures (Sydney: ABC Books, 1992).

CHAPTER 4

breaking down. Western Australia, he noted in a 2008 history of the State, had become more complex and adversarial.[7] The public role he had inherited from Alexander, serving on the boards of institutions such as the State Library of Western Australia and the Western Australian Museum, no longer carried the same clout. He looked back nostalgically to 'the easy and frequent access to ministers and senior public servants' enjoyed by his predecessors. Amidst the bounty of the mining boom, he deplored the poverty of the State's cultural institutions. 'It would be disgraceful if ... our generation went down to posterity as a generation of philistine, provincial pygmies.'[8] Enough of the *ancien régime* survived for Geoffrey to remain a powerful advocate and patron, but its days were numbered.

By the 1980s, many of Geoffrey's younger colleagues, led by Tom Stannage and including Rob Pascoe, Lenore Layman, Jenny Gregory and Charlie Fox, had begun to challenge that consensus. Stannage's *The People of Perth* (1979) and *A New History of Western Australia* (1981) were the opening salvoes of an attack on what they called, mischievously, 'the gentry view' of Western Australian history. Lenore Layman's critical studies of the State's development ideology, Anna Haebich's studies of Aboriginal policy and Jenny Gregory's *City of Light* exposed fissures in the fabric of a society Bolton had portrayed as relatively harmonious.[9] While some of these works were written

---

7   Bolton, *Land of Vision and Mirage*, p. 3.
8   Town Hall Forum, 19 October 2009.
9   Lenore Layman, 'Making a Difference: Tom Stannage and the UWA Tradition of Engagement', *Studies in Western Australian History*, 29 (2015) pp. 69-79; C.T. Stannage, *The People of Perth* (Perth: Perth City Council, 1979), and C.T. Stannage (ed.), *A New History of Western Australia* (Perth: University of Western Australia Press, 1981); Lenore Layman, 'Development Ideology in Western Australia 1933–1965', *Historical Studies*, 20, 79 (1982), pp. 234-60; Anna Haebich, *For Their Own Good: Aborigines and Government in the South-west of Western Australia* (Perth: University of Western Australia Press, 1992); Jenny Gregory, *City of Light: A History of Perth since the 1950s* (Perth: City of Perth, 2003).

under State or city patronage, they exemplified a shift in the public role of the historian from insider to outsider, and from a celebratory to a critical vision of history.[10] Towards the end of his life, Geoffrey Bolton often adopted the stance of prophet to shame the State's politicians into funding a new building for the Western Australian Museum, and to denounce the destruction of Perth's Esplanade to make way for Elizabeth Quay.

The Coming of Public History

It was at about this time that Australian historians began to speak of 'public history'. They borrowed the term from the United States to describe the diverse forms of historical activity being undertaken by academically-trained historians in places outside the academy, such as museums, heritage agencies, national parks and the like. 'Public history', according to its advocates, denoted an engagement in 'the public process'. It was a notion that resonated with high-minded American conceptions of liberal democracy and kindred terms such as 'public interest', 'public service' and 'public philosophy'.[11] It gained currency, one might argue, not because the historians were *more* engaged in the public domain than their predecessors, but less. As the universities expanded during the 1960s and 1970s, academic history had looked inwards, developing its own specialisms and technical language. Only when the boom ended did they begin to look outwards again. Public history was the motto for that re-engagement.

At its simplest, public history was a marketing strategy: an attempt to increase the demand for the products of academic history, and to

---

10   Graeme Davison, *The Use and Abuse of Australian History* (Sydney: Allen & Unwin, 2000), pp. 9-17.
11   Robert Kelley, 'Public History: Its Origins, Nature and Prospects', *The Public Historian*, 1, 1 (1978), p. 16.

CHAPTER 4

protect the competitive position of practitioners already in the field. Historians often faced cutthroat competition from journalists and other 'unqualified' historians offering to do the same work – whether it was a commissioned local history, a heritage study or a museum brief. Potential employers simply did not understand the research and literary skills involved in writing a good history. 'It's not a hobby! That's my livelihood', Terri McCormack had to remind slow-paying clients.[12] In founding the Centre for Western Australian History in 1985, Tom Stannage and Brian de Garis were offering a home to the growing number of academically trained historians seeking a livelihood outside the university. The Victorian and New South Wales History Councils, formed at about this time, had similar objectives. Over the past thirty years, under the leadership of Jenny Gregory and her colleagues, the Centre has produced an impressive volume of commissioned histories, heritage reports, edited collections and oral history archives.

Traditionalists sometimes sneered at the idea of 'public history'. There seemed to be something vaguely distasteful and intellectually dubious about it, Grace Karskens recalled.[13] Some regarded it as a form of academic slumming, while others objected to the inference that, as academics, they were not already engaged in a public activity. In Australia it became a flag of convenience under which historians outside the academy and their academic fellow travellers could happily sail together. The two-way traffic between academic history and public history, we were convinced, would be mutually beneficial, bringing the best insights of the academics into the work

---

12   'That's My Livelihood', *Phanfare*, 205 (2004).
13   Grace Karskens, 'Public History-Academic History: The Common Ground', *Public History Review*, (1992), p. 23.

of heritage consultants, museum curators and other public historians, and heightening awareness of the uses of the past within the academy. The movement gained impetus as the humanities responded to the utilitarian challenge of the 'Dawkins Revolution' in higher education. As president of the Australian Historical Association in 1988–89, I responded to the Green Paper with a two-pronged defence: insisting on the value of history as a humanistic study while also advocating the skills it taught to potential employers.[14]

Over the following two decades, several universities introduced graduate programs in public history, although only two – at Monash University and the University of Technology in Sydney – lasted for more than a few years. The Monash program began as a fourth-year honours subject, History in the Field, taught jointly by Ann McGrath, who had recently returned from the Northern Territory where she had researched on Aboriginal Land Claims, and Graeme Davison, then chair of the Victorian Historic Buildings Council (now Heritage Council). Keen student interest – the subject attracted more than half the final honours cohort – persuaded us to offer a Masters program in 1988. From the first, the program combined critical classroom discussion with experience in the field. To underline its 'real world' orientation and foster links with downtown cultural institutions, it was based at Monash's city campus. Under Chris McConville and Tom Griffiths, assisted by archaeologist Annie Bickford and architect Richard Aitken, students engaged in a range of 'hands-on' projects in heritage, environmental history and museums, supported by weekend fieldwork excursions and internships.

---

14   Graeme Davison, 'History and Higher Education: A Response to *Higher Education: A Policy Discussion Paper*', *Australian Historical Association Bulletin*, 55 (1988), pp. 29-36.

CHAPTER 4

Describing the program in 1992, I emphasised 'practical skills of interpretation and communication' and immersion in 'real world experience'.[15] One of its first by-products, *A Heritage Handbook*, was funded by the Hawke government's inquiry into Australian Studies, and combined critical essays on the idea of heritage and case studies of notable heritage battles with practical advice on 'reading a building' and 'presenting a case'.[16] Tom Griffiths' *Secrets of the Forest* (1992) and the Monash Public History Group's *Macalister Landscapes* (1994) originated as student fieldwork projects in cooperation with the Centre for Gippsland Studies and the Victorian Department of Conservation.[17] Like its American counterparts, the Monash Public History course sought to equip its graduates to engage in 'the public process'. The demand for salaried historians in public institutions, like museums and government heritage bodies, had evened out by the late 1980s; most of the Monash graduates became freelance historians, Jills-of-all trades, mixing heritage consultancies, commissioned histories, research assistance and other short-term projects.

Public history was outdoor history, a history of the field rather than the cloister. In this, we were not pioneering but building on an earlier tradition. When Fred Alexander sent Geoffrey Bolton north to the Kimberley, and Keith Hancock directed him to write a history of North Queensland, they were following this tradition.

---

15 Graeme Davison, 'Paradigms of Public History', *Australian Historical Studies*, special issue, *Packaging the Past*, edited by John Rickard and Peter Spearritt, 24, 96 (1991), pp. 4-15.

16 Graeme Davison and Chris McConville (eds), *A Heritage Handbook* (Sydney: Allen and Unwin, 1991).

17 Tom Griffiths, *Secrets of the Forest: Discovering History in Melbourne's Ash Range* (Sydney: Allen & Unwin, 1992), republished in a revised version as *Forests of Ash: An Environmental History* (Melbourne: Cambridge University Press, 2001); Monash Public History Group, *Macalister Landscapes: History and Heritage in Maffra Shire* (Bairnsdale: Kapana Press, 1994).

Max Crawford had previously arranged for a young Geoffrey Blainey to write a history of the Mount Lyell Mining Company in the remote northwest of Tasmania. Soon afterwards John Mulvaney was recruiting his friends in the first archaeological expeditions to Fromm's Landing. The weekend field trips that became a feature of the Monash Public History course followed their example, teaching hands-on skills and cultivating an ethos of collaboration as an antidote to the more solitary life of the archive-bound historian.[18]

The decade leading up to the Australian Bicentenary had brought a notable quickening of debate within the academy, as well as outside, about the public uses of history. Many historians had participated in the multi-volume Australian Bicentennial History Project launched by Ken Inglis and his colleagues at the ANU, or in other commemorative history projects such as the four-volume *People's History of Australia*, published by Penguin and dedicated to 'analysing the lives of the oppressed', or the more orthodox narrative *Oxford History of Australia* edited by Geoffrey Bolton. 'There was a great deal of confusion about what it meant to be Australian', Bolton noted in his own concluding volume of the series.[19] Some of the confusion was circumstantial, produced by the events and personalities of the moment; but more of it derived from intractable differences of opinion among historians, as well as citizens, about how the past was implicated in 'what it meant to be Australian'. Geoffrey's even-handed, rather Olympian narrative of these conflicts led him towards a characteristic conclusion, in praise of Australian subtlety and the sensible 'middle way'. For other historians, however, the Bicentenary

---

18 Tom Griffiths, *The Art of Time Travel: Historians and Their Craft* (Melbourne: Black Inc., 2016), p. 22.
19 Geoffrey Bolton, *The Oxford History of Australia. Volume 5, 1942–1988: The Middle Way* (Melbourne: Oxford University Press, 1990), p. 288.

CHAPTER 4

had elicited questions about the uses of history that demanded closer investigation.

While Monash was launching its Masters program, historians at the University of Technology, Sydney (UTS) led by Ann Curthoys and Paula Hamilton established a graduate diploma in Applied History. Located in downtown Sydney, in a School of Communications close to the ABC and the Powerhouse Museum, it defined public history as 'a concern with audience and an awareness of the complex relationship between audience, historical practice and institutional context'.[20] Curthoys' interest in cultural theory and Hamilton's in journalism, coupled with Paul Ashton's decade-long experience in heritage and local history, gave the program its distinctive focus. Over the following two decades, UTS became the principal national clearinghouse for debate on how Australians use the past. *The Public History Review*, established in 1992 in cooperation with the Professional Historians Association of New South Wales, carries articles, commentaries and reviews on the full range of public histories, including heritage, museums, theme parks, environmental history, new media, school history, commemorations, re-enactments, memorials, film and television.

Public history represented a shift in the traditional public role of the academic historian. Rather than an oracle standing above the fray, the historian, it suggested, was a participant in the 'public process', alternating between the roles of patron, consultant, mentor, collaborator, commentator and critic. In 'going public' we expected to learn from our fellow citizens as well as teach them. Every person, we sometimes said, could be their own historian, and as professionals

---

20 Ann Curthoys and Paula Hamilton, 'What Makes History Public?', *Public History Review*, 1 (1992), p. 11.

we had no proprietary rights to the past. Yet, when it came down to it, we also believed – as did the public, most of the time at least – that academic expertise conferred a degree of authority. Those on the frontline, like history teachers in schools and professional historians working in the community, grew nervous when the academics engaged in 'trendy exercise[s] to deconstruct the study of history'. It was hard enough to win the respect of students and clients without their academic colleagues 'going to water behind us'.[21] If the professors didn't believe in their claims as truth-tellers, who would believe in their students'?

Public History and the Politics of Identity

If there was a theme to public history during the 1980s and 1990s, it was the idea of identity. Whether one thinks of heritage, museums, monuments, commemorations, school histories, commissioned histories or national history, the historian's job was to appropriate the past in order to reinforce – or to contest – a personal or group identity. 'History is identity', Mayor Frank Sartor writes in his introduction to Shirley Fitzgerald's 1992 history of Sydney.[22] Projecting that identity into the public realm was what made that history public. More often than not, the client was the state, in its local, State or national manifestation. Public history was not necessarily official or authorised history, and historians employed in public institutions often enjoyed considerable freedom in how they did their job. Shirley Fitzgerald claims she had more personal autonomy as historian of Sydney than she did in her previous academic job. She was more like a consultant

---

21 Tony Prescott, 'The Relevance of History', *Phanfare*, 210 (January–February 2005), p. 7.
22 Shirley Fitzgerald, *Sydney 1842–1992* (Sydney: Hale & Iremonger, 1992), p. 7.

CHAPTER 4

than an employee ('I never committed the sin of saying "us" when I meant "them"') and was frank about admitting the political nature of her role. Writing history for a patron, she noted, could often be 'a delicate and compromising affair' yet she had not found it so.[23]

I have experienced the role of 'official historian' myself, both as an outsider co-editing a history of the Powerhouse Museum, and as an insider co-writing a commissioned history of my own university, Monash. In one of our last conversations, Geoffrey and I discussed the challenges of writing the history of one's own university. He had written a ten-year history of Murdoch and was planning a volume to commemorate its fiftieth. Who were we writing for? Were we seeking to reinforce our institution's sense of its own identity, or to question it? How far were we bound by the expectations of employers or our colleagues? Neither the Powerhouse nor Monash attempted to censor what I wrote, yet loyalty, peer perceptions, even a desire for vindication, could subtly influence one's approach. Aware of my own biases, I consciously attempted to counter them by engaging a co-author with a different perspective. At the Powerhouse, I relied on the collegial relationships and institutional memory of long-time curator Kimberley Webber. At Monash, where I was the insider, Kate Murphy, a relative newcomer, brought a perspective closer to that of the younger generation of post-Dawkins students and staff.[24] Behind the decision was the assumption that the public historian is, at least partly, a servant of the community whose story he or she tells.

---

23 Shirley Fitzgerald and Kathryn Evans, 'Reflections on the Commissioning Process', *Public History Review*, 2 (1993), pp. 130-31; Fitzgerald, *Sydney 1842–1992*, p. 9.

24 Graeme Davison and Kimberley Webber, *Yesterday's Tomorrows: The Powerhouse Museum and its Precursors 1880–2005* (Sydney: Powerhouse Publishing, UNSW Press, 2005); Graeme Davison and Kate Murphy, *University Unlimited: The Monash Story* (Sydney: Allen & Unwin, 2012).

'Identity' can be a demanding mistress, and the higher the historian climbs towards the pinnacle of 'national identity', the more onerous its demands become. 'Practising the essentially critical discipline of history in a conservative institution confronts staff with unavoidable choices and occasional conflicts', Peter Stanley, long-time historian at the Australian War Memorial, observed mildly in 1992.[25] With the election of the Howard government and the promotion of Anzac as the primary historical focus for national identity, that challenge became more acute. During the 1980s the Memorial's Historical Section, begun under deputy-director Michael McKernan, had fostered a broad-ranging conversation between military and social historians. But under new director Steve Gower, the renamed Military History Section became 'less comfortable with the diversity and contention' that had previously characterised it. Stanley's departure, first to the National Museum and then to the University of New South Wales, the appointment of a person without qualifications in academic history as head of the section, and the emergence of the website 'Honest History' as a vigorous but not altogether unfriendly critic of the historical activity at the Memorial, charts a widening gap between the roles of the official historian and the public historian, especially as a guardian of the nation's most sacred story.[26]

In 1999, Geoffrey Bolton, John Mulvaney and I served as historical advisors to the National Museum of Australia during the completion of the Acton Peninsula museum. Engaged originally to advise the

---

25 Peter Stanley, 'Happy Birthday HRS: A Decade of the Australian War Memorial's Historical Research Section', *Public History Review*, 2 (1993), p. 58, and 'In the "Street of the Historians": Practising History at the Australian War Memorial', *Dialogue* (Academy of the Social Sciences), 26 (2/2007), pp. 30-38.

26 Peter Stanley, 'War without End', in Anna Clark and Paul Ashton (eds), *Australian History Now* (Sydney: New South, 2013), pp. 90-106.

historians on the Museum's staff, we soon found ourselves mediating between the professional staff of the Museum and two conservative members of the Museum's Council, Christopher Pearson and David Barnett. As a skirmish in the so-called 'History Wars', the episode was usually presented as a conflict between opposing left-liberal and conservative views of the Australian past, especially on the politically charged issue of settler violence towards Aborigines.[27] Because they engaged deep-seated beliefs about personal and national identity, the issues were seldom to be settled by appeal to evidence alone. The history that enhanced one citizen's sense of identity could too easily threaten another's.

Simmering below the surface, but seldom coming into clear focus — even in conversations between the three advisors — were competing notions of historical truth, professional responsibility, and political reality. Were we historians there as fact-checkers, mediators, arbitrators — or none of the above? Characteristically, Geoffrey recalled our negotiations as 'serious and civilised' and our conservative interlocutors — bar one irreconcilable — as amenable to persuasion and eager for consensus.[28] He pleaded for the critics to respect the academic

---

27   Stuart Macintyre and Anna Clark, *The History Wars* (Melbourne: Melbourne University Press, 2003), pp. 191-215; Bain Attwood and S.G. Foster (eds), *Frontier Conflict: The Australian Experience* (Canberra: National Museum of Australia, 2003).

28   Graeme Davison, 'A Historian in the Museum: The Ethics of Public History', in Stuart Macintyre (ed.), *The Historian's Conscience* (Melbourne: Melbourne University Press, 2004), pp. 49-63; 'What Should a National Museum Do?' in Marilyn Lake (ed.), *Memory, Monuments and Museums* (Melbourne: Melbourne University Press, 2006), pp. 91-109; 'Museums and the Culture Wars: In Defence of Civic Pluralism', *Open Museum Journal*, August 2006 (journal now defunct but archived on Pandora, National Library of Australia). Bolton and Davison submissions to the Carroll Review are available on the website of the National Museum of Australia. For a useful critique, see David Dean and Peter E. Rider, 'Museums, Nation and Political History in the Australian National Museum and the Canadian Museum of Civilization', *Museum and Society*, 3, 1 (2005), pp. 35-50.

expertise of museum in-house historical staff and for the council to adopt 'guidelines' reflecting a hoped-for consensus. My own memories are less sanguine. Despite our best endeavours, and agreement on many matters of detail, there appeared to be no satisfactory basis for an interpretative consensus. I was worried, in any case, that a consensus that papered over the differences of perspective among past actors and later historians would impoverish public understanding rather than advance it.

As the debate rumbled on without clear resolution, I reached for a conception of the public historian's role – 'civic pluralism' I called it – as a participant or moderator in a national conversation. Rather than a church presenting an authorised version of the nation's past, I thought of the National Museum as a public square where debate was welcomed and difference celebrated. I was drawn to the view of another of the Museum's advisors, the American curator Elaine Gurian, who described it as a 'safe place for the expression of unsafe ideas'.[29] Historians working in museums, I suggested, should be publicly identified as authors of the exhibitions they designed and subjected to critical scrutiny like their colleagues who wrote books, made documentary films, or advised film directors. By 'going public' in this way, the historian submitted to the critical discipline experienced by any speaker in the public square. If the institution's view of history became disconnected from its audience, it would be corrected by public and professional opinion rather than an official directive.

This was a hopeful perspective and it has borne some fruit. The leading historical journals, for example, now frequently review museum exhibitions along with books. But I now doubt that 'civic

---

29   Elaine Gurian, *Civilising the Museum: The Collected Writings of Elaine Neumann Gurian* (London and New York: Routledge, 2006).

CHAPTER 4

pluralism' can withstand the powerful pressures upon individual practitioners, or that their superiors will allow sufficient creative liberty to make it an effective model of public engagement. I was disappointed to discover that some public historians actually prefer institutional anonymity rather than the risks of public criticism. In such settings, the public historian becomes a public servant: sometimes outspoken within the institution but subject, in the end, to managerial control. From the vantage point of the academic, for whom intellectual autonomy is paramount, this may seem like a kind of surrender, although others may ask why a historian working within a public institution, with access to large budgets and audiences, should expect the taxpayer to subsidise a personal vision of the past rather than one grounded in a community consensus.

Public History Now

The end of the History Wars coincided with a decline of Public History, as we had used that term since the mid-1980s. Public history was turning into professional history as the graduates of the public history courses begun at Monash and UTS filled up the diminishing number of jobs in heritage, museums and other state-sponsored institutions and captured most of the commissions for local histories and heritage studies. Between 1971 and 2011 the number of academic historians in Australia had more halved from 750 to approximately 310, and were fewer than the number of professional historians (410) enrolled in the various branches of the Professional Historians Associations (PHA). Victoria (180), New South Wales (85) and Queensland (80) were the largest branches. Overwhelmingly, the profession is female (approximately 80 per cent) and most of its bread and butter comes from heritage studies, local and institutional histories and museums.[30] Long-time member Terry Kass credits the PHA with a significant improvement in the remuneration, public recognition and morale of the profession.[31] Even so, the lot of the independent historian, living from one contract to the next, is a precarious one, with little scope, one might suppose, for courageous independent inquiry. Some younger practitioners have formed small companies ('HistorySmiths', 'Way Back When', 'Historica') for mutual support and business advantage. Despite the pressures of earning a livelihood, however, the professional historians constitute a vigorous and self-critical intellectual community. A forthcoming conference of the Victorian branch includes sessions on such topics as 'Negotiating Complexity', 'History and Policy' and 'Challenging Grand Narratives'. Artisanal in structure, collegial in ethos, professional history retains much of the critical edge of public history. Earning a livelihood, it often seems, is a means to supporting the historian's vocation, not an end in itself.

Even today, the relationship between academic and professional history remains strong. Many of the most original of the present generation of Australian historians, including Tom Griffiths, Grace Karskens, Ann McGrath, Peter Stanley, Clare Wright and Alison Alexander, served their apprenticeship as public historians, working for public institutions, writing commissioned histories, or making film or television before returning to the academy in mid-career. Sometimes they coupled their work as public historians with teaching postgraduates who also aspired to work outside academia. As

---

30 For figures on academic staff and professional historians I am indebted to Mary Sheehan. Fields of activity is based on Members' Work Database in *Phanfare*, 230 (July–August 2008), pp. 8-9. Sex ratio estimated from current membership lists of Victorian and New South Wales branches of PHA.
31 Terry Kass, 'What Use is the PHA?', *Phanfare*, 242 (May–June 2010), pp, 4-5.

CHAPTER 4

Griffiths has persuasively argued, this experience in the field, including even the economic insecurity that went with it, imparted a sense of public relevance and urgency to their work, as well as a deeper appreciation of the contribution of colleagues in adjacent fields of archaeology, architecture and museology.[32]

Public history was not only an interim vocation for the academics of the next generation; by breaking down the walls of the ivory tower, it made historians more conscious of the broader dimensions of their practice. For fellow travellers in the public history movement, this was one of its prime rewards. Despite its provocative title, my book *The Use and Abuse of Australian History* (2000) was more curious about the uses of history than it was vigilant in policing its abuses. As sociologists of our discipline, we became more conscious of the effects of our practice on audiences. When we found insights in the work of historians outside the university we were more likely to incorporate them in our own work.

Paula Hamilton and Paul Ashton's national survey of Australians' attitudes to the past, modelled on Roy Rosenzweig and David Thelen's similar American survey, confirmed how important the past is to people's private and public identity. But the forms of history making that mattered to them, such as family history, were often very different from those esteemed by the academy.[33] The past, to many Australians, was not another country. It was not even their own country, as academic historians considered it, but an extension of their private selves. 'It's when history touches us personally that it tends to really take

---

32 Griffiths, *The Art of Time Travel*, pp, 278-79.
33 Roy Rozenzweig and David Thelen, *The Presence of the Past: Popular Uses of History in American Life* (New York: Columbia University Press, 1998); Paul Ashton and Paula Hamilton, *History at the Crossroads: Australians and the Past* (Sydney: Halstead Press, 2007); see also the special issue of *Australian Cultural History*, 22 (2003).

hold', writes Anna Clark in her recent *Private Lives, Public History*.[34] Like some other academics, I tended to look down on family history, seeing it as a retreat from the public domain. Only recently when I researched the history of my own family, setting it in the larger contexts of locality, religion, nation and empire, did I begin to see how genealogy, memory and history could become partners in a new kind of public history, one that acknowledged the need to link the public past with the private one, and stretched sympathy with one's own kin to solidarity with others who shared their fortunes, good and bad.[35]

Public history, as a self-conscious movement, had arrived in Australia by way of the United States. During the 1980s and 1990s, it elicited little interest among my British colleagues. Public history had affinities with the People's History movement championed by Raphael Samuel at Ruskin House in Oxford but its origins in the Workers' Educational Association and its explicit socialism set it apart from the more pragmatic and professional character of both the American and Australian public history movements. 'When "public history" is mentioned', an English sympathiser Jill Liddington observed in 2002, 'people still wrinkle their nose at the unfamiliarity'. Perhaps it smacked too much of American pragmatism, and of public relations rather than public good. Only towards the turn of the century did British historians surprisingly begin to follow Australia's lead. Ironically, Liddington notes, 'it was not from America but from

---

34   Anna Clark, *Private Lives, Public History* (Melbourne: Melbourne University Press, 2016), p. 25.
35   Graeme Davison, *Lost Relations: Fortunes of My Family in Australia's Golden Age* (Sydney: Allen & Unwin, 2015) and compare *The Use and Abuse of Australian History*, pp. 80-109 and 'Speed-relating: Family History in a Digital Age', *History Australia*, 6, 2 (2009), pp. 43.1-10.

CHAPTER 4

Australia that the key inspiration and crispest thinking about Public History in Britain flowed'.[36]

Over the past decade, as enrolments in British history departments slowed under the pressure of increased undergraduate fees, and more searching inquiries about the employment prospects of history graduates, academics began to think more earnestly about the public uses of history. The debate gained a sharper edge from the demand of politicians, on both the left and right, for history to play a part in instilling 'British values' and encouraging active citizenship.[37] John Tosh's *Why History Matters* (2008) is a balanced assessment of the opportunities and challenges of the new national mood. Wary of demands for history to supply 'pre-determined identities', he nevertheless insists on critical historical study as one of the foundations of an active citizenship.[38] The role of the public historian is not only to discredit myths – one of the key tenets of Richard Evans' 1997 book *In Defence of History* – but to bear testimony to uncomfortable truths about the past, giving voice to those whose histories have been distorted or suppressed. As he acknowledges, public history has often taken this more forensic turn in countries like Australia and New Zealand where indigenous peoples have sought redress from the wrongs of colonial rule.[39] While recognising the inevitable links between history and identity, public history, Tosh argues, must

---

36 Jill Liddington, 'What Is Public History? Publics and their Pasts, Meanings and Practices', *Oral History*, 30, 1 (2002), pp. 84-86.

37 Graeme Davison, 'Testing Times: Citizenship and "National Values" in Britain and Australia', in Raimond Gaita (ed.), *Essays on Muslims and Multiculturalism* (Melbourne: Text Publishing, 2011), pp. 119-53.

38 John Tosh, *Why History Matters* (Basingstoke: Palgrave Macmillan, 2008), pp. vii-ix.

39 Tosh, *Why History Matters*, p. 107; Graeme Davison, 'History on the Witness Stand: Interrogating the Past', in Iain McCalman and Ann McGrath (eds), *Proof & Truth: The Humanist as Expert* (Canberra: The Australian Academy of the Humanities, 2003), pp. 53-65.

maintain a critical distance. His image of the public historian – disinterested, public spirited, benevolent – is more than most humble practitioners, beset by conflicting interests and swayed by competing loyalties, could claim to be. Yet without a notion of 'public good' what can it mean to be a 'public historian'?[40]

The Future of Public History

After thirty years, public history has chalked up some successes: it has found careers outside the academy for many history graduates; it has strengthened the links between academic history and the public; it has made academic historians more self-critical about their discipline and their public roles as oracles and advocates, mediators and critics. Geoffrey Bolton, who alternated between several of these roles, remained cautious about pressing their limits. He recognised that, however much historians might aspire to lead public debate, their ability to do so depended on the willingness of their fellow citizens to be led. His public role as Western Australia's Mr History rested on a shrewdly judged combination of scholarly authority, narrative skill and native charm.

During the History Wars, as questions of national identity became paramount, that relationship often became fraught. In a timely survey in 2006, Ann Curthoys warned against 'the undeniable blandishments of national history'. It is tempting, she acknowledged, 'to be told one is valuable for the nation, and to see one's work as having national value', but that role could easily threaten the historian's critical independence. 'Let's keep a fearless critical edge … and be wary of the excesses into which a discourse of national

---

40   John Tosh, 'Public History, Civic Engagement and the Historical Profession in Britain', *History*, 99, 335 (2014), pp. 191-212.

CHAPTER 4

cohesion can draw us', she urged. Fortunately, civil society offered more than one source of patronage and the public historian working for a mix of clients, in local, State and national governments, as well as various public and private agencies, could retain a measure of critical independence.[41]

The History Wars were a battle that had to be fought, but, once the strife subsided, many historians yearned for a public role less ideologically charged, and perhaps more useful, than the one they had been conscripted into over the previous decade. There had been too much attention to the misuse of history and not enough to its value. 'It is time for us to rise above these ideological battles and champion the use of history', Western Australian historian Cathie Clement declared in 2008.[42] Too much energy, she implied, had gone into defending history, not enough into demonstrating its practical usefulness.

Two decades ago, in a review of 'paradigms of public history', I worried that too much public history had been devoted to 'salvaging the past'. Preserving buildings, curating museum exhibitions and writing commemorative histories: all were activities that seemed to look backward rather than forward. 'What had become of the grander aspirations for a public history that would help to shape the future as well as save the past?'[43] I was thinking of American 'applied historians' like Ernest May and Peter Stearns who aspired to make history a tool of public policy and Australians like Noel Butlin and Hugh Stretton who had shown how it could be done. Historians, Stretton argued, were well equipped by their training to weigh hard and soft

---

41 Ann Curthoys, 'History in the Howard Era', *Phanfare*, 219 (July–August 2006), pp. 5-8.
42 'After Summit', *Phanfare*, 230, (July–August 2008), p. 15.
43 Graeme Davison, 'Paradigms of Public History', pp. 10-11.

data, to see wholes as well as parts, to acknowledge the contingent and unforeseen in human affairs and to be critical of the values influencing public policy, including their own.[44] In his *Spoils and Spoilers*, Geoffrey Bolton had invoked Stretton's example in pleading for an environmental history that could inform his compatriots' choices about the future.[45]

In the 1990s that plea largely fell on deaf ears, including my own. The demands of identity politics for recognition and redress overrode the aspiration to progressive reform, while postmodern critiques of historical knowledge undermined our confidence that history could serve as an instrument of 'evidence-based' public policy. Only quite recently, in the United Kingdom and the United States, has public policy re-emerged as the focus for a new kind of public history. Some of the most 'wicked' policy dilemmas we now face – our responses to climate change and urbanisation, for example – require us to confront intractable patterns of path-dependence and to frame policy responses over longer time-scales than policy-makers usually employ. In *The History Manifesto* (2014), David Armitage and Jo Guldi call upon their fellow historians, accustomed to handling 'big data' and in thinking long-term, to guide their fellow citizens along the perilous path from past to future. 'We must, all of us, engage the big picture, and do so together', they exhort.[46]

Most reviewers responded sceptically, and even angrily, to the *Manifesto*'s apocalyptic tone and intellectual overreach. Those who

---

44　Hugh Stretton, 'The Botany Bay Project: Historians and the Study of Cities', *Historical Studies*, 19, 76 (1981), pp. 430-39, and *Political Essays* (Melbourne: Georgian House, 1987), pp. 167-83, 190-94.

45　Geoffrey Bolton, *Spoils and Spoilers: Australians Make Their Environment 1788–1880* (Sydney: Allen & Unwin, 1981), pp. 168-74.

46　David Armitage and Jo Guldi, *The History Manifesto* (Cambridge: Cambridge University Press, 2014), p. 13.

CHAPTER 4

shared the authors' desire to apply historical thinking to public policy did not necessarily agree that 'big data' and 'big history' were the best or only way of achieving it.[47] The historians in Cambridge and London who had been cooperating in a 'History and Policy' centre for more than a decade avowed more modest objectives and a more self-reflective tone. 'History is a discipline infused with particularity, irony, and contingency', three of them noted.[48] The historians' instinct was to complicate rather than to simplify. In policy debates, they more easily fell into the role of critic, dousing the over-confident prognoses of fellow social scientists with the cold water of historical realism, rather than of preacher or prophet.

For all their British reserve, however, participants in the 'History and Policy' website sponsored by Cambridge and King's College London have now built up an impressive archive of policy papers on subjects ranging from climate change and environment to families and children. More than five-hundred British historians are affiliated with the site and it has sponsored conferences and workshops on key conceptual and methodological issues. Australian historians have as yet been slow to follow their example, although the Policy and History Network founded by David Lowe and his colleagues at Deakin University, with links to the Museum of Australian Democracy, is a promising beginning on a path that more Australian public historians may follow.[49]

---

47 Deborah Cohen and Peter Mandler, 'AHR Exchange: *The History Manifesto*: A Critique', *American Historical Review*, 120, 2 (2015), pp. 530-42; Marc Parry, 'Historians Attack the Data and the Ethics of Colleagues' Manifesto', *The Chronicle of Higher Education*, 17 April 2015, Academic Onefile, 21 June 2016.
48 Lucy Delap, Simon Szreter and Paul Warde, 'History & Policy: A Decade of Bridge-building in the United Kingdom', *Scandia*, 80, 1 (2014), pp. 97-118.
49 For further information, see the website at http://aph.org.au.

A HISTORIAN FOR ALL SEASONS

As Tom Griffiths has argued, we live on a continent where some of the most urgent problems we face – in Aboriginal policy, climate change, fire-control, urban sprawl – are grounded in a deep past that constantly impinges on the present and constrains the future. What light can public historians throw on the historical path dependencies that govern our use of water, land and fire, for example? For almost two centuries Australians believed that they inhabited a young country, and that their future was theirs alone to make. As we adjust to a new understanding of our situation, historians have the opportunity to play a creative public role, not just in saving the past, or guarding against its misuse, but in navigating our way to a safer future.

Chapter 5

GEOFFREY BOLTON AND THE BRITISH WORLD

Carl Bridge

'till he should build a city and bring his gods to Latium'

Virgil, *The Aeneid*, Book 1, ll.5-6

In the last twenty years or so some historians of the British Empire have been exploring what we now call the British World. That is, the networks of social, cultural, economic, and political connections that held the self-governing countries of the British Empire together. We have been interested in the complex flows of people, ideas and products in all directions, not simply from the metropole outwards, but importantly back from the periphery and across and around the wheel as well as along its spokes, as the peripheries turned into metropolitan centres in their own right.[1] Historians of earlier generations,

---

My thanks to the editors and to Kent Fedorowich and Simon Potter for their comments on this piece.

much more so than now, were products of, active participants in and analysts of these phenomena. Geoffrey Bolton's life and career were deeply enmeshed in the British World and very much shaped by it. He lived in it, taught and wrote about it, and was one of its relatively unsung exemplars. Here, as one of the successor generation, I wish to bear witness to his achievement and to use a British World perspective to unlock some of these connections. Elsewhere in this volume, colleagues have assessed his magnificent contribution to Australian historiography, which also was infused in many ways with his British World experience and perspectives.

A Late Imperial Career

The pattern and substance of Geoffrey Bolton's career marked him as an exemplar of the British World. A perennial scholarship boy, he ascended the ladder of educational success from North Perth Primary School to the University of Western Australia, and as a Hackett Fellow then climbed to the top rung, in his case Balliol College, Oxford.[2] At the University of Western Australia he was taught by Fred Alexander, a Victorian Rhodes Scholar who himself had been at Balliol in the early 1920s. In Oxford Bolton wrote a

---

[1] The definitive statement of the approach is Carl Bridge and Kent Fedorowich, 'Mapping the British World', *Journal of Imperial and Commonwealth History*, 31, 2 (2003), pp. 1-15. For further examples, see Phillip Buckner and R. Douglas Francis (eds), *Rediscovering the British World* (Calgary: University of Calgary Press, 2005), and their *Canada and the British World* (Vancouver: UBC Press, 2006); Kate Darian-Smith et al. (eds), *Britishness Abroad* (Melbourne: Melbourne University Press, 2007); Simon Potter, *News and the British World: The Emergence of an Imperial Press System, 1876–1922* (Oxford: Oxford University Press, 2003), and *Broadcasting Empire: The BBC and the British World, 1922–1970* (Oxford: Oxford University Press, 2012), and Tamson Pietsch, *Empire of Scholars: Universities, Networks and the British Academic World, 1850–1939* (Manchester: Manchester University Press, 2013).

[2] See Ged Martin, 'Geoffrey Bolton 1931–2015: A Tribute', in *Martinalia* at ged.martin.net accessed 18 July 2016.

CHAPTER 5

thesis, which became a book, *The Passing of the Irish Act of Union: A Study in Parliamentary Politics*.[3] Back in Australia he worked with another Rhodes Scholar from Victoria, Sir Keith Hancock, as a research fellow, and then taught at Monash University, where all three professors, John Legge, Alan McBriar and A.G.L. Shaw were Australians who had graduated from Oxford. In due course Bolton was appointed Professor of History at the University of Western Australia. His later career was punctuated by sabbaticals in England: at the University of Kent in 1971 during which he wrote a book on the rise and fall of the British Empire, *Britain's Legacy Overseas*;[4] as Visiting Commonwealth Fellow, St John's College, Cambridge, 1978–79, when he wrote his environmental history of Australia, *Spoils and Spoilers*;[5] and as Senior Scholar in Residence, All Souls College, Oxford, 1995, when he began work on his biography of Australia's first prime minister, Edmund Barton.[6] He was also, most significantly, the foundation Professor and Head of the Australian Studies Centre (now Menzies Centre) at the Institute of Commonwealth Studies, University of London, from 1982 to 1985. Besides being elected a Fellow of the Academy of the Humanities in Australia and the Australian Academy of Social Sciences, he was made a Fellow of the Royal Historical Society in London. Within Australia, at various times he held history chairs at the University of Queensland, and Murdoch and Edith Cowan universities.

---

[3] G.C. Bolton, *The Passing of the Irish Act of Union: A Study in Parliamentary Politics* (London: Oxford University Press, 1966).

[4] G.C. Bolton, *Britain's Legacy Overseas* (Oxford: Oxford University Press, 1973).

[5] Geoffrey Bolton, *Spoils and Spoilers: Australians Make Their Environment 1788–1980* (Sydney: Allen & Unwin, 1981; 2nd edn, 1992).

[6] Geoffrey Bolton, *Edmund Barton: The One Man for the Job* (Sydney: Allen & Unwin, 2000).

The Irish Act of Union

After completing his Masters thesis on the cattle country in Western Australia's north, the young Bolton proceeded in 1955 to Oxford, eventually to enrol in doctoral studies. There he was supervised by John B. Owen, just back in Oxford himself after teaching for five years at the University of Canterbury, New Zealand, and destined for history chairs in Calgary and Halifax.[7] Bolton also attended the Imperial History research seminar convened by Professor Vincent T. Harlow, who coined the phrase 'the swing to the East' to characterise the trajectory of the second British Empire after the secession of the thirteen North American colonies.[8] Owen, a British historian and Namierite, encouraged the close analysis of political connections and material interests as underpinning political thought and policy in the limited world of eighteenth-century politics. Harlow, on the other hand, was concerned with the broad sweep of empire and encouraged looking for patterns, flows and movements. Elsewhere in the Oxford History Faculty, A.J.P. Taylor, Hugh Trevor-Roper and Christopher Hill were in their prime. Nationally, during Bolton's first academic year the Suez Crisis was played out, Anthony Eden fell on his sword as prime minister and his successor Harold Macmillan came in to wind up what was left of the empire.

Owen suggested to Bolton that for his dissertation topic he should go to the personal records of the Irish and British gentry and aristocracy in the public archives and libraries and in the muniment rooms of their country houses and seek out the inside story of the passing of

---

7   Owen would soon publish *The Rise of the Pelhams* (London: Methuen, 1957).
8   Harlow's principal work was *The Founding of the Second British Empire, 1763–1793*, vol. 1 (London: Longman Green, 1952).

CHAPTER 5

the Irish Act of Union of 1801. It was an intriguing subject: he had to discover why, in the midst of the American and French Revolutions, and following the failed uprising of 1798, the Irish Protestant Ascendancy had chosen to abandon their own parliament and plump for direct British rule and a hundred seats in the Westminster parliament. Bolton must have seen parallels with the secessionist debate in his own State of Western Australia in the 1930s and with Western Australia's earlier decision to join the Australian federation in 1901. His thesis and the subsequent book would look behind the rhetorical analysis of the parliamentary debates which characterised the existing historiography and drill down into the political and commercial deal-making, factions, office-seeking and preferment which, clothed in ideological respectability, according to the Namierites were the real stuff of politics.[9] Bolton's findings stepped back from reductive Namierism, while still benefiting from its insights, to allow a more independent role for ideas, sentiments and friendships. He wrote in his book's final paragraph:

> To regard the ruling class who passed the Union as preternaturally corrupt does not help us understand the actions of its members. Many of them accepted the framework and conventions of politics as they found them, and too often forgot larger issues in the scuffles and manoeuvres of party feuding. But when all this is allowed, the story of the Union presents a recognisable narrative of the relations between a colonial ruling minority and the metropolitan power, understandable in terms of commercial, religious, social, and personal relationships. In such a narrative there can be no heroes or villains, but simply the attempt to understand the action and motives of men

---

9   Bolton, *The Passing of the Irish Act of Union*. The first footnote, on p. 2, is to Harlow's *Founding of the Second British Empire*, vol. 1.

confronted with a problem in administering the affairs of their fellows.[10]

Bolton could never be straitjacketed.

Britain's Legacy Overseas

Bolton's next excursion into British history ventured more fully into and well beyond Harlowian territory. This was his most ambitious imperial work, *Britain's Legacy Overseas*, commissioned for Oxford's OPUS series of 'authoritative introductions to … important branches of the humanities and sciences', and written mostly in Westgate-on-Sea while he was on study leave at the University of Kent in 1971.[11] In five mercurial essays, somewhat reminiscent in their bravura and span of the work of another of his mentors, Sir Keith Hancock,[12] Bolton offered a revisionist critique and thoughtful conclusions aimed partly at encouraging the next generation of imperial historians to break free from the suffocating, self-congratulatory whiggish 'colonies-to-independence' paradigm that dominated the established historiography. Refreshingly, he suggested that commerce and culture were often more important than administration and politics, and that the colonies were seedbeds of change which outgrew one-way influences from the metropole and took on lives of their own, in some cases even exporting new forms back to the mother country or to each other.[13] Here he anticipated British World historiography by nearly thirty years, and was concurrent with New Zealander

---

10   Ibid., p. 222.
11   Bolton, *Britain's Legacy Overseas*, Preface and back cover. Martin, 'A Tribute', notes the authorial transition from 'G.C.' to 'Geoffrey'.
12   See, for example, Hancock's *Professing History* (Sydney: Sydney University Press, 1976).
13   Bolton, *Britain's Legacy Overseas*, pp. 1-3.

CHAPTER 5

J.G.A. Pocock, whose seminal essay on 'neo-Britains' proved to be the work from which British World historiography eventually took its cue.[14] Written in the form of a powerful manifesto in the wake of Britain joining the European Economic Community, Pocock's punchy essay fired the imagination of later scholars and set out a program for future study, while Bolton's more nuanced and descriptive book went largely unnoticed.

Bolton was at pains in *Britain's Legacy Overseas* to point out that while trade and naval power had made the empire, its most important legacies were the English language and adapted British institutions. Furthermore, once the colonies of settlement (and later those of conquest) became economically viable, they lost little time in negotiating agreeable terms for their relationships with Britain. The Anglican Church was disestablished, franchises widened (and sometimes narrowed), restrictive immigration and protective tariffs introduced, constitutions amended, locals appointed to high office, civil services and judiciaries occasionally unduly politicised, and so on. Police forces (sometimes armed and mounted) and education systems were more likely to follow Irish and Scottish models than English. He remarked on the extraordinary longevity in office of some 'colonial' premiers and parties, such as Sir Oliver Mowat in Ontario, Sir Thomas Playford in South Australia or the Australian Labor Party in New South Wales. Democracy was refashioned to local circumstance. It might be Americanised or abandoned altogether, and he noted gnomically, as despotism came to characterise some of the New Commonwealth, that 'Sandhurst appeared to be

---

14   J.G.A. Pocock, 'British History: A Plea for a New Subject', *New Zealand Journal of History*, 8 (1974), pp. 3-21.

replacing Oxford as a nursery for national leaders'.[15] In his astute estimation, imperial sentiment peaked in and around the world wars and the Great Depression, when it coincided with white dominion and metropolitan self-interest (though not in Ireland and only partly in South Africa), but waned at other times and collapsed after the Suez debacle and Britain's joining the Common Market.

Geoffrey Bolton's eye for the quirky and apposite was unerring. Witness his evident delight when he wrote of the Elizabethan explorer Martin Frobisher's landing in Greenland in 1577 to get his sailors to mine 200 tons of 'gold'-bearing ore to take home to a delighted Elizabeth I only to discover on a later voyage that it was iron pyrites (fool's gold). Or when he quoted William Cobbett's admonishment to prospective emigrants, 'leave those horrible regions' to the bears and the savages; or Edmund Burke's wonderful 'colour-blind' defence of the rights of Indians in a letter to Miss Palmer: '[They] have none of your Lilies and Roses in their faces; but … are the images of the great pattern as well as you and I. I know what I am doing; whether the white people like it or not.' And Bolton noticed Jawaharlal Nehru's telling remark when dismissing the idea of Hindi as the Indian national language that the English language 'is the major window for us of the outside world'.[16]

This analysis in *Britain's Legacy Overseas*, while very perceptive, has a strangely valedictory, even elegiac tone. He could not have foreseen Britain's referendum-based decision in 2016 to 'Brexit' from the European Union and the subsequent scramble for free trade deals with Anglosphere (read former imperial) countries, among them the USA, Canada, Australia and New Zealand, or anticipated Five

---

15   Bolton, *Britain's Legacy Overseas*, p. 140.
16   Ibid., pp. 8, 64, 108.

CHAPTER 5

Eyes security and the associated 'coalitions of the willing' in recent international military interventions, based around the same countries, or the perennial popularity of Australian soap operas for British television viewers. The British imperial 'legacy' is more alive than would have seemed possible in the 1970s. Other developments which might have surprised him would have been the central role played by the Commonwealth (led by Rajiv Gandhi and Bob Hawke among others) in the ending of apartheid in South Africa and that country's decision to rejoin the Commonwealth; India's rise as the cricketing superpower, at least financially; and the thirty-year insurgency in Sri Lanka. The empire, its successor Commonwealth, and the wider British World are proving extraordinarily long-lasting in their influences, however mercurial and consensual these might be.

The 'British World' School

Had Bolton's generation the methodological tools of the 'British World' school – digital technology to dissect censuses or search newspapers for key words; funds for international comparative research in depth; network and globalisation theory, among others – they might have discovered more of what he sensed intuitively, such as the larger than imagined cash-flows from migrants back to Britain (so-called 'migrapounds'), the extraordinary to-ing and fro-ing of return and boomerang migration, and the complexities of national identities clustered around British race patriotism or other civic forms in the case, say, of some anglophile Indians, East and South-East Asians, Africans, Quebeckers and Afrikaners, among others.[17]

---

17 See, for example, Paul Magee and Andrew Thompson, *Empire and Globalisation: Networks of People, Goods and Capital in the British World, c. 1850–1914* (Cambridge: Cambridge University Press, 2010); James Belich, *Replenishing the Earth: The Settler Revolution and the Rise of the Anglo-World, 1783–1939* (Oxford: Oxford University

Here is a flavour of some of the British World school's work. 'Migrapounds' could only be unlocked by digital analysis of voluminous postal note records; as could the multinational newspaper 'word searching' that enabled the tracing of the shift in connotation of the word 'immigrant' from negative to positive from mid-nineteenth century and the rise of the 'settler'; or, similarly, the detailed study of the transnational outrage that followed the execution of Edith Cavell.[18] Making the England and Wales census electronically searchable revealed that there were 15,295 Australian-born in England and Wales at the time, the population was evenly spread across the whole country, they were overwhelmingly skilled workers of one sort or another, they were disproportionately from Victoria, their average age was 27, and two-thirds of the adults were female.[19] The international multi-archival approach has also uncovered the extraordinary and varied complexities of Edwardian newspaper and banking networks; the markedly transnational nature of the trade union movement; the different causes, trajectories and meanings of the rise of multiculturalism in Canada and Australia; the significant contribution of indigenous soldiers to the imperial effort in World War I; the vital role played by the old dominions in propping up Britain, in terms of manpower,

---

Press, 2009); Kent Fedorowich and Andrew Thompson (eds), *Empire, Migration and Identity in the British World* (Manchester: Manchester University Press, 2014); Stuart Ward, *Australia and the British Embrace: The Demise of the Imperial Ideal* (Melbourne: Melbourne University Press, 2001); James Curran and Stuart Ward, *The Unknown Nation: Australia after Empire* (Melbourne: Melbourne University Press 2010), and the works cited in note 1 above.

18 Magee and Thompson, *Empire and Globalisation*, ch. 3; Belich, *Replenishing the Earth*, ch. 5; and Katie Pickles, *Transnational Outrage: The Death and Commemoration of Edith Cavell* (Basingstoke: Palgrave Macmillan, 2007).

19 Carl Bridge, 'Australians in the England and Wales Census of 1901: A Demographic Survey', in Carl Bridge, Robert Crawford and David Dunstan (eds), *Australians in Britain: The Twentieth Century Experience* (Melbourne: Monash University ePress, 2009), ch. 4.

commodities and finances, while it ostensibly stood 'alone' against Germany and Italy before the United States entered World War II; and how the Nawab of Nawanagar, Prince Ranjitsinhji, while in many ways quintessentially British traded on his position as an outsider-insider.[20] These findings only scratch the surface.

Professing Australian Studies on the European Frontier

Throughout his career Bolton was drawn to establishing new institutions and departments. Monash was in its infancy when he went there to his first lectureship, and he was later to found the history programs at Murdoch and guide that at the Western Australian College of Advanced Education when it became Edith Cowan University. But perhaps his most challenging effort in this regard was when he was appointed foundation Head of the Australian Studies Centre at the Institute of Commonwealth Studies in London in 1982. The Institute's first director, when it was set up in 1949, had been Sir Keith Hancock, who we have seen was one of Bolton's Australian predecessors at Balliol and was the man who had appointed Bolton to his first research fellowship at the Australian National University.[21]

---

20 Simon J. Potter, *News and the British World*; Andrew Dilley, *Australia, Canada, and the City of London, c. 1896–1914* (Basingstoke: Palgrave Macmillan, 2012); Jonathan Hyslop, 'The Imperial Working Class Makes Itself "White": White Labourism in Britain, Australia and South Africa before the First World War', *Journal of Historical Sociology*, 12, 2 (1999), pp. 389-421; Timothy Winegard, *For King and Kanata: Canadian Indians and the First World War* (Winnipeg: University of Manitoba Press, 2012); Jatinder Mann, *The Search for a New National Identity: The Rise of Multiculturalism in Canada and Australia, 1890s–1970s* (New York: Peter Lang, 2016); Iain E. Johnston, *The British Commonwealth and Victory in the Second World War* (Basingstoke: Palgrave Macmillan, 2016); Satadru Sen, 'The Migrant's Empire: Loyalty and Imperial Citizenship at the League of Nations', in Buckner and Francis (eds), *Rediscovering the British World*, pp. 305-20.

21 Hancock mused about his own British World career in his *Country and Calling* (London: Faber, 1954); see also Jim Davidson's biography, *A Three-Cornered Life: The Historian W.K. Hancock* (Sydney: UNSW Press, 2010).

Bolton was appointed to London for three years (it was intended that the post would have a series of such distinguished appointees on short-term secondments from Australia) and to assist him he in turn recruited a young political scientist, Dr John Warhurst, as lecturer on a two-year contract (the lecturers were also to be parachuted in from Australia) and a Commonwealth Public Service Fellow, the economist, Bob Lim. Professor Anthony Low, another Hancock man, Oxonian and former ANU colleague of Bolton's, was at the time chairman of the board of the Institute of Commonwealth Studies, and Sir Zelman Cowen, the former Australian Governor-General and yet another Rhodes Scholar, then provost of Oriel College, Oxford, was made chair of the Australian Studies Centre's board.[22]

The Australian Studies Centre was the product of two intersecting moments – the Institute of Commonwealth Studies' need to replace its Australianist, Trevor Reese, who had died tragically young of motor neurone disease in 1976, and a concern in Australian government circles that after Britain had joined the European Common Market in 1973 cultural and academic interest in Australia had declined there. Thus, when a delegation from the Institute approached the Fraser government they got a sympathetic hearing. Funding initially came from an annual subvention from the Department of Foreign Affairs.

As he later explained it, Bolton had two main tasks in the UK. The first was to establish an institutional infrastructure and create the tools for the job. The second was to make the British and wider European public aware of the Centre's existence and mission. University

---

22 Much in this section comes from personal knowledge, as I was one of John Warhurst's successors in the lectureship, 1987–89, and one of Bolton's as Head, 1997–2014 (Centre staff became tenured in 1999). Bolton also published a memoir about his time in London, 'The Shoals of Celebrity', *Meanjin*, 63, 3 (2004), pp. 144-48.

courses in History were started at the University of London. Grants were begun for British academics to visit Australia and others to enhance library collections. Seminars, symposia, literary readings, book launches and conferences were convened. Papers and books were published, among them a comprehensive survey of all Australian research collections in the UK, done in association with the British Library.[23] The recently established British Australian Studies Association (known as Bazza to initiates) was encouraged. And there was a very proactive campaign of media engagement.

Bolton's was an inspired appointment. Professor Robert Holland, who was one of the History lecturers at the Institute of Commonwealth Studies in Bolton's time and now a seasoned judge, recalled in an email to me:

> He had that knack of being highly intelligent and yet accessible and pitched in exactly the right note or mood. I would say that in my experience he would be in the top five or so absolutely riveting speakers I have heard – possibly no one better.

And further:

> He also of course embodied – like such New Zealand contemporaries as … Sir Keith Sinclair – a post-war era of Anglo-Australasian intimacy, especially in the academic sphere. You and I (but you much more obviously) caught the end of that. It would not mean a great deal to a younger generation, at least not in the same way.[24]

---

23   Valerie Bloomfield, *Resources for Australian and New Zealand Studies: A Guide to Library Holdings in the United Kingdom* (London: Australian Studies Centre and the British Library, 1986).

24   Robert J. Holland to Carl Bridge, 27 July 2016, email in my possession. I recall sitting in an enthralled audience at a conference at Bond University while Bolton, years before 'what if-ery' became fashionable, riffed on his *Australian Dictionary of Biography* entry on H.V. Evatt, and gave a fanciful (and I think extempore and sadly unpublished) lecture on what would have happened to Australia had 'Doc' Evatt won the 1954 federal election, as well he might have done before he was derailed by the Petrov affair.

John Warhurst saw and admired the same qualities in Bolton: he was a great 'raconteur' who loved London and the British universities, happily transacting business over lunches in the Athenaeum (a London gentlemen's club where he was a member); 'He was clearly "Aussie" but he also fitted in'.[25]

In short, Geoffrey Bolton was a model citizen of the British World.

In an early press interview Bolton had said that the Centre's task was to go beyond the prevailing stereotypes peddled in the media by the likes of Barry Humphries and the now disgraced Rolf Harris, and foster a more sophisticated and accurate understanding of contemporary Australia. Predictably, and on cue, Humphries, who had a stage show in London at the time, turned up as that old reprobate the former Australian cultural attaché to the Court of St James 'Sir Les Patterson' outside the Centre with a television camera crew and claimed to be barred from entry. Humphries also wrote an illustrated piece for *Punch* (reproduced in *Quadrant*), which included 'all the predictable kitsch', and featured a secretary in 'crotchless bikini pants'.[26] Needless to say this sharp satire annoyed the actual secretary who was a blameless middle-aged Irish spinster and some of the board. Bolton smarted at this lampooning of his job and his Centre, noting in his diary that Humphries' television skit was a 'malicious effort', but he cannily saw that all publicity is good and ordered reprints to

---

25 John Warhurst to Carl Bridge, 2 August 2016, email in my possession.
26 Barry Humphries, 'Professor Patterson's Christmas Package for the Poms', *Quadrant*, 27, 1 (January/February 1983), pp. 36-37. Humphries would return to the charge over the years, claiming in his fictional biographies to have an honorary doctorate in Australian Studies from the University of Sydney and to be Emeritus Vice-Chancellor of the London School of Australian Studies (*Twelve Inches of Les*, LP sleeve notes, 1985, and theatre programme notes, *Look at Me when I'm Talking to You*, 1995).

CHAPTER 5

use for advertising purposes.[27] In the Centre archives there is a gracious letter from Humphries, on his characteristic lavender stationery, with a message printed across the bottom: 'Keep this. It'll be valuable one day'. Humphries – as himself and not Patterson and minus the cameraman – had visited the Centre, charmed the secretary, and presented the library with a copy of his latest book; though for some reason, and despite overtures from mutual friends Ross Fitzgerald and Humphrey McQueen, Humphries was never to meet Bolton, who continued in private to find the whole episode hurtful.[28] One of the conceits Bolton used to employ was that it was the Centre's task, located as it was on the far-flung cultural frontier of Australia among the British barbarians, to spread Antipodean civilisation among the untutored Britons. This he and his staff did very effectively and the tradition continues over thirty years on[29]

Bringing His Gods to Latium

The Roman poet and brilliant propagandist Virgil in his *Aeneid* has his eponymous Greek hero bear his household gods from Troy to the mouth of the Tiber and, in founding Rome, graft the values of classical Greek civilisation onto a virile Italian root. The process of migration, conquest and settlement, which is at the heart of British imperialism, long fascinated Geoffrey Bolton, as he was like so many of us a product of it. He described and analysed the process of founding a neo-Britain in Australia – bringing the old gods to a new place

---

27 Bolton Diary, 19 July 1983 (I owe this reference to Stuart Macintyre); Bolton, 'The Shoals of Celebrity', p. 145.
28 Information from Stuart Macintyre.
29 The Menzies Centre for Australian Studies now teaches over a hundred students annually, offering History, Literature and Film courses at undergraduate and graduate levels, and supervising half-a-dozen doctoral students.

– and the subtle changes wrought in these by the new environment and circumstances. He also ventured to a further stage and wondered how the various elements of British-derived societies interacted with and cross-fertilised each other. In so doing, Latium, in Virgil the most civilised of places, evolved from a common root but manifested itself in multiple, if related, forms and locales; the same but interestingly different.[30]

---

30 For the parallel case of Manning Clark and Virgil, see J.S. Ryan, 'A History of Australia as Epic', in Carl Bridge (ed.), *Manning Clark: Essays on His Place in History* (Melbourne: Melbourne University Press), pp. 61-69.

Chapter 6

'DO UNTO OTHERS'

Australia and the Anglican Conscience, 1840–56 and Afterwards

Alan Atkinson

In 1967 Geoffrey Bolton published, in the second volume of the *Australian Dictionary of Biography*, his biographical sketch of the Anglican clergyman, John Ramsden Wollaston, one of the pioneers of Christianity in Western Australia. Bolton afterwards pursued his interest in Wollaston with an address to the congregation of Holy Trinity church, York, Western Australia, in September 1985, which was published in pamphlet form by that church. Encouraged by the rector, Peter Mold, and working with the historian Heather Vose, he then undertook a new edition of Wollaston's journals, covering the period from Wollaston's departure from England in 1840 to his death in 1856. These appeared in three volumes from 1991 to 2006, though Bolton was apparently not much involved with the final volume. In short, Geoffrey Bolton was actively interested in Wollaston for a large part of his academic career.[1]

---

1   Geoffrey Bolton, *John Ramsden Wollaston: The Making of a Pioneer Priest* (York, W.A.: Holy Trinity Church York Society, 1985); Geoffrey Bolton and Heather Vose with

It would be wrong to make too much of this lengthy scholarly relationship. After all, few Australian scholars have gathered and stored so much information, over so long a period, about so many figures of Western Australian, and indeed Australian, history, as Geoffrey Bolton. Nor did religion figure very largely in Bolton's scholarship. However, he was comfortable with many of the formalities and presumptions of Christianity. His father, Frank Bolton, had been a lay reader in the Church of England in North Perth, and his mother's background was Baptist (as Winnie Ransley she had sung in the little Baptist church at Pingelly, south of York), while Bolton himself went to a Methodist school (Wesley College, South Perth).[2]

Bolton was less obviously interested in religion than, say, Manning Clark, and yet, as with Clark, there was something religious implicit in Bolton's imagination. Both his parents appear in his account of the community of his childhood, called *Daphne Street* (1996), and he refers only very briefly, and with a perfectly even hand, to their religious concerns and those of their neighbours. And yet *Daphne Street* opens with a long quotation from Ecclesiasticus and it ends with another, much shorter, from Isaiah. And, while it made little difference to his writing, certainly, in life and in death, Bolton defined himself as Anglican.[3]

***

Genelle Jones (eds), *The Wollaston Journals*, vol. 1 (1840–42) (Perth: University of Western Australia Press, 1991); Geoffrey Bolton, Heather Vose and Allan Watson with Suzanne Lewis (eds), *The Wollaston Journals*, vol. 2 (1842–44) (Perth: University of Western Australia Press, 1992); Helen Walker Mann (ed.), *The Wollaston Journals*, vol. 3 (1848–56) (Perth: University of Western Australia Press, 2006).

2   *Pingelly Leader*, 4 November 1912, 20 April, 4 May 1916.

3   Geoffrey Bolton, *Daphne Street* (Fremantle: Fremantle Arts Centre Press, 1996); information very kindly supplied by Carol Bolton, 4 May 2016.

CHAPTER 6

What did this mean? Bolton was a forward-thinking, open-minded visionary, but he was intrigued, amused and even delighted with questions of form, protocol and intricate interconnection. About the time he wrote on Wollaston for the *Australian Dictionary of Biography*, he also composed an article for *Historical Studies* entitled 'The Idea of a Colonial Gentry'. In it he displayed the fruits of his recent Namierite training at Oxford, including a grasp of patrician family networks, and he spoke of leading colonial settlers as typically possessed of 'an Anglican and hierarchical view of society', and as such typically reactionary in every respect. Their ideal society, he said, consisted of 'village communities, in which an obedient and industrious tenantry enjoyed the public libraries and mechanics institutes, the ploughing matches and hospitable sporting events, organised and controlled by the landed gentry'. In Western Australia, in particular, there existed 'an "English" society where everyone kept their proper places'.[4]

These two publications proved Bolton's capacity to break the mould of Australian history-writing by taking seriously phenomena which previous writers had dismissed as irrelevant to the national story, in this case the Anglican Church and the colonial landed gentry. By definition, pioneers open the way for others, and in due course Bolton was to be a remarkable mentor for the next generation of scholars, including myself. However, such others are bound, almost from the start, to improve on their masters' pioneering formulations, if they can. Hence this present attempt.

There is a question begged even within the above quotation. Ploughing matches were largely a creation of the agricultural societies which flourished in the 1820s, and were symptomatic of a new

---

[4] G.C. Bolton, 'The Idea of a Colonial Gentry', *Historical Studies*, 13, 51 (1968), pp. 319, 321.

approach to the use of the soil, in Britain and Australia, while the energetic promotion of literacy among small farmers – among entire populations – dates from much the same period. Bolton tended to equate hierarchy with rigidity. And yet for many characterised as 'gentry' in this period, in Britain and its colonies, hierarchy was just as much a medium for moral and material progress, and for general, if gradual, enlightenment. Certainly, Bolton implies that the fluidity and novelty of colonial circumstances converted some individuals who might have represented stand-still Toryism in England to 'developmental conservatism' in the colonies, defined by a concern for material progress.[5] And yet, something like the opposite might be true. Colonial circumstances could stifle or attenuate ideas about reform. Great movements for change depend on good communications, easy contact with new ideas and the stimulus of continuing argument. With these things there may be a sense of new direction and, with the right material resources, the chance of acting on it.

Bolton states that John Wollaston, as 'a conservative and traditionalist by instinct', was not much affected by the great theological questions of his day, including even the Oxford Movement, which, from 1833, aimed at the total reinvigoration of the English Church.[6] But I suggest that Wollaston's instincts were not entirely reactionary. In 1842 he told his diary that '[p]ublic institutions, as well as private individuals are almost always needing reformation'. And, he went on, 'the more sensibly this is felt & attended to, the more extensive will be the good conferred, both by precept & example, on Mankind at large'.[7] These are statements consistent with Tractarian hopes for a

---

5   Bolton, 'The Idea of a Colonial Gentry', p. 321.
6   Bolton, Introduction, in Bolton and Vose with Jones (eds), *The Wollaston Journals*, vol. 1, pp. xii, xxiv-xxv, xxx.
7   Wollaston journal, 12 December 1842, *The Wollaston Journals*, vol. 2, p. 3.

CHAPTER 6

connection between individual piety and public life, and for sweeping change in both. If Wollaston looks like a Tory, it may be because, in Western Australia, where progress of this sort had to be piecemeal and gradual at best, his habits of mind fell into a type of ideological default.

It was different on the other side of the continent. In his recent study of the Church of England throughout Australia up to 1850, Michael Gladwin has described a great inrush of Anglican clergy to the colonies from the mid-1830s. Recruiting efforts in England and Ireland multiplied their number five times. Supply and demand grew together because of the intellectual and spiritual revival of the English Church. With increasing numbers, and more frequent movement and communication, family and recruiting networks now connected the Church in Australia more closely to the Church in England.[8]

In Western Australia, with its population, including its clergy, so few and so widely scattered, even under these new conditions the bare survival of religious institutions might seem good enough. But in the east, clergy and sympathetic laymen gathered in a kind of critical mass, and with some wealth at their command. This happened in New South Wales precisely while Wollaston was fighting his battles in the west. Anne Coote has sketched the consolidation in vivid detail. During the 1840s there was, she says, the beginning of 'national feeling' within New South Wales, a sense of collective purpose centred on Sydney but reaching out at least to the main provincial centres. She has described the rapid expansion of a reading culture. The number of newspaper titles greatly increased in the early

---

8   Michael Gladwin, *Anglican Clergy in Australia 1788–1850: Building a British World* (Woodbridge, Suffolk: Boydell & Brewer, 2015), pp. 37-56, 75-7, 85-91, 177-8.

1840s, and the number of newspaper copies grew mightily through the period, thanks partly to expanding postal services. Figures available for 1836 and 1854 show more than a ten-fold increase in papers distributed, most of it apparently before the gold rush. The network of conversation, of all kinds, was more tightly drawn and the rhetoric of rising politicians of all persuasions was fraught with what Coote calls 'a sense of community and national feeling', the nation, I repeat, being New South Wales. A distinctly moral tone was also unmistakable.[9] The anti-transportation movement of this period is a well-known case in point, but it was by no means all.

The gold rush of the 1850s added momentum and complexity, but in New South Wales it was not such a fundamental turning point as historians once believed. In Victoria the impact of gold was deep and immediate. In New South Wales community was two generations older, and recent 'national' feeling had enough substance already to continue in the same form for several years beyond the discovery of gold. I am concerned, then, with the decade and a half from the end of convict transportation to New South Wales to the first instalment of democracy, 1840–56, which is, by coincidence, also the period between John Wollaston's departure from England and his death.

Michael Roe's *Quest for Authority in Eastern Australia, 1835–1851* (1965) – as innovative for its time as Bolton's work – uses the conventional periodisation (a gold-rush turning point), and Roe's argument features 'moral enlightenment' very largely. But by 'moral enlightenment' Roe means a movement for personal and social reform concentrated on such issues as intemperance and improvidence, a movement which was individualist rather than social, and egalitarian rather

---

[9] Anne Coote, 'Space, Time and Sovereignty: Literate Culture and Colonial Nationhood in New South Wales up to 1860', Ph.D. thesis, University of New England, 2004, pp. 98-115, 235.

CHAPTER 6

than hierarchical.[10] This chapter sketches another type of moral enlightenment, including a theology of social justice, clearly identifiable with social hierarchy of a traditional kind and with Anglicanism. I suggest clear links, for instance, with the English Christian Socialist movement of the 1840s and 1850s, led by Frederick Denison Maurice and Charles Kingsley, both Anglican clergymen, and founders, for instance, of the Working Men's College in London, a project in which the young John Ruskin was also involved.

This chapter considers theology as an aspect of ordinary idealism, and as an ingredient of world-view, of *mentalité*. In its origins, Christian Socialism belonged to the mid-nineteenth-century intellectual and moral revival of the Church of England, a revival which involved the renegotiation of the relationship of Church and state, and the redefinition of English citizenship. The education of the poor and disadvantaged was a means of social justice and the Working Men's College was perfectly symptomatic of this large, powerful but amorphous phenomenon. Note, for instance, Maurice's account of a good college as:

> a society for fellow-work, a society of which teachers and learners are equally members, a society in which men are not held together by the bond of buying and selling, a society in which they meet not as belonging to a class or a caste, but as having a common life which God has given them and which he will cultivate in them.[11]

Under the new Anglican rubric, national community was to have the same characteristics, and teaching, nation-wide, was understood from a dynamic and progressive point of view.

---

10   Michael Roe, *Quest for Authority in Eastern Australia, 1835–1851* (Melbourne: Melbourne University Press, 1965). Roe has an account of the gentry on pp. 35-57.
11   *The Reasoner* (ed. G. J. Holyoake), vol. 17 (1854), p. 262.

As Samuel Taylor Coleridge put it in setting out his notion of 'clerisy', social superiority itself must be partly didactic. Truly equal membership of the national society was compatible with, and even dependent on, rank being conscientiously used. So, Coleridge said, 'there can be no true notions of religion among men at large without just notions of philosophy in the higher classes'.[12] Most of all, conscience must be trained.

Here was an understanding of equality different from that of democratic liberalism. In New South Wales, it was an understanding Christian and bureaucratic at the same time. Individuals were to have equal membership in a spiritual sense – equality within an earthly Jerusalem – though some were teachers and some were learners, some far-sighted initiators and some only subjects of the state. By this means all possessed a common life. The driving ideas were to have the deep inclusiveness of the New Testament message, or, as some were calling it, Bible Christianity, but also of the nominal listings which had underpinned government since the First Fleet. They also took for granted, all at once, the old kind of social hierarchy and a driving, centralised sovereign conscience.

A program so comprehensive in origin and aims could only have come from a body with enormous resources and with an idea of itself as a national church, exclusive in its power but all-inclusive in its reach, and with quasi-governmental responsibilities. As an aspect of Australian history, the Church of England needs to considered as a body of ideas, as much as a hierarchy with religious impact. Not just in England but throughout the British Empire, it was a powerful, pervasive and sometimes highly creative phenomenon.

---

12   Ben Knights, *The Idea of the Clerisy in the Nineteenth Century* (Cambridge: Cambridge University Press, 1978), pp. 44, 68-72.

CHAPTER 6

In every part of the British Empire the main levers of official authority were in the hands of members of the Church, and in the 1840s and 1850s many were more or less up to date in their religious understanding. In New South Wales, for other reasons as well, as Michael Roe says, this was a time of new moral beginnings. Convict transportation had ended in 1840 and during the mid-1840s the community emerged from a serious economic depression, the question of pastoral land rights was resolved and the arrival of a new governor, plus a general election in 1848, progressively cleared the way for a large program of reform. As I now show, that included social, educational and economic legislation. The single-chamber legislature was, as ever, led by Anglicans, who shaped it more or less – sometimes much more and sometimes much less – to Anglican purposes. Their achievements included a new constitution in 1855–56, which in spite of their best efforts also introduced liberal democracy and led very quickly to their own demise. But meanwhile they made a difference on their own terms.

William Charles Wentworth, James Macarthur (these being the two pre-eminent figures), Edward Deas Thomson, James Martin, G.R. Nicholls, Henry Grattan Douglas, James Darvall and their allies were all concerned, more or less, with giving their own branch of English Christianity a new and more distinctly self-aware national and communal form. The discovery of gold in 1851, so Macarthur said, meant that New South Wales must soon become 'a magnificent nation', but well before that their agenda was clear. Their individual priorities differed. Wentworth had a power all his own, with physical presence and intellectual force combined. But James Macarthur's authority was equal in its way, as a result of his landed property, his English connections, his intellectual and moral integrity and his patient, detailed attention to principle. For Macarthur, a nation was defined by its spiritual possibilities and collective capacity for good and his idea of national magnificence involved, as he put it, 'great moral and social improvement'. During a visit to England in the 1830s Macarthur had enjoyed some long consultations with the young W.E. Gladstone. He shared Gladstone's concern for 'our national religion' ('national' here means English and imperial), and his idea that nationality was contingent on moral and spiritual ambition, on social discipline and social justice.[13]

The leaders' program was diverse. During 1849–54, from one general election to the next, the legislature passed 40 public Acts per annum, compared with 27 during the previous Council, and it instigated an even more remarkable number of select committees. The inquiries themselves were wide-ranging beyond precedent in Britain or elsewhere. One historian has argued that the select committees were so substantial, in number and purpose, that they might be seen as a type of second chamber. For the first time, an Aboriginal was interviewed in committee, and also a woman (Caroline Chisholm), as well as several labouring men. Members thereby drew interest groups of all kinds into the legislative process, substantially preparing the way for popular self-government.[14]

The leadership was also decidedly interventionist. It made smallpox vaccination compulsory, it founded a new system of elementary schools, which doubled the number of such schools within four years,

---

13   James Macarthur to W.E. Gladstone, 24 March 1838, Gladstone Papers, Hawarden, UK; *The Sydney Morning Herald*, 8 September 1852; Alan Atkinson, 'The Political Life of James Macarthur', Ph.D. thesis, Australian National University, 1976, pp. 195-99.

14   Alan Atkinson, 'Time, Place and Paternalism: Early Conservative Thinking in New South Wales', *Australian Historical Studies*, 23, 90 (1988), p. 3; Kerry Mills, 'Lawmakers, Select Committees and the Birth of Democracy in New South Wales, 1843–1855', *Journal of Australian Colonial History*, 14 (2012), pp. 135-53.

CHAPTER 6

and it extended the colonial tariff in a mildly protectionist spirit, aiming to raise the price of beer, spirits and tobacco, but also, as the members responsible said, to protect the wages of working men. A lengthy series of bills tackled child welfare, urban health and, in an age of raw capitalism, the vulnerability of tenants and debtors, and, implicitly, all the evils apparently incident on urban agglomeration.[15]

In principle and practice, they were ready to be innovative. Much of what they attempted was already underway in Britain, but they were prepared to copy reforms still on the drawing board there, and to work out their own. Their confident moral attitude is evidence in itself that their ideas had emerged from something far beyond their own immediate time and place. Their Public Health Bill would have given nominated government boards extensive power over homes and workplaces, and made life more difficult for landlords and employers. Its purpose was almost utopian: to provide 'to the working classes, the blessing of comfortable houses, fresh air and pure water'.[16] Their plan to criminalise the sale of poisonous drugs was easily attacked as 'over-legislation', and their ideas about state responsibility for neglected children, including the morally neglected, were plausibly said to depend on 'a principle unknown to British law'.[17]

Such ambition was feasible because the government still had some of the centralised energy of the old convict administration, though less, as it turned out, than the leadership needed for all it wanted to do. Since the 1820s that energy was expressed in equally idealistic reform in the colonial prisons and convict assignment system. On Norfolk Island, for instance, when Alexander Maconochie was

---

15 Atkinson, 'Time, Place and Paternalism', pp. 2-10.
16 *The Sydney Morning Herald*, 21 July 1854.
17 *The Sydney Morning Herald*, 30 June 1852.

commandant, in 1840–44, dealings between subject and government were face-to-face and personal, and yet entirely, even obsessively, systematic. These schemes taught one crucial lesson, well learnt by the leadership in Sydney, who had served a kind of apprenticeship during the convict regime. Moral progress, including equity on the ground, could not be kept up on a large scale without system – without an efficient, centralised, pervasive and comprehensive state, far-reaching but fully capable of dealing with its subjects on a case-by-case basis.

Their measures, coming as novelties from above, were condemned as undemocratic, and better suited to Czarist Russia than to a British colony. In setting up as '"uncle" for the people', said one member of the Legislative Council, a squatter, these leaders attacked the rights of property owners and the principles of laissez faire. And indeed, they explicitly challenged any argument at odds with the dictates of simple Christianity, as they understood it. They wanted to place what James Macarthur called 'the protecting shield of the law' between the poor and sick on the one hand and ruthless entrepreneurs on the other.[18] They would deal head on, said James Darvall, with the 'cold-blooded calculations of the advocates of free-trade'.[19]

This particular brand of idealism had been evident in the British parliament in the 1830s, mainly in the work of the eccentric Tory factory reformer Michael Sadler. Sadler's speeches had focused on the stark inequity of unregulated industrial relations – a disequilibrium of power – in all cases, but especially for children. At one level, this was a matter of contractual relations, which, Sadler thought, must take better account of the real human beings involved. But it was also a matter of social policy and of the need for a government

---

18   Atkinson, 'Time, Place and Paternalism', pp. 2-10.
19   *The Sydney Morning Herald*, 15 July 1854.

CHAPTER 6

strong enough to deal equally with all comers. In New South Wales, Macarthur appealed to the principle of the Sermon on the Mount, 'Do as you would be done by', which must apply both to the people among themselves and to rulers in their relationship with all parties.[20]

The same principle underpinned the attempt to reconcile secular and sacred teaching in the schools, using a model designed for Ireland in 1832. Dealing equally with all denominations, but with emphasis on the leading four, Anglican, Catholic and Presbyterian, and later the Wesleyan Methodists, they also encouraged each to deal similarly with the others. This was not a secular, or proto-secular, state catering for a range of more-or-less voluntary bodies. This was a professedly Christian state extending the practical application of Christianity, applying moral imagination, with some intellectual rigour, to a rapidly changing world.

* * *

This essay is designed to consider a particular moral-religious attitude, and in a new way. It aims to come to terms, in a provisional fashion, with the reality of past spiritual life, considered not as a static set of beliefs, but as something intimate and subjective, and at the same time processual and dynamic. From 1929, in France, the *Annales* school set about exploring the idea of *mentalité*, the intellectual world-views shared by large numbers in the past. Such methods are certainly useful here, but the scholars of the *Annales* school limited themselves to historic circumstances which could be

---

20   Kim Lawes, 'Michael Thomas Sadler and the Idea of the Paternal State: A Study of Paternalism and the Formulation of Social Policy in Early Nineteenth-Century Britain', Ph.D. thesis, University of New England, 1996.

thought of as more or less static. They also wrote about periods when individuality of belief was not the norm, so that variations of *mentalité* were rare and easily traced. And yet, during the same years, anthropologists and sociologists of religion were also struggling to understand how shared faith might operate within a rapidly changing, industrialised world. Relevant for what I say later on is the work of A.P. Elkin (1891–1979), an Anglican clergyman and anthropologist, who used his experience of Australian Indigenous culture to explore the dynamic relationship of the individual with mass cultural, political and religious commitment in Western societies. Elkin insisted on the importance of the individual's free response to, and reverence for, something beyond structure and static definition. As an essential aspect of subjectivity, this liveliness is hard to pin down in historical argument. It is a real aspect of history nevertheless, to be considered on its own terms, free of what E.P. Thompson called 'the enormous condescension of posterity'. And, echoing Thompson again, faith, like class and like love, is 'a relationship, and not a thing'. It is an event and might be an impulse for change.[21]

The new Anglican understanding of the 1830s rested on the same premise. It had emerged from a university, and from a university college (Oriel), and it put more emphasis on training and instruction than on the contagion of spiritual enthusiasm. The Church of England was a government church, and the new understanding was also concerned with order – intellectual order and refinement of conscience, as well as public order. But it depended even more on a sense

---

21   A.P. Elkin, 'The Present Social Function of Religion', *Morpeth Review*, 18 (December 1918), pp. 29-32; E.P. Thompson, *The Making of the English Working Class* (London: Penguin edn, 1968), pp. 9-10, 13; J.A. Lane, 'Anchorage in Aboriginal Affairs: A.P. Elkin on Religious Continuity and Civic Obligation', Ph.D. thesis, University of Sydney 2007, pp. 226-31.

CHAPTER 6

of lively transcendence and of forward movement, interpreted as continuous revelation. The question of conscience, especially (What was conscience? How was it to be educated and managed? How did it shape the life of each individual in the ordinary circumstances of their existence? How did it affect the moral destiny of nations?) occupied many minds in one way or another during these years.

The novelist George Eliot was one such. George Eliot was partly a historian, though she grappled with large historical developments, including changes in religious sensibility, through the medium of fiction. Eliot followed the vagaries of moral decision-making in all her books, ending with the deeply theological story of *Daniel Deronda* (1876). By then she had moved far beyond her preoccupations at mid-century, but she continued to explore ideas and human relationships (momentary, everyday exchanges) as a single parcel because to her mind they could not be separated. Her concerns were fundamentally religious and, in a broad sense, theological.[22]

Two of George Eliot's stories, *Felix Holt* (1866) and *Middlemarch* (1871–72), concentrate on a deep shift in the moral sense of English men and women, including Anglican landed families, in the early 1830s. In *Felix Holt* a minor character, the local MP, Philip Debarry, is shown subscribing to a simple but challenging principle of moral reciprocity involving Anglican gentry, such as his own family, on the one hand, and radicals and dissenters on the other. The issue was apparently small. Should someone, however otherwise despicable, who stepped willingly out of the way for you, or who picked up your hat for you, be thanked and thought of, within that simple transaction, as an equal? Debarry's father, an old-world squire, saw this as a redundant

---

22 Peter C. Hodgson, *Theology in the Fiction of George Eliot: The Mystery beneath the Real* (London: SCM Press, 2001), p. 29.

'superfineness of consideration'. '[H]e ... did not quite trust the dim vision opened by Phil's new words and new notions'. So Eliot sketched a new moral and intellectual energy to be found in a certain type of new-generation Anglican, which during the 1830s and 1840s was to draw some to the Oxford Movement, and to carry a few to further extremes. Searching as far as possible for a fresh moral discipline, Philip Debarry, she says, 'died fifteen years later, a convert to Catholicism'.[23]

Samuel Taylor Coleridge, a crucial figure for the new Anglicanism, had already articulated this transformation most keenly. In 1838 he explored the question of conscience in his 'Essay on Faith'. Humanity was in essence spiritual and moral. Conscience, Coleridge said, was 'the root of all consciousness' and so it was 'the precondition of all [human] experience'. He made this a matter of logic. In the experience of each individual, he said, 'there can be no I without a Thou [a singular second person], and ... a Thou is only possible by an equation in which I is taken as equal to Thou, and yet not the same'. And again, 'the equation of Thou and I, by means of a free act, negativing the sameness in order to establish the equality, is the true definition of conscience'. Beyond that, there were social and national implications. As the outcome of consciousness and conscience, we all merge in a common spiritual existence, and there is a 'synthesis of the *alter et idem*, myself and my neighbour'.[24]

Coleridge's equation and Coleridge's synthesis, if dimly felt, intrigued the Anglican leadership in mid-century New South Wales. As James Macarthur put it, the governing principle of political action, the end if not the means, was 'Do as you would be done by'. With

---

23 George Eliot, *Felix Holt, the Radical* (New York: Harper & Brothers, 1966), pp. 181-2, 234.
24 S.T. Coleridge, 'Essay on Faith', in H.N. Coleridge (ed.), *The Literary Remains of Samuel Taylor Coleridge* (London: William Pickering, 1838), pp. 428, 434.

CHAPTER 6

diverse views on Coleridge, if they read him at all, on the Oxford Movement and so on, these individuals lived, as they thought, at a turning point in the civilising process. Few of them were figures of real 'intellectual preoccupation', like the fictional Debarry and the real Coleridge, but they did believe that such turning points could only be managed by educated elites such as themselves. They were not only parties to the Coleridgean equation. In their self-idealising mind's eye, they also stood over and above the equation, oiling its machinery and keeping it precise.

All social action must have a spiritual and a social bearing, and all laws must leave room for conscience. Speaking of this period in Australia, Wayne Hudson, in his new book *Australian Religious Thought*, calls this 'a sacral view of the secular'.[25] The alternative, said the legislative leadership, was un-Christian and 'cold-blooded', as unpromising for civilisation as unrestrained free trade. It all depended on a thorough spirit of mutuality and on education. In 1849 the Australian Mutual Provident Society (AMP) was formed in Sydney to encourage the lower middle class to pool their savings in a self-managed corporation, as insurance against future risk. Mutuality in insurance was newly fashionable, and it gave material form to Coleridge's ideas about both equation and synthesis. The AMP's three original founders were all Anglican churchmen, including two who were keenly involved in the moral and spiritual reinvigoration of their Church, namely William Horatio Walsh, rector of Christ Church St Laurence in Sydney, and his close friend, the businessman Thomas Sutcliffe Mort.[26]

---

25 Wayne Hudson, *Australian Religious Thought* (Melbourne: Monash University Publishing, 2016), p. 78.
26 Alan Barnard, *Visions and Profits: Studies in the Business Career of Thomas Sutcliffe Mort* (Melbourne: Melbourne University Press, 1961), pp. 38-40; Geoffrey Blainey, *A History of the AMP 1848–1998* (Sydney: Allen & Unwin, 1999), pp. 1-6.

In England, the established and national Church had always taken responsibility for education, from Oxford and Cambridge down to parish schools, and it had long been driven by the need to extend its authority to new centres of population in England and elsewhere in the empire. In New South Wales, Anglican clergy and churchmen clung to this responsibility, making use of the moral and spiritual energies which drove the Oxford Movement. The Anglican educational program which unfolded in the colony between about 1840 and 1856 was hesitant and superficial to start with but its end-point looks like a remarkable climax to the legislative scheme already outlined.

In the beginning, in 1840, William Grant Broughton, Bishop of Australia, founded St James's Grammar School, in King Street. This foundation, said Broughton, 'though not Collegiate, should always be regarded as introductory to an institution of higher pretensions'.[27] In 1846 he announced accordingly the foundation of St James's College, at Lyndhurst in Glebe, which within two years was doing well enough to justify Broughton's hopeful description of it as 'the germ of some future illustrious university'.[28]

In London, in 1836, the Anglican King's College had been combined with an unchartered but flourishing non-denominational foundation to create the University of London. In Toronto, in 1849, another King's, also Anglican, was simply taken over and renamed as the University of Toronto, with its staff largely undisturbed.[29] St James's, Lyndhurst, was Sydney's obvious equivalent, and in that sense it might indeed have been the germ of a university. The founding legislation of Sydney University, worked out during 1849–50, stated

---

27 *The Sydney Morning Herald*, 25 November 1841.
28 *The Sydney Morning Herald*, 22 December 1846.
29 Martin L. Friedland, *The University of Toronto: A History*, 2nd edn (Toronto: University of Toronto Press, 2013), pp. 26-35.

CHAPTER 6

accordingly that it might include colleges 'already instituted', as well as those which might be founded in future. Besides St James's the only thing like a college 'already instituted' was a Roman Catholic school, St Mary's, which took boys to the late teenage level. As the more ambitious foundation, St James's appeared as the central pillar of the new university. In the case of Toronto, the Anglican hierarchy had objected to their college being taken from them, but King's College, London, had been easily included within a larger whole. This was the model Wentworth, as initiator of the new project, looked to. '[W]hy', he said, 'should not the College at Lyndhurst do the same[?]'.[30]

However, St James's – all too Tractarian – was now under attack from churchmen suspicious of popery, students were withdrawn and it collapsed as the University Bill passed through Council. Efforts to revive it on a better foundation and as an integral part of the new university led in 1854 to legislation pushed through by Anglican churchmen, which allowed the government funding of affiliated colleges and to a new foundation, called St Paul's, in 1856. This was an Anglican effort and, while there was equitable provision for other churches, only the Roman Catholics responded for the time being. The first Warden of St Paul's, Henry Hose, a graduate of Trinity College, Cambridge, had been among the original Christian Socialists, with F.D. Maurice and Charles Kingsley, and had taught at the Working Men's College, as well as at the new College for Ladies in Bedford Square.[31]

---

30   *The Sydney Morning Herald*, 7 September, 5 October 1849; *University of Sydney Act*, 1850, c. 11.

31   F.J. Furnivall, *Early History of the Working Men's College* (London: no publisher given, 1891; reprinted from the *Working Men's College Magazine*, 2 [1860]), p. 3; A.D. Murray (ed.), *John Ludlow: The Autobiography of a Christian Socialist* (London: Frank Cass, 1981), p. 169 (name misspelt 'Hope'); C.W. Kilmister, 'The Teaching of Mathematics in the University of London', *Bulletin of the London Mathematical Society*, 18 (1986), pp. 323-4.

The university itself was to teach secular knowledge, but it did not follow that it was to be a secular institution. The precise implications of secularity were another issue of current topicality. In England, the freethinker, George Jacob Holyoake, described himself as a secularist – an advocate of secularism – and to explain what he meant in 1851 he published a small book called *The Principles of Secularism Illustrated*. 'Secularism', he said, 'means the moral duty of man in this life deduced from considerations which pertain to this life alone'. He drew a clear distinction with secular education. 'Secular education simply means imparting Secular knowledge separately – by itself, without admixture of Theology with it. The advocate of Secular education', Holyoake went on, 'may be, and generally is, also an advocate of religion; but he would teach religion at another time and treat it as a distinct subject'. Secularism was 'a policy of life'. Secular education was only a way of organising instruction.[32]

Sydney University offered secular education, and none of the founders of the university and of its original college subscribed to secularism as 'a policy of life'. For them all, in varying degrees, the secular was to be understood through the medium of the sacred. It is unsafe to assume the contrary even of Wentworth. And on the other hand, while many may have subscribed, more or less, to 'an Anglican and hierarchical view of society', it was not as Geoffrey Bolton believed when he made that attribution.

Most of the individuals mentioned earlier, not only Wentworth but also Macarthur, Nicholls and Douglass, were involved in the foundation of the university. Walsh, Mort and several other Anglican

---

32 George Jacob Holyoake, *The Principles of Secularism Illustrated* (London: Austin & Co., 1871; first publ. 1851), p. 27; Michael Rectenwald, *Nineteenth-Century British Secularism: Science, Religion and Literature* (Basingstoke: Palgrave Macmillan, 2015), pp. 71-106.

CHAPTER 6

founders of the AMP were also founders of its original college. As Wentworth himself said in October 1849, the university was to be dedicated to 'proving the divinity of the great Christian code' and to training the minds of 'those who trusted and relied upon [that code]', a code which, for such men, used comprehensive principles of equity and mutuality. At the same time Wentworth said, much more famously, that the university was to be 'a fountain of knowledge at whose springs all might drink, be they Christian, Mahomedan, Jew, or Heathen', but as with secular education this possibility was contingent on its main purpose. Certainly, Wentworth's own career, as capitalist and politician, had never shown much of the spirit of mutuality. He also loathed the priestly mysteries embedded in the Anglo-Catholic dimension of the Oxford Movement. And yet, he said, it was only among a people educated at a university such as Sydney's that 'the great truths of Christianity' were really safe.[33]

The more advanced intellectual leaders of the Church understood that genuine Christianity must allow for such diversity. By the same token, universities must reinforce traditional faith with scientific discovery. Darwin's *Origin of Species* was published in 1859, but figures such as William Whewell, Master of Henry Hose's college, Trinity at Cambridge (and another participant in the debate about conscience), had already made great strides in such reconciliation. Central to Anglican thought was the idea of variety within unity, and the Holy Trinity offered powerful imagery for scholarship beyond the theological. Whewell invented the term 'consilience', meaning an inner logic across all intellectual inquiry, an idea recently revived from the perspective of human biology. For Whewell, new scientific

---

33   *The Sydney Morning Herald*, 5 October 1849.

discoveries sprang immediately from the human relationship with God. They made the deeper laws of creation 'more and more mysterious', drawing us closer, he said, quoting Milton, to 'the darkness which surrounds the throne of light'.[34]

In 1853, discussion on the precise form of the university benefited from the intervention of George Selwyn, Bishop of New Zealand, who had an English reputation as a public intellectual of the first rank. Selwyn was in step with the new understanding of university education which was bringing reform to Oxford and Cambridge. He was happy to distinguish secular studies from religious studies, despite their ultimate interdependence, borrowing here from Adam Smith. 'The division of intellectual as of mechanical labour', he said, 'makes each man perfect in his own department, by shutting out in a great measure every other thought and action from his mind'. As with the doctrine of the triune God, the key to understanding creation was not unity alone, but difference within unity.[35]

No other legislative creation in New South Wales during 1840–56 says more than Sydney University about the 'national' aspirations of the men with whom this essay has been most concerned. In the founding of the university, the advocate of secular education was also an advocate of religion, and of religious education. Echoing Holyoake, the university was designed to guide and enliven conscience in New South Wales, at first among men likely to be in positions of power.[36] It was to do so, not for secularist reasons, but because of the religious

---

34 William Whewell, quoted in Peter Searby, *A History of the University of Cambridge*, vol. 3 (Cambridge: Cambridge University Press, 1997), p. 350; Edward O. Wilson, *Consilience: The Unity of Knowledge* (New York: Vintage Books, 1998), pp. 6-7.

35 G.A. Selwyn, *'A Little One Shall Become a Thousand': A Sermon Preached at the Opening of the Cuddesdon Theological Institution, on Thursday, June 15, 1854* (Oxford: J. Vincent, 1854), at http://anglicanhistory.org/nz/selwyn/cuddesdon1854.html

36 Holyoake, *The Principles of Secularism Illustrated*, p. 30.

CHAPTER 6

priorities of that small group which for a decade and a half controlled the legislative agenda.

* * *

Anglicanism had always had a territorial dimension. It was designed to make its presence felt on the national landscape, however 'national' might be defined. The great neo-gothic front of Sydney University was built between 1854 and 1859, under the direction of the ecclesiastical architect Edmund Blacket, and it was positioned to overlook the city. Vastly more ambitious than the church buildings John Wollaston was struggling to erect in Western Australia at the same time, Sydney University expresses a churchmanship similar to Wollaston's, a churchmanship of 'reform', but within a larger and more intricate vision. Included around its Great Hall was a scattering of angels. Angels flanking the dais in the hall proclaimed on scrolls *'Timor Domini, principium Sapientiae'* ('Fear of the Lord is the beginning of wisdom') and *'Scientia inflat, Caritas aedificat'* ('Knowledge puffs up, love edifies') and perched on the apex outside a winged figure representing 'Christian philosophy' gazed across a valley to the spires of Christ Church St Laurence and St Paul's, Redfern. (Renamed 'the Angel of Knowledge', she was removed as dangerous in 1874.) These buildings, and St Paul's College, were all more or less Blacket creations. So the architect, on behalf of his patrons, cast a neo-gothic and Christian scheme over this piece of antipodean landscape, as if to sacralise not just knowledge but the country itself.[37]

---

37   *The Sydney Morning Herald*, 13 July 1859.

In the late 1850s the leadership group I have been concerned with succumbed to an increasingly highly organised campaign for liberal democracy, hurried along by responsible government and manhood suffrage. The new regime identified the old one with military government, class privilege and the near-slavery of convict assignment. Note Daniel Deniehy's celebrated bunyip-aristocracy speech in Sydney in 1853. In the same spirit, in 1859 a parliamentary committee spoke scornfully of the university itself, and of its vastly expensive buildings, ridiculous with griffins, unicorns and other 'monstrous shapes'.[38]

The legislative achievements exemplified by the university were a thorough application of visionary idealism to Australian circumstances. Nor was that idealism now quite dead. For instance, the 1890s saw the emergence of the 'bush brotherhoods', organisations of young, celibate, highly mobile Anglican clergymen which brought a distinctive form of highly ritualised spiritual support to the remoter parts of Queensland, New South Wales, and Western and South Australia. Just as outlandish, to some eyes, as bunyips and griffins, their origins lay with the missions to English slums instigated by young men, of Tractarian habits of mind, from the colleges of Oxford and Cambridge. Even more distinctly than Blacket's architecture, they represent an attempted détente between Anglican spirituality and Australian community and landscape.[39]

Clergy of various denominations were involved in the Australian federation movement. Among concentrated efforts to sacralise the

---

[38] Clifford Turney, Ursula Bygott and Peter Chippendale, *A History of the University of Sydney*, vol. 1, 1850–1939 (Sydney: Hale & Ironmonger, 1991), pp. 117-20; Alan Atkinson, *The Europeans in Australia: A History*, vol. 2 (Sydney: UNSW Press, 2016; first publ. 2004), pp. 358-59.

[39] R.M. Frappell, 'The Australian Bush Brotherhoods and Their English Origins', *Journal of Ecclesiastical History*, 47, 1 (1996), pp. 82-97.

CHAPTER 6

new nation and to invest it with a collective soul, Charles Strong's Australian Church was the most substantial, and its origins were Presbyterian. If Anglicans made a less memorable impression, it was probably because they relied more on formality and hierarchy, and on imposing policy from above. However, during the years immediately before and after 1901, Anglican clergy certainly took the lead in arguing for a 'national conscience', especially in Aboriginal affairs, and in that they were ahead of their time.[40]

The field for action was enlarged with a new generation of public opinion between the two world wars. The *Morpeth Review* was a quarterly, published during 1927–34 from St John's College, an Anglican clergy training college at Morpeth, near Newcastle. One of the most intellectually significant Australian periodicals of the inter-war period, the *Morpeth Review* was managed by three clergy who had been students at St Paul's College at Sydney University, namely Ernest Burgmann, A.P. Elkin (mentioned above), and Roy Stuart Lee, later an Oxford theologian who wrote on faith and Freudian psychology.[41] Like the original Tractarians, their purpose showed a distinct sense of national responsibility, and it too was didactic. The *Review* was designed to prepare the way for a university at Morpeth, in which Christian purpose would underpin free inquiry, so that an inspirited and integrated understanding of humanity might grow up in place of the materialised and specialised forms of knowledge then apparently in vogue. 'In life', said Burgmann, 'one and the same man is religious, ethical, political, economic, and artistic, and it is a fallacy to exalt any

---

40   Sir Alfred Stephen, evidence, select committee on Division of the Legal Profession Abolition Bill, NSW Legislative Council *Votes and Proceedings*, 1847, vol. 2, pp. 469-70; Alan Atkinson, *The Europeans in Australia: A History*, vol. 3 (Sydney: UNSW Press, 2014), pp. 276-80, 290, 332-5.

41   See, for instance, R.S. Lee, *Freud and Christianity* (London: James Clark, 1948), and R.S. Lee, *Psychology and Worship* (London: SCM Press, 1955).

of these elements in him to the exclusion or depreciation of any of the others'. University curricula ought to reflect that understanding.[42]

Burgmann saw his rural university as an exercise in social justice. It would bring higher education to remote places just as the bush brotherhoods had brought spiritual succour. The same idea led J.S. Moyes, Bishop of Armidale, a Christian Socialist and writer in the *Morpeth Review*, to help in the foundation of a university at Armidale in 1954 (the University of New England). Meanwhile, as Bishop of Goulburn, including Canberra from 1934, Burgmann worked for a 'national cathedral', which among other things might testify to a national conscience, and he was part of the movement for a national university in the capital.[43]

In 1840–56 the Anglican imagination (and of course other imaginations) had been especially preoccupied with questions of individual understanding of right and wrong, possibly because of the way conscience might now so easily jar with an ever-changing but anonymous national public opinion. By the 1920s and 1930s the concern was more with the interweaving and underpinning of community, and with doing something about the vast (in Australia, geographically vast), fragmentary and superficial character of industrial civilisation. Love for one's neighbour was still a central issue, but whereas Coleridge's contemporaries had asked about the impulse of conscience itself, now the main question was 'Who is my neighbour?'.[44]

---

42 E.H. Burgmann, 'The Morpeth Review', *Morpeth Review*, 18 (December 1931), pp. 7-8; Tod Moore, 'The "Morpeth Mind" and Australian Politics 1927–1934', paper at Australasian Political Studies Association conference, University of Newcastle, 25–27 September 2006 (www.newcastle.edu.au/Resources/Schools/Newcastle Business School/APSA/ANZPOL/Moore-Tod.pdf; seen 15 May 2016); Ian Tregenza, 'The Political Theology of *The Morpeth Review*, 1927–1934', *Journal of Religious History*, 38, 3 (2014), pp. 413-28; Lane, 'Anchorage in Aboriginal Affairs', pp. 164-68.

43 Matthew Jordan, *A Spirit of True Learning: The Jubilee History of the University of New England* (Sydney: UNSW Press, 2004), pp. 27, 67.

44 Lane, 'Anchorage in Aboriginal Affairs', p. 50.

CHAPTER 6

Australian historians have moved on just as completely from the questions asked about religion by Geoffrey Bolton and others in the 1960s. Books such as Barry Hill's *Broken Song* (2002), Robert Kenny's *The Lamb Enters the Dreaming* (2007) and Wayne Hudson's *Australian Religious Thought* (2016) suggest a more complex historical understanding of religiosity.[45] In a particularly fine doctoral thesis at the University of Sydney, Jonathon Lane has recently drawn a line directly from the Tractarians and Christian Socialists of the mid-nineteenth century to T.H. Green and the New Idealism, and so to Ernest Burgmann, the *Morpeth Review* and A.P. Elkin, in order to uncover the origins of Elkin's anthropological and advocacy work among Australian Indigenous peoples.[46]

Reflecting Coleridge's definition of clerisy, as a student Elkin had written about national consciousness: 'It may be only to the brighter intellects and to the best statesman that the nation will be motive to, or the criterion of, acts'. Later on, so Lane points out, he developed this idea in connection with the power of medicine men in Indigenous society, or as he also called them 'Aboriginal men of high degree'. In every case, said Elkin, these were 'the intellectual, imaginative and courageous élite', who, in their own learning, embodied their society's sacred and cultural traditions. If sufficiently courageous, it was these individuals who would, 'for some cause or other – social, intellectual, psychopathological – endeavour to initiate changes, and often succeed directly or indirectly, sooner or later'.[47]

---

45 Barry Hill, *Broken Song: T.G.H. Strehlow and Aboriginal Possession* (Sydney: Knopf, 2002); Robert Kenny, *The Lamb Enters the Dreaming: Nathanael Pepper and the Ruptured World* (Melbourne: Scribe, 2007); Hudson, *Australian Religious Thought*.
46 Lane, 'Anchorage in Aboriginal Affairs'.
47 A.P. Elkin, *Society, the Individual and Change: With Special Reference to War and Other Present-Day Problems* (Sydney: Camden College, 1940), p. 65; A.P. Elkin, *Aboriginal Men of High Degree: Initiation and Sorcery in the World's Oldest Tradition* (Sydney: Australasian Publishing, 1944); Lane, 'Anchorage in Aboriginal Affairs',

Elkin believed that worthy change depended on such élites taking initiatives consistent with continuing sacred tradition. His carefully conservative world-view explains Elkin's fundamental contribution to the understanding of Indigenous religiosity, and his opinion about the way in which Indigenous and White Australians might properly share the continent. As Lane says:

> Elkin propagated a consistent, precise, and systematic account of Aborigines, carrying the authority of science. But he built this account upon a moral imperative, inspired by a religious vision; and only thence a political strategy.

In short, as with his Anglican predecessors a century earlier, and for both Indigenous and White Australians, Elkin understood the secular by way of the sacred. From this understanding emerged that common view of the Dreaming, which Elkin's student, W.E.H. Stanner, spelt out in the 1950s, and which was to be fundamental to Indigenous politics in following decades – that Indigenous life was beyond all else spiritual, and that it was in some sense, like archetypal Anglicanism, a merger of past and present, and, on top of that, somehow single and comprehensive nation-wide.[48]

These are some of the adventures of the Tractarian world-view, transported and reshaped for antipodean use. They deserve a central place in the Australian story, but just as important is the way in which they suggest new ways of exploring past minds.

---

pp. 25-7, 36, 38, 62 (quoting Elkin, 'Nation and National Consciousness: Australian National Consciousness', B.A. thesis, University of Sydney, 1915), pp. 255-56; Marnie Hughes-Warrington and Ian Tregenza, 'State and Civilization in Australian New Idealism', *History of Political Thought*, 29 (2008), pp. 90-108.

48 W.E.H. Stanner, 'The Dreaming' (first published 1956), in Stanner, *The Dreaming and Other Essays* (ed. Robert Manne) (Melbourne: Black Inc., 2009), pp. 57-72; Lane, 'Anchorage in Aboriginal Affairs', pp. 37-38.

Chapter 7

SPOILS AND SPOILERS

Geoffrey Bolton's Environmental History

Andrea Gaynor and Tom Griffiths

In *Spoils and Spoilers*, Geoffrey Bolton wrote what we might consider to be Australia's first national synthesis of environmental history. It was published in 1981, that stellar year in Australian historical literature: the poet Judith Wright wrote to Bolton, saying 'We all seem to be writing "man and environment" books just now'.[1] Wright's own environmental and social history of the southern Queensland frontier, *The Cry for the Dead*, was published that year, as was Henry Reynolds' *The Other Side of the Frontier* and Eric Rolls' *A Million Wild Acres*. The burgeoning ecological consciousness that underpinned the new conservation politics of the late 1960s and 1970s was having its impact on historical scholarship.

In later years Geoffrey was to look back on this period of his life – around 1981 – as a time when he renewed his confidence about his academic career. In the previous decade he had harboured some self-doubt about his capacity to be a national historian of the stature of

---

1   Judith Wright to Geoffrey Bolton, 26/11/80, Bolton Papers, NLA Acc.05/139 Box 3.

his successful contemporaries Geoffrey Blainey and Ken Inglis. He felt his scholarly recognition had stalled, and he was also a bit dissatisfied with the impact of his earlier books.[2] But *Spoils and Spoilers* was a shot in the arm: it was widely and positively reviewed, and it had *span*, as Keith Hancock would have put it. It was a national history, a grand narrative, a synthesis. And about the same time as *Spoils and Spoilers* was published, Bolton was approached to be general editor of a five-volume *Oxford History of Australia* to anticipate the Bicentenary. As a further endorsement of his stature, he was appointed in late 1981 as the foundation head of the Australian Studies Centre at the University of London. Bolton was always grateful for the opportunity to write *Spoils and Spoilers*, for, as he recalled, it 'really got me back into productivity'.[3] Aged 50 when it was published, the book boosted his confidence about tackling Australia-wide questions; it also carried a message about national self-confidence.

Geoffrey Bolton was born into the middle of the Depression years and had strong childhood memories of a society struggling with poverty and unemployment, of people knocking at the door looking for work; such experiences would shape his historical curiosity and compassion. He grew up in a Perth suburban neighbourhood that he remembered as a lively, face-to-face community, with home deliveries by horse and cart. Some of his earliest memories were of domestic spaces, including the chooks, almond tree and grapevine of the family's productive backyard, though he also vividly remembered horse teams from an early visit to the wheatbelt. Geoff's grandfather had taken up farming in Pingelly in 1912 and the family maintained

---

2   Geoffrey Bolton, interviewed by Stuart Reid, July 1994 – March 1985, OH 2618, transcript, p. 144, State Library of Western Australia (SLWA).
3   Reid interview, p. 149.

CHAPTER 7

connections with the region throughout his childhood.[4] But he never seemed to regret his suburban upbringing. Visitors to Perth's Hyde Park can press a button at a heritage installation to hear the voice of Geoff as an elderly man, recalling how his childhood self saw the islands in the Park's lakes as sites of imagination, places where exciting things might happen. His early experience of the urban domestic and material world as lively and absorbing infiltrated many of his histories.

Spoils and Spoilers was a culmination of years of experience and thinking. As a postgraduate student, influenced by Fred Alexander's *Moving Frontiers*, Bolton had set out to apply Frederick Jackson Turner's frontier thesis to the Australian setting; in the early 1950s he worked in the Kimberley while researching a Masters thesis on the history of pastoralism. So at the age of 21 he found himself in remote rugged country looking at the land, talking to the people and pecking away at his typewriter, getting to the station journals before the white ants did, talking to the old hands before they died. He took the fieldwork seriously, staying in the region for more than three months. He didn't want to be seen as 'just some young bloke trying to take a winter holiday'.[5] 1952 was a drought year, there was scalded country, erosion on the watercourses, and cattle feed was scarce; Geoff became interested in the *unintentional* changes to the land as a result of white settlement. He was also fascinated by the local technologies and skills developed by settler Australians as they grappled with the distinctive environment of the northwest.[6] This admiration for settler ingenuity fuelled his emerging conviction, elaborated in

---

4   Reid interview, p. 2.
5   Reid interview, p. 43.
6   Reid interview, p. 46.

Spoils and Spoilers, that many environmental problems arose from the tendency to privilege imported ideas and models over locally derived knowledge and solutions.

In 1954 Geoff won a Hackett Fellowship that enabled him to trade the limestone of the University of Western Australia for the sandstone of Balliol College, Oxford. There, like Fred Alexander and Keith Hancock before him, he read History. Hancock at this time was the director of the Institute of Commonwealth Studies within the University of London. As a student, Geoff had heard about Hancock and read his books, and he 'devoured' Hancock's autobiography *Country and Calling* when it came out in 1954.[7] Bolton later called himself a 'disciple' of Hancock's, and even his half-century of devotion to the *Australian Dictionary of Biography* can be seen in part as a kind of tribute to a creation of Hancock's. As he left for London, Fred Alexander and a local doctor, Bruce Hunt, provided Bolton with personal introductions to Hancock. The two historians had much in common. Hancock had experience at the University of Western Australia, having worked as an assistant lecturer there in 1919 under Edward Shann, who encouraged him to develop his interest in land use.[8] During those lively days Hancock was also introduced to the Western Australian flora by his house-mate Desmond Herbert, an acquaintance from his Melbourne school days who had recently been appointed government botanist of Western Australia.[9] An interest in the land always permeated Hancock's work and over time, as 'environment' emerged as an object of public concern and

---

7   Reid interview, p. 65.
8   Trevor Daly, 'Discovering Hancock: A Profile of an Australian Environmental Historian (W.K. Hancock)', *Limina*, 4 (1998), p. 71.
9   Jim Davidson, *A Three-Cornered Life: The Historian W.K. Hancock* (Sydney: UNSW Press, 2014), p. 40.

CHAPTER 7

activism, these themes became more pronounced in his writing. His *Australia* (1930), though principally an analysis of the cultural, political and economic life of the nation, included a much-quoted section which, in the vein of George Perkins Marsh, railed against the environmental damage wrought by colonial economic development: 'in the second half of the nineteenth century tree murder by ringbarking devastated the country on a gigantic scale', he wrote. Bolton would later take the 'invaders" hatred of trees, identified by Hancock, as a basis for a chapter of *Spoils and Spoilers*.

Bolton was completing his D.Phil. when he was asked by Hancock to take up a research fellowship at the Australian National University in Canberra, where Hancock had recently been appointed director of the Research School of Social Sciences and Professor of History. It was a nourishing environment in which to develop interdisciplinary scholarship. One model was the Wool Seminar, convened by Hancock from 1957 to 1959. Scholars from a range of disciplines – history, economics, geography, political science, and the natural sciences – came together to discuss wool, which interested Hancock not only because of its economic importance, but also 'its talismanic value as an index of Australian distinctiveness.' Bolton later observed that the Wool Seminar 'revived and kindled that interest in environmental history already foreshadowed in *Australia*' and which distinguished much of Hancock's later scholarship.[10]

In 1959 Bolton also found himself on another northern field trip, with 'environment' as a sub-theme of a regional study; he had been commissioned to write a history of North Queensland by the North

---

10   Geoffrey Bolton, 'Rediscovering Australia: Hancock and the Wool Seminar', *Journal of Australian Studies*, 23, 62 (1999), pp. 160, 168.

Queensland Local Authorities Association.[11] Published in 1963 as *A Thousand Miles Away*, this project helped to sustain Geoff's broad interest in relationships between people and place. In a preface he argued that settlers arrived in North Queensland at a time when Australians:

> had not yet learned to understand their environment. The result was a prodigal waste of resources ... It was only when the newcomers had learned to adapt to their environment, to husband their land and co-operate in planning its development, that permanent white settlement in North Queensland was assured.[12]

The dual theme of settler environmental understanding and adaptation would feature centrally in *Spoils and Spoilers*. By the mid-1970s, however, Bolton regarded *A Thousand Miles Away* as engaging insufficiently with environmental issues. In a telling reflection on the way in which understandings of the category 'environmental' were being clarified – and narrowed – at that time, he suggested that the lack of attention paid to environment in *A Thousand Miles Away* put him 'no further forward' than the approach of economic historian Edward Shann thirty years earlier.[13] From a contemporary perspective, the value of 'land use' studies as environmental histories is more clear.

After Bolton's return to Western Australia in 1966, his old boss and mentor began to research an environmental history of Canberra's

---

11   Lyndon Megarrity, 'Geoffrey Bolton's *A Thousand Miles Away*: Origins, Influence and Impact', *History Australia*, 12, 3 (2015), pp. 7-29.

12   Geoffrey Bolton, *A Thousand Miles Away: A History of North Queensland to 1920* (Brisbane: Jacaranda in association with the Australian National University, 1963), p. viii.

13   Geoffrey Bolton, 'The Historian as Artist and Interpreter of the Environment', in George Seddon and Mari Davis (eds), *Man and Landscape in Australia: Towards an Ecological Vision* (Canberra: Australian Government Publishing Service, 1976), p. 121. This was the case even though, as he later recalled, environment was not as prominent a theme in the North Queensland context; Reid interview, p. 79.

mountain hinterland. Published in 1972 as *Discovering Monaro*, Hancock's book also used the concept of 'land-use' but drew additionally on botany, forestry and ecology, thus anticipating the cooperative alliance of historians and ecologists that would flower in the 'forest history' of the 1980s.[14] Hancock's work, written in the midst of an archaeological revolution (Australia's Pleistocene human past was confirmed in the 1960s), was quick to integrate deep time into a regional narrative and to incorporate insights into Aboriginal burning regimes by archaeologist Rhys Jones. Manning Clark, writing in *The Bulletin*, considered *Discovering Monaro* 'the first significant look at our past through what might be called the "pollution or ecology window"'.[15] In the same year, Bolton completed his social history of the 1930s Depression in Western Australia, *A Fine Country to Starve In*. In following the distinctive responses of the Western Australian community to a global crisis (and the donation of all royalties to two charities) it conveyed Bolton's keen sense of social justice, but environmental themes were not prominent.

However, this was a time in which environment could not readily be ignored: the Western Australian government had recently established an Environmental Protection Authority, which had immediately acted to prevent development of an alumina refinery in the Swan Valley. Environmental campaigns, including the Great Barrier Reef, Little Desert and Lake Pedder, were making headlines nationally. It was in this climate that Bolton joined forces with his undergraduate friend David Hutchison at the Western Australian Museum to produce a study of 'European Man in Southwestern Australia',

---

14 See, for example, the *Australia's Ever-Changing Forests* series published by the Australian Forest History Society from 1988; also Tom Griffiths, *Secrets of the Forest: Discovering History in Melbourne's Ash Range* (Sydney: Allen & Unwin, 1992).

15 Manning Clark, *Bulletin*, 8 July 1972, pp. 45-46.

published in 1973.[16] Drawing on the work of local and regional historians and historical geographers, it comprised an early survey of the environmental history of the southwest and a call for further research. While giving a nod to the 'subtle environmental awareness' of *Discovering Monaro*, it was a work of synthesis that would not be followed up with a deeper, more engaged study of Bolton's native region: whereas the retired Hancock, raised in Gippsland, had pursued his fascination with and desire for attachment to country in Monaro, Bolton was to return to his suburban roots in his first retirement project, a detailed history of the street in which he was raised.[17]

In 1973, on taking up the foundation chair of history at Murdoch, the new 'bush university' in the southern suburbs of Perth, Geoff received funding from the US State Department to travel around the USA and see how American Studies was taught there.[18] During this visit he met with Roderick Nash, who in 1970 had launched a course at the University of California, Santa Barbara, in 'American environmental history'. Though Nash was later criticised for his parochial neglect of foreign precedents, from the English and French as well as geographers and anthropologists,[19] Geoff was impressed by his efforts to develop the area as a sub-field of American history, later describing him as 'the leading environmental historian – young and bright'.[20]

---

16   Geoffrey Bolton and David Hutchison, 'European Man in Southwestern Australia', *Journal of the Royal Society of Western Australia*, 56, 1–2 (1973), pp. 56-64.
17   Tom Griffiths, *The Art of Time Travel: Historians and Their Craft* (Melbourne: Black Inc., 2016), pp. 45, 56, 58; Geoffrey Bolton, *Daphne Street* (Fremantle: Fremantle Arts Centre Press, 1997).
18   Reid interview, p. 141.
19   Richard Grove and Vinita Damodaran, 'Imperialism, Intellectual Networks, and Environmental Change: Origins and Evolution of Global Environmental History, 1676–2000: Part II', *Economic and Political Weekly*, 41, 42 (2006), pp. 4500-501.
20   *Spoils and Spoilers* marketing questionnaire, Bolton Papers, NLA Acc.05/139 Box 3. Folder 'Spoils and Spoilers'.

CHAPTER 7

Bolton himself was always quick to acknowledge the pioneering work of Australian historical geographers, who for years had colonised ground ahead of the historians. Graeme Wynn has characterised the late 1960s as a time of introspection and some pessimism among historical geographers in Australasia, in response to the challenge of developing more quantitative and theoretical approaches.[21] However, the early 1970s saw a flourishing empirical scholarship in the field. Perception, evaluation and transformation of land were key themes, evident for example in the work of Keith Moon and Michael Williams on the South Australian landscape, Les Heathcote on arid lands arising from his influential 1965 study, and Jim Cameron on early colonial Western Australia.[22] In Sydney, Dennis Jeans produced the first book-length historical geography of colonial New South Wales, while in Melbourne Joe Powell commenced a study of land policy in nineteenth century Victoria. Powell, who arrived from England at Monash University in 1964 (overlapping briefly with Bolton there), also continued the earlier focus on perception, producing influential books on the role of images and image-making in the colonisation of Australia. He would go on to become Australia's leading scholar on the history of environmental management.[23]

---

21 Graeme Wynn, 'Discovering the Antipodes: A Review of Historical Geography in Australia and New Zealand 1969–1975, With a Bibliography', *Journal of Historical Geography*, 3 (1977), p. 251.

22 Keith Moon, 'Perception and Appraisal of the South Australian Landscape 1836–1850', *Proceedings of the Royal Geographical Society of Australasia (South Australian Branch)* 70 (1969), pp. 41-64; Michael Williams, *The Making of the South Australian Landscape* (London: Academic Press, 1974); R.L. Heathcote, 'The Vision of Australia 1770–1970', in Amos Rapoport (ed.), *Australia as Human Setting* (Sydney: Angus & Robertson, 1972), pp.77-98; J.M.R. Cameron, 'Prelude to Colonization: James Stirling's Examination of Swan River, March 1827', *Australian Geographer*, 12 (1973), pp. 309-27.

23 D.N. Jeans, *An Historical Geography of New South Wales to 1901* (Sydney: Reed Education), 1972; J.M. Powell, *The Public Lands of Australia Felix* (Melbourne: Oxford University Press, 1970); Geoffrey Bolton, 'Environmental History in Western Australia before 1980', *Studies in Western Australian History*, 27 (2011), p. 5.

On his return from the USA in 1974, Geoff attended a conference convened by George Seddon as part of the UNESCO Man and the Biosphere program. In the proceedings, he mused that:

> It would be particularly useful if some intrepid scholar were to venture upon a history of Australians acting upon their environment. Such a book would be bound to attract much criticism in detail, but given the right use of written, oral, and photographic material, it would be a stimulus and a necessity. Then we might follow the American examples and introduce the teaching of Australian environmental history in a number of Australian universities.[24]

Bolton would be that 'intrepid scholar', though the teaching preceded the textbook by five years.

The historical geographers' interest in environmental perception was prominent in the 'Australian Environmental History' course Geoff launched in 1976: the brief handbook entry lists 'European man in 1788 – preconceptions about landscape' and 'Australian visions of Australia' among the areas covered.[25] A second-year course with no prerequisites, it was designed for the kinds of students attracted to the new university in Perth, for Murdoch was consciously innovative and multidisciplinary and many of the students who took Geoff's course were studying the environmental and biological sciences. The different perspectives of the science and arts students led to frequent debates, making it 'a good lively subject'.[26] The course had legs, running with its original title until 2010 and then onward with a new one.

The course began by considering 'Aborigines and their effect on the environment'. Aboriginal people didn't figure prominently in

---

24 Bolton, 'The Historian as Artist and Interpreter of the Environment', pp. 122-23.
25 *Murdoch University Handbook & Calendar 1976*, p. 120.
26 Reid interview, p. 136.

CHAPTER 7

Geoff's work on the Kimberley: he'd had little contact with them in his youth, and during his fieldwork he felt hampered by his lack of ease with Aboriginal informants.[27] Yet, as he later recalled, he returned from the Kimberley having 'learned respect for Aboriginal capacity'.[28] In the mid-1970s this perspective nurtured his interest in recent work on Aboriginal environmental impacts, from Rhys Jones and John Mulvaney in the east, to Duncan Merrilees and Sylvia Hallam in the west.[29] He saw Aboriginal people as key agents in environmental change, anticipating Bill Gammage's later work in his claim that 'The whole of Australia was their farm, and it was a farm which they exploited with care for the needs of later generations'.[30] However, he was careful to reject the static and essentialising 'ecological indian' stereotype, pointing out that some prehistoric Aboriginal practices may have led to environmental impoverishment.

Geoff's conviction of the importance of Aboriginal agency was strengthened by Tom Stannage's invitation to contribute a chapter on twentieth-century Aboriginal–settler relations to *A New History of Western Australia*. Geoff worked on this in parallel with *Spoils and Spoilers*, using Western Australian Aborigines Department records to show how Aboriginal people were not 'passive victims' but had often mobilised to provide for their own needs in the face of state

---

27 Reid interview, p. 44.
28 Bolton, 'Portrait of the Historian as a Young Learner', in Duncan Graham (ed.), *Being Whitefella* (Fremantle: Fremantle Arts Centre Press, 1994), pp. 119-20.
29 Duncan Merrilees, 'Man the Destroyer', *Journal of the Royal Society of Western Australia*, 51 (1968), pp. 1-24; S.J. Hallam, *Fire and Hearth: A Study of Aboriginal Usage and European Usurpation in South-Western Australia* (Canberra: Australian Institute of Aboriginal Studies, 1975).
30 *Spoils and Spoilers: Australians Make Their Environment 1788–1980* (Sydney: Allen & Unwin, 1981), p. 8; Bill Gammage, *The Biggest Estate on Earth: How Aborigines Made Australia* (Sydney: Allen & Unwin, 2014).

exclusion and neglect.[31] The two projects were mutually supportive; both contributed to Geoff's trajectory of increasing support for Aboriginal rights and later reconciliation, as well as his confidence in the utility and significance of his own historical work.[32]

The invitation to write *Spoils and Spoilers* came from Heather Radi, a historian at the University of Sydney and a friend of Geoff, who was commissioning books for a new Allen & Unwin series of thematic histories on 'The Australian Experience'. Heather knew of the environmental history course and, as Geoff later recalled, 'it always concentrates the mind if someone says that, "We want you to do this and here is a contract."'[33] Always intended to be a general survey, the book drew on the material gathered for the course, as well as new research. Written partly while Geoff was a visiting fellow at Cambridge, but mostly in a small, tranquil cottage in an orchard near the southwest town of Balingup, it was dedicated to the Murdoch staff and students who participated in the course's creation. Curiously, given Geoff's earlier work, the north of Australia received scant attention, though these experiences of regional and rural history had familiarised him with the most useful types of primary source material. Michal Bosworth, then working on her own ground-breaking environmental history school textbook, which was also published in 1981, researched and provided many of the images.[34]

---

31 Reid interview, p. 152; Geoffrey Bolton, 'Black and White after 1897', in C.T. Stannage (ed.), *A New History of Western Australia* (Perth: University of Western Australia Press, 1981), pp. 124-78.

32 Deborah Gare, 'A Journey in Australian History: Geoffrey Bolton and the "Middle Way"', *Limina*, 4 (1998), p. 86.

33 Reid interview, p. 149.

34 Michal Bosworth, *Environment Australia* (Sydney: Methuen Australia, 1981); Heather Radi to Geoff Bolton, 29 June 1980, NLA Acc 05/139 Box 3, Folder 'Spoils and Spoilers'.

CHAPTER 7

The title of *Spoils and Spoilers* is enigmatic. It is a phrase that evokes plunder and pillage; a dual sense of destruction and theft in an ongoing conflict between settler Australians and the land. It appears to mark out the work as a declensionist narrative of fall from ecological harmony and abundance, unredeemed by hope. This is, however, at odds with the book's content, which is rather more balanced and optimistic. How might we account for this dissonance? The initial working title, appearing in 1977 when the book was contracted, was 'Man-made Australia'. As the book neared production in March 1980, Heather Radi looked forward to seeing Geoff with a manuscript and new title; by June it was still undecided, with publisher John Iremonger asking Geoff and Heather 'Has a small muse of fire ascended the brightest heaven of invention and brought you both back a title?'[35] Heather then wrote to Geoff, with some exasperation, that 'noone yet seems to have agreed on a title!', finishing the letter with her hope that they would arrive at a decision between 'Cutting down building up' and 'Tearing down and building up: Australians making their environment'. These versions, invoking both destructive and creative impulses, more accurately reflect the tone of the book than the final title, which emerged sometime in the following two months. In August, while Heather Radi was visiting Perth, Geoff wrote to John that 'The choice of title and sub-title seemed alright to me, so I have not bothered to write about that'. In his reply, John had Spoils and Spoilers as the subject line, and indicated that he was glad Geoff liked 'the final choice of title'.[36] It seems that the

---

35 Patrick Gallagher to Geoffrey Bolton, 18 November 1977; John Iremonger to Heather Radi, cc Geoffrey Bolton, 10 June 1980, Folder 'Spoils and Spoilers'.
36 Heather Radi to Geoffrey Bolton, 13 June 1980; Bolton to Iremonger, 19 August 1980; Iremonger to Bolton, 25 June 1980, Folder 'Spoils and Spoilers'.

title was the publisher's and while Geoff's feelings on the title appear lukewarm, he declined to contest it.

Early sales of *Spoils and Spoilers* were 'extremely encouraging', with more than eight hundred copies sold in the first two months.[37] Reviews appeared in a very wide range of publications, from Perth newspapers to *The Bulletin* and the American *Journal of Environmental Quality*. Reviewers generally saw the book as significant and timely, with the notable exception of George Seddon, discussed below. Having set out to write a book with popular appeal, Geoff would have been pleased with the review appearing in the *Daily News*, Perth's 'underdog' newspaper for afternoon commuters, which deemed the book 'one of the most valuable, stimulating and important Australian books to appear for some time'.[38] Of all the reviews, this was the only one to identify an 'overriding theme' of hope. By contrast, the reviewer for *The West Australian* portrayed it as an unremitting tale of devastation, ignorance and greed, of settler Australians' hatred of the land.[39] Most reviewers were struck by Geoff's gloomy prognosis for the future – of increasing exploitation in a period of economic downturn and steadily degrading urban environments under increasing population pressure – and it appears this coloured their interpretation of the text as a whole.

In an era of proliferating and increasingly obvious environmental challenges, most reviewers acknowledged the book's importance and utility: this was a history from which we could – indeed, needed to – learn. The Queensland History Teachers' Association newsletter

---

37 Patrick Gallagher to Geoffrey Bolton, 13 June 1981, Folder 'Spoils and Spoilers'.
38 Mark Dixon, 'Lust to Conquer the Land', *Daily News*, 17 June 1981, p. 23.
39 Alex Harris, 'Why Conservation Is So Important', *The West Australian*, 18 July 1981, p. 43.

declared that the subject matter of *Spoils and Spoilers* 'should be central to every course in Australian history or social studies', while Keith Hancock expressed his hope, in a private letter to Geoff, that the book would 'have some impact on the policy-makers'.[40] Reviewers also appreciated its 'readability', achieved through evocative and clear prose, with Edmund Campion for *The Bulletin* particularly emphasising its literary qualities.[41] The principal academic reviewers were geographers: Dennis Jeans found it 'difficult to think of a more insightful overview' of the forces shaping urban environments over time, while Murray McCaskill was impressed by its 'apt and challenging generalisations'.[42] Both criticised the book for its lack of attention to international contexts, though this was no impediment to the sole North American reviewer, a bureaucrat in the Ontario Ministry of Natural Resources, for whom parallels between the Australian and North American experiences were self-evident.[43]

Academic reviews were spread across the disciplinary spectrum, from Pacific studies, political science and history to geography and environmental management. The multidisciplinary dimensions of the book were part of its innovation in the new field of 'environmental history'. Bolton was influenced by Hancock's *Discovering Monaro* in his integration of ecological perspectives. From the 1960s, ecology had gained power as both a science and a metaphor, and ideas of

---

40 Bob Riley, review of *Spoils and Spoilers* in *The History Teacher*; W.K. Hancock to Geoffrey Bolton, 9 November 1981, Folder 'Spoils and Spoilers'; see also C.F.H. Jenkins, 'Looking Back – and Learning', *The West Australian*, 29 May 1982, p. 43.

41 Edmund Campion, 'Four Aspects of Australian History Unfold', *Bulletin*, March 1982, p. 76.

42 D.N. Jeans, review of *Spoils and Spoilers*, *Australian Geographer*, 15, 3 (1982), p. 187; Murray McCaskill, review of *Spoils and Spoilers*, *Historical Studies*, 20, 80 (1983), p. 476.

43 Arthur D. Latornell, review of *Spoils and Spoilers*, *Journal of Environmental Quality*, 11, 2 (1981), pp. 330-31.

community, webs and relationships became influential in environmental and social thought. In the writing of his late classic in environmental history, Hancock had walked the paddocks of the high plains with soil scientists, botanists and foresters, and one of his heroes was Baldur Byles, a forester who gathered evidence of soil erosion on his hands and knees and passionately advocated the protection of the mountain water catchments from grazing cattle. In *Spoils and Spoilers* Bolton referred not only to 'land' and 'nature' but also to *ecology* and *ecosystems*, and he brought a keen attention to the interrelatedness of climate, soil, biota and humans – although Hancock wrote to Geoff saying he would have liked to see more about soil chemists and agricultural botanists.[44] By contrast, Geoffrey Blainey's book *A Land Half Won*, published in the same year as Bolton's, was more geographical than ecological and was less responsive to the environmental politics of the time. When Bolton later reflected on the course he taught at Murdoch in the 1970s he said: 'I wasn't preaching, but some of [my students] did become very green in their thinking'.[45]

Venturing across the science–humanities divide got him into trouble too. Bolton's friend the environmental scholar George Seddon, who had a doctorate in geology, wrote a highly critical review of *Spoils and Spoilers* which consisted mostly of carping about geological and biological errors made by this trespasser from the humanities.[46] Seddon considered the national historical synthesis to be 'premature', but that

---

44 Keith Hancock to Geoffrey Bolton, 9 November 1981, Folder 'Spoils and Spoilers'.
45 Reid interview, p. 141.
46 The most obvious of the errors, which a number of readers picked up, was a geological one – the description of Sydney as being founded on limestone, instead of sandstone. This was corrected in the second edition, but Bolton considered many of Seddon's other complaints to be 'trivial'. Geoffrey Bolton to John Iremonger, 30 August 1982, Folder 'Spoils and Spoilers'. For George Seddon's review, see *Overland*, 1982, 87 (May 1983), pp. 55-60.

CHAPTER 7

was exactly Bolton's challenge. Bolton himself was generous about Seddon's inspiring body of work and even his 'caustic wit' – and he happily acknowledged the disciplinary breadth and promiscuity of Seddon's intellect. Seddon's books on *Swan River Landscapes* (1970) and *Sense of Place* (1972) were highly original studies, Bolton noted, ones that built on a tradition of topographical essays in English literature that might be said to go back to Gilbert White's *The Natural History and Antiquities of Selborne*, first published in the year of the French Revolution. Bolton explained that it was 'a genre which before the coming of photography required the combination of literary grace and a sharp eye for natural phenomena'. He valued Seddon's combination of scientific observation with 'the good old-fashioned art, the Augustan art, of connoisseurship of landscape'. Bolton and Seddon shared an interest in combining studies of the natural and built environments and in scholarship that enabled intelligent environmental stewardship. Bolton approvingly quoted Seddon's definition of ecology as 'the science of good housekeeping'.[47]

This points us to another, neglected source of strength in *Spoils and Spoilers*. Bolton drew on an organic, local, vernacular tradition of writing often overlooked by academics. This is what he appreciated about Seddon's work, for he saw him as working in that nature-writing tradition. So we find Bolton invoking on the first page of *Spoils and Spoilers* the zoologist Hedley Finlayson whose book *The Red Centre*, published in 1934, was one of the great pieces of Australian nature writing; we find him drawing on Francis Ratcliffe, whose 1938 book *Flying Fox and Drifting Sand* was of the same lineage; and we find him starting a chapter with the feisty zoologist, Jock Marshall,

---

47 Geoffrey Bolton, 'Environmental History in Western Australia before 1980', pp. 7-10; Bolton, 'The Historian as Artist and Interpreter of the Environment', p. 122.

and his 'fine angry title', *The Great Extermination: A Guide to Anglo-Australian Cupidity, Wickedness and Waste* (1966). In an assessment of environmental history influences in Western Australia, Bolton honoured two naturalists who closely observed and described intimate seasonal changes in plant and animal life. One was Vincent Serventy whose book *Dryandra* (1970) described a eucalyptus woodland reserve in 1934, and the other was Barbara York Main, an arachnologist whose book *Between Wodjil and Tor* (1967) became a celebrated piece of scientific prose poetry about the wheatbelt.[48] Bolton was always a strong advocate of local and regional history – that's where his own career began – and he saw environmental history as a natural development of that literature of place.

Spoils and Spoilers therefore grew out of Bolton's strong advocacy for local and regional history, which was part of his 'view from the edge', part of his identity as a Western Australian. His doctoral thesis at Oxford had focused on a populace marginal to the UK, the Anglo-Irish of the eighteenth century, and his histories of the Kimberley and North Queensland were both studies (as he put it) of 'a frontier society on the margin of white Australian civilisation'.[49] In a 1999 memoir, Bolton elaborated his 'Provincial Viewpoint' as being more than geographical; it was also 'a habit of mind' that was expressed in an awareness of diversity, fidelity to grassroots sources and a mistrust of bold generalisations. He made fun of his younger self as 'a bigoted empiricist'.[50] He certainly liked to build his arguments from the

---

48 Bolton, 'Environmental History in Western Australia before 1980', pp. 6-7. See Tony Hughes-d'Aeth, 'Islands of Yesterday: The Ecological Writing of Barbara York Main', *Westerly*, 53 (2008), pp. 12-26.

49 Geoffrey Bolton, 'A Provincial Viewpoint', in Bruce Bennett (ed.), *Australia In Between Cultures: Specialist Session Papers from the 1998 Australian Academy of the Humanities Symposium* (Canberra: Australian Academy of Humanities, 1999), p. 82.

50 Bolton, 'A Provincial Viewpoint', p. 81.

CHAPTER 7

ground up and was thus intellectually inclined to regionalism. Bolton was interested in the history of regionalism as a political movement and in the writing of regional history, and he saw his study of North Queensland as part of an academic rediscovery of regional history from the late 1950s, as evidenced by the work of Margaret Kiddle on the Western District of Victoria, Duncan Waterson on the Darling Downs and R.B. Walker on New England.[51] Even Bolton's work in London, as foundation head of what became the Menzies Centre, had an edginess he relished. As Geoff put it, in London he was pursuing 'one of my own persistent themes, that within Australia as a Western Australian, within Britain as an Australian, you are there to stand up for the provincials, for the people on the periphery'.[52] Although he also feared provincialism and occasionally felt the isolation of Western Australia, he was determined to make an advantage of his geography.

Bolton's early literary models included Lytton Strachey, Edward Gibbon and Thomas Babington Macaulay; he admired good, compelling prose.[53] As a young man he met Miles Franklin, Henrietta Drake-Brockman and Mary Durack and he was introduced to the Fellowship of Australian Writers, where he participated in a poetry group. He had been active as a student journalist and took pride in publishing the early poems of Randolph Stow. He recalled a 'strong consciousness of trying to keep alive the traditions of Australian

---

51 Margaret Kiddle, *Men of Yesterday: A Social History of the Western District of Victoria, 1834–1890* (Melbourne: Melbourne University Press, 1961); Duncan Waterson, *Squatter, Selector and Storekeeper: A History of the Darling Downs, 1859–93* (Sydney: Sydney University Press, 1968); R.B. Walker, *Old New England: A History of the Northern Tablelands of New South Wales, 1818–1900* (Sydney: Sydney University Press, 1966).
52 Reid interview, p. 65.
53 Reid interview, p. 41.

literature'.[54] When he sparred with Geoffrey Blainey in the pages of *Historical Studies* over the reasons for the founding of the British colony of New South Wales, he saw their debate as an echo of Henry Lawson's literary stoush with Banjo Paterson. Geoff Bolton was a literary historian. He called himself 'the least ideological of creatures' and as a scholar he claimed to be 'a tortoise, basically, rather than a hare';[55] he liked to earth himself in place, period and people and to allow patterns to emerge from that mastery. Thus he respected writing embedded in locale, and wisdom that grew from experience. This spirit underlies *Spoils and Spoilers* – and it shapes its analysis too, for Geoff told his publishers that the book argued that 'Australians have done best when they discarded ideas and models brought from Britain and North America' and that 'the worst mistakes have taken place through disregarding the native experience'.[56] By the turn of the millennium 'native experience' included Aboriginal lore, and Australian regional and environmental histories had become essays also about settlers' relationships to Aboriginal country – as seen, for example, in Tom Griffiths' *Hunters and Collectors* (1996), Peter Read's *Belonging* (2000), Tim Bonyhady's *The Colonial Earth* (2002) and Mark McKenna's *Looking for Blackfellas' Point* (2002).

Another striking aspect of *Spoils and Spoilers*, read from an early twenty-first century perspective, is its attentiveness to urban and domestic environments. The cities and the suburbs are the sites of a substantial part of Bolton's 'environmental' history – he takes us into the intimate, noisy, smoky worlds of domestic houses and fenced yards, the streets and lanes of traffic, abattoirs and incinerators. Two-thirds

---

54 Reid interview, p. 59.
55 Reid interview, p. 42.
56 *Spoils and Spoilers* marketing questionnaire, Folder 'Spoils and Spoilers'.

CHAPTER 7

of its chapters are principally or wholly devoted to urban settings and issues. Sometimes, in describing the development of the field of environmental history, we have fallen into the American habit of saying that urban history was long neglected in favour of forests, 'wilderness', and the preservation of the 'natural' world. Yet for Bolton environmental history and urban history were seamlessly integrated in a national narrative from the start. Like Hugh Stretton, he suggested that the origins of Australian environmentalism were to be found in the very suburbia disdained by intellectuals. He described how conservation thinking emerged at the same time that Australians were turning the bush into suburbs. So Bolton's interest in the built environment, the little blocks and boxes, the nature strips and backyards, is part of his argument about the bush and what the loss of it came to mean. *Spoils and Spoilers* was written and taught in the same years that Graeme Davison presented his compelling critique of Russel Ward's *The Australian Legend*, arguing the urban origins of 'the Australian Legend' – and Bolton's book also offered a counter-narrative to the Ward thesis.

This urban emphasis seems at first surprising: Bolton had pursued environmental themes most prominently in his work on rural and regional environments – the Kimberley river frontages, the steamy canefields of North Queensland. Look a little closer, however, and a lineage emerges. Bolton's early 1970s work with David Hutchison on southwestern Australia delves into the way in which Perth's urban infrastructure and geography shaped the experience of its inhabitants, from opportunities for recreation to class differentiation according to environmental amenity. This incipient interest was nurtured by a period of frenetic activity in Australian urban history. Tom Stannage was working on *The People of Perth*, which shocked and dismayed

Perth conservatives when it hit the bookstores in 1979. The Sydney History Group's first publication, *Nineteenth-Century Sydney: Essays in Urban History*, was launched in 1978, an exceptional year for urban history which also saw the publication of Graeme Davison's *The Rise and Fall of Marvellous Melbourne*, Weston Bate's *Lucky City* and Peter Spearritt's *Sydney since the Twenties*. Bolton himself collaborated with young Murdoch graduate Su-Jane Hunt, who was working on a history of Perth's Metropolitan Water Supply, Sewerage and Drainage Board, to produce an article of enduring significance on the early water supply and sanitation of Perth.[57] Beyond the discipline of history, Max Neutze and Hugh Stretton were producing influential works engaging with postwar urbanisation.[58]

Surveying the advent of town life in Australia, Bolton not only described the planning and administration of colonial settlements but also evoked what it *felt* like to live in these places of unmade roads, rudimentary or non-existent organised waste disposal and ubiquitous flies. Partly a literary strategy, this approach also yielded new insights: Australians' failure to develop a Mediterranean 'al fresco' culture, for example, arose not from their lack of sophistication, but the sensory deterrents exercised by dust, mud, flies and stench; these elements of the urban environment also shaped, from very early on, a preference for vehicular transport that insulated occupants from the experience of inhospitable streets.[59] Decades before the 'material turn' in the humanities, Bolton provided fresh insights into the

---

57 Su-Jane Hunt and Geoffrey Bolton, 'Cleansing the Dunghill: Water Supply and Sanitation in Perth 1878–1912', *Studies in Western Australian History*, 2 (1978), pp. 1-17.

58 See, for example, Max Neutze, *Urban Development in Australia: A Descriptive Analysis* (Sydney: Allen & Unwin, 1977); Hugh Stretton, *Ideas for Australian Cities* (Melbourne: Georgian House, 1971).

59 Bolton, *Spoils and Spoilers*, pp. 63-4.

CHAPTER 7

manifold ways in which materiality and embodied experience shaped significant features of Australian cultural life.

Within this analysis is nested a keen sense of social justice, leading to an early articulation of the concerns that would later inform much work on environmental justice. Bolton emphasised the ways in which the material and social processes of urbanisation produced quite different outcomes for rich and poor. For example, writing at a time when the first civil suits against the siting of landfill facilities were taking place in the United States, and drawing on Tom Stannage's groundbreaking history of Perth, Bolton highlighted the practice of locating rubbish tips in the poorest suburbs. His analysis of urban environmental issues led to an understated yet profound conclusion: 'It was the same with environmental hazards always. If they could be kept out of sight of the prosperous and influential remedial action was slow in coming.'[60] Drawing both a chapter title and one of the key themes guiding his exploration of the urban scene from J.K. Galbraith's 1958 classic *The Affluent Society*, Bolton proposed that the relative neglect of public spaces and infrastructure, aggravated from the mid-nineteenth century by the advent of a 'weak and lopsided system of local government',[61] bore hardest on those migrant and working-class families with the fewest resources to invest in their private surroundings. Meanwhile, the seemingly intractable problems of public spaces encouraged many urban residents to devote their efforts to carving out more agreeable private environments in the home and garden – a finding that featured prominently in reviews of the book.

Bolton examines these 'private' environments in some detail, pointing for example to the fact that in the 1920s most Australians

---

60 Bolton, *Spoils and Spoilers*, p. 124.
61 *Spoils and Spoilers*, p. 110.

did not have access to spaces that were entirely private. Even bedrooms were shared: with siblings when young, and later spouses. 'This meant that most people seldom had the opportunity of asking: "What sort of environment would I create for myself if I were planning for myself alone?"'[62] Here 'environment' is domestic and intimate: the living spaces and conditions that shaped most Australians' everyday subjectivities. Household life is evoked in unexpected detail for an environmental history – the manifold daily uses of the kitchen table, the customary prints adorning the walls: 'a solitary Arab with his camel gazing over the endless Sahara sands, or a handsome couple in evening dress conversing in a Mediterranean garden'.[63] A lively and sympathetic historical imagination is exercised for analytical ends: Bolton concludes that the lack of opportunity for most suburban Australians to effectively shape their private environments meant that they also had no expectations of controlling the public environments in which they met and moved. Meanwhile, increasing access to beaches and hills meant that many suburban families began to visualise alternative home environments; dreams that were often pursued in the context of postwar prosperity.[64] The underlying concern here is with the way in which people's views are shaped in interaction with their immediate, proximate surrounds. Similar approaches became popular in the first decades of the twenty-first century, inspired by anthropologist Tim Ingold's philosophy of dwelling and bodily engagement, among other influences.[65]

---

62 *Spoils and Spoilers*, p. 130.
63 *Spoils and Spoilers*, p. 132.
64 *Spoils and Spoilers*, p. 134.
65 Tim Ingold, *The Perception of the Environment: Essays on Livelihood, Dwelling and Skill* (London: Routledge, 2000).

CHAPTER 7

Bolton's commitment to and interest in urban environments increased over time: while he finished the first edition of the book with a hope that Australians might come to regard the earth as their mother, in the 1992 revised edition he accepted that perhaps this tradition 'was insufficient in a nation whose environmental issues were increasingly those of the urban environment'.[66] He also took issue with the longstanding tendency of conservation and environmental activists to focus on issues of 'wilderness' remote from the daily lives of most Australians. Even in the first edition, he asked: 'what if the ACF started to intervene in urban Australia' where most people lived and property rights were most entrenched?[67] By 1992 the criticism was more overt:

> conservation was often seen as the protection of 'nature' or rural habitats, although the environment was often an artifact, most characteristically in the city and its suburbs. Even the more radical 'green' movement of the 1980s and early 1990s concentrated on the preservation of forest or wilderness rather than looking at the problems of the urban environment which was home to most Australians. The 'greens', who at one time had seemed a potent force for change, were in danger of marginalisation.[68]

For Bolton, cities were *the* big environmental issue, and a failure to address the environmental inequities and challenges in the places where most Australians lived threatened to make environmentalism a concern of a privileged minority. But while Bolton deeply respected the desires and choices of ordinary Australians and the visions of reformers who sought to provide them with a spacious and leafy environment, he also recognised the collective problems generated by

---

66   Bolton, *Spoils and Spoilers*, 2nd edn (Sydney: Allen & Unwin, 1992), p. 178.
67   Bolton, *Spoils and Spoilers*, p. 163.
68   Bolton *Spoils and Spoilers*, 2nd edn, p. 177.

'suburban sprawl'. It is a tension that is unresolved in the book, and remains one of the key challenges facing Australian cities.

In the late 1980s and early 1990s, leading American environmental historians vigorously debated whether cities should be included within the scope of the field: were they insufficiently 'natural', or were they important as sites where nature was encountered, transformed, represented and managed? In Australia, while many key environmental conflicts took place outside the cities and the historians tended to follow them there, still some, like Geoff, recognised the importance of cities and suburbs as environments. Dan Coward (now Huon), who had worked as a research assistant to Keith Hancock for *Discovering Monaro*, marked Sydney's environmental history as a story of pollution and public health in *Out of Sight* (1988). Inner urban contagion and pollution also featured in other studies around this time, while George Seddon and David Ravine bucked the trend with their innovative application of art history and historical geography to the study of Perth in *A City and its Setting* (1986).[69] Subsequently, amid debates over urban consolidation and the establishment of federal programs to combat 'sprawl', planning and economic historians pursued environmental themes in work on town planning and suburban expansion.[70] Another factor bringing together the study of cultural and natural landscapes was environmental history's emergence in the 1980s as an instrument of heritage practice, as a way in which

---

69   Dan Coward, *Out of Sight: Sydney's Environmental History, 1851–1981* (Canberra: Dept of Economic History, Australian National University, 1988).
70   See, for example, Robert Freestone, *Model Communities: The Garden City Movement in Australia* (Melbourne: Nelson, 1989); Lionel Frost, *The New Urban Frontier: Urbanisation and City-Building in Australasia and the American West* (Sydney: New South Wales University Press, 1991); Lionel Frost and Tony Dingle, 'Sustaining Suburbia: An Historical Perspective on Australia's Growth', in Patrick Troy (ed.), *Australian Cities: Issues, Strategies and Policies for Urban Australia in the 1990s* (Cambridge: Cambridge University Press, 1995), pp. 20-38.

CHAPTER 7

public historians could talk to natural scientists and heritage practitioners across the nature–culture divide. *Spoils and Spoilers* encouraged that dialogue.

In the early twenty-first century, historians regarded urban environments from a range of angles. A growing number of works on town planning, gardens, political mobilisation and local history explored environmental themes and expanded our knowledge of how urban environments were transformed, regarded and used for livelihood or profit. Others aimed to achieve a more integrated storying of urban ecologies and societies: Heather Goodall and Alison Cadzow linked the ecologies of Sydney's Georges River to its critical role as a centre of networks, enterprise and ultimately survival for Aboriginal people; Graeme Davison with Sheryl Yelland showed how the car was drawn into Australian cultures where it worked to transform both the structure and the very air of our cities; Grace Karskens, attentive to the material culture of the residents of early Sydney, took us into their homes and helped us understand what it felt like to live in a two-roomed hut in the growing township, and to contemplate the vast bush beyond.[71] Andrea Gaynor, with an eye to the future and a notice served by a local council ranger ('Nah, you can't keep chooks here!'), explored suburban food production as a practice connecting minds and bodies to the broader urban environment.[72] It turned out that the eviction of her chooks occurred in the dying days of a middle-class project of suburban modernisation, undertaken over the

---

71 Heather Goodall and Allison Cadzow, *Rivers and Resilience: Aboriginal People on Sydney's Georges River* (Sydney: UNSW Press, 2009); Graeme Davison and Sheryl Yelland, *Car Wars: How the Car Won our Hearts and Conquered our Cities* (Sydney: Allen & Unwin, 2004); Grace Karskens, *The Colony: A History of Early Sydney* (Sydney: Allen & Unwin, 2009).

72 Andrea Gaynor, *Harvest of the Suburbs: An Environmental History of Growing Food in Australian Cities* (Perth: University of Western Australia Press, 2006).

twentieth century at the expense of (largely) working-class capacity for self-provisioning.

While these works consciously engaged with contemporary environmental problems, they avoided the polemical approach taken by William Lines in *Taming the Great South Land* (1991).[73] The first national environmental history to appear since *Spoils and Spoilers*, it lacked the empathy, humour and balance of its predecessor. The revised edition of *Spoils and Spoilers* (1992) contained relatively few changes, principal among them a new final chapter that combined discussion of the escalating environmental problems and conflicts of the 1980s and early 1990s with a strong critique of economic rationalism as a force increasingly shaping relations between society and environment. A more subtle change involved the subtitle, from 'Australians make their environment 1788–1980' to the softening of human agency in 'A history of Australians shaping their environment'. Funding was sought from Film Australia to develop a pitch for a TV documentary based on the book, to coincide with the release of the revised edition; despite much enthusiasm for this proposal around Canberra, it never got off the ground.

* * *

In London in 1982, as mentioned earlier in this volume, Geoffrey Bolton had a disagreement with Barry Humphries who, in the guise of Australia's 'Cultural Attaché' Sir Les Patterson, had imagined a rather different representative of Australia in Britain. Geoff's mission

---

73 William J. Lines, *Taming the Great South Land* (Sydney: Allen & Unwin, 1991); see also his *False Economy: Australia in the Twentieth Century* (Fremantle: Fremantle Arts Centre Press, 1998).

was seriously in tension with that of the comedian. Jim Davidson wrote to Bolton in 1982, saying: 'If you manage to bury Sir Les Patterson, you'll have done a good job'.[74] Ten years later, in his 1992 Boyer Lectures, Bolton continued to ask: 'So why do we [Australians] so often succumb to self-hatred and self-mockery, why do we accept Les Patterson and Sylvania Waters as icons of Australia?'[75]

This stand-off between Australian icons at the heart of the old empire reminds us that one of Bolton's causes as a historian was to foster 'a collective Australian self-confidence'. He felt again that his experience in the west and north of the continent delivered an advantage, for they were 'regions whose errors have often been errors of too much optimism rather than too little. But some of that quality of optimism is needed in Australia today.'[76] Optimism and cultural confidence could be valuable, he argued, if they strengthened trust in home-grown wisdom and local solutions – and this was very much the message of *Spoils and Spoilers*.

Australian historians living at the margins of their continent, beyond the 'golden triangle' (as Bolton called it), can become serious nationalists and keen students of federalism. Bolton's view of the robustness of regional identity and the origins of Australia as 'an archipelago of city states, each with their own hinterland' led him to argue that 'the achievement of the politicians who put together the Australian Federation must be seen as impressive'.[77] He was attracted to a biography of Barton because he was a leading figure who saw

---

74   Jim Davidson to Geoffrey Bolton, 21 September 1982, Bolton Papers, NLA Acc.05/139, Box 1.

75   Geoffrey Bolton, *A View from the Edge: An Australian Stocktaking* (Sydney: ABC Books, 1992), p. 69.

76   Bolton, *A View from the Edge*, pp. 69-70.

77   Bolton, *A View from the Edge*, pp. 25, 29.

federation 'as a means of reconciling provincial diversity with the establishment of a national polity'; thus Barton enabled Bolton to resolve some of his own tensions between the metropolitan and the marginal.[78] One of his favourite metaphors was 'The Belly and the Limbs', drawn from Shakespeare's *Coriolanus*, which argues the interdependence of belly and body. The central belly or Commonwealth, however much resented for 'cupboarding the viand', does digest and distribute nourishment to the limbs of the States.[79] Throughout his life Geoff was a strong and thoughtful champion of the federal invention that is Canberra. 'Most other nations would be proud of such an achievement', he declared in his Boyer Lectures. 'It is a symptom of the Australian disease of self-hatred that we knock it.'[80]

Spoils and Spoilers, then, was upbeat, ecological, literary, federal and urban. Bolton, like Barry Humphries, drew inspiration from Australian suburbia – but for him it was not a source of self-mockery but of a rather surprising radicalism. When the revised edition was published in 1992 – a time Bolton described as replete with gloom – his publishers assured readers that 'Professor Bolton ... reaffirms the message of hope from the first edition, that Australians can influence governments and markets to ensure the quality of urban and rural environments.' And Geoff wanted his book to make a difference. He advised his publishers: 'Every member of parliament should have [a copy] – at least those who read'.[81]

---

78 Bolton, 'A Provincial Viewpoint', p. 85.
79 G.C. Bolton, 'The Belly and the Limbs', *Victorian Historical Journal*, 53, 1 (1982), pp. 5-23.
80 Bolton, *A View from the Edge*, p. 25.
81 *Spoils and Spoilers* marketing questionnaire, Folder 'Spoils and Spoilers'.

Chapter 8

THE PERIPATETIC PROFESSOR AND A SENSE OF PLACE

Jenny Gregory

With an alliteration that he may have enjoyed, Geoff Bolton was sometimes referred to as the peripatetic professor. Like most of us, his horizons enlarged as he aged. Born and schooled in North Perth, he travelled over the Swan River to South Perth for his secondary education and then to Crawley in Perth's western suburbs for university. He journeyed to the State's far north to research his Masters thesis and then voyaged by ship across oceans to undertake doctoral studies in Oxford, with research in Dublin. Offered a position at the ANU in Canberra, he returned to Australia, but then travelled to northern Queensland to research the book that became *A Thousand Miles Away* and after a year or so went south to take up a position at Melbourne's Monash University until he returned to Perth to take up a chair at the University of Western Australia. And so it continued: from UWA to Murdoch to Queensland to London and back, to Edith Cowan and then to Murdoch, with sabbaticals in the United

Kingdom along the way, trips to the United States, and frequent trips to the eastern capitals. While today academic historians frequently jet around the world to conferences and for research, as Stuart Macintyre observes in this volume, Geoff was 'the most ... widely travelled of his generation of Australian historians'.

This chapter will consider Geoff's journeying and several of his key works to ask what they reveal about his sense of place. Can a sense of place be nurtured and strengthened during such a peripatetic career? I will first discuss some of the key aspects of his career that give clues to his sense of place. Then I will reflect on three of his books that seem to most clearly exhibit aspects of his sense of his own place – *A Fine Country to Starve In*, *Claremont* and *Daphne Street* – before turning to a broader discussion of the idea of place and case studies from my own work in which I have explored reactions to the loss of place.

Both Geoff's career and his writings complicate our understanding of his sense of place. Several aspects can be discerned. As Stuart Macintyre suggests, there was increasing tension between his 'deep attachment to his native Western Australia' and his career ambitions. Geoff's realisation of this tension surfaced in his 1981 paper 'The Belly and the Limbs' when he referred to the 'golden triangle of south-eastern Australia' and delineated some of 'the grievances that weigh upon those of us who live and work on the outer periphery'.[1] He became increasingly irritated by dominance of the golden triangle, voicing his concern pointedly in a 1994 interview: 'There is, I think, a sense particularly in Melbourne that its version of Australia

---

1   G.C. Bolton, 'The Belly and the Limbs', Augustus Wolskel Memorial Lecture delivered to the Royal Historical Society of Victoria, *Victorian Historical Journal*, 53, 1 (1982), p. 6.

CHAPTER 8

is normality and that the regions are just picturesque aberrations'.[2] He voiced this publicly in 2013:

> It is not narrowly parochial to suggest that the writing and teaching of Australian history have sometimes been too much dominated by the point of view of what Geoffrey Blainey called the 'Hume Highway axis' – Melbourne-Canberra-Sydney.[3]

Andrea Gaynor and Tom Griffiths comment on Geoff's continuing connection with his home State in this volume, proposing that his 'strong advocacy for local and regional history ... was part of his "view from the edge", part of his identity as a Western Australian'. His concern for the land had deep roots. Perhaps imprinted during boyhood visits to the southwest, it seems to have been reawakened in the 1950s during research in the Kimberley and later under Keith Hancock at the ANU, emerging during the writing of *A Thousand Miles Away* (1963), apparent in *A Fine Country to Starve In* (1972), more fully developed during the delivery of his Australian Environmental History unit at Murdoch and consolidated in *Spoils and Spoilers* (1981). They observe that 'he liked to earth himself in place, period and people and to allow patterns to emerge from that mastery'.

What of his sense of place as it related to the urban environment? Griffiths and Gaynor also argue that 'cities and the suburbs are the sites of a substantial part of Geoff's "environmental" history'. While that may hold true for *Spoils and Spoilers* and for occasional pieces like 'Cleansing the Dunghill', I'm not so sure about *A Fine Country to*

---

2   Deborah Gare, 'Images from a Life in Australian History: An Interview with Geoffrey Bolton', *Limina*, 4 (1998), p. 94.
3   Emeritus Professor Geoffrey Bolton, Address at the Wesfarmers Chair in Australian History signing ceremony, University of Western Australia, 12 March 2013, reported in *The West Australian*, 13 March 2013.

Starve In. While Geoff begins the book with a marvellous evocation of the 1929 Centenary Parade through the streets of Perth, he does not engage strongly with the suffering experienced in the city and its suburbs. He situates much of the experience of hardship amongst group settlers and wheat farmers – the groupies and the cockies. His examination of the plight of the urban unemployed was limited and for this he was criticised by labour historians.[4]

Yet two of Bolton's books – *Claremont* and *Daphne Street* – are firmly situated within suburban society and demonstrate a deep engagement. Geoff and his family lived in Claremont from 1967. Shortly after the Claremont Museum was established in 1975, he agreed to write a history of the suburb with research assistance provided by a host of volunteers from the museum. As his introduction to *Claremont* notes, the pressures of his academic career and 'guilty procrastination' slowed progress, a factor that some locals did not understand, particularly as the centenary of the suburb approached. Fortuitously, my doctoral thesis on the manufacture of middle-class suburbia, using Claremont as one of its case studies, was completed in 1988. This provided an opportunity for more speedy completion. An agreement was reached, sections on Claremont were drawn from the thesis and seamlessly woven into the book, eyewitness accounts from the 1930s by Paul Hasluck and the 1960s by George Seddon were inserted, and the manuscript was ready for publication in 1998, the year of Claremont's centenary.[5]

While defined by place, the book is about the people of Claremont over time, recalling Gaynor and Griffiths' observation about the roles

---

4 See, for example, the review of *A Fine Country to Starve In* by H.J. Gibbney, *Labour History*, 25 (1973), pp. 83-84.

5 Geoff reflects on the progress of the book in his introduction to Geoffrey Bolton and Jenny Gregory, *Claremont: A History* (Nedlands: UWA Press, 1999).

CHAPTER 8

of 'place, period and people' in Geoff's work. It traces the suburb from its years as a depot for convicts and a settlement for pensioner guards until the coming of the railway in 1883 brought in land speculators and developers. Then the emerging suburb became socially differentiated with a resident gentry living in large establishments overlooking the river, served by working people from wooden houses that jostled together on small blocks. The twin pillars of paternalism and deference were writ large. Further suburban development resulted from the population surge of the gold rushes so that by the interwar years Claremont was noted as a home for a comfortable upper middle-class: civil servants, rising young professionals and businessmen, and affluent semi-retired pastoralists. There was a 'wrong side of the tracks' in Claremont. On the 'other' side of the railway on the suburb's periphery, Aborigines camped near the local swamp, as they had since time immemorial (until removed by the Council in 1957), the Agricultural Society's show grounds were established and a hospital for the insane was built. Nevertheless, Claremont's growing population consolidated its reputation as a pleasant leafy riverside suburb, despite the incursion of a few high-rise developments during the mineral boom of the late 1960s.

Where then is Geoff's sense of the place? People and their activities dominate *Claremont*, but now and again the natural environment asserts itself in relation to the life of the people. He described Claremont in its earliest years of white settlement as a:

> pleasant bush environment. There was always the river with its plentiful fish, and any number of wise old Aborigines who could tell the colonial lads where the best spots for bream or tailor might be found.[6]

---

6   Bolton and Gregory, *Claremont*, p. 31.

'For the majority of Claremont residents at the turn of the century it was the river that gave their suburb its special character', he wrote, quoting one elderly resident who reminisced:

> It was a lovely river – you could look down ten to fifteen feet, crystal clear to the bottom. It was too far to go to the ocean, but we had this river and it was really a wonderful playground. We used to go crabbing, prawning, and fishing ...[7]

According to Paul Hasluck's memories of the 1930s in Claremont '[m]uch of the life of Claremont was focused on the river'.[8] He described activities at the yacht club, the jetty 'always thronged with youngsters fishing', picnicking and rivers cruises, supplementing Geoff's descriptions of the swimming baths, 'remembered by hundreds ... as the venue where they learned to swim'.[9]

Nevertheless, the environmental impact of nutrients that washed into the river was not welcome. Algal growth in the river was a regular problem in summer from the 1920s onwards, unwelcome to those living nearest to the river who regularly complained to the council as the algae decomposed.[10] Seddon, in his section of the book, gloriously recalled one resident's consolation to another: 'My dear, think of it as the smell of money'.[11]

For some, the natural environment of Claremont was used productively. Geoff writes of one Claremont family during the Depression who 'sold and cleaned chickens and ducks, caught fish, and grew vegetables ... remind[ing] us that Freshwater Bay and the country

---

7   Bolton and Gregory, *Claremont*, pp. 95-96.
8   Paul Hasluck, 'Claremont in the 1920s and 1930s', in Bolton and Gregory, *Claremont*, p. 190.
9   Bolton and Gregory, *Claremont*, p. 98.
10 Bolton and Gregory, *Claremont*, p. 169.
11 George Seddon, 'Claremont in the 1960s', in Bolton and Gregory, *Claremont*, p. 212.

CHAPTER 8

around it had been a source of nourishment for its people since Nyoongar times'.[12] And as Hasluck confirms, fruit trees – lemons, figs, grapes and oranges – and backyard vegetable patches were to be found in many Claremont gardens up to the 1950s.[13]

In the final pages of the book, Geoff describes Perth's high life of the 1980s as it was played out in affluent Claremont, quoting a newspaper report describing the main shopping area as a scene of 'badly parked Porsches and colour-coordinated toddlers'.[14] He moves then to Claremont's nightlife of the late 1990s and the community's shock at the tragedies of the Claremont serial killings. His final paragraph, however, is both a summary passage and a reflection on the suburban environment. It includes a degree of nostalgia:

> Yet, as so often in the past, Claremont's sense of identity was stamped by its environment. There were still continuities with the environment which the Nyoongar had known and enjoyed, where the Pensioners found themselves a living, where the professionals of late Victorian and Edwardian Claremont had tried to create a village community; generations of children of every background had enjoyed the river and the back lanes and the trees and the sense of growing up in an established community.[15]

For Geoff, it was largely the relationship between the people and the natural environment that defined Claremont's identity and his own sense of the place.

Daphne Street had been completed two years earlier in 1997.[16] It too was some years in the making, begun when Geoff lived in Brisbane.

---

12 Bolton and Gregory, *Claremont*, p. 171.
13 Hasluck, in Bolton and Gregory, *Claremont*, p. 191.
14 *Sunday Times*, 8 November 1987 quoted in Bolton and Gregory, *Claremont*, p. 225.
15 Bolton and Gregory, *Claremont*, p. 226.
16 See also Jenny Gregory, review of Geoffrey Bolton, *Daphne Street* (Fremantle: Fremantle Arts Centre Press, 1997), *Studies in Western Australian History*, 19 (1999), pp. 241-43.

As he revealed in an interview, he 'wanted some Western Australian projects to justify to the taxation people my frequent flights to Perth and I began a project ... writing the history of the street in which I grew up, Daphne St'.[17] This was the street that helped shape his understanding of the world and he lovingly reconstructed the lives of its people. As he reflected, 'These are my people and it is right that I should be their chronicler'.[18] Place, people and period dominate the book. It is a nostalgic world of backyard chooks and vegie growing, of back lanes, plumbago hedges and corner stores, a book of the heart, a mark of filial piety.

The residents of Daphne Street who inhabit this book were largely respectable working-class and lower middle class folk. Even the absentee landowners of Daphne Street were not that dissimilar from residents. Perhaps just a rung further up the ladder – small investors who had managed to get together a little capital and who saw the land as a good opportunity to make that capital grow perhaps to help support them in their retirement.

The lives of the people of Daphne Street, however, are rich in contrasts. Geoff had an eye for the poignant story and for some residents life was extraordinarily difficult. A World War I veteran crumbles under the long-term impact of war service and takes a fatal dose of cyanide, despite a wife and child and a steady job.[19] A young mother cries during the Depression as she tries to feed her baby – 'How can I make milk when I only have lettuce to eat?'[20] But generally Daphne Street seems to have been a fairly cheerful sort of place. By

---

17   Geoffrey Bolton interviewed by Stuart Reid, Battye Library Collection, State Library of Western Australia (SLWA), OH2618, 1994–1995, transcript, p. 207.
18   Bolton, *Daphne Street*, p. 14.
19   Bolton, *Daphne Street*, p. 89.
20   Bolton, *Daphne Street*, p. 88.

CHAPTER 8

the 1930s most of its residents were in the lower rungs of the middle class. Many were civil servants and, although their salaries were cut, they remained in work and some did quite well out of a lower cost of living and the ability to pick up properties cheaply as the less fortunate fell by the wayside. By 1936 all the breadwinners of the street were back in work, either part- or full-time. Home ownership, which had dipped during the Depression, returned to its World War I rate of over 50 per cent by the 1950s.[21] Geoff lived in Daphne Street between 1939 and 1954 and it is this period that colours his sense of the place.

The Daphne Street experiences that he charts mirror many of the most profound changes in Australian society over the twentieth century; eastern depression and western goldrushes, World War I, migration from Britain in the prosperous twenties, Depression, World War II, migration from Europe, gentrification. By the end of the twentieth century, Daphne Street, with its smattering of European migrants, newly built flats, and the movement of young couples into the street intent on 'restoring' the street's early twentieth-century homes, bears the traces of these transformations.

Geoff was a narrator par excellence. The parade of mostly engaging characters and their stories underlines that for Geoff it is the people of streets like Daphne Street throughout the nation who maintain 'the fabric of the world'.[22] And paraphrasing E.P. Thompson's famous phrase, he argues that it is 'time the suburbs were rescued from ... the condescension of social critics', echoing Hugh Stretton's call made nearly thirty years earlier.[23] A study of Geoff's analysis of this

---

21 Bolton, *Daphne Street*, pp. 67, 96, 134.
22 Ecclesiasticus, 38:34, part of the epigraph of Bolton, *Daphne Street*, p. 11.
23 Bolton, *Daphne Street*, p. 134; Hugh Stretton, *Ideas for Australian Cities* (Adelaide: self-published, 1970).

world, his place, tells us much about his view of history. But his claim that the history of the nation can be read through the history of the people of Daphne Street misleads. Can a single street be a microcosm for Australia's diverse history? To argue this is to deny the range of experience – from Toorak or Peppermint Grove to Redfern or Balga – that makes up Australian life. Daphne Street represents a middle way; it is a middling place, and its history a lyrical and nostalgic evocation of a place that is lost.

* * *

Like Geoff, most people have strong cultural attachments to familiar places. This is reflected in the extensive literature on the meanings of place by scholars such as Henri Lefebvre, Yi-Fu Tuan, David Harvey and Edward Soja. As the urban historian and architect Dolores Hayden has argued:

> [u]rban landscapes are storehouses for … social memories, because natural features such as hills or harbors, as well as streets, buildings and patterns of settlement frame the lives of many people and often outlast many lifetimes.[24]

Memories contribute to our attachment to place, helping to explain why both communities and individuals mourn for places lost to urban renewal. This is in part nostalgia, which in its modern sense involves spatial and temporal dislocation and includes dispossession, so that we feel nostalgia for a place that we love but have lost.[25] But

---

24 Dolores Hayden, *The Power of Place: Urban Landscapes as Public History* (Cambridge: MA: MIT Press, 1995), p. 9.
25 Irwin Altman and Setha Low, *Place Attachment (Human Behavior and Environment)*, (New York: Plenum Press, 1992); Peter Read, *Returning to Nothing: The Meaning of Lost Places* (Cambridge: Cambridge University Press, 1996).

the distress we feel when a loved place is under assault or is transformed has been called 'solastalgia' – derived from solace, desolation and nostalgia – a term coined by philosopher Glenn Albrecht. We feel solastalgia when a loved place is threatened so that our sense of place attachment and identity is undermined.[26]

The influence of emotions such as nostalgia and solastalgia on people's sense of place has been highlighted in much recent literature as part of the 'affective turn'. As Sarah Dunant and Roy Porter observed, the rapid transformation of the later twentieth century and beyond has eroded older values, leading many people to feel loss of control and uncertainty about the future.[27] A study of their emotions can reveal the attachments that hold people in place and connect them to the world, and in the remainder of this chapter I discuss three case studies that demonstrate the way people respond to loss of place.

Protesting against Loss of Place

In another work I have argued that the protest surrounding the part-demolition of Perth's Pensioner Barracks, which was intended to culminate in a rally through the city streets in March 1966, would have been the first heritage rally in an Australian city if the police had not thwarted it.[28] The Battle for the Barracks was long running. It began in the late 1950s when, to make way for freeway development, planners first proposed the demolition of the old Pensioner

---

26 Glenn Albrecht, '"Solastalgia": A New Concept in Health and Identity', *PAN (Philosophy, Activism and Nature)*, 3 (2005), pp. 45-46.

27 Sarah Dunant and Roy Porter (eds), *The Age of Anxiety* (London: Virago, 1996), p. xi, cited in Sara Ahmed, *The Cultural History of Emotions* (Edinburgh: Edinburgh University Press, 2004), p. 72.

28 Some of the following is taken from previous research published in Jenny Gregory, *City of Light: A History of Perth since the 1950s* (Perth: City of Perth, 2003), ch. 3.

Guard Barracks built in 1866. These were situated at the head of St George's Terrace, the city's most prestigious thoroughfare, blocking the view of Parliament House.

In 1961, the best-selling West Australian novelist Dorothy Sanders expressed the reaction of many to the threat of demolition of the Barracks through the voice of one of her heroines, a daughter of one of Perth's old families:

> At the top of the hill she could see the old red brick Barracks with their mock battlements.
>
> A town planner from abroad had advised West Australians to remove that old historical building in order to allow a finer vista down the length of the Terrace from Parliament House. The Barracks were not architecturally beautiful, he had informed the citizens.
>
> This advice had been received in courteous silence. West Australians could not explain to a man from abroad that the Barracks held a beauty for them he would never be able to see with foreign eyes. That building stood for their history, their birth pangs. As a nation they had not come trailing clouds of glory from some other world. Their primordial memory was one of discovery ships, pioneer ships, convict ships, immigrant ships. The Barracks, relic of the birth of a nation, reminded the citizens they were not born of privilege but of hardship, endurance and the will to survive.[29]

Defenders coalesced to form the Barracks Defence Council (BDC) in 1961 with Bishop Tom Riley as president. They were mainly mature men and women and included influential members of Perth society who were active in the (Royal) Western Australian Historical Society, the newly-formed National Trust, and other community groups such as the Citizens' Committee for the Defence of Kings Park, the Tree

---

29 Lucy Walker (aka Dorothy Sanders), *Monday in Summer* (London: Hodder and Stoughton, 1961), p. 173.

CHAPTER 8

Society, the WA Fellowship of Writers, the Women's Service Guild and the National Council of Women. Ranged against them were a determined premier, David Brand, and the ruling Liberal-Country Party coalition.

With many of its members already seasoned by campaigns against development in Kings Park, the BDC had considerable organisational skill. They printed pamphlets and stickers depicting the Barracks arch in silhouette flying a black banner with the words 'Preserve Democracy' emblazoned on it, and organised a public opinion poll, speakers and media publicity.[30] They arranged for the visiting chairman of the English National Trust to make a well-publicised call on the premier, for visiting Poet Laureate John Betjeman to come out in support of the Barracks, and for the visiting chairman of the National Trust in New South Wales, Mr Justice McClemens, to speak out against demolition.[31]

The arguments went on and on over the next few years. The BDC held meetings with government planning committees, ideas were batted about, and petitions were submitted. The government proposed a compromise: the arch would be retained and only the wings demolished. It was rejected by the BDC. A radio station conducted a public opinion poll, resulting in 2688 votes for retention and only 59 for demolition. The premier tried to minimise the poll, leading Bishop Riley to 'warn the government of the mounting public opinion against the sacrifice of the Barracks on the altar of an engineering

---

30 Mrs Ray Oldham, Hon. Secretary Barracks Defence Council, to Bessie Rischbieth, 27 June 1962, Bessie Rischbieth Papers, 'Correspondence, Newspaper Cutting re the Preservation of Perth Barracks', Battye Library, SLWA MN 634/1, Acc.2552, Item No.22, 1961–62; and sticker, Bishop C.L. Riley Papers, 'Papers re Barracks Defence Council', Battye Library, SLWA MN 567, Acc.2425A, Item No.6, 1962, SLWA.
31 *The West Australian*, 7 July 1966.

Moloch'.³² Ironically, demolition of the wings began just as Perth residents received copies of the new phone directory carrying a colour photo of the Barracks on the cover.

After demolition of the wings was completed in July 1966, leaving the archway in front of the deep scar that marked the freeway works, *The West Australian* took a poll of passers-by to gauge the public's views on its appearance. 'I think the archway looks marvellous. It gives distinct character to this end of the terrace', said a housewife. A taxi driver thought that 'it looks like a pimple on a pumpkin'. But the majority were on the side of the arch, describing it as 'striking', 'mellow', 'picturesque', 'elegant', and declaring that 'It is not a public nuisance. Posterity will thank us', and 'It helps hold back the concrete jungle'.³³ The premier, however, firmly in the grip of modernist urban planning and development, believed that people who were against a proposal would always be the most vocal and were best ignored. 'The tendency to be influenced by our emotions' should be put aside for the sake of town planning and the demands of the car.³⁴

Continuing pressure against the demolition of the archway forced the government to commission a Gallup Poll on the issue.³⁵ It showed that most people were against demolition. A panel of experts discussed the results on television. Their opinions were evenly divided,

---

32 Bishop C.L. Riley, public statement after Barracks Defence Council meeting, 24 March 1966, endorsed at special conference of member organisations on 5 April 1966, Riley Papers.
33 *The West Australian*, 15 July 1966.
34 Premier David Brand to Right Reverend C.L. Riley, President, Barracks Defence Council, 25 July 1966.
35 *Daily News*, 14 October 1966: '$800 Barracks Poll Bill Called Waste', Riley Papers. There were at least three polls conducted in 1966: one organised by local radio station 6IX (2688 people for retention, 59 for demolition), a McNair poll commissioned by TV Channel TVW 7 (44% for retention, 32% for demolition, 24% undecided) and the Gallup poll commissioned by the government (49% for retention, 39% for demolition).

CHAPTER 8

with those in favour of retention speaking of the archway's personal, sentimental and historical attachments and the controversial City Planner, Paul Ritter, threatening to jump from the top if they tried to pull it down.[36]

The premier decided to put the issue to parliament in a non-party vote. The crowded public gallery broke into applause when, in an historic division (twenty-six to eighteen with thirteen backbenchers voting with the Opposition), the Legislative Assembly rejected the premier's motion for the removal of the archway.[37] As the *Daily News* explained later, in an editorial in October 1966 headlined 'Big Brother Rebuffed':

> the Barracks archway became a symbol. People tended to identify its planned destruction with so much of the recent casual scarring of the city in the name of progress – and, in a general sense, with governmental and departmental arrogance. It may be that many people who protested about the planned demolition of the archway would not have felt deeply about it if they were not already resentful. Whatever the aesthetic value of the archway, it is to be hoped that the successful fight for its survival has taught the Government a lesson – that it cannot consistently act on the basis that Big Brother knows best.[38]

Geoff missed the public meetings, polls, the media and parliamentary debates on the fate of the Barracks. He came in at the tail end of the controversy when he returned to Western Australia to take up the Chair of Modern History at the University of Western Australia in 1966. But he was aware of the dispute and the increasing loss of place in Perth that it signalled. Over the next two decades many

---

36 'TV Panel Divided over Archway' and 'Survey Retain Arch', unsourced newspaper cuttings, 4 October 1966, Riley Papers.
37 *The West Australian*, 20 October 1966.
38 *Daily News*, 20 October 1966.

nineteenth and early twentieth-century buildings in St George's Terrace, which gave it the appearance of a European boulevard, came tumbling down, replaced by high-rise buildings and transforming the city into a US-style skyscraper city. But intriguingly, during Western Australia's 'four-on-the-floor' development era of the 1980s, Geoff wrote of a protest in earlier times. He quoted an editorial condemning a 1931 proposal to alienate 35 acres of Perth's Kings Park for a new public hospital. Tellingly he noted that it concluded in language which could apply equally today: 'There is a tendency in these unrelenting days for … things to be done "under the lap" in the belief that public agitation will die quickly'.[39]

Then, in 1994, he contributed a chapter on 'The Good Name of Parliament' to a history of the WA parliament. He devoted five of its eighteen pages to the Barracks controversy, justifying this with the statement that 'no single episode so clearly epitomis[es] the public view of Parliament's role and standing'.[40] He did not take a position on the merits or otherwise of the protest, but argued that '[f]rom being a controversy about the historical and architectural merits of the Barracks, it began to take on the character of an attack on the alleged tendency of politicians to override public opinion'.[41]

That same year he wrote an article which he entitled 'The Price of Protest'. This time he wrote of a complex legal case in Perth in 1870 when criticism of an uncompromising decision by Western Australia's only judge by an up-and-coming lawyer made its way into several newspapers. The result was that the lawyer was fined and

---

39 G.C. Bolton, 'Newspapers for a Depression Child', *Westerly*, 31, 4 (1986), p. 78.
40 Geoffrey Bolton, 'The Good Name of Parliament, 1890–1990', in David Black (ed.), *The House on the Hill: A History of the Parliament of Western Australia 1832–1990* (Perth: Parliament of Western Australia, 1991), p. 490.
41 Bolton, 'The Good Name of Parliament', p. 488.

required to apologise, and the editors were gaoled (later remitted to payment of a substantial fine) and ordered to write abject letters of apology for publishing 'a gross and scandalous libel on the Supreme Court'. One of the editors, distraught at his imprisonment, died a few months later. While the judge was privately castigated for acting tyrannically, as Geoff noted, the press had been muzzled and would be careful to keep its criticisms within safe limits for the next twenty years.[42] It was a cautionary tale, with Geoff clearly recognising the consequences that protest could have on careers.

Mourning and Celebrating Lost Places on Social Media[43]

During the controversy over the demolition of the Barracks, an architect had observed that the public should be reminded that it 'was not the only historic building on Death Row'.[44] Perth soon lost an unprecedented number of historic buildings as developers cut a swathe through the city. This may partly explain the interest in Perth's lost places that has appeared in social media, with several Facebook groups – 'Beautiful Buildings and Cool Places Perth has Lost – a photo history', 'Lost Perth', 'Lost Perth Found' – launched in recent years. The oldest is the 'Beautiful Old Perth …' group, launched in 2009, and its activities are discussed here.[45]

---

42 Geoffrey Bolton, 'The Price of Protest: Press and Judiciary in 1870', *Studies in Western Australian History*, 15 (1994), pp. 14-22. See also O.K. Battye, 'Arthur Shenton (1816–1871)', *Australian Dictionary of Biography*, vol. 6 (1976), pp. 117-18; and Sheila McClemans, 'Sir Archibald Paull Burt (1810–1879)', *Australian Dictionary of Biography*, vol. 3 (1969), pp. 307-8.

43 This subject is explored further in Jenny Gregory, 'Connecting with the Past Through Social Media: The "Beautiful Buildings and Cool Places Perth has lost" Facebook Group', *International Journal of Heritage Studies*, 21, 1 (2015), pp. 22-45.

44 Julius Elischer, quoted in 'TV Panel Divided Over Archway', newspaper cutting, 4 October 1966, Riley Papers.

45 For convenience I refer to it as 'Beautiful Old Perth'. The group's activities can be viewed at www.facebook.com/groups/129206433137 (accessed 29 October 2016).

The places discussed by members of 'Beautiful Old Perth' are places lost through demolition or obliteration that they wish had been kept for the future. They have recreated these places in digital form through online photos that conjure up a past era. These photographic representations of lost places create a visual discourse that draws members of 'Beautiful Old Perth' together. The group shares an 'architecture of the heart ... a place within [them] that holds onto the emoting memory of a place'.[46]

Nostalgia for the past is at the core of many of the emotions expressed by members of the 'Beautiful Old Perth' group. Thirty years ago David Lowenthal included an extensive discussion of nostalgia in *The Past is a Foreign Country*, suggesting that 'nostalgic dreams have become almost habitual, if not epidemic'.[47] More recently, the role of nostalgia in heritage has been discussed by a number of writers who have critiqued the scholarly dismissal of nostalgia, arguing that it is not simply a matter of wallowing in sentiment.[48] Nostalgia is a negotiation between past and present, between continuity and discontinuity: 'it insists on the bond between our present selves and a certain fragment of the past, but also on the force of our separation from what we have lost'.[49]

Nostalgia and the response to historic photographs have been the subjects of much scholarly discussion. In famously analysing the nature of photography, Susan Sontag wrote that '[p]hotographs turn

---

46   Shelley Hornstein, *Losing Site: Architecture, Memory and Place* (Burlington: Ashgate, 2011), p. 3.
47   David Lowenthal, *The Past is a Foreign Country* (Cambridge: Cambridge University Press, 1985, 2nd edn 2013), pp. 4-13.
48   Stuart Tannock, 'Nostalgia Critique', *Cultural Studies*, 9, 3 (1995), p. 454.
49   Nadia Atia and Jeremy Davies, 'Nostalgia and the Shapes of History: Editorial', *Memory Studies*, 3, 3 (2010), p. 183.

CHAPTER 8

the past into an object of tender regard, scrambling moral distinctions and disarming historical judgements by the generalized pathos of looking at time past'.[50] Raphael Samuel later mused that the popularity of historic photographs in Britain demonstrated a postmodern turn to nostalgia in which lost Edens were created in the public imagination.[51] He argued that while they have created an 'iconography of the national past ... The loved one [or thing] no longer exists ... the original bond, or relationship, has been irretrievably shattered', so that keeping an old photo 'is a grasping after shadows'. The moment of the photo cannot ever be repeated, and this is part of the nostalgia that people feel for the places, events or people depicted. However, it has been empirically shown that nostalgia, even though it can be generated by psychological threats such as loneliness and meaningless, has a positive effect on psychological health because it increases social connectedness, enhances positive self-regard, improves mood, and contributes to perceptions of the meaning of life by linking the past and the present.[52]

The members of 'Beautiful Old Perth' have responded to the dramatic changes in the built environment of the central business district of Perth over the previous fifty years by development of an online photo history. Through this they both mourn and celebrate the lost places of Perth. Within a few hours of setting up 'Beautiful Old Perth' and posting the first photos, its creator/curator had attracted several comments. This was the first exchange:

---

50 Susan Sontag, *On Photography* (London: Penguin, 1977), p. 71.
51 Raphael Samuel, *Theatres of Memory* (London: Verso, 1994), pp. 323, 356, 375.
52 Clay Routledge, Tim Wildschut, Constantine Sedikides and Jacob Juhl, 'Nostalgia as a Resource for Psychological Health and Well-being', *Social and Personality Psychology Compass*, 7, 11 (2013), p. 812.

S1: 'Michelle, I share your passion and grieve for the loss of these beautiful buildings too! Thanks for sharing your awesome photos and creating this group!!'

Michelle: 'No probs. I also wanted younger people who might not know much about Perth's history to see what vibrant city we used to have culture-wise.' (17 September 2009)

Over the following two years Michelle shared nearly eight hundred photos with the group. They were mainly of theatres or cinemas, houses, hotels and office buildings. Group members left hundreds of comments in response to these photographs. While many can also be viewed on the State Library of Western Australia's website, a catalogue search is necessary to find them. Michelle has curated an archive of photographs, which is immediately accessible *en masse* and thus has a more immediate impact.

In mid-2011 the group had attracted nearly 7000 members, though only just over five hundred made regular comments and it is their commentary that is discussed here. Although the gender of a few could not be identified (it's impossible to assign a gender to a pseudonym like 'Noisy Corella', for example), the group seems almost equally split between men and women. Their age was rarely revealed, but could be estimated by their response to the photos of lost heritage places, with nearly 20 per cent likely to be aged over forty.

N1: 'Thanks so much for a wonderful group. The photos of Boans bought a smile and a tear to my eye. Fond memories of my grandmothers taking me there as a little girl to see the Christmas decorations and window displays.' (7 November 2009)

B2: 'What a wonderful walk down memory lane! I lament what Perth has done ... I remember the George Hotel when I was a child as my father and his mates went there to have a

CHAPTER 8

drink after the Anzac Day Parades. And of course I screamed at Billy Thorpe at the Capitol Theatre in the 60s and had drinks at the Palace before heading down the hill to the Embassy Ballroom in our beautiful ball dresses, about the same era.' (12 November 2009)

For more than 80 per cent of members of the 'Beautiful Old Perth' group, however, the lost buildings in the photos were a revelation. These members are likely to be either recent arrivals to Perth or aged under forty. Their tone and language suggests that many were considerably younger:

> S3: *'Wow I had no idea*!!!! What brilliant photos. It is such a shame these beautiful buildings have now been demolished.' (2 November 2009)

> E1: *'I had no idea we had all this stuff in Perth*, it is tragic to see it all gone and in its place just buildings, no heart, no history ... shame.' (3 December 2009)

The responses of younger members do not have the warm glow generated by nostalgic reminiscences. While they appear to feel a generalised nostalgia for the past, it is not a past that they have experienced. Their responses tend to be tinged with the emotions of, at best, disappointment, or, at worst, shame and anger.

The 'Beautiful Old Perth' group became an emotional community of shared values created via social media. It demonstrates, through the response of members to photographs of lost buildings and places, the sense of loss that many people feel when a heritage building or place is demolished. Those who remembered the lost places shown in photos tended to reminisce nostalgically about their experience of the place so that, although lamenting its loss, they recalled positive memories. Those who had not previously seen or experienced these lost places were more likely to express negative emotions of loss and their anger was directed towards those who had been responsible for their demolition or obliteration. Some of the members of 'Beautiful Old Perth' have gone further, sheeting home blame to city property developers and government. Moreover, the considerable social capital that the group developed has led to increased civic engagement among members, who have shared links to like-minded groups, signed petitions, and actively protested against the loss of heritage.

Obliterating Place: Elizabeth Quay[53]

In December 2013, after months of excavation with bulldozers digging and back-filling soil and sand, and barges dredging sediment and slurry, water from the Swan River flooded through a cutting in Perth's Esplanade Reserve, known simply as the Esplanade. It was in the process of being redeveloped as Elizabeth Quay. Not so long before, the Esplanade, which lay at the foot of the Perth's Central Business District near the Swan River's edge, was a ten-hectare swathe of grassed parkland bounded by immense Moreton Bay fig trees on three sides, and separated from the edge of the river by a four-lane riverside drive. The redevelopment of the Esplanade, which remains permanently listed on the Western Australian State Register of Heritage Places despite its obliteration, gave rise to huge public controversy.

Fundamental to this controversy was the loss that many Perth citizens felt when the redevelopment of this historic site was announced and which intensified as its destruction became imminent. This sense

---

53 This subject is explored further in Jenny Gregory, 'The Esplanade and the City Gatekeepers: Contesting the Limits of Urban Heritage Protection', in Alicia Marchant (ed.), *Emotions and Heritage: Blood, Stone and Land* (London: Routledge, forthcoming).

CHAPTER 8

of loss was expressed through a range of heightened emotional responses. Many were angered by the proposed destruction of the historic parkland and the trees that edged it; others were incensed that government protection – the 1880 Crown Grant reserving the land for public recreation and the Heritage Act protecting the site because of its heritage significance – was being ignored; others were alarmed by the traffic congestion that would be created by the redevelopment; others were shocked and angered by the cost, and some simply saddened by the assault on the city's past.

The Esplanade did not always exist. Originally reed beds in shallow river flats, it was a fishing place for many generations of the Whadjuck Noongar people, who knew it as Gumap.[54] The area was reclaimed from the river in fits and starts between 1866 and 1880 and given to 'the Council and Burgesses of the City of Perth … their successors and assigns, upon trust for the purposes of a place of recreation for the city forever' with the proviso that the Crown could resume the land for 'works of public utility or convenience' on payment of compensation.[55]

The Esplanade quickly became a place for sport, especially cricket, and for passive recreation. People enjoyed promenading there, listening to band performances and watching parades of troops. Civic events were held on the Esplanade: the Perth Intercolonial Exhibition (1881), the proclamation of self-government (1890), and celebrations when the Australian colonies federated to form the Commonwealth of Australia (1901). The annual Anzac Day march was held there from 1916 onwards. From the 1890s to the 1960s

---

54   Debra Hughes-Hallet, 'Indigenous History of the Swan and Canning Rivers', Curtin University project with the Swan River Trust, 2010, pp. 41-3.
55   Crown Grant 1066, Title no. 5066, 31 March 1880.

there was a 'speakers corner' on the Esplanade. Almost every Sunday, hundreds would turn up to hear the 'stump orators'. Radical organisations held rallies there and marches by protestors, from the unemployed of the 1930s to supporters of nuclear disarmament in the 1980s, always began there. It was also the site of celebrations attended by many thousands of Perth people for Australia II's victory in the America's Cup in 1983 and for the CHOGM Barbeque for Queen Elizabeth II in 2011. It was for all these reasons that the Esplanade Reserve was entered onto the State Heritage Register in 2003.[56]

There had been numerous threats to the Esplanade in the years prior to its entry on the State Heritage Register.[57] None eventuated but extensive public consultation in the 1990s showed that people did not want the Esplanade or the foreshore to be built on.[58] Then in 2008, a plan by Melbourne architects again threatened the Esplanade with destruction. It was to be 'transformed into a cove surrounded by skyscrapers' with 'new roads and bridges, man-made river inlets and an island shaped like a swan'.[59] Riverfront land was to be sold or leased to developers to build shops, bars and apartments. The editor of *The West Australian* newspaper judged the proposal 'bold and visionary', but warned that it was likely to be met with 'guarded scepticism, if not downright cynicism, as well as the usual flurry of instant protest

---

56   Heritage Council of Western Australia, Register of Heritage Places – Assessment Documentation – Esplanade Reserve, October 2003, http://inherit.stateheritage.wa.gov.au/Public/Inventory/Details/4e6affb3-79ce-49c5-9bec-0bbbbbf7abf7 (accessed 15 October 2016).

57   Julian Bolleter has made a detailed examination of many of these plans in *Take Me to the River: The Story of Perth's Foreshore* (Perth: UWA Publishing, 2015). He estimates that since 1833 there have been more 200 proposals for the Perth Foreshore. These proposals, he argues, are 'symbolic pointers' to changes in Perth's collective psyche over time.

58   City of Perth, Council Minutes, 13 April 1992.

59   *The West Australian*, 14 February 2008.

CHAPTER 8

that any plan for significant development on a Perth waterway faces. This time, wrote the editor, 'the Government should say no to the naysayers and go for it'.[60]

Those in favour of the development began to talk about 'getting rid of the old front lawn', in reference to the Esplanade; 'the day we start digging up that lawn will be the start of Perth's renewal'.[61] The State Architect rejected suggestions that the proposed development looked like Dubai or Disneyland.[62] The City Architect gave a scathing critique of the development and the City of Perth's Planning Committee rejected the plan, noting that the buildings were too big, destroyed view corridors, replaced too much open space (the Esplanade) and posed engineering problems.[63] It was not long before a local independent think-tank, 'City Vision', comprised of well-known planners, architects, heritage and arts practitioners, came up with an alternative plan, quickly slammed by 'FuturePerth', which consisted mainly of young planners.[64] Public consultation, organised by the government, showed that 66 per cent of 'official community feedback' was in favour of the development.[65]

A change in government in early 2009 signalled a modification of the plans. 'A new vision for Perth' was announced. Now labelled 'an integrated river port', its towers were reduced to seven storeys near the river ranging up to thirty storeys near the city centre. The swan-shaped island, widely critiqued as kitsch, was now to be amoeba-shaped. Further sweeteners included a long-promised Aboriginal

---

60   *The West Australian*, 15 February 2008.
61   Paul Murray in *West Australian*, 16 February 2008.
62   Professor Geoffrey London in *West Australian*, 10 March 2008.
63   *The West Australian*, 16, 18 April 2008.
64   *The West Australian*, 19 June 2008.
65   *The West Australian*, 20 June 2008.

art centre and a cable car to King's Park (neither of which has eventuated). The new Liberal Party premier, Colin Barnett, said that the project offered 'the best real estate in Australia', with land sales expected to recoup much of the government's infrastructure costs.[66] *The West Australian* newspaper talked up the project, citing the long history of waterfront plans and expressing frustration at potential delays.[67] The government announced Cabinet approval of the $440 million project in early 2011. The Lord Mayor greeted the announcement as an 'opportunity to rebrand Perth on the global stage'.[68] By the end of the year the city agreed to the resumption of the Esplanade Reserve by the State, with the unanimous agreement of councillors.[69] By then a sudden decline in the price of iron ore suggested that Western Australia's mining boom might be beginning to cool and the property sector began to cast doubt on the ability of the market to absorb the development.[70] Ignoring such signs, the premier announced that the development would proceed. It would be called Elizabeth Quay to commemorate Queen Elizabeth II's Diamond Jubilee.[71] His royalist sentiments did not reflect the mood of the public and provided a dream subject for the cartoonists.

A coalition of around twenty-one planners, architects, historians, politicians and other disaffected citizens was formed in late 2011 to protest against the development. They were indignant that land

---

66   *The West Australian*, 14 December 2009.
67   *The West Australian*, 15 December 2009.
68   *The West Australian*, 16 February 2011.
69   City of Perth, Council Minutes, 8 November 2011.
70   In October 2011 the iron ore price fell sharply from its highest points in 2010, corrected a little, then fell further in April 2012. There were a couple of brief resurgences in 2012–13 before it began a steady downward trend at about the end of 2013.
71   *The West Australian*, 28 May 2012.

CHAPTER 8

belonging to the people was to be sold to private developers, albeit with conditions; angry that the historic values of the Esplanade were being ignored; distressed that the mighty Moreton Bay fig trees bordering the Esplanade would be destroyed; concerned by the environmental impact on the Swan River; and nearby ferry operators were fearful (correctly as it transpired) that their businesses would be badly affected during development. There was much focus on likely traffic chaos as members believed that that was the key political issue that would garner support from the public and local government authorities adjacent to the city.[72] The group gave themselves a collective label, 'City Gatekeepers'.

Rather than suggesting watchfulness as anticipated, the name that the group adopted suggested people who control or block access. They were soon cast as '"yesterday's men and women" trying to use worn-out ideas to argue against change and progress'.[73] Indeed, the group drew on nostalgia for the protest movements of the 1960s and 1970s. Emails from its leader, urban planner Linley Lutton, all ended with a quotation from Margaret Mead – 'Never doubt that a small group of thoughtful, committed citizens can change the world' – and the group adopted the standard tactics of past protest movements: public rallies and petitions. A People's Rally that they organised on the Esplanade to 'Demand a Better Plan' attracted around 2000 people, but the Esplanade was a large space that could hold more than 100,000, and the crowd looked small in such an expansive area. Hopes focused on a petition, signed by more than 13,000 people and presented to parliament before the Legislative Council vote on the

---

72   Linley Lutton, City Gatekeepers, letter to supporters, 14 February 2012.
73   Joe Lenzo, Executive Director, Property Council of Australia, letter to editor, *The West Australian*, 18 January 2012.

amendment needed to make the waterfront development a reality.[74] Despite a three-hour debate that was watched by many Gatekeepers who packed the public gallery, the Opposition's disallowance motion to block the amendment failed.[75]

In a carefully orchestrated media event, work began on the Perth Waterfront Project on 26 April 2012, when the premier and the minister for planning turned the first sods on the Esplanade. The ten hectares of riverfront land were to be transformed into a 'vibrant contemporary development', said the minister.[76]

The last ditch stand by protesters was a unique Citizens' Enquiry announced in November 2012 by City Vision, the urban think-tank closely associated with the Gatekeepers. It was headed by three leading retired professionals – a judge, a historian (Geoffrey Bolton), and an architect – and called for submissions from twelve invited experts. Its findings were announced two months later, just prior to the State election. It recommended that the project be halted immediately and that a full enquiry be held, as 'the process followed has been badly flawed, resulting in a flawed scheme and design'.[77] But with

---

74 An Opposition Member of the WA Legislative Council moved that the Metropolitan Regional Scheme, Amendment No. 1203/41 – Perth Waterfront, published in the *Government Gazette* on 14 October 2011 and tabled in the Legislative Council on 18 October 2011 under the *Planning and Development Act 2005*, be disallowed. Linley Lutton refers to 13,000 signatures in his account of Elizabeth Quay as an example of community disempowerment and poor planning, December 2013.

75 WA Legislative Council, *Votes and Proceedings*, 7 March 2012.

76 WA Today, 26 April 2012, www.watoday.com.au/wa-news/work-begins-on-440-million-perth-waterfront-project-20120426-1xn20.html (accessed 15 October 2016).

77 City Vision, 'Report on Written Submissions of Invited Experts on Difficulties in the Perth City Waterfront Development (Elizabeth Quay), prepared by an independent committee constituted by The Hon Robert Nicholson AO, Emeritus Professor Geoffrey Bolton AO, and retired Associate Professor of Architecture David Standen AM', 31 January 2013, and CityVision, 'The Perth Waterfront Development (Elizabeth Quay) Project: Summary Report of Submissions by Invited Experts and Conclusions and Recommendations', 31 January 2013.

CHAPTER 8

the emphatic re-election of the Liberal government, its findings were ignored.

The government responded to community concerns about the loss of place in several ways. A 1928 kiosk was rebuilt on the small island in the inlet.[78] The statue of World War I hero, Sir Joseph John Talbot Hobbs, which had stood on the site of the inlet since 1940 watching over Anzac parades, was moved to an adjacent site.[79] Two public art works were commissioned to commemorate the site's history. The most successful was a striking five-metre-tall cast-aluminium sculpture of a large bird in a boat, representing the Noongar people's first sight of distant European sailing ships.[80] The statue of feminist and social activist Bessie Rischbieth that was erected in 2016, however, seemed to parody the iconic 1964 press photo of her standing in front of a bulldozer in an attempt to stop the reclamation of nearby Mounts Bay to build a freeway interchange. Many suggested that she would roll in her grave knowing she was part of the redevelopment. The newly created streets around the Quay were also named, most after early river ferries perhaps as a sop to the irate ferry owners who had lost business during the redevelopment.[81]

Ironically, the government named the main street that crossed the north side of the Quay Geoffrey Bolton Avenue. Ostensibly this was to acknowledge his contribution 'in conserving, recording and

---

78   Hon. John Day, Minister for Planning, Culture and the Arts, Media Statement, 11 November 2012.
79   Neville Green, historian, letter to editor, *The West Australian*, 3 November 2014.
80   'Giant Bird Comes Home To Roost at Quay', *The West Australian*, 16 December 2015; Laetitia Wilson, 'Quay Art Opens Up Our Hearts and Minds', *The West Australian*, 13 February 2016.
81   Hon. John Day, Minister for Planning, Culture and the Arts, Media Statement, 15 October 2015, www.mediastatements.wa.gov.au/Pages/Barnett/2015/10/Ahoy-to-EQ-street-names-with-a-nautical-twist--.aspx (accessed 16 October 2016).

teaching Western Australian history', but there were suspicions that it was to silence those historians who had protested against the development. Before accepting the honour, and well aware of the potential reaction, he discussed the pros and cons of accepting it with a few colleagues. Rightly so. Within a few days of the announcement, letters appeared in the press castigating him for accepting it. But in his letter countering the criticism, Geoff explained his reasons, arguing that he had accepted the honour as 'a representative of all those historians ... who had laboured to recover and record' the 50,000 years of history in Western Australia and 'to secure recognition for their work'.[82]

Elizabeth Quay was opened on 29 January 2016. The next day, *The West Australian*, which at an editorial level had resolutely supported the project, reported enthusiastically arguing that 'Critics must give the Quay a fair go'.[83] The community was still split. Complaints continued. Some thought the premier 'a strong fearless leader', others lampooned him as the dictatorial creator of 'Barnett's Billabong'.[84] The project continued to be plagued by problems. The premier's assertion that it could be five years or more before developers built the proposed skyscrapers around the inlet was amplified by a past director of planning with the City of Perth: 'Elizabeth Quay will be a construction site for 30 years'.[85] Meantime, the placemakers of the Metropolitan Regional Authority have activated the site with market days, festivals and concerts, and sporting events, in a faint echo of

---

82   *The West Australian*, 16, 24 October 2015.
83   *The West Australian*, 30 January 2016.
84   Suzanne Fielding, *Post*, 23 January 2016; Alston, Cartoon, *The West Australian*, 11 December 2015; Sean Woods, letter to editor, *The West Australian*, 30 January 2016.
85   'Barnett Sets a Quay Time Limit', *The West Australian*, 11 December 2014; Max Hipkins, past director of planning, City of Perth, in *The West Australian*, 15 December 2014.

CHAPTER 8

the past. Is it possible that the Esplanade in its new incarnation as Elizabeth Quay might continue as a place of recreation for the people of Perth or will it be overshadowed by upmarket high-rise apartments, hotels and office blocks?

* * *

In the final chapter of *A Fine Country to Starve In* that reflects on the impact of the development ethos and the re-emergence of mining in the 1960s, Geoff mused that '[as] Western Australians moved too rapidly into an unpredictable future ... the older among them looked back nostalgically to a past that was simpler'.[86] Is that what loss of the past represents? Are these case studies simply reactions to inevitable change?

The Barracks Archway was preserved in the 1960s as a reminder of Western Australia's convict heritage, but it was also a declaration that politicians were subject to the will of the people. Advocates for retention of the Barracks were influential members of society speaking on behalf of their long relationship to the city. Their call for retention became a popular cause that was played out within the parliament. The Facebook group 'Beautiful Old Perth', while mourning and celebrating lost places, also provided individuals with a way of caring for places already lost. Their responses to photographs posted online may be in part nostalgia for places and times past, but this too has become political as the images encouraged civic engagement to prevent further loss of heritage. The protest against the loss of the Esplanade was not simply a nostalgic desire to prevent change. Protesters made it clear that, if public land was to be sold to developers, they wanted a

---

86 Bolton, *A Fine Country to Starve In*, p. 267.

better plan, a better outcome. They, however, lacked the level of support or the leverage of those who had protested against demolition of the Barracks. While community organisations such as the National Trust and the Historical Society were still active, the public service under the ultimate control of a minister of the Crown was now the regulator of heritage protection which had become enmeshed in political decision-making and dominated by the will of the government.

Geoff's works that focus on his home place are infused with an understanding of the impact of loss on a society and its people. While he viewed this as nostalgia, he recognised that at times it could become a matter of contemporary political dispute. During his career, he was loath to participate in public controversy and saw clearly what the price of protest could be. His way was a middle way.

Towards the end of his life, however, he increasingly took a public stand. He became a trustee of the WA Museum in 2005. The following year, as Western Australia's mining boom gathered pace, he pointed to the grand infrastructure works of the 1890s gold boom, asking "will we develop industries and skills where we can add value or are we going to be content to be a quarry?"[87] By 2009 his concerns were directed towards the state of the arts and culture in Western Australia. He argued publicly that while previous mining booms had seen the birth of iconic cultural institutions in Perth, the present boom had left 'the major cultural institutions ... under-staffed, beset by continual demands to reduce spending and struggling to maintain services'.[88] The following year he launched 'a stinging attack' on government, saying that:

---

87 Victoria Laurie, 'A New Wave of Wealth', *The Australian*, 14 August 2006.
88 Bolton, Address to History Council of WA Forum, 'History at Mercy of Razor Gang', *The West Australian*, 2 November 2009.

CHAPTER 8

posterity will severely judge 'a generation of provincial philistine pygmies' if they continue to ignore the parlous state of Perth's cultural institutions ... WA's approach to periods of surplus wealth resembles a boa constrictor ... ingesting huge meals and then lapsing into a torpor while it sleeps off the process of digestion.[89]

Continuing public pressure and the appointment of a lively new museum director eventually led to a funding commitment and plans for a new museum. Geoff continued to take a stand. As we have seen, in 2012 he was one of three heading the Citizen's Enquiry into Elizabeth Quay.

By then his status and the esteem with which he was held had cemented his place in the Western Australian psyche. Remembrance of the heritage that he left through a remarkable corpus of historical research and writing was inscribed on the landscape by the naming of Geoffrey Bolton Avenue.

---

89 Bolton, Address to City Vision forum, reported by Victoria Laurie, 'Mining Boom Fails To Turn into Gold for Cultural Groups', *The Australian*, 30 March 2010.

Chapter 9

'THE NORTH'

Colonial Hegemony and Indigenous Stratification

Tim Rowse and Elizabeth Watt

How are we to write the history of northern Australia? In this essay we will illustrate some possible approaches to the history of the north by reference to Bolton's work on the regions of Australia. We will then point to a theme of 'northern history' that is barely present in his work – race-based status differences among Indigenous Australians. We will devote much of our essay to demonstrating the importance of this neglected theme.

Regional Differences and State Differences

Bolton once remarked that 'It may be that the central theme of twentieth century Australian history is the conflict between the search for a national identity and the obstinate persistence of regional loyalties and prejudices'.[1] He later remarked that he had a 'vested interest in disputing' a sense, 'particularly in Melbourne, that its version of

---

1   G.C. Bolton, 'Regional History in Australia', in John A. Moses (ed.), *Historical Disciplines and Culture in Australasia: An Assessment* (Brisbane: University of Queensland Press, 1979), p. 223.

CHAPTER 9

Australia is normality and that the regions are just picturesque aberrations'.² However, in disputing Melbourne's normality, he sometimes evoked the particularities of a State (Western Australia) and at other times evoked regional distinctiveness. It is important that we do not conflate State-focused and region-focused historical writing.

Reviewing Paul Hasluck's *Mucking About*, Bolton argued that 'many of the themes and preconceptions of mainstream Australian history are inapplicable, or at least substantially altered, in the Western Australian setting'.³ In Western Australia, he suggested, class and religion had been weaker factors in determining a person's access to elites. Ancestry had been more significant: Western Australians credited lineage from free immigrants of the nineteenth century. Success in pastoralism and gold did not produce an entrenched capitalist class, he continued, and those with wealth were esteemed to the extent that they used it philanthropically. Self-improvement was possible by public education (Perth Modern, without private school rivals until the 1950s; a university that did not charge fees) and by working the abundant land (though many family farms failed). Bolton referred to his State's 'easy-going sense of *gemeinschaft*', though he wondered – writing in the 1970s – how much longer this ethos could last.⁴ He seemed ambivalent about this community: dissenters were tolerated 'provided that they are good Western Australians'.⁵ In 1981 (referring to Western Australia's response to the 1904 Roth Report) he wrote of 'the usual response of Western Australians to

---

2 Deborah Gare, 'Images from a Life in Australian History: An Interview with Geoffrey Bolton', *Limina*, 4 (1998), p. 94.
3 Geoffrey Bolton, 'A Local Identity: Paul Hasluck and the Western Australian Self-concept', *Westerly*, 22, 4 (1977), p. 72.
4 Bolton, 'A Local Identity', p. 76.
5 Bolton, 'A Local Identity', p. 75.

outside criticism: challenge and belittlement', and in the same essay he asserted: 'More than most other communities in the world, white Western Australians were simply not habituated to the possibility of a plural society'.[6]

Along with this argument for Western Australia's distinctive pattern of social hierarchy, social mobility and boundary-formation, we find other passages about regional differences *within* Western Australia and Queensland. Each had a 'north', and the problem facing all of Australia's 'norths' was that each State hinterland was oriented to its 'metropolitan government for the provision of police, schools, postal services, and eventually telegraphs and railways'.[7] The 'co-ordinated planning for Australia's North was always to be complicated by the necessity of persuading three different governments to reconcile their conflicting interests and agree on common policies'.[8] Writing about regional differences within States, Bolton saw each 'north' as estranged, to a degree, from its 'south'. On the geography of Western Australia, Bolton remarked that although Western Australia was naturally separated from the rest of Australia by the Nullarbor Plain and by the Great Sandy Desert, 'there is little logic in dividing the Kimberley district from the western part of the Northern Territory.'[9]

---

6   Geoffrey Bolton, 'Black and White after 1897', in C.T. Stannage (ed.), *A New History of Western Australia* (Perth: University of Western Australia Press, 1981), pp. 130, 177.

7   Geoffrey Bolton, 'The Spread of Colonization', in John Hardy & Alan Frost (eds), *Studies from Terra Australis to Australia* (Canberra: Australian Academy of the Humanities, Occasional Paper 6, 1989), p. 192.

8   G.C. Bolton, 'The Development of the North', in Richard Preston (ed.), *Contemporary Australia: Studies in History, Politics, and Economics* (Durham, NC: Duke University Press, 1969), p. 124.

9   Geoffrey Bolton, 'Western Australian History – The Next Assignments: Address to the History Council of Western Australia', *History Australia*, 2, 2 (2005), p. 48.1-7.

CHAPTER 9

A 'region' is an observer's construct, an argued analytical proposition, not a 'thing' that simply awaits our discovery. The historian must justify representing phenomena as 'regional'. For example, Martinez and Vickers have recently argued that 'the Pearl Frontier' was a region or 'zone' based on an industry whose 'commodity relations' (pearls and labour power as the two key commodities) straddled the borders of Australia (including Broome, Darwin and the Torres Strait) and the Dutch East Indies; the bosses and workers enacting these relations were of many ethnicities, and the Aboriginal–Indonesian intermarriage that these commodity relations encouraged were problematic from the point of view of the nations and empires that sought to effect political boundaries within the region.[10] The authors' analytical approach – to describe political and social relationships that subtended certain commodity relations – persuasively constructs the object of historical inquiry: a 'frontier'/region/zone whose conditions of existence are historically intelligible. Bolton's fascination with Western Australia's distinctiveness as a State does not theorise 'Western Australia' as a region so much as take it for granted as a formal jurisdiction.[11] His more consistently argued regionalism was his concern with Australia's 'north', or 'norths'.

Thus the Kimberley and northwest were distinct zones within Western Australia in ways that were, for Bolton, historically significant. The social stratification of Western Australia's north reminded him of Ireland: 'the behaviour of the Anglo-Irish, or the Protestant

---

10 Julia Martinez and Adrian Vickers, *The Pearl Frontier: Indonesian Labor and Indigenous Encounters in Australia's Northern Trading Network* (Honolulu: University of Hawai'i Press, 2015), p. 7.
11 He sometimes referred to States as 'provinces': Geoffrey Bolton, 'A Provincial Viewpoint', in Bruce Bennett (ed.), *Australia In between Cultures* (Canberra: Australian Academy of the Humanities, 1999), pp. 79-85.

Ascendancy, in the eighteenth century was very much like pastoralists with Aborigines in northern Australia. It is another variant of a colonial elite.'[12] This repeated what he had written in 1981: after violent clashes in the settlement of the Fitzroy and Ord valleys, 'the relationship between pastoralists and Aborigines came to resemble the quasi-feudal status quo already established in the other northern pastoral districts between the Pilbara and the Gascoyne'.[13] In earlier work on Alexander Forrest, Bolton had characterised the northern electorates as 'rotten boroughs', neither East Kimberley nor West Kimberley having more than 200 (white) voters.[14] Perhaps 'gemeinschaft' was a southern thing?

Perhaps not. Bolton once suggested that race relations in Western Australia reached their nadir in the Depression; he seems to have had Perth and the southwest in mind, where certain people were rounded up and taken to Moore River – an institution (that he condemned) enabling what 'most communities in the Great Southern district demanded ... virtually a complete system of apartheid'.[15] We can put this 'nadir' in a longer term perspective. Bolton noticed the regionally differentiated 'contribution made by Aboriginal labour to primary production in Western Australia: crucial in the northern districts between 1900 and the 1960s, and more vulnerable to fluctuating demand in the South-West'.[16]

---

12 Bolton, 'Images from a Life', p. 92.
13 Bolton, 'Black and White', p. 126.
14 G.C. Bolton, *Alexander Forrest: His Life and Times* (Melbourne: Melbourne University Press in association with the University of Western Australia Press, 1958), p. 93.
15 Bolton, 'Black and White' pp. 143, 149.
16 Bolton, 'Western Australian History', pp. 48-6. For an account of the racial dynamics of the southwest that emphasises the mutual accommodation of Nyungar and whites within a rural labour market, see Sally Hodson, 'Nyungars and Work: Aboriginal Experiences in the Rural Economy of the Great Southern Region of Western Australia', *Aboriginal History*, 17, 1 (1993), pp. 73-92.

CHAPTER 9

Thus two problems trouble Bolton's 1977 observations about the distinctive political culture of Western Australia (in addition to the possibility that, by then, it had passed). First, he discerned different social patterns in the north and south of the State: 'easy going *gemeinschaft*' versus Kimberley 'feudalism'. Second, he noticed that gemeinschaft's Other was not only pesky dissenters and critics but also the Aborigines in excess of southern labour requirements. As a historian of regional differences which trouble national identity, Bolton achieved more by his description of 'the north' – extending across Western Australia, the Northern Territory and Queensland – than by evoking a distinct Western Australian ethos.

Bolton's treatments of 'the north' consisted of two sets of writings: those barely mentioning Aboriginal people and those with Aborigines at the centre of attention.

The North (1): Aborigines Marginal

Bolton's 'The Development of the North' (1969) synthesises much of two previous works: a long article (1954) about the Kimberley pastoral industry from the 1880s to around 1950 and a monograph (1963) on North Queensland up to 1920. His themes in 1969 were the obstacles to colonial enterprise in the north – both physical (climate, soils, distance from markets) and human (Aboriginal opposition, shortages of labour and capital) – and the emergence of political solutions, of varying quality, to these problems. Bolton saw white settler attachment to the Kimberley as tenuous. 'The native question, the trying climate, the general lack of amenities fostered little love for their surroundings.'[17] After describing Broome, Derby

---

17   G.C. Bolton, 'The Kimberley Pastoral Industry', *University Studies in History and Economics*, 2, 2 (1954), p. 18.

and Wyndham, he wrote: 'Contemporary attitudes towards the North ... eliminated any thought of building attractive residences suited to semi-tropical living conditions'.[18] The 1928 Durack Royal Commission into the Meat Industry exposed absentee owners who left management 'to ageing stockmen of conservative and unenterprising tendencies, assisted by aborigines and half-castes'.[19] Bolton implied that reliance on native labour was the resort of poor management and unmotivated investors: by the early 1950s, the public, the investor and the government still lacked a vision for the Kimberley. Contrast North Queensland. 'One hundred years after settlement', he wrote in 1963, 'North Queensland was securely established as a "white man's tropics". Prosperity was evident at every point from Sarina to Mossman.'[20]

Bolton's Kimberley and North Queensland studies are exemplary of the artistic and conceptual integration of economic, social and cultural history. His thesis about northern Australia, in his 1969 essay, was about factors of production.

> The only industries to survive unsubsidised in northern Australia have been those yielding a high return on labour input. Since Australian workingmen have traditionally expected a high standard of wages, this has implied either exploiting reserves of raw material for which there is currently a high demand (such as pearling and most forms of mining) or condoning the use of cheap non-European workers (such as the Pacific Islanders in the nineteenth century sugar industry, and the aborigines employed for many years in raising beef cattle).[21]

---

18 Bolton, 'The Kimberley', p. 29.
19 Bolton, 'The Kimberley', p. 41.
20 Geoffrey Bolton, *A Thousand Miles Away: A History of North Queensland to 1920* (Brisbane: Jacaranda in association with the Australian National University, 1963), p. 323.
21 Bolton, 'The Development of the North', p. 121.

CHAPTER 9

The essay then narrated the waves of interest in pastoral production (wool and beef), mining, pearling and agriculture – noting the importance of Aboriginal labour in the pastoral industry, of Asian and Aboriginal labour in pearling, of Pacific Islanders in the sugar industry and the attraction of Italian immigrants to agriculture in Queensland's north in the 1920s. Having illustrated the unlikelihood of sustained financial return from northern investment, he turned to public policy efforts to 'develop the north' – particularly after World War II had underlined the north's vulnerability. At this point Bolton noted the rise of Australia's first 'company town' – Mt Isa – where a private corporation sought to assure a long-term supply of labour by sharing with government the responsibility for providing urban amenities. The last third of the essay reviewed: the increasing capitalisation of the beef industry, the rising cost of Aboriginal labour, the discovery of many valuable mineral deposits, the uncertain market for agricultural produce, and the tensions between two States and the Commonwealth about infrastructure costs. He considered the gap between an economic realism that is aware of the north's low returns and a nation-building perspective favouring public investment in defence and infrastructure. Uncertainty of profits from cotton made it impossible, he advised, to judge whether the Ord River irrigation scheme was the basis of sustainable northern settlement or another instance of State boosterism.[22] 'The Development of the North' can be read as exploring, in one regional instance, one of the abiding themes of Imperial history: 'the transplantation of British institutions – the perceptions of class, the social attitudes, the concepts of politics, education, religion – to a new and very different environment'.[23]

---

22   Bolton, 'The Development of the North', pp. 148-49.
23   Bolton, 'Regional History', p. 220.

The North (2): Colonisation as Hegemony

In *A Thousand Miles*, examining North Queensland's claim to be 'the first successful instance in the British Empire of white settlement in the tropics', Bolton also began to represent settlement as invasion.[24] His Kimberley study had noted that 'the blacks were troublesome' because of their stock-killing in the 1880s, and he had attributed to Aboriginal resistance the failure of the Canning Stock route to become a 'major outlet'.[25] The North Queensland book offered more, particularly the chapter 'Squatters and Aborigines, 1870–90': 'the old cycle of misunderstanding, hostility, and reprisal' between colonists and Aboriginal people.[26] However, Bolton's perspective was still close to the colonists':

> Though the wealth and population of North Queensland were chiefly derived from the mining and sugar industries [by 1890], the pastoralist could claim to have made productive a wide region which would otherwise have remained a mere hunting ground for Aborigines. Some there were who regretted that the white man's penetration of the country had caused such hostility and wrought such destruction among the natives. Most authorities agreed, however, that the Aborigines were a dying race … [giving way] to those who were better able to develop the land and its resources; such was the thought of the times, and in truth the Aborigines who lived under the paternalism of a North Queensland cattle station were not, in 1890, the least fortunate of their race.[27]

This use of comparison to parry criticism of colonial violence echoed a remark in his biography of Alexander Forrest: 'Any case in

---

24 Bolton, 'Regional History', p. 220.
25 Bolton, 'The Kimberley', pp. 14, 16, 18, 24.
26 Bolton, *A Thousand Miles Away*, p. 94.
27 Bolton, *A Thousand Miles Away*, p. 108.

CHAPTER 9

which a northern settler could be shown to have acted callously towards the aborigines was played up and exaggerated [by Forrest's political opponents] although there is no evidence that the riff-raff of the gold fields treated the blacks more humanely'.[28] In a 1977 essay on Western Australia with the celebratory title 'History: 150 Years of Rapid Growth', he made no reference to the northern frontier, but mentioned Aborigines in the south as a 'defeated race' that had offered 'sporadic resistance'.[29] His main point about Aboriginal people in that piece was their insignificance as a labour force, necessitating Western Australia's willingness (1850–1868) to receive convicts.

By 1979, looking back on *A Thousand Miles*, he acknowledged that he had presented things 'too much through the eyes of the white Australian land-takers'.[30] And 'while I felt no sense of pressure because of the financial and other support given by the North Queensland Local Authorities Association, I was reluctant to express judgments that might give pain to the friendly and hospitable local residents whose co-operation helped my research'.[31]

Bolton had by then become more interested in Aborigines' adaptations to the colonists. In 1992, delivering his inaugural lecture at the University of Queensland, he said that he had understated Aboriginal agency; he warned against 'too gloomy a view of the Australian past' that denies 'the working class or the Aborigines any capacity for initiative or agency to resist pressure from the powerful'.[32] Bolton's

---

28 Bolton, *Alexander Forrest*, p. 171.
29 Geoffrey Bolton, 'History: 150 years of Rapid Growth', in Richard Woldendorp (ed.), *Looking West* (Perth: Day Dawn Press, 1977), p. 16.
30 Bolton, 'Regional History', p. 216.
31 Bolton, 'Regional History', p. 219.
32 Geoffrey Bolton, *Who Owns Australia's Past?* Inaugural lecture delivered at the University of Queensland, 18 March 1992 (Brisbane: University of Queensland Press, 1993), p. 4.

second thoughts thus added Aboriginal people of initiative to colonists of initiative to make a more balanced history of colonisation.

In 'Black and White after 1897' Bolton developed this 'agency' theme: 'the search ... for structures through which the Aborigines of Western Australia could organize their lives'. He argued that theirs was a regionally differentiated quest, giving rise to two pathways of adaptation. 'Western Australia supported two Aboriginal populations very different in ethnic mixture and in strength of adherence to the law and sanctions of traditional Aboriginal society, though the geographic division between the two populations was not nearly clear-cut enough for administrative tidiness.' He adopted the terms 'Aborigines' (the north) and 'part-Aborigines' (the south) to distinguish the protagonists.[33]

Adaptation by 'part-Aboriginal' people in the southwest of the State was more difficult. First, they had a 'less vigorous sense of ancestral tradition on which to build. Without effective sources of authority of their own they needed beliefs from which they could create a sense of communal self-respect and pride.' Second, the legislative sequel of the 1904 Roth Report's exposé of colonial relationships in Western Australia – laws dedicated to 'protection' – created 'grievous problems for the part-Aborigines of the south-west, many of whom now found themselves brought under official surveillance for the first time'. He attributed to A.O. Neville – the public servant implementing 'protection' from 1915 to 1940 – a perception that Aborigines were 'most attractive when most remote from the mainstream of Australian society' and that those with more contact were generally more degraded and deserving of intrusive supervision. Bolton gave instances of the Aborigines of the south demonstrating

---

33 Bolton, 'Black and White', pp. 175, 162.

capacity for self-organisation and recovery, but he lamented that they were hampered by their misfortunes in a fluctuating rural economy (droughts, depressed markets) and by heavy-handed official responses to their perceived incapacity. By contrast, because of demand for their labour, 'for the northern station Aborigines a stable and comparatively secure way of life developed ... [and] ... Aboriginal society in the northern pastoral districts continued to survive and regenerate itself'.[34] He endorsed Ronald Berndt's observation that in the north it was not clear what Aborigines – still so traditional – were being asked to assimilate to; and he illustrated the resilience of Aboriginal Law in the face of mission and governmental pressures.

While 'the part-Aborigines of the south-west' benefited most from the 'assimilation' reforms pursued by Stanley Middleton (1948–60), in their urbanisation they 'experienced considerable difficulty in achieving a style of life which was either acceptable to the white majority or productive of their own happiness and self-respect', and 'they found few acceptable means of integrating themselves into the wider community, and were so forced back into channelling their emotional loyalties into family allegiances of such intensity that violence was likely to result'. On violence he commented: 'It would be misleading to see these feuds as an archaic revival of tribal loyalties, since the breakdown of traditional society in the south-west had taken place by the 1890s'.[35]

Distinctions among Aboriginal People

Bolton's term 'part-Aborigines' combined reference to hybridity of descent with an historical argument about the attrition, in the south,

---

34 Bolton, 'Black and White', pp. 176, 131, 138, 139-40.
35 Bolton, 'Black and White', pp. 160, 169, 175, 174-75.

of traditional Aboriginal institutions, as if one may stand for (if not explain) the other. In the same year that his essay was published, Marcia Langton criticised such terms for their failure to grasp in a positive way what 'urban' Aboriginal people were becoming: their difference from 'traditional' Aboriginal people was not their 'loss' or their departure from a classical ideal constructed from ethnographies of the least colonised peoples of the north.[36] We imagine that Bolton – wishing to note Aboriginal adaptation – would have seen her point. In the remainder of this essay we raise a different problem: the term 'Aboriginal' is insensitive to distinctions that have been meaningful to those who inhabit the north – in particular the status difference between Aborigines known as 'full blood' and those known as 'half caste'.

Historians are wary of making this distinction central to their account of northern colonial hegemony. Notwithstanding Bruce Shaw's report that, in the East Kimberley, the term 'half-caste' is an inoffensive way to refer to a 'person of mixed European (or other nationality) and Aboriginal descent', some find the language of 'caste' offensive.[37] At the 1994 'Going Home' conference in Darwin, delegates identifying as Stolen Generations condemned such 'racist and derogatory terminology' as 'coloured', 'half caste' and 'full-blood'; they urged 'all Aboriginal and non-Aboriginal people to stop using such language'.[38] Reluctance to distinguish between Aboriginal people based on their skin hue is an understandable response to racial policies

---

36 Marcia Langton, 'Urbanizing Aborigines: The Social Scientists' Great Deception', *Social Alternatives*, 2, 2 (1981), pp. 16-22.

37 Bruce Shaw, *When the Dust Come In Between: Aboriginal Viewpoints in the East Kimberley prior to 1982* (Canberra: Aboriginal Studies Press, 1992), p. 330.

38 Jacqui Katona and Chips Mackinolty (eds), *The Long Road Home ... The Going Home Conference 3–6 October* (Darwin: Karu Aboriginal Child Care Agency, 1995), p. 28.

CHAPTER 9

that categorised the Indigenous population according to degrees of descent (as 'full bloods', 'half-castes', 'quadroons' and 'octoroons') and sought to prise those in the latter categories away from their Aboriginal peers.

At the risk of offending some readers, we will argue that colonial hegemony in the north will not be understood if we do not examine the changing significance of these distinctions. Bolton was aware of the half-caste/full blood distinction. In 1954, he referred to the Kimberley workforce as 'aborigines and half castes', and in his 1994 memoir of his youthful Kimberley travels he quotes from letters to his parents in which he used the phrase 'natives and half-castes'.[39] However, his work never explored how this distinction operated to effect colonial hegemony in the north. Distinctions of 'caste' functioned in the north to create a variety of subaltern subjectivities.

Missions were important classifiers of the Aboriginal population. Discussing the Aboriginal understanding of 'yeller feller' in the Gulf region (straddling the Northern Territory and Queensland), David Trigger noted that – as in the Kimberley – the removal of half-caste children to missions and government institutions was part of the system of colonial rule. In the Gulf region the legacy of this practice, he argued, was a continuing sense of distinction: phenotypic features associated with differences of skill and outlook.[40] Trigger's survey of the literature mentioned observations by Terwiel-Powell on the salience of colour distinctions at Hope Vale Mission. One of the authors of this paper (Watt) has built on Terwiel-Powell's work, and

---

39 Bolton, 'The Kimberley', p. 41; Geoffrey Bolton 'Portrait of the Historian as a Young Learner', in Duncan Graham (ed.), *Being Whitefella* (Fremantle: Fremantle Arts Centre Press, 1994), p. 124.

40 David Trigger, 'Racial Ideologies in Australia's Gulf Country', *Ethnic and Racial Studies*, 12, 2 (1989), pp. 208-32.

so we will focus on Hope Vale as our North Queensland instance of caste/class distinction.

Hope Vale

The history of the Hope Vale community begins with the *Guugu Yimithirr* language group. In the pre-colonial era, *Guugu Yimithirr* was spoken over a wide area from contemporary Cooktown in the South to the McIvor River in the north.[41] The *Guugu Yimithirr* speakers did not have sustained contact with Europeans until gold was discovered on the Palmer River in 1873.[42] From that time their homelands were flooded with miners and pastoralists.[43] Their resistance to the colonists was soon crushed by disease, settler violence and the Native Mounted Police.[44] By the 1880s most of *Guugu Yimithirr* were begging, stealing and prostituting themselves in camps near Cooktown, or working irregularly as divers on boats collecting trochus shell and *bêche-de-mer*.[45] The conditions in these camps caught the attention of German Lutheran missionaries who responded by establishing the Cape Bedford mission on the 50,000 acre Aboriginal reserve north of Cooktown.

---

41 John Haviland, 'Last Look at Cook's Guugu Yimidhirr Word List', *Oceania*, 44, 3 (1974), p. 216.

42 Leslie and John Haviland, 'How Much Food Will There Be in Heaven? Lutherans and Aborigines around Cooktown to 1900', *Aboriginal History*, 4 (1980), pp. 119-49.

43 Haviland, 'How Much Food', pp. 120-21.

44 Noel Loos, 'Aboriginal Resistance in North Queensland', *Lectures on North Queensland History*, 3rd series (Townsville: James Cook University, 1978) p. 238; Belinda McKay, 'Constructing a Life on the Northern Frontier: E.A.C. Olive of Cooktown', *Queensland Review*, 7, 2 (2000), pp. 2, 47-65; Haviland, 'How Much Food'.

45 Fiona Terwiel-Powell, 'Developments in the Kinship System of the Hope Vale Aborigines: An Analysis of Changes in the Kinship Nomenclature and Social Structure of the Kuuku-Yimityirr Aborigines', Ph.D. thesis, School of Social Science, University of Queensland, 1976, p. 21.

CHAPTER 9

Two Bavarian missionaries, Wilhelm Poland and George Schwarz, encouraged the *Guugu Yimithirr* to adopt agriculture, but many Aboriginal people visited the mission for food without committing themselves to growing it.[46] Eventually, the Cape Bedford missionaries persuaded some of the *Guugu Yimithirr* people to leave their children and young wives behind at the mission. Many boys absconded from the segregated dormitories to travel to Cooktown or to participate in ceremonial life, but most of the girls stayed on and converted to Christianity.[47] The diminishing number of *Guugu Yimithirr* women outside the mission gave the Lutherans leverage: they offered marital partners only to those men who demonstrated commitment to settled village life and Christianity.[48]

Poland played an important role in the establishment of the Cape Bedford mission by running the girls' dormitory with the help of his wife, but it was Schwarz (who stayed on 33 years after Poland left in 1909) who had the greater influence over *Guugu Yimithirr* history. According to Noel Pearson's 1989 history, Schwarz cultivated a 'shepherd and sheep model' of social relations by positioning himself as his peoples' religious saviour.[49] *Muni,* as he became known, preached and taught in a standardised and Romanised version of the *Guugu Yimithirr* coastal dialect, encouraged by the German romantic

---

46 Haviland, 'How Much Food', pp. 128-30.
47 Noel Loos, 'Concern and Contempt: Church and Missionary Attitudes Towards Aborigines in North Queensland in the Nineteenth Century', in Tony Swain and Deborah Bird Rose (eds), *Aboriginal Australians and Christian Missions: Ethnographic and Historical Studies* (Adelaide: Australian Society for the Study of Religions, 1988), p. 110.
48 Haviland, 'How Much Food', p. 147.
49 Noel Pearson, 'Ngumu-Ngaadyar, Muuri Bunggaga and Midha Mini in Guugu Yimidhirr History', in Jan Kociumbas (ed.), *Maps, Dreams, History: Race and Representation in Australia* (Sydney: University of Sydney Department of History, 1998), p. 221.

view that language was the 'soul' of the *volk*, and he tolerated pre-colonial practices that he considered useful or relatively innocuous, such as classical stories, identification with clans (*pupuwarras*), elements of the traditional marriage system and hunting and gathering.[50] Yet most of the 'old ways' were cast as 'un-Christian', to be replaced with 'Protestant ethical values centering on chastity, sobriety, monogamy, obedience to authority, good work habits and the maintenance of a settled way of life'. Terwiel-Powell claims that while all Cape Bedford residents 'accepted Muni's opinions' and came to see traditional ceremonies as 'something that only "myall" and heathenish Aborigines did', some residents identified with the new Protestant values more than others.[51] Divisions emerged after the passing of Queensland's *Aboriginal Protection and Restriction of the Sale of Opium Act* in 1897, which empowered the state to relocate Aboriginal people to reserves or missions. Aboriginal people were brought into the mission from defunct Lutheran missions in the regions, followed by 'a continual stream of children from other parts of Queensland' from 1910.[52] Unlike the *Guugu Yimithirr* people, who were mostly 'full blood' Aborigines, many of these new residents had some European ancestry. All children, either taken involuntarily or with their parents' consent, learnt *Guugu Yimithirr* and were adopted into local families and *pupuwarras*, but *Muni* favoured those with a lighter complexion, indicating European heritage: he gave them a better education and greater responsibility on the mission when they came of age. *Muni* also reportedly prevented

---

50 Terwiel-Powell, 'Developments in the Kinship System', p. 115. Muni is a translation of Schwarz, meaning 'black' in German.
51 Terwiel-Powell, 'Developments in the Kinship System', pp. 28, 42.
52 John Haviland, 'The Life of a Speech Community: Guugu Yimidhirr at Hope Vale', *Aboriginal History*, 9 (1985), p. 177.

CHAPTER 9

these paler mission residents from marrying darker-skinned *Guugu Yimithirr* people, banishing one couple who defied this dictate to an outstation.[53]

This preferential treatment had an enduring impact on *Guugu Yimithirr* social organisation. In the early 1970s Terwiel-Powell observed a 'hierarchy of worthiness'.[54] At the top sat an exclusively light-skinned elite, who thought of themselves as 'hardworking, clean-living, God-fearing, honest people' and strove 'to demonstrate it in their lifestyle'.[55] The male breadwinners of this group had closer relations with the mission staff, greater responsibilities and higher incomes than other *Guugu Yimithirr* men. Their wives dedicated more time to ensuring that their families were clean and neatly dressed, and that their orderly homes and flourishing gardens resembled those of the mission staff, where most had worked before marriage.[56] Through 'saving and careful budgeting', Terwiel-Powell noted, these light-skinned elite women were able to purchase furnishings such as curtains, beddings, washing machines, refrigerators and petrol irons, and to balance their weekly budget so that they wouldn't need to rely on their family.[57] Members of the lower class groups often had difficulty saving for substantial items because of lower incomes, which they were obliged to share with their poorer relations, including the exclusively dark-skinned *Guugu Yimithirr* group, who made up the lowest class on the mission.[58] The light-skinned elite reportedly considered this stigmatised group a 'disgrace to the mission' because

---

53 Terwiel-Powell, 'Developments in the Kinship System', p. 313.
54 Terwiel-Powell, 'Developments in the Kinship System', p. 318.
55 Terwiel-Powell, 'Developments in the Kinship System', pp. 306, 308.
56 Terwiel-Powell, 'Developments in the Kinship System' p. 304.
57 Terwiel-Powell, 'Developments in the Kinship System', p. 309.
58 Terwiel-Powell, 'Developments in the Kinship System', p. 310.

they 'lived like blackfellows' or 'camp' people: more sprawling and spontaneous lives on the edge of the settled mission.[59]

According to Terwiel-Powell, the dark-skinned lower class demonstrated little concern about the upkeep of their homes and gardens and about the opinions of the mission staff. They did not pursue sobriety, financial independence and material accumulation. The elite described this dark-skinned group as 'dirty, lazy and ignorant' who were 'sponging off' relatives, believing 'what's yours is mine' and spending what little money they had on 'alcohol and "unnecessary goods"'.[60] The dark-skinned residents reportedly responded to these aspersions by stressing their own racial purity and describing the light-skinned *Guugu Yimidhirr* as 'red cattle', 'bastards' and 'yellow-mongrels'.[61] Some explained their lowly position on the mission as a consequence of discrimination, but others denounced the values hierarchy that the light-skin families subscribed to: accusing them of being 'stuck-up', 'colour proud', 'snooty' and 'snobbish' folk, who did not look after their kin and 'like to pretend they are white'.[62]

Caste in the Kimberley

In the Kimberley, children recognised as 'half caste' were taken to Beagle Bay or Forrest River missions or to the government cattle station Moola Bulla or far south to Moore River – to be trained. Some were seized by police, to the shattering sorrow of their mothers; some were sent by their white fathers, and some were kept on the station because their parents connived with the station-owner to persuade or

---

59 Terwiel-Powell, 'Developments in the Kinship System', p. 308.
60 Terwiel-Powell, 'Developments in the Kinship System', pp. 306, 308.
61 Terwiel-Powell, 'Developments in the Kinship System', pp. 307, 315.
62 Terwiel-Powell, 'Developments in the Kinship System', p. 313.

CHAPTER 9

deceive the visiting police. Kimberley leader Johnny Watson owes his knowledge of Nyikina tradition to the fact that his mixed-descent father, William Watson, sent him and his younger brother to grow up with family on other stations. William Watson, as a highly valued mixed-descent head stockman on Mount Anderson (south of Derby), seems to have been afforded more freedom as a parent.[63] The autobiography of Lucy Marshall, a Nyikina woman born on Mount Anderson Station in 1933, further illuminates William Watson's delegated authority over other Aborigines on Mount Anderson:

> Watsons were in the same category as the Europeans. We wasn't allowed to talk to them people except if they were working. Never went to their place, never went to their quarters. We weren't allowed. Even my stepfather [her mother's 'tribal way' husband Smuggler (Binyjirr)] wasn't allowed to talk to them.[64]

Head stockman William Watson was familiar not only with the local Aboriginal languages and law but also with the station's women.

> William Watson used to run amok with us girls. He used to be a very rough spade. We used to be frightened. We used to be shaking, oh yeah! Used to grab us by the throat. We wasn't game to tell our step-fathers or our mothers. Wasn't game to report him to the boss.[65]

Lucy Marshall got pregnant to him and, at the age of seventeen, bore a son (Paddy) at the Native Hospital in Derby. According to Lucy, so high was the standing of the Watson family that they were permitted to take responsibility for him, when Paddy was two years

---

63 Harry Watson and Johnny Watson in Paul Marshall (ed.), *Raparapa Kularr Martuwarra* (Broome: Magabala Books, 1988), p. 112, 220-21.
64 Lucy Marshall and Colleen Hattersley, *Reflections of a Kimberley Woman* (Broome: Madjulla Inc., 2004), p. 47.
65 Marshall and Hattersley, *Reflections of a Kimberley Woman*, p. 45.

old: 'We'll take him with us and we'll grow'm up. We got a better home than you so we take Paddy with us 'cos Paddy is ours.'[66] They took Paddy to Derby; Lucy Marshall believes that he was told that his mother was dead.

Products of this colonial system could base their identity on racial distinctions. Bruce Shaw interviewed Sandy McDonald (born in 1908) on five occasions between 1970 and 1974. McDonald told him that in his family there were 'three half caste and two black people'. The generation above him did not put him through initiation, as they regarded a half-caste youth as 'gone to the white man'. According to McDonald, many 'half castes', but no 'full bloods', in the Kimberley and Northern Territory had rifles; he recalls brandishing his at a bullying white boss. He told Shaw that he once said to a Mr George: 'Don't try to stand over me … I'm not like those Aborigines you've got over there. I always have something in my swag. I was not dragged up. I was brought up.' In the late 1960s, when 'Native Welfare' had offered him and his wife a house on an Aboriginal reserve, he refused, saying 'you want to push me back in the native camp'.[67] McDonald's sense of distinction from 'full bloods' helped him to survive, with dignity, in a racially ordered society in which whites assumed authority over non-whites.

This limited but real privileging of 'half castes' was essential to Donald Pwerle Ross's upbringing in Kaytetye country, north of Alice Springs, but it made him uneasy. Don Ross (1915–1999) was born at Barrow Creek Telegraph Station. His mother was the Kaytetye Hettie Hayes; his father (with whom he had little contact) was Alec

---

66   As Marshall recalls in Marshall and Hattersely, *Reflections of a Kimberley Woman*, p. 45.
67   Bruce Shaw and Sandy McDonald, 'They Did It Themselves: Reminiscences of Seventy Years', *Aboriginal History*, 2, 2 (1978), pp. 125, 127, 129–30.

CHAPTER 9

Ross. Don was raised under the authority of Old George Hayes, his mother's white father, a telegraph linesman who took up Neutral Junction pastoral lease in 1910. His playmates as a child on Neutral Junction were Aboriginal children of the station's workers: 'I was the only yellow bugger amongst them'.

> The Kaytetye boys used to live in the camp with their parents, in windbreaks, in the open, in anything they could pick up. Canvas, grass – they made them out of spinifex too. They used to come in the shed [where Don and Hettie lived] in the rain time. I'd have liked to have had the boys, the kids, you know, with me, at the station. I was feeling a bit crooked about that. I should have had them. It was no good. My mother thought it was no good, but she couldn't do nothing. George Hayes wouldn't have them. She knew he wouldn't come up with that. He'd have the workers all right, and the bloody kewayes (women), but no outsiders. He tried to make a white man out of me, see. He used to say to me, 'Don't you talk Language (Kaytetye).'

Old George thought highly of child Don, but Don was both fond and 'a bit scared' of him. Neutral Junction's gardener, a well-educated Englishman, taught Don reading, writing and numbers. His grandfather did not prevent his mixing with the Kaytetye workers, but Don was careful not to use Kaytetye within his grandfather's presence (Kaytetye words are sprinkled through his autobiography). Once old enough to ride and work, he got a Kaytetye education during work time: 'all them working boys, riding around all the time, they'd tell me about bush tucker'.[68]

As a 'coloured' man and 'better looking', Don was the object of the sexual interest of the Kaytetye women. He says that his marital

---

[68] Alexander Donald Pwerle Ross and Terry Whitebeach, *The Versatile Man: The Life and Times of Don Ross, Kaytetye Stockman* (Alice Springs: IAD Press, 2007), pp. 16, 17, 23, 81.

partners were in the appropriate kin class for a Pwerle (section) man. One of his wives (Aileen/Eileen) was 'promised', but he was careful not to let the police know that he was with a Kaytetye woman: 'We wasn't allowed to have gins'. He regrets having a sexual relationship with a Kaytetye woman who was 'wrong skin for me'. His mother did not like this unlawful affair either, but 'she only took notice of old George Hayes'. At one point in his life he was in a relationship with two women, each willing to marry him – a white and a black. He decided to marry 'a woman of me own colour' and his mother agreed. In a marital row with a white woman, 'she'd be calling me all the black-Bs and everything. That mattered.'[69]

Asked what he thought of living in a world in which darker people had fewer liberties, he answered: 'I did think about that, when I was growing up, but I was frightened. I couldn't do much.' Don Ross lived almost his whole life on Kaytetye country, working the cattle with local Aboriginal labour, and was for a few years (1947–51) the lessee of Neutral Junction. He was reminded where he stood in the white man's law when, in his absence from Neutral Junction, one of his children was taken to be raised at the Bungalow ('Half Caste Institution' in Alice Springs). But if police questioned his right to drink, he showed them a letter (a character reference) from the Northern Territory MP Macalister Blain.[70]

Charlie McAdam was born in the east Kimberley in 1935 or 1936, and raised at Beagle Bay and Moola Bulla, as his white father required, and so had the status of being 'half caste'. To be told that he was not 'a blackfeller ... made me cocky in my young days'. Recounting his life to Elizabeth Tregenza, Charlie labelled the 'half

---

69 Ross and Whitebeach, *The Versatile Man*, pp. 32–33, 69, 76–77.
70 Ross and Whitebeach, *The Versatile Man*, pp. 63, 73, 98.

CHAPTER 9

caste'/'full blood' distinction 'poison', because his 'yeller feller' identity had caused him trouble. He explains how he was 'poisoned'. After leaving Beagle Bay as a teenager, he had returned to Springvale Station (east Kimberley) – a station that his white father had sold to the Quilty family in 1948. The Quilty brothers drummed into him that he was 'not a blackfeller', and:

> Even my mother was poisoned. She said to me in lingo, 'You not blackfeller. You ngilaping [half caste]. You don't want to mix up with black women or anything like that.' Said this when I came back to Springvale. She always worked for white people all her life, and I suppose my father told her that, or the Quiltys, she probably got it from the white man's influence. I tried not to take much notice but actually at one stage I started to believe them because of my colour.

Thus empowered, he obeyed a Quilty instruction to shoot all the dogs in the Aboriginal camp. His grandfather (mother's father) upbraided him in Kija:

> 'We brought you up. We looked after you all those years and now you shoot our dogs. Do you think you're katiya [white man]?' I'll always remember that.

Charlie later worked as head stockman on Lake Nash Station, with 'twenty-four full-blood Aboriginal people working for me' – some of whom he sacked for not working to his standards. Eventually the men challenged him 'because they reckoned I was cheeky', and Charlie used his fists to show he was boss. The police were called and backed Charlie. One of them said to the recalcitrant workers: '"Pity Charlie never shot the whole lot of you bastards." That was what the copper said. I felt sorry then.'[71]

---

71   Charlie McAdam and Family (as told to Elizabeth Tregenza), *Boundary Lines* (Melbourne: McPhee Gribble Publishers, 1995), pp. 118, 153.

Transition to 'Trusteeship'

The circumstances in which a 'yeller feller' was expected to assert himself over the 'black feller' on behalf (or with the permission) of the 'white feller' boss changed in the late 1960s when industrial awards began to include Aboriginal stock workers. Facing a higher wage bill, stations ceased to employ many Aboriginal workers. At the same time, the Australian government was making it easier for Aboriginal people to get social security benefits. The shift from rations to cash had begun with 1959 amendments to the *Social Security Act* and climaxed in the mid-1970s with the effective universal eligibility of Aboriginal people for unemployment benefits.

Noel Pearson has highlighted the ill effects of this conjuncture of changes in labour market and welfare status, and his writings have persuaded governments to constitute the trusteeship of well-functioning Aboriginal people such as himself over those whose perceived dysfunction is rooted in their chronic unemployment and welfare dependency. The Cape York Welfare Reform Trials (CYWRT) commenced in 2008. The State and Commonwealth governments have entrusted certain Aboriginal leaders and organisations to select which people's welfare payments are replaced (in part) with a card that can be spent only on certain items. By constituting Indigenous trusteeship since the 1970s, in this and in other ways, the state has effected a transition from 'assimilation' to 'self-determination'; that is, the state has dealt with the emergence of a surplus, welfare-dependent remote Indigenous population by adapting the northern style of hegemony: some people of Aboriginal descent have become trustees over others.

In two papers about the Kimberley since 1968, Tony Smith presents 'trusteeship' as the State and Commonwealth response to the

CHAPTER 9

social crisis that the conjuncture of equal wages and welfare created in the Kimberley: the rapid relocation of the surplus Aboriginal population to Halls Creek, Wyndham, Derby, Fitzroy Crossing and Turkey Creek. In the Western Australian policy of 'trusteeship' governments transferred assets to Indigenous people so that they could start enterprises, including cattle stations purchased by the government from white leaseholders on behalf of the Aborigines on whose country the leases stood. In 1972 the Western Australian government established the Aboriginal Lands Trust, run by Aboriginal appointees, with a potential land base of 47 million acres of reserve land and acquired leases. The government also set up an Aboriginal Advisory Council. The Trust and Council were composed of appointed Aboriginal people, mandated to develop land as an asset. The policy imagined Aborigines to live in communities, and 'community development' was its goal.

The better educated Aborigines with some management experience were suitable recruits as Aboriginal community leaders and entrepreneurs. Smith sees Ernie Bridge, a man of mixed descent from the East Kimberley, as exemplary of the emerging Aboriginal business class as it expanded in the Kimberley under this policy.[72] Bridge was not only a businessman but also a member of the Aboriginal Land Trust and of the Commonwealth government's Aboriginal Land Fund Commission. He was elected as the member for Kimberley in 1980 and held portfolios of Aboriginal Affairs, Small Business and Agriculture, Water Resources and the North West in the Western Australian government. Economic development policies aimed to absorb surplus Aboriginal labour, and the more traditional Aboriginal people came

---

72 Tony Smith, 'Indigenous Accumulation in the Territory in the Early Years of "Self-Determination": 1968–75', *Australian Economic History Review*, 42, 1 (2002), p. 22.

under the trusteeship of Aboriginal people such as Bridge who, in an earlier era, would have been head stockmen acting under the authority of their white bosses.

Some white pastoralists did not like the rise of the Aboriginal pastoralist.[73] However, white pastoralists and black trustees were structurally similar. According to Smith, the Aboriginal business class, like white pastoralists (their predecessors and contemporaries), had to confront a tension between the business and welfare rationales of their enterprises: any surplus generated had to be apportioned either to investment or to immediate consumption by workers and residents.[74] In his interview-based study of the Kimberley's Aboriginal cattle bosses, Paul Marshall found that Harry and John Watson had much to say about the terms on which State and Commonwealth agencies viewed their trusteeship of the cattle stations that had passed into communal ownership and were thus under their management.[75]

Both State and Commonwealth approaches to 'trusteeship' encouraged Indigenous communities to form corporations that receive public funds to discharge public services to the Aboriginal people of the Kimberley, including representing them legally and politically as traditional owners of the region. According to Patrick Sullivan, these bodies have been cultural mediators between two very different political cultures, sustained by 'an alliance between white sympathisers, educated mixed-descent Aborigines and the Kimberley "blackfellers"

---

73   Smith, 'Indigenous Accumulation', p. 27.

74   Smith, 'Indigenous Accumulation', pp. 29-30; Tony Smith, 'Welfare, Enterprise and Aboriginal Community: The Case of the Western Australian Kimberley Region, 1968–1976', *Australian Economic History Review*, 46, 3 (2006), p. 261.

75   Marshall (ed.), *Raparapa Kularr Martuwarra*, pp. 107-10 (Harry Watson), pp. 208-19 (John Watson).

increasingly liberated from the restraints of mission and station'.[76] Sullivan cautions that 'mixed descent Aborigine' is a category that 'covers a wide variety of experience, origins, opinions and abilities that need not in all cases reflect significant understanding of, or identification with, traditional Aboriginal culture'.[77] 'Town' includes Derby, Broome, Wyndham and Halls Creek, where some people from Kimberley Aboriginal families were schooled and employed. The Kimberley Land Council (KLC) resulted from 'an increasing awareness of the potential for leadership and mediation by a number of mixed-descent Aborigines who were at that time [early 1980s] working for the departments of Aboriginal Affairs and Community Welfare, and the Aboriginal Legal Service'.[78] John Watson, son of William Watson, was a founder of the KLC and served as chair from 1981 to 1986 and 1991 to 1993.

Pearson's Scheme for Trusteeship

Hope Vale's persistent social distinctions are manifest in the reception of the CYWRT.[79] Reviews of the Trial suggest that, of the four communities involved, Hope Vale residents are the most vocally opposed to the scheme. Yet the CYWRT's primary architect – Noel Pearson – derives both reform inspiration and moral authority from his upbringing in Hope Vale. Even more surprising is the fact that the resistance to CYWRT is led by Hope Vale's wage-earning

---

76   Patrick Sullivan, *All Free Man Now: Culture, Community and Politics in the Kimberley Region, North-Western Australia* (Canberra: Australian Institute of Aboriginal and Torres Strait Islander Studies, 1996), p. 30.
77   Sullivan, *All Free Man Now*, pp. 86, 89.
78   Sullivan, *All Free Man Now*, p. 106.
79   Elizabeth Watt, 'Mission Modern: An Ethno-Historical Explanation of the Origins and Reception of the Cape York Welfare Reform Trial in Hope Vale', Ph.D. thesis, Australian National University, 2015.

'spectators' of the reforms, rather than by the welfare-dependent 'subjects' of the reforms themselves.[80]

The employed 'spectators' of the CYWRT are mostly descendants of the lighter-skinned elite, who were favoured by the Lutherans during the mission era, while the welfare dependent 'subjects' are more likely to be descendants of the neglected darker-skinned families. Even though the CYWRT is heavily influenced by Pearson's upbringing as part of this mission upper class, the same upbringing has inspired his peers' hostility to his reforms.

Having been socialised to value domesticity, industry, self-improvement and material accumulation, the elite members were better placed to seize educational and employment opportunities that became available under Joh Bjelke-Petersen (supporter of the *Guugu Yimithirr* elite, as chair of the Hope Vale mission prior to becoming premier). While Bjelke-Petersen's schemes were designed to assimilate this group into broader Queensland society, they had the unintended consequence of exposing the elite to 'modern thinking' about Indigenous pride and self-determination emanating from urban centres since the 1970s.[81] Upon returning to Hope Vale, members of this more educated, liberal group – including Noel Pearson – were eager to take total control of the administration of their town from the Lutheran Church.[82] While Pearson has reassessed his views on this transition in recent years, many of the educated stratum to which he belongs still hold strongly to rights-based and utilitarian arguments

---

80   Colmar Brunton, *Cape York Social Change Research Study: Hope Vale Community Reports, prepared for the Department of Families, Community Services and Indigenous Affairs* (Canberra: Colmar Brunton, 2012).

81   Terwiel-Powell, 'Developments in the Kinship System', p. 322.

82   Michael Limerick, 'What Makes an Aboriginal Council Successful? Case Studies of Aboriginal Community Government Performance in Far North Queensland', Ph.D. thesis, Griffith University, 2009, p. 266.

against paternalistic systems of government. This leads them to denounce Pearson's approach as undemocratic, and to liken his interventionist initiatives to the Lutherans' efforts in the past. Members of the elite wish to preserve their financial base and influence the local council – the primary source of employment, authority and prestige since the decline of Hope Vale's private market in the 1990s. They see the CYWRT as a threat to their organisation because it has replaced many of their existing social programs with better-funded alternatives and drawn political attention away from the councillors.

While the members of the elite identify more strongly with the values underpinning Pearson's reform, they are also more likely to take offence at his public criticisms of their home town's mores. The marginalised *Guugu Yimithirr* families are less likely to feel stigmatised by the new interventionist policy paradigm than the elite, despite being the primary targets of welfare quarantining schemes, because their frame of socio-political reference is largely restricted to the town's 'Blackfella domain'.[83] Very different Indigenous identity constructions prevail in this more private, inward-looking domain, and behaviour that triggers quarantining of their welfare payments – such as welfare dependence, drinking, truancy, violence and tenancy violations – is normalised. Hope Vale's lower classes are less likely to experience shame in relation to the CYWRT, and they tend to base their views on personal, tangible experiences of the scheme rather than on broader politico-philosophical principles or interests. Members of the *Guugu Yimithirr* lower class who are not quarantined are usually ambivalent about or ignorant of the Trials, and many find the Trials' restriction of their spending useful or relatively innocuous.

---

83 David Trigger, *Whitefella Comin': Aboriginal Responses to Colonialism in Northern Australia* (Melbourne: Cambridge University Press, 1992).

Any who are opposed to welfare quarantining and other interventionists measures, such as the Alcohol Management Plans, resist by thwarting restrictions rather than by articulating a critique that can be recorded in surveys or public forums.

Conclusion: Languages of Unity and Distinction

Bolton speculated to Deborah Gare in 1998 that he might one day write 'a general history of northern Australia as the meeting place of Aboriginal, Asian and European culture'.[84] One possible explanation for his not doing so is that others did.[85] In such a history, the author must find terms to refer to collective actors. Bolton continued to be thoughtful about the problem of nomenclature, and in 2005 he mused about the many meanings of 'indigenous', and noted the rising salience of terms of regional distinction such as Bardi or Bunuba or Yamadji.[86]

The historian of the north must also consider what to do with the terminology of 'caste'? To abandon it is to respect the view that it has been an ideological feature of colonial authority, divisive of colonised people whose unity is strength. When Paul Marshall interviewed the members of the Watson family (Harry, Ivan and John) a generation younger than William Watson, in the mid-1980s, Ivan presented this inclusive notion of 'Aboriginal': 'The white people use the name "half-caste" for some kids, but to us they're all Aboriginal people'.[87] His inclusiveness can be read as part of the language of trusteeship,

---

84   Bolton, 'Images from a Life', p. 95.
85   For example, Henry Reynolds *North of Capricorn: The Untold Story of Australia's North* (Sydney: Allen & Unwin, 2003), and Regina Ganter (with Julia Martinez and Gary Lee), *Mixed Relations: Asian–Aboriginal Contact in North Australia* (Perth: University of Western Australia Press, 2006).
86   Bolton, 'Western Australian History', p. 48-6.
87   Marshall (ed.), *Raparapa Kularr Martuwarra*, (Ivan Watson), p. 126.

CHAPTER 9

in which certain Aboriginal people have become empowered to speak for and act in the interests of all Aboriginal people. The language of unity – suppressing memory of differentiating processes – is no less a political artefact than the language of distinction.

Bolton once noted, paradoxically, that Ernie Bridge's career was 'somewhat exceptional proof that race was no bar to achievement in the Kimberleys'.[88] We see figures such as Bridge as exemplary of the evolution of northern colonial hegemony: the adaptation of the stratified racial relations into a project of state-authorised trusteeship. We make no judgment against the politics of trusteeship. We merely call attention to its socio-historical roots in what Terwiel-Powell called the 'hierarchy of worthiness' – sharply defined in Hope Vale in the 1970s, but evident also in the cattle industry in other parts of northern Australia where caste distinctions meant something to those caught up in them.

This 'northern' pattern of differentiation has been modified in two ways since around 1970. First, the terminology of caste and colour distinction has come under severe reproach as a colonial imposition, a threat to the putative unity of Aborigines as a colonised people. Second, faced with a worrying surplus of Indigenous labour supply over the colonial economy's demand for workers, governments have initiated policies of trusteeship over land and state transfer incomes. Such 'self-determination' empowers Aboriginal people with skills of brokerage. The historical roots of their leadership role are in the practices of delegated authority – based on formerly explicit distinctions of caste and colour – nurtured by missions and pastoral stations.

---

88   Bolton, 'Black and White', p. 174.

Chapter 10

FEAR, AFFECTION AND *WURNAN*

Reframing Station History in the Kimberley through Jack Wherra's Art

Mary Anne Jebb

In early 2015 Geoffrey Bolton and I decided we should rewrite and publish a chapter we had co-written in 1994 on the Kimberley pastoral industry from 1912 to 1967. The collection in which it was to appear was not published but remains a useful manuscript of historical essays covering such topics as Aboriginal people and missions, stations, health, government policy and the pearling industry.[1] At that time Geoffrey was keen to return to his 1953 research interest and collaborate with an early career student who was working with Kimberley Aboriginal people, using oral history recordings and written documents to analyse Kimberley pastoral station relationships. He was aware that his earlier history (and to some extent our 1994 chapter) was written from official records with a view from the

---

1   Geoffrey Bolton and Mary Anne Jebb, 'The Kimberley 1912–1967', in Sarah Yu (ed.), 'In Our Own Country' (unpublished manuscript, 1994).

CHAPTER 10

administrative south and the station owners' verandahs. It failed to present a picture of Kimberley pastoral station history that explained the emotional context for the relative peace of the 1950s and later.

This essay provides an opportunity to reframe that earlier work and explore the sentiments of Kimberley pastoral station lives. It utilises a corpus of hundreds of carved boab nut images created by Ngarinyin artist Jack Wherra, mostly in 1964 and 1965, which depict events and relationships in the Kimberley from the period of first contact to the time of welfare and town reserves in the 1960s. Wherra's realist images provide an Aboriginal historical document of Kimberley station relationships that conveys personal experiences and expressions of power. They concern men whom Geoffrey Bolton referred to as the 'salt beef and damper men', or the 'battlers of the Leopolds', and whom I called the nomad whites, those who lived closely with Aboriginal people at the margins of the pastoral industry.[2] I use Wherra's art to explore the social relationships between the marginal men and Aboriginal people of the Leopold Ranges, particularly in the 1920s and 1930s.

Hidden Relations

In his 1953 Masters thesis Geoffrey Bolton traced the economic rise and fall of the pastoral industry from the 1880s to the 1950s, identifying the Fitzroy Valley and Ord River pastoralists as central figures in a history of economic development.[3] He did not consider the Aboriginal people or their relationships with station leaseholders and

---

2   Mary Anne Jebb, *Blood, Sweat and Welfare: A History of White Bosses and Aboriginal Pastoral Workers* (Perth: University of Western Australia Press, 2002).

3   Geoffrey Curgenven Bolton, 'A Survey of the Kimberley Pastoral Industry from 1885 to the Present', M.A thesis, University of Western Australia, 1953.

managers. His account of labour relations in the Kimberley in 1953 is summed up in the statement from a pastoralist: 'we depend on our black labour and we find it dependable'.[4]

In the thesis Geoffrey exposed characteristics of the Kimberley pastoral industry that drove smallholders into the Leopold Ranges region while large landholders and companies monopolised the more accessible land around the Ord and Fitzroy rivers. He wrote of the Western Australian government's legislative attempts after 1920 to change the system of large leaseholders controlling huge areas of land, which had resulted in a 'polite legal fiction'. 'Capitalists', as Geoffrey called them, had the money to pay managers, erect fences, develop water points and, most importantly, live in the south and leave their Kimberley pastoral stations to a manager. They did not view the Kimberley as a place to make the family home. 'It was, instead, a district in which to make money before retiring to the South and leave a manager to work the station.' To reinforce his point he quoted Edwin Rose's 1896 journal entry on his return to Quanban station: 'Back to this dismal hole, after glorious six months holidays south'.[5]

The area 'over the ranges' was opened for leasing in 1903 and occupied mostly by smallholders and battlers, the marginal men who had worked for the larger stations or were soldier settlers. Geoffrey noted that these men each had a few hundred cattle 'and maintained a rough and precarious living'. He mentioned that they were especially dependent on Aboriginal people to run their stations, even more so than the pastoralists with some capital and resources behind them. In the first decades after 1900 many of these marginal smallholders

---

4 Bolton, 'A Survey of the Kimberley Pastoral Industry', p. 236.
5 Bolton, 'A Survey of the Kimberley Pastoral Industry', p. 65.

CHAPTER 10

lived with Aboriginal women and relied on their children with those women to work the station. Geoffrey noted but did not expand on the idea that the Aborigines Protection Acts, especially the 1905 Act, marked a turning point in relationships between Aboriginal women and white men in the Kimberley. Prior to this Act, relationships were relatively open. Afterwards they were hidden, at least from an official written history view.

In 1981 Geoffrey prefaced his chapter 'Black and White after 1897' in Tom Stannage's *New History of Western Australia* with the comment that there was 'insufficient material' available at that time to write a history 'from the Aboriginal point of view'.[6] He observed that a reliance on administrative files created a one-sided view of history and that source materials had to expand to include oral histories from Aboriginal people. At that time, he wrote, 'only Jack Davis among Aboriginal historians offered an overview of white–Aboriginal relations (in drama form)'. In 1953 and in 1981 Geoffrey acknowledged that all pastoral stations in the Kimberley were started with the assistance of black labour to a greater or lesser degree, and were established within a violent frontier environment. He acknowledged there was some 'spirited militant resistance', but claimed that by 1905 Aboriginal people were by and large 'habituated' to a 'quasi-feudal' relationship on pastoral stations.[7] Within this regime bosses varied – one or two were sadistic, some eccentric and most resorted to physical means to discipline Aboriginal people.

In 1953 Geoffrey stated that he would make some attempt to describe the men and women concerned in the conduct of the

---

6 G. Bolton, 'Black and White after 1897', in C.T. Stannage (ed.), *A New History of Western Australia* (Perth: University of Western Australia Press, 1981), pp. 124-78.
7 Bolton, 'Black and White after 1897', p. 127.

Kimberley but would not rely on the more colourful traditions of the 'old timers' unless their stories were confirmed in written documents.[8] He believed the history of the Leopold battlers was elusive since there was little written information, 'although interesting traditions exist in stories, which, if true, give evidence of a code of morality differing somewhat from city conventions'. The Leopold battlers presented an anomaly for Geoffrey as their lives retained aspects of the frontier no longer spoken of and hidden from official histories. Twenty years earlier in 1934, Ion Idriess visited Derby and the Leopold Ranges and transposed bar room conversations with some of the battlers into dialogue in his books. Idriess' books were attractive to Geoffrey, who sought to achieve a similar vivacity in his own writing. In *Outlaws of the Leopolds* Idriess referred to the resistance hero Jandamarra and Bunuba people in the 1890s and presented the white men 'over the ranges' as almost as exotic as the 'natives'. Their emotional attachment was to each other, not to women or the south. In government records the white men in the Leopolds were also labelled the 'outlaws'.[9] While a few held pastoral leases in their own names, most had few possessions and they all struggled to stay within the law, especially the Aborigines Protection Acts which outlawed living permanently with Aboriginal women. Many had participated in the violent invasion and pacification of the Kimberley.[10] One particular police file investigating the alleged murder in 1913 of a white man by Scotty Sadler gives gruesome details about his relationship with an Aboriginal woman and his direction to destroy evidence of her

---

8   Bolton, 'A Survey of the Kimberley Pastoral Industry', p. 4.
9   Jebb, *Blood, Sweat and Welfare*, pp. 80-102.
10 Kate Auty, 'Patrick Bernard O'Leary and the Forrest River Massacres, Western Australia: Examining "Wodgil" and the Significance of 8 June 1926', *Aboriginal History*, 28 (2004), pp. 122-55.

CHAPTER 10

pregnancies to him.[11] The file includes a parade of Leopold battlers, including Jack Connaughton, Mick O'Conner, Jack Wilson, Jack Dale, Scotty Sadler and Alec Thompson. They survived by selling dingo scalps or a few cattle, working for others on musters or managing teams of Aboriginal people to build fences and yards. Many had been boundary riders, occupying land leased by someone else. The moral problem for the men of the Leopolds was partly their hard-drinking lifestyle and their small wood and brush huts, with a likeness to those of the natives, but a lack of a connection to the south and their relationships with Aboriginal women set them apart. They survived because they lived with Aboriginal people and developed long term relationships with them. They came to depend on the few 'half-caste' children they allowed to live and stay about their camps.

Jack Wherra's art provides a window onto the intertwined working and living relationships of the Leopolds that goes beyond the polite fictions of economic interdependence and the impermeable social divisions of the black camps and homesteads. His images depict events and relationships that are echoed in and supported by oral histories recorded by Aboriginal men and women who grew up and lived with the Leopold Ranges battlers.[12] These oral and visual forms of history provide information about the informal social relationships in the Kimberley from an Aboriginal standpoint. They carry 'emotional freight' from the past that helps to reconcile survival within systems dominated by fear and unequal power relations.[13]

---

11   'Bowers Supposed Lost, Murder of, from Broome', Police Department (PD) 1531/1917, Cons 430 Series 76, State Records Office of Western Australia (SROWA).
12   Mordni Munro, Weeda Nyanulla, Banjo Wirrenmurra and Daisy Angajit in Morndi Munro with Mary Anne Jebb (ed.), *Emerarra: A Man of Merarra*, (Broome: Magabala Books, 1996).
13   Jock Willis, historian and general editor of *Te Ara: The Encyclopedia of New Zealand*, suggests the term 'emotional freight' for affects contained within oral histories that

Wurnan

When I began my research into Kimberley pastoral station relationships in 1989 I was struck by the ability of Aboriginal people to describe some bosses as 'bad', 'cheeky' or 'cruel' men who perpetrated a litany of abuses, but also as 'good' managers. I felt this could be interpreted as meaning that these men were good stockmen who taught their off-siders to be skilled and good stock workers. This effort from Aboriginal people to acknowledge such 'good' qualities reflects their views of their past and their agency in making that history. The anthropologist Anthony Redmond and historian Fiona Skyring tackle this tension through an analysis of *Wurnan* and its application to relationships on Kurunjie station, one of the stations over the Leopolds.[14] *Wurnan* is the overarching social institution adhered to by Aboriginal people across the north Kimberley and throughout the ranges country.[15] It shaped (and still shapes) the way Aboriginal people dealt with outsiders. It was more than sharing, more than exchange. *Wurnan* animates and organises sharing and exchange relationships for ceremonial and non-ceremonial items. It operates through a delayed and complex system of trading partners who are bound by personal and group social relationships. It enables objects with little value from one social and economic world to be valued and increase status in a different social world.[16]

---

    can be otherwise hidden in written records; personal communication, 2016.

14 Anthony Redmond and Fiona Skyring, 'Exchange and Appropriation: The *Wurnan* Economy and Aboriginal Land and Labour at Karunjie Station, North-Western Australia', in Ian Keen (ed.), *Indigenous Participation in Australian Economies: Historical and Anthropological Perspectives* (Canberra: ANU Press, 2012) pp. 73-90.

15 Valda Blundell, and Donny Woolagoodja, *Keeping the Wanjinas Fresh: Sam Woolagoodja and the Enduring Power of Lalai* (Fremantle: Fremantle Arts Centre Press, 2005).

16 Anthony Redmond, 'Tracking Wurnan: Transformations in the Trade and Exchange of Resources in the Northern Kimberley', in Natasha Fijn, Ian Keen,

CHAPTER 10

Redmond and Skyring note that Aboriginal people's descriptions of their relations with white men on stations often use 'idioms of emotional interdependency' to characterise their agency in these unequal relationships. They ascribe an active role to themselves in making the 'boss into a good boss'.[17] Relationships such as being a 'private boy' or 'off-sider' to the white boss synchronised with relationships in their own social world and opened possibilities for increasing status within their own system of power. *Wurnan* made economic interdependence and exploitation in one system socially meaningful in another.

Women's relationships with white men were fundamental in this interconnected system. Even though these relationships started badly and continued in a context of persistent fear, over time the 'networks that developed between the station bosses and local clans became assimilated into Ngarinyin expectations about the obligations of kinship'.[18] They created an 'expansive politics that extended human networks, territory, and resources'.[19] White men were drawn into the *Wurnan* system, which transformed a process of survival into a form of resistance and value production against an economic system that was designed to 'strip them of power'.[20] *Wurnan* operated in the Leopolds in the 1920s and 1930s and at Mowanjum in the 1960s; it underpins Jack Wherra's art.

Christopher Lloyd and Michael Pickering (eds), *Indigenous Participation in Australian Economies II: Historical Engagements and Current Enterprises* (ANU E Press, Canberra, 2012), pp. 57-72.
17   Redmond and Skyring, 'Exchange and Appropriation'.
18   Redmond and Skyring, 'Exchange and Appropriation'.
19   Ann McGrath, *Illicit Love: Interracial Sex and Marriage in the United States and Australia* (Lincoln, NE and London: University of Nebraska Press, 2015), p. 27.
20   Redmond and Skyring, 'Exchange and Appropriation'.

Jack Wherra, 'The Michelangelo of the Rugged Kimberleys'[21]

Jack Wherra was a Ngarinyin man, born in 1922 near Kunmunya mission on the Kimberley coast north of Derby. He died in 1980.[22] He was born during the 'early days', before things 'settled down'. His father was not one of the bosses' off-siders and his mother (Janungnarri) was not a white man's concubine. His family moved between Kunmunya Mission, Munja government ration station (from 1926) and white men's camps. They worked occasionally for Fred Merry at the small Sale River station in the 1920s and 1930s.[23] Wherra lived closely with the white men over the ranges, especially Scotty Salmond, Jack Wilson and Fred Merry.

In 1934, when Jack Wilson was ordered by the Protector of Aborigines to give up his fair-skinned child to missionaries, Fred Merry gave him Jack Wherra, who was staying in the camp at Merry's station. Jack allegedly tried to poison Wilson. Because of his youth, he was sent for a short time to the government ration station in the central Kimberley, Moola Bulla. He was soon sent back to Fred Merry and his family at the advice of the Moola Bulla manager and government officials, who agreed that he was a quiet and sensible boy who had probably been defending himself from Jack Wilson, a known drunk and bad character.[24] In 1940 Wherra and two of his brothers, Ivan and Sandy, were involved in a killing at Kunmunya Presbyterian Mission and jailed at Broome for five years for a 'tribal

---

21 *Australasian Post*, 11 December 1969.
22 Jack Wherra's exact date of death is unknown. It is not registered with the Registrar General, nor on his personal file created by Native Welfare. A search of police files and Derby hospital files has been unsuccessful.
23 Fred Merry to Manager Munja, 25 September 1935, Native Affairs 330/1935, 'Full Blood – Wherra @ Jack – Personal file', SROWA.
24 Native Affairs 330/1935, SROWA.

CHAPTER 10

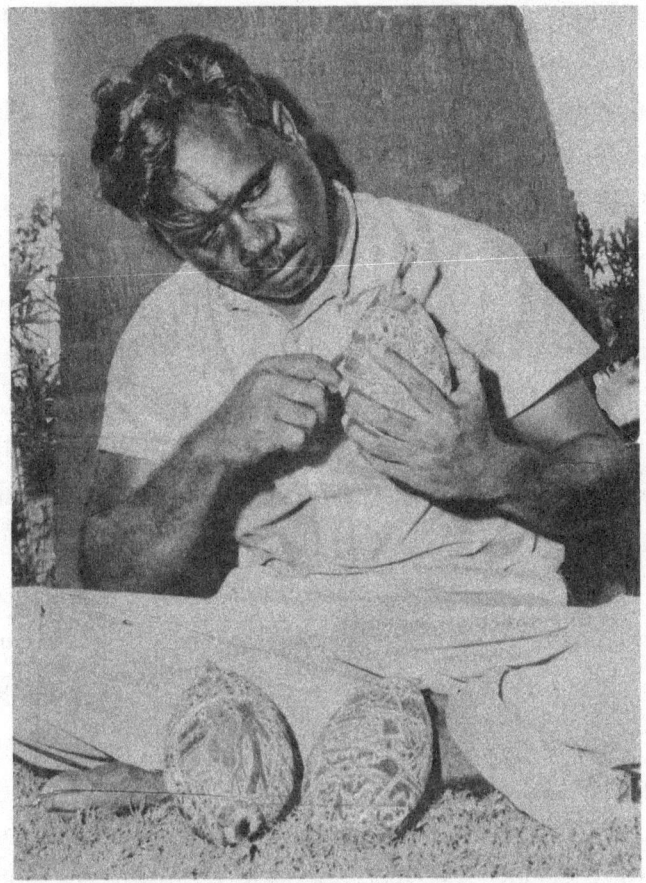

10.1 Jack Wherra outside Broome prison, 1963. Courtesy Bauer Media Pty Ltd.[25]

murder' over marriage infringements.[26] His law boss, Mungalili (also known as Rattler) was demanding justice, to be dealt by younger Ngarinyin and Worrorra men from the bush on men camped at the mission over a series of marriages at the mission that had broken tribal law.

---

25 All images of jack Wherra reproduced with permission of Gwen Puemorra and Janet Oobagooma.
26 Kate Auty, *Black Glass: Western Australian Courts of Native Affairs 1936–1954* (Fremantle: Fremantle Art Centre Press, 2005), pp. 89-126, refers to Wherra's two trials.

In April 1942, the prison was needed for the internment of enemy aliens and Wherra was released to his country, Munja, and the care of the superintendent.[27] Wherra's wife disappeared from Munja in 1946 and he was suspected by the police and the station manager of murdering her, but there was no evidence and no body. In 1947 he was sent to Moola Bulla, again on the advice of the manager at Munja. He escaped from Moola Bulla in 1947 and walked over 250 kilometres across the ranges to his own country and back to Munja. In 1948 he was jailed again for being involved in the murder of two men from Sunday Island who were staying at Munja and allegedly flirting with Munja women. This time, there was no 'tribal murder' plea and he was jailed for life.

Wherra was a model prisoner. He carved hundreds of boab nuts in prison and became a well-known figure (see image 10.1). He came and went from the prison to care for the ducks and work in the garden, to wash the warder's car and to meet people who wanted to talk to him about his boab nut carving. On his release from prison in 1964, Wherra had a small amount of money in a bank account from the sales of his carvings, sales that had been coordinated by the prison warders. He had also given his carvings to visitors, the warders' sons and family, and exchanged them for tobacco or items such as *Phantom* or *Buck Rogers* comics or cowboy and indian books about the American western frontier.[28] The prison authorities argued that Wherra should be released from prison because he would be able to

---

27   Commissioner of Native Affairs to Minister, 25 March 1942, Native Affairs 330/1935, SROWA.

28   Brian Waterer, interviewed by Mary Anne Jebb, 15 August 2005. Brian was a prison warder's son who lived in the Broome prison with Wherra from 1941 to 1942. Brian Naughton, another prison warder's son who also lived in the Broome prison with Wherra from 1941 to about 1953, remembered sharing comics with Wherra.

CHAPTER 10

support himself with his carving.[29] He had become widely known locally and through newspaper articles for his art work, although his place as a recognised artist was ambiguous. While a very few carved boab nuts were sent to museums from the 1890s onwards, they were mostly considered to be curios and not recognised as fine art, or as an authentic 'ethnographic' reproduction of past cultural practices. Wherra's carvings were sought as tourist items in Broome and Derby after his release from prison. They were appreciated and kept for decades in collections in people's sitting rooms and homes.[30] However, his celebrity as an artist was consistently overshadowed in press articles and in the memories of the twenty-five people I interviewed by his notoriety as a 'tribal murderer'.[31]

The anthropologist John McCaffrey came to Mowanjum in 1964 and 1965, and commissioned Wherra to carve boab nuts and paid him for his time to record explanations of what he had carved and how he carved. Through the carvings, Wherra recorded elements of his own story and a more general history of his people over the ranges. The narrative is echoed in later histories depicting an Australia-wide pattern of pacification, fear and conflict with police and white men.[32] Through his support, McCaffrey provided Wherra

---

29 Native Affairs 934/1950 'Full Blood – Wherra @ Jack – Personal file', SROWA record viewed at Department of Community Development.

30 I interviewed 25 people who had, from 1941 to 1970, bought or been given Jack Wherra carved boab nuts and found a wide range of stories of appreciation for his artwork.

31 'Killer Will See Queen', *Daily News*, 18 March 1963; 'Wherra Jack', *People*, 20 November 1963, p. 24; 'Old Man of Death', *Australasian Post*, 11 December 1969.

32 Bain Attwood and S.G. Foster (eds), *Frontier Conflict: The Australian Experience* (Canberra: National Museum of Australia, 2003); Raymond Evans, '"Plenty Shoot 'Em": The Destruction of Aboriginal Societies along the Queensland Frontier', in A. Dirk Moses (ed.), *Genocide and Settler Society: Frontier Violence and Stolen Indigenous Children in Australian History* (New York: Berghahn Books, 2004), pp. 150-72; Noel Loos, *Invasion and Resistance: Aboriginal–European Relations on the North Queensland Frontier* (Canberra: Australian National University Press,

with the means to make a series of images that were not sold off one-by-one at the local pub or to welfare officers, teachers and police. They present a form of narrative production that can be read by outsiders. Wherra's visual narratives render the feelings in pastoral station histories as complex and emergent; they portray social relationships including dance, humour, fear and violence in camps and the bush and around station homesteads, which are linked by characters, causes and consequences. He depicted a range of feelings in his characters, including happiness, tenderness, shock, fear, anger, shame and grief.

Framed Action Narratives

There are striking similarities in Jack Wherra's work with comic-book heroes, especially the Phantom.[33] The nuts are divided horizontally and vertically, with some having as many as twelve miniature framed images. The framed panel arrangement operates as a device for establishing complex narratives for a broad audience.[34] Each image contains a self-contained story but also relates to others on the same nut, and to other nuts, contributing to a larger narrative. Wherra gently cut, pressed and scraped into the brown outer shell of the nut to expose the creamy layers below the surface. He used glass, wire, a pocket knife, a sharpened butter knife and screwdriver to create shading, cross hatching, feathering, dots and clean lines. He developed landscape scenes with perspective and light and consistently

---

1982); Henry Reynolds, *Frontier: Aborigines, Settlers and Land*, (Sydney: Allen & Unwin, 1987); Henry Reynolds, *The Other Side of the Frontier: Aboriginal Resistance to the European Invasion of Australia* (Ringwood: Penguin Books, 1990).

33   Wherra was the first Aboriginal artist to engage with action-figure style to produce his own narratives. Phantom figures became the symbol for health programs from the early 1970s.

34   Gaye Sculthorpe suggested that the frame developed after 1950 within the growing tourist trade; Gaye Sculthorpe, 'Designs on Carved Boab Nuts', *COMA: Bulletin of the Conference of Museum Anthropologists*, 23 (1990), pp. 37-47.

CHAPTER 10

10.2 Carved boab nuts by Jack Wherra, 1964–66. Courtesy Sotheby's. Photograph by Graham Baring.

referenced the Leopold Ranges of his country. He used elements of a shared and continuous iconography seen on pre-contact artefacts, dance paraphernalia and body decorations such as half-circles of the moon at the top and base of the nuts, the geometric framing and dots. Unlike comics, he does not use text-balloons; he did not read or write, confining text to his name and occasionally a date on carvings that especially pleased him. His narrative and use of action figures with exaggerated movements and facial expressions set him apart from other artists at Mowanjum or the Kimberley.

Gwen Puemorra, Wherra's close descendant (called granddaughter), described the story in the six-framed nut (image 10.2) as starting when the real 'flash stockmen' came into town, 'all cashed up', and one asks a husband for his woman (bottom left frame). They play cards. The visitor wins, picks up his winnings and the fight starts. The police arrive and lock the woman and her husband in the old Derby jail. She ends up in court. Senior Wunambal woman Pudja Barunga, also working with Gwen Puemorra to interpret image 2, provided the

A HISTORIAN FOR ALL SEASONS

10.3 Carved boab nut by Jack Wherra, 1964–66. Courtesy National Museum of Australia. Photograph by the author.

words for the court image (top left frame), focusing particularly on the woman's hand signal to the magistrate: 'she played her last card'.[35]

After days of reviewing and reconstructing more than 400 images, his granddaughter Gwen Puemorra selected one particular frame (image 10.3) that epitomised his artistry. She described the scene of the spearing: 'no-one ever did that, every meaning in there'.[36] I believe she is referring here to Wherra's extraordinary skill for depicting movement and his ranges country, as well as reproducing images of Kimberley history that referred to Aboriginal peoples' attempts to settle the mess caused by the frontier.

Fear: 'if I was born in the bush I wasn't here'

Fear of violence dominated the emotional culture of the stations. Jack Wherra's carvings (see images 4 to 9) reflect the violence of

---

35 Pudja Barunga notes on interview with Mary Anne Jebb, 17 April 2005, Mowanjum Derby. All subsequent interviews are by Mary Anne Jebb unless indicated otherwise.
36 Gwen Puemorra, 11 April 2005, interview notes by author.

CHAPTER 10

the frontier. Morndi Munro, who was relatively protected on the stations, described the situation: 'I was born in the station me, if I was born in the bush I wasn't here'.[37] His stockmen and managers of the 1920s in the western region of the Leopold ranges were Jack Lloyd, Frank Gairdner, Fred Easton, Harry Bannon and Alec Thomson. 'They was good cattlemen ... that's where I learned my experience.' They were 'rough', hard and capable of shooting to wound, kill or frighten.

Harry Howendon (Martin) did not become a head-stockman. He, like Jack Wherra's family, lived in the region between Kunmunya Mission and Munja ration station and could move between them and the white men's camps. He did not become a permanent 'offsider' to a white boss. Like Morndi Munro, he identified broad themes and turning-points in relationships with white men. He was a bushman. He spoke of change for the better once Scotty Salmond, Dave Rust and managers of that era were replaced by a new regime of 'Queenslanders' in the 1950s. Before, he said, it was all 'sneaking' into the stock-workers' camp at night to claim tobacco from the workers.

> Right that manager findem track now. Followem followem followem me fella. Findem me fella. Chasem me fella. Huntem up me fella, every way. That the olden time. We never been come close up. This time you can walk outside. If I come from bush I can come up straight up to camp.[38]

Harry Howendon remembered that during the time of the Leopold battlers, if white men asked for people to be removed, the police took them away. The local white men destroyed spears and killed dogs:

---

37 Morndi (Bill) Munro, interviewed 17 May 1989.
38 Harry Howendon (Martin), interviewed 4 April 1992.

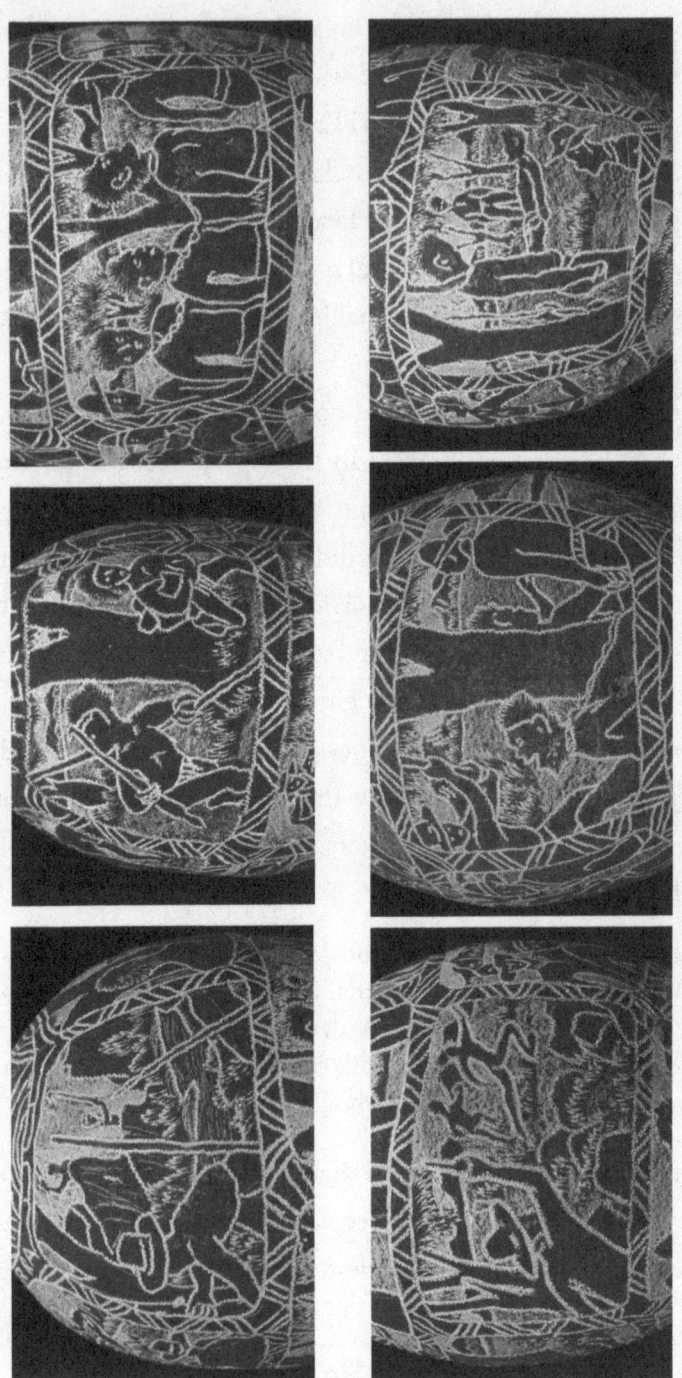

10.4, 10.5, 10.6, 10.7, 10.8, 10.9 Carved boab nuts by Jack Wherra, 1964–66. Courtesy National Museum of Australia. Photographs by Graham Baring.

CHAPTER 10

> Our old policeman more better, little bit. He never do nothing. He only been tie im up and take him way. See. White men been have em trouble, well he been take em way. White people he been gettem all the dog, finishem up all the spear, everything broke em up. Broke em. Make a big fire, burn em all the spear. … He had a chain. We had the collars …[39]

One police file from 1944 on the investigation of the murder of 'Elsie' by the Aboriginal man Rattler, in the region over the ranges, provides detailed information from witnesses, including Harry Howendon, about the lifestyle of Aboriginal people at this time.[40] They travelled often between camps and stations with the express purpose of meeting and hiding women from white men and competitors from groups at Missions or the government ration station. Their access to the right women had to be negotiated within the altered situation dominated by white men on stations, in camps and on missions and ration stations.

Yvonne Burgu, who lived at Gibb River station in the ranges and was Harry Howendon's close relation, reconstructed the story around one of Jack Wherra's carvings as the story about Harry Howendon when he was falsely accused of killing his wife, who in reality had been killed by Rattler (see image 10.10), Wherra's law boss – also known as Mungalili. Wherra, she said, 'was carving what happened in the early days'.[41] She explained that the key to understanding this image is the sack:

---

39   Harry Howendon (Martin), interviewed 5 April 1992.
40   'Alleged murder of Cilgualla @ Elsie by Mongulgillin @ Rattler at Phillips Range June 1944', PD4458/1944, Cons 430 Series 76, SROWA.
41   Yvonne Burgu, Perth, 15 October 2005, interview notes by author.

10.10 Carved boab nut by Jack Wherra, 1964-66. Courtesy Sotheby's. Photograph by Graham Baring.

Harry went out and had to carry the bag of bones back over his shoulder. Uncle Harry stole Elsie from Kunmunya. They left Maudie (Yvonne's mother) in Gibb River. They went to Dingan – Mount Barnett fishing spot. Rattler burnt the body there. They (the police) made Harry carry the body stinking on his back. ... Every time they pull up to sleep they said "Use it as your pillow." And the stink is all over his body.

Alliances, Agency and *Wurnan*

Wherra created some scenes of domestic bliss (see images 10.11 and 10.12). In image 12 a young couple meet away from their main camp for romance. Wherra described image 11 as the 'start' of this story, with the old man and his wife and baby. This scene he said represented how things should be for the 'Ngarinyin tribe' and all the 'natives' of the Kimberley. It showed how the Law worked and how marriage systems operated. In this scene the old man was 'very proud of this little boy or girl'.[42] Wherra also used wavy, almost transparent

---

42   Jack Wherra, interview by John McCaffrey, 4 April 1965, Australian Institute of Aboriginal and Torres Strait Islander Studies (AIATSIS) McCaffrey_Jo1 tape LA16997.

CHAPTER 10

lines to depict scenes about death or heightened emotions. In image 10.13 the wronged man sees the illicit lovers and fumes with jealousy. In other frames he punishes both the man and woman for breaking marriage rules. Wrong marriages were central to Wherra's carvings and to his jailing.

10.11 Carved boab nut by Jack Wherra, 1964–66. Courtesy Sotheby's. Photograph by Graham Baring.

10.12 Carved boab nut by Jack Wherra, 1964–66. Courtesy Brian Noughton. Photograph by the author.

– 255 –

10.13 Carved boab nut by Jack Wherra, 1964–66. Courtesy Powerhouse Museum. Photograph by the author.

Affection: The Verandah Kiss is the 'start of it'

Gwen Puemorra interpreted images 10.14 to 10.16 as part of a story when the station manager took an old man's wife away and 'forced her to stay with him'. The woman ran away from the manager and the couple was 'hunted' by the police. The station manager identified the husband as a 'cattle killer' to the police, and he was 'hunted' and killed by the policeman and manager.[43]

In images 10.17 and 10.18 Wherra's carvings depict a fight between Scotty Salmond and Jack Wilson over the control of a child. This incident is referred to by Daisy Angajit and recorded in government files. Daisy Angajit was brought up living with Jack Wilson in the 1920s and described it as a 'good life'.[44] She described her marriage to Bill Munro as 'arranged' by Jack Wilson. This arrangement ran counter to the 'promise' of her family to an individual but was within the Law of marrying across moiety groups. However, it

---

43   Gwen Puemorra, 5 April 2005, interview notes by author.
44   Daisy Angajit, in Morndi Munro with Mary Anne Jebb (ed.), *Emerarra*, p. 100.

CHAPTER 10

10.14, 10.15 and 10.16 Carved boab nuts by Jack Wherra, 1964–66. Courtesy Sotheby's. Photographs by Graham Baring.

created conflict with the man to whom she had been promised at birth within her own social world. She told also how Wilson's son, her brother, was taken by 'old Tom Street', the missionary.[45] It is clear from government records that Wilson did not want to give up his fair-skinned children but had been forced to in the early 1920s and again in 1934. In this fight over the child he and Salmond are recorded as resembling 'gunslingers' as both drew pistols.[46]

---

45 H. Reid, Munja Station, to Chief Protector of Aborigines, 1 October 1934, 195/1929 'Establishment of a Mission near Mt Barnett', Acc. 993 An1/7, SROWA.

46 Mathew Touhy, Police Inspector Broome 27 January 1935, Native Affairs 330/1935, 'Full Blood – Wherra @ Jack – Personal file', SROWA record viewed at Department of Community Development. Touhy refers to police file 5436/1930 DO 432/30.

10.17 and 10.18 Carved boab nuts by Jack Wherra, 1964–66. Courtesy Sotheby's. Photographs by Graham Baring.

These are round nuts, with no physical beginning. They can be read in many different directions to embody different versions of similar histories. This arrangement presents a history that has multiple interpretations. It allowed Wherra to negotiate two social systems. To members of his community, Wherra kept the Law and was jailed for that. Penny Bidd, a Ngarinyin woman and artist at Mowanjum, remembered watching him carve in the 1960s when she was a girl. For her Wherra carved:

> what happened to him, how gardia come to the land and how old people used to be frighten and run away in the bush. How Baba (grandfather) used to be treated. ... He draws from his life.[47]

Heather Umbagai, a Worrorra woman who also watched him carve when she was a child, recalled him as a quiet man whose carvings provided an historical narrative for the community to 'look back on that and have the chance of writing'.[48] Senior Wunambal woman, Pudja Barunga, who was only a few years younger than Jack Wherra

---

47 Penny Bidd, Mowanjum Hall, 2 September 2005, interview notes by author.
48 Heather Umbagai and Pudja Barunga, interviewed 23 March 2005.

CHAPTER 10

and whose daughter was offered to Wherra as his wife, emphasised that his carvings applied generally to Kimberley history: 'He's not only talking about himself, it's other people too in the carving'.[49] The Ngarinyin artist and head-stockman Jack Dale, also Wherra's contemporary, emphasised these carved images were not 'comics', they were 'true'.

Creating Carved Histories

There is an unusually rich amount of information from Jack Wherra about his art production, primarily because of the recordings and documentation created by the anthropologist John McCaffrey.[50] He arrived in Derby in September 1964 and stayed for about eight months. He sought out leaders and artists at Mowanjum, eventually collecting three hundred paintings and artefacts, and dozens of carved boab nuts executed by Jack Wherra, which he transported to the USA. A collection of these carved boab nuts was sold by McCaffrey's widow in 2003; twenty-one were bought by the National Museum of Australia, seventeen by the Powerhouse Museum in Sydney and five for the late Kerry Packer's private collection.

John McCaffrey spent weeks with Jack Wherra in late 1964 and early 1965, and then for a short time in 1966. Wherra had been out of prison for only six months when McCaffrey arrived to do his fieldwork on Aboriginal art production. In addition to the artworks, McCaffrey left an extensive record of his time at Mowanjum: over three hundred pages of notebook entries and more than eighty hours

---

49 Pudja Barunga, 11 April 2005, interview notes by author.
50 McCaffrey was born in 1928 in San Diego and in 1964 received a Fulbright scholarship to do fieldwork in Western Australia; Tim Kingender (compiler), *The John McCaffrey Collection of Kimberley Art* (Sotheby's 2003).

of taped discussions, mainly with Jack Wherra.[51] The recordings provide an extraordinary insight into an artist's daily life at Mowanjum community in the 1960s and into his art production. Although they are mainly of Wherra's voice, they also present an unusual sound record of McCaffrey's research process and relationship with Wherra.

McCaffrey used the tape recordings to back up his field inquiries. He was not recording a formal interview with the intention of sound production. He often kept the tape running through interruptions by children (asking for things usually), nearby arguments and dog fights. McCaffrey, an expressive and philosophical person, was intensely interested in the art production process. There are occasional times of laughter between the men but there are also moments when it sounds like McCaffrey is pushing too hard and digging too deeply with his questions, and Wherra laughs nervously or sounds worried or decides he is tired.[52]

In his notebooks McCaffrey described in detail the setting for the artists, their homes, postures, conversations, food, clothes and families. He recorded his thoughts about their moods, their unspoken communications and signals. He also recorded his perception of what the artists thought about him and their relationship to him. On several occasions McCaffrey notes that he feels he is unwanted or a nuisance, or that he seems to have upset someone with a comment or question. Of significance for this essay are descriptions of establishing

---

51 These tapes are archived at AIATSIS. The author received a research grant in 2005 from AIATSIS to work collaboratively with the Mowanjum community to transcribe them. The community has not yet cleared them for public access, as they contain a great deal of personal and sensitive information, so the project continues. There are also a small number of recorded discussions with David Mowaljarlai.

52 My own collection of hundreds of hours of recordings with Kimberley men and women in the 1990s contains numerous similar incidents of cross-cultural errors. It touches on the complex question of what ethically should be kept and reproduced from recordings that contain material that is inadvertently being created.

CHAPTER 10

his social place with the senior men of Mowanjum and four of the artists. His scrupulous notes describe the negotiations with the artists as they draw him into the *Wurnan*, not through his relationships with women, as with men of the Leopold Ranges, but through gifts, payments and resources that he brought into the community. He is given a 'boss', Watty Ngerdu, and told 'good you belonga this camp, you belong this country now'. He was also shown that money could become part of the *Wurnan* to connect different social worlds. He noted with disappointment that a man approached him as he sat in camp one day, pointing surreptitiously to something secret hidden in his shirt and whispering. McCaffrey thought he must have sacred boards, but it was 'only money'.[53]

He records the time he told the Wunambal artists that he had no money to pay them and Long Wattie was so upset that he was 'almost crying' and 'shaking with rage'. Mickey Bunguni laughed a few times and then 'finally told me to stop *talking*'.[54] Long Wattie and Bunguni said they wanted to sleep and Albert Barunga approached him and said he would need to pay his (Barunga's) power bill and took £2 from McCaffrey, commenting that the days of anthropologists paying in tobacco were over. McCaffrey had been given a place to pass resources to others so they could continue to pass them along *Wurnan* channels that were expanding to link work and money. The Mowanjum men were able to convert the money and resources into their own social system within limitations. McCaffrey saw the power of the *Wurnan* and the possibilities for conflict and rage if it was broken.

---

53   John McCaffrey Notebook, n.d., p. 70, in Kim Akerman (transcriber), 'Field Notes of John McCaffrey, Kimberley 1964–66', 2002, copy held by author.

54   McCaffrey Notebook, p. 72; emphasis in the original.

Jack Wherra mapped elements of the *Wurnan* system for McCaffrey and explained that he had to give things to his brother Sandy to get them to Gibb River station following the *Wurnan* channel through specific stations and in a specific direction. He explained how his time in prison came after killings that involved his 'brothers' and their 'bosses', and breaking laws through wrong marriages. The strict hierarchy of place and people that determined who could give and receive items could also be linked to the recognisably different system of building a bank account and paying wages. Jack Wherra explained to McCaffrey that there was another layer of relationships that he now negotiated as a professional artist who was paid money for his carvings by many people. He was allowed to get these 'presents' from anyone but he would buy shell for his brother Sandy and pay his brother Ivan regularly for harvesting boab nuts.[55]

The McCaffrey and Jack Wherra recordings are all in English. Having been in prison for nineteen years in close contact with the warders, their children and other Europeans, Wherra conversed relatively easily in English. He was acutely aware and seemed to take pride in the fact that his carvings had meanings that could be understood outside his cultural frame by tradesmen, visitors, tourists, school-teachers and publicans. When asked what he thought about Albert Namatjira's paintings, he told McCaffrey that his carvings were better able to tell a story. According to Wherra, Namatjira's paintings did not 'tell stories'; they depicted places that were 'real', whereas Wherra populated his carvings with animals, people and their behaviour; Wherra 'told a story'.[56]

---

55   McCaffrey Notebook, pp. 140-41.
56   McCaffrey Notebook, p. 51.

CHAPTER 10

McCaffrey's interest, intellect and character converged with Wherra's and his desire to tell his own story of his jailing for a wide audience and the need to uphold his laws. He referred to his carvings as a 'book' and told McCaffrey that he wants people to 'read that book' and 'think of me'. The viewer, according to Wherra, would say:

> What we gonna do with that man? He got real story … those things he carves they got meanings on it … He got nothing against me after that criminal name I had. I make paper for myself I got someone to know this.[57]

'But I can't give up my old mate'

John McCaffery engaged a Canadian photographer, Neil Tildon, to capture the setting at Mowanjum and make a detailed record of the art production process. These beautiful photographs, coupled with the notebooks and recordings, allow for a close reading of Wherra's art practices and his emotional engagement with each nut and image. McCaffrey wrote that Wherra described his image creation process as one that 'grows up with the nut'. He did not always carve from memory and was often prompted by what he saw in the surface of the nut. Each had its own particular imagery, which belonged to it.[58]

> Jack uses the slight bumps and color changes of the nut to suggest the imagery. He studies the play of light on the lumpy surface of the nut and the white-black color lines of the nut.[59]

Jack Wherra described to McCaffrey how he always had a 'good watch' to see if an image was an emu or a person or 'anything'; 'that's

---

57 Jack Wherra, n.d. [1964/65], John McCaffrey audio collection, AIATSIS McCaffrey JO_17006.
58 McCaffrey Notebook, p. 126.
59 McCaffrey Notebook, p. 189.

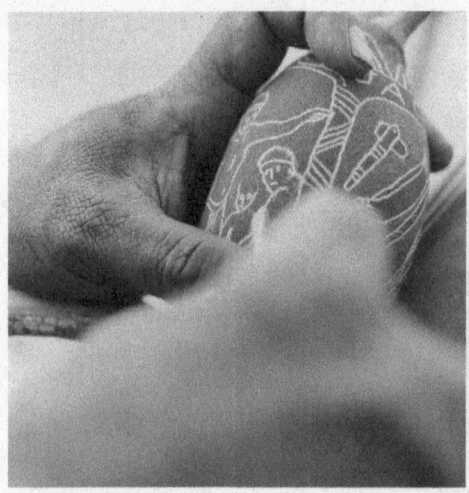 

10.19 and 10.20 Carved boab nuts by Jack Wherra, 1964–66. Courtesy AIATSIS, McCaffrey collection. Photographs by Neil Tilden.

how I do all this. All this thing, now picture, I only done it by seeing them, not by memory.'[60] He engaged intently, humorously and tenderly with the boab nut and at times laughed at the images that began to emerge and form a scene as he carved.[61]

Jeffrey Burgu, a senior Ngarinyin man, knew Wherra well, was closely related and a similar age. He described Wherra's carving process: 'When he carve he used his tool to let the spirit out'.[62] McCaffrey's photographs capture how the images emerged and Wherra's skill at presenting a story of intense human relationships. Images 10.19 and 10.20, for example, show a man turning to face the viewer and look toward the adjoining frame where a woman accused of wrongdoing is shamed and shocked at her discovery. The image also faces Wherra.

---

60   Jack Wherra, interviewed by John McCaffrey, 27 and 30 April 1965, AIATSIS McCaffrey_Jo1 tape LA16997.
61   McCaffrey Notebook, p. 136.
62   Jeffrey Burgu, Mowanjum Hall, 2 September 2005, interview notes by author.

CHAPTER 10

10.21 Carved boab nut by Jack Wherra, 1964–66. Courtesy Sotheby's. Photograph by Graham Baring.

Jack Wherra did not always look so intently for images in the surface of nuts he carved. He produced hundreds, perhaps many hundreds, of carvings without deep engagement; some duplicated images for quick sale and others small carvings to meet obligations to locals for a drink at the pub, or a ride or just to make some money.[63]

McCaffrey's collection contains one nut (see image 10.21) with a series of images depicting an anthropologist being taken into the ranges country. This is McCaffrey. In each frame he is accompanied across different countries or clan lands from Ngarinyin north into Wunambal country. His Aboriginal guide asks permission from one large man to take him into his country. The words Pudja Barunga suggested to accompany this image were: 'The big man is smiling for Havelock [tobacco], tea and sugar and trouser. He (the guide) is saying "I can bring this gardia?"' The anthropologist is shown in one frame dancing and clapping and in another with a senior man in full ceremonial headdress in the 'sun cave'

---

63   McCaffrey Notebook, p. 181.

in Wunambal country.[64] I have previously referred to this series of images as 'closing the circle, recording the recorder recording his people'. But this does not do justice to the depth and dynamism of the relationship of visitors, outsiders, historians or anthropologists with Aboriginal people from the Kimberley ranges. It is not just a flat circle of 'watchers', for it brings McCaffrey into the narrative at the same time as it offers something to McCaffrey. It, like the Wurnan itself, is 'evidence' of a relationship; it is also constitutive of the relationships.

Jack Wherra's carved images challenge myths of a peaceful frontier by presenting images of resistance, alliances and active entanglements. They also contain autobiographical images, and explicit depictions of conflict between Aboriginal families, of punishments for law breaking, narratives of men and women hunting, pastoral work and life on the reserve. They speak to a struggle over land and sovereignty as well as domestic and ceremonial life of his community. These images also depict the *Wurnan* channel or 'road', as it is more often called, and the social 'glue' that formed relationships with the Leopold battlers and with McCaffrey in the 1960s. They operate as metaphors for sovereignty of land and knowledge, and they probably contain the people who were Wherra's closest *Wurnan* partners at Mowanjum. The big man who is 'smiling for Havelock' could well be his 'boss', Big Wattie, carved into his own country, in a bush outfit of naga or cockrag, holding his spears, and smiling from a position of power with responsibility to look after the small young fellow, the anthropologist who will eventually also look after him.

---

64   I draw here on Pudja Barunga's interpretation of the scenes and some of her dialogue as recorded in interview and discussion; Pudja Barunga interview, Mowanjum, 17 April 2005.

CHAPTER 10

Conclusion

Wherra was an innovator who departed from convention amongst West Kimberley boab nut carvers, who in the main depicted animal iconography of rock shelters, their own clan groups and closely associated ancestral beings.[65] His carvings embodied what Ian McLeod referred to as 'radical creativity' to produce histories in art that referred to uncomfortable events and relationships in a visual language that could be understood by non-Aboriginal, non-Kimberley people.[66] They did not create a 'rupture' with his culture or social norms but extended his art production into an individualistic and economic business realm that he said himself was 'different'.[67] He engaged in a 'value creation process' that was both economic and his own cultural production within the 'arenas of the encompassing society'.[68] The system of *Wurnan* provided a means to negotiate the divide between economics and culture, and draw McCaffrey into his social world. *Wurnan* helps to understand how Aboriginal people experienced asymmetrical power relations and violent demands for sex and labour from white men, and the changing circumstances of radically altered marriage systems. *Wurnan* underpins survival and gives history and value to agency.

Geoffrey Bolton did not meet Jack Wherra in 1953 when he travelled to the Kimberley to see for himself how the stations operated.

---

65 Some carved pearl shells contained images of people, boats and trucks; see Kim Akerman and J.E. Stanton, *Riji and Jakuli: Kimberley Pearlshell in Aboriginal Australia*, Monograph Series No. 4 (Darwin: Northern Territory Museum of Arts and Sciences, 1994).

66 Ian McLeod (ed.), *Double Desire: Transculturation and Indigenous Contemporary Art* (Newcastle: Cambridge Scholars Publishing, 2014), p. 4.

67 Howard Morphy, *Becoming Art: Exploring cross-cultural categories* (Sydney: UNSW Press, 2008).

68 Morphy, *Becoming Art*, p. xv; see also Blundell and Woolagoodja, *Keeping the Wanjinas Fresh*.

A HISTORIAN FOR ALL SEASONS

Wherra was in the prison, gaoled for punishments meted out to his own people by his brothers and Law bosses. Nor did Geoffrey manage to obtain one of Wherra's boab nut carvings. He was, however, fascinated by the images and the artistry contained within them, providing me with an enthusiastic and convincing reference for a Manning Clarke House writing fellowship in 2009 to research Jack Wherra's biography and the history in his art.

In Wherra's images of the frontier there is a full range of emotions and relationships within a frame of violence. The stories told through Wherra's boab nut carvings were ones generated by the Kimberley regimen Geoffrey encountered in 1953. He was then, by his own admission, a young man encountering a world quite different from down south, not fully comfortable in his conversations with Indigenous men and women, and in any case working within the same framework of frontier settlement and pioneer enterprise that put Wherra in prison, and gave him no way of expressing in writing the complexity of relationships.

There were hints that Geoffrey would approach Kimberley history very differently, given the opportunity. In 2008 as dinner speaker for the Western Australian Oral History conference in Broome, he reflected on his 1953 visit to Broome and stories told to him by a pioneer pearler and pastoralist of youthful adventures decades before and his Aboriginal descendants and workers. Geoffrey seemed to be making the point that this was not a tale of shame, victimisation or regret, nor was it cruelly intended. In the audience were descendants who had an oral tradition of the same white ancestor that had been fractured by government policies of removal and laws that made intimate relationships with Aboriginal women illicit. Geoffrey's anecdote bridged the intervening 50 years and admitted closeness not

CHAPTER 10

usually spoken of in public and missing from most government records. Had he the chance to redraft our 1994 chapter of station lives, I hope he would have added the emotional freight of anecdotes and experiences like this from the conversational and emergent space between official, written, oral and visual histories.

Chapter 11

THE CHALLENGES OF FAMILY AGEING 1920–64

Nettie and Vance Palmer

Pat Jalland

The history of ageing in Australia has been a neglected field of study until quite recently.[1] Australian history textbooks and other syntheses mostly omitted older age as a significant period in Australian life. Geoffrey Bolton's 1990 *Oxford History of Australia* volume, *1942–1988: The Middle Way*, was a pioneering exception, including a thoughtful analysis of major trends in ageing and health in the 1960s.[2] Geoffrey noted that women survived longer – 60 per cent of people over 75 were women, many with very limited means. Only about a quarter of the workforce had some form of superannuation, with most living off a non-contributory old-age pension that was subject to a means test. The more fortunate older people owned their own homes and had supportive families, though even the better off

---

1   See Pat Jalland, *Old Age in Australia: A History* (Melbourne: Melbourne University Press, 2015).
2   Geoffrey Bolton, *The Oxford History of Australia. Volume 5, 1942–1988: The Middle Way* (Melbourne: Oxford University Press, 1990), pp. 136-38, 331 (index entry).

CHAPTER 11

needed to be careful about money in later years. Geoffrey was also struck by 'the surprising diversity of the approaches to old age policy in different parts of Australia, not only in the nineteenth century but even recently'.[3]

Different regional, family, and individual experiences of ageing necessarily require specialist studies of older age, especially as the history of old age has largely been written in terms of public policy relating to issues like pensions, housing, health and nursing homes. Historians need to humanise these policy and institutional studies of ageing with biographical approaches to family experiences of older age. Individual and family biographies are some of the most revealing genres about human life, and of particular value for the investigation of ageing, as Geoffrey recognised.[4] For example, at the best, individuals such as Paul Hasluck, a former Governor-General, could look forward to 'a vigorous retirement', but the physical decline and frailty of older people like Alexandra Hasluck, Paul's wife, was a more common and problematic experience for many individuals and families.[5]

The personal papers of Australian writers are an especially valuable source for understanding the history of the challenges of ageing. For example, the Nettie and Vance Palmer family created an unusually rich and substantially neglected archive relevant to older age. Nettie

---

3   Geoffrey Bolton to Pat Jalland, personal email, 6 Nov. 2012, commenting, with characteristic generosity, on drafts of Pat Jalland's *Old Age in Australia*.

4   Geoffrey Bolton published seven biographies, as well as a remarkable 91 entries for the *Australian Dictionary of Biography*. These 91 entries reflected his view that the *Australian Dictionary of Biography* was 'probably the most momentous step to promote biography in the history of Australian scholarship'; Geoffrey Bolton, 'The Art of Australian Political Biography', in Tracey Arklay, John Nethercote and John Wanna (eds), *Australian Political Lives: Chronicling Political Careers and Administrative Histories* (Canberra: ANU E Press, 2006), p. 4.

5   Geoffrey Bolton, *Paul Hasluck: A Life* (Perth: UWA Publishing, 2014), pp. 460-73.

and Vance were central figures in Australian literary and wider cultural life in the first half of the twentieth century. They were very widely recognised as significant authors and cultural contacts. Indeed, the Western Australian historian Paul Hasluck included a visit to Nettie and Vance on his first visit to the eastern States in 1933.[6] The Palmers were also examples of the trends in ageing which Geoffrey had emphasised. They illustrated the gradual ageing of the population and the impacts of illness and deaths on the family. Heart disease killed almost one-third of those who died in the 1960s.[7] Vance Palmer died suddenly of a heart attack at the age of 74 in 1959, surviving longer than most.[8]

This essay on Vance and Nettie Palmer and their family will explore their individual and family experiences of old age, illuminating the realities of the daily life of ageing, especially when facing illness, as in Vance Palmer's case; or when confronted by the challenge of protracted decline, as was Nettie Palmer's fate. I have drawn largely for primary sources on the extensive and revealing Palmer family correspondence and Nettie's diary deposited in the National Library of Australia. These sources offer a daily account of how time was spent and how poor health and the death of loved ones was experienced. They demonstrate the advantages of family support, though at considerable cost to female members of the family, and the value of adequate financial resources to reduce the effects of dependence and frailty.

---

6   Ibid., p. 56.
7   Bolton, *The Oxford History of Australia*, vol. 5, p. 137.
8   Geoffrey Serle, 'Edward Vivian (Vance) Palmer (1885–1959)', *Australian Dictionary of Biography*, vol. 11 (Melbourne: Melbourne University Press, 1985), pp. 126-28.

CHAPTER 11

Janet Gertrude ('Nettie') Palmer (1885–1964) was born in 1885 in Victoria to Irish-born Baptist parents.[9] She was educated at Presbyterian Ladies' College from 1900 to 1904, which demonstrated her parent's financial capacity and commitment to her formal schooling. Nettie's formative years were influenced by the women's movement and the rise of socialism. She met her future husband, Vance Palmer (1885–1959), while she was at Melbourne University from 1905 to 1909 (B.A. 1909, M.A. 1912) and married him in 1914.[10] Their daughter Aileen was born in 1915 and Helen in 1917. Deborah Jordan's excellent study *Nettie Palmer: Search for an Aesthetic* describes Nettie as 'a prolific, influential and widely read cultural critic' by the 1920s, following the publication of her *Modern Australian Literature (1900–23)* in 1924. Nettie became influential as a journalist-reviewer, commentator and broadcaster, a vital force in promoting creative writing and encouraging a distinctive Australian literature.[11]

In all her achievements Nettie Palmer worked closely with Vance, also a distinguished writer, in an intimate and inspiring partnership. Nettie established 'a network of contact and encouragement' between numerous Australian writers, especially younger women, including Eleanor Dark and Marjorie Barnard. Nettie was highly intelligent,

---

9   See D.J. Jordan, 'Janet Gertrude (Nettie) Palmer (1885–1964)', *Australian Dictionary of Biography*, vol. 11, pp. 129-31; William H. Wilde, Joy Hooton and Barry Andrews, *The Oxford Companion to Australian Literature*, 2nd edn (Melbourne: Oxford University Press, 1994), pp. 601-2.

10 Serle, 'Edward Vivian (Vance) Palmer'; Wilde et al., *The Oxford Companion to Australian Literature*, pp. 602-3.

11 Deborah Jordan, *Nettie Palmer: Search for an Aesthetic* (Melbourne: History Department, University of Melbourne History Monograph 24, 1999), p. 182. Drusilla Modjeska argued earlier that Nettie 'was of central importance to the cultural history of the period [1920s] as a critic, sponsor and correspondent of many writers'; *Exiles at Home: Australian Women Writers 1925–1945* (Sydney: Angus & Robertson, 1981), p. 8; see also pp. 50-89. Modjeska is especially valuable on Nettie's female literary networks in the 1930s.

warm, generous and self-assured. Her books included her autobiographical *Fourteen Years* in 1948, and her biographical studies of Henry Bournes Higgins in 1931, Henry Handel Richardson in 1950 and Bernard O'Dowd in 1954.[12]

Nettie Palmer as Carer for Her Parents in Old Age, 1920s–1944

Nettie was intimately involved in caring for both her parents in old age – her father John Higgins (d. 1929), an Irish-born accountant, in the 1920s, and her mother Catharine (Katie) MacDonald (1859–1944) in the following decade. Both parents were Baptists who believed in 'High Thinking and Plain Living'.[13]

From the 1880s daughters and other female family members were subject to considerable social pressure to care for frail elderly parents. Valerie Braithwaite has emphasised the toll of this 'burden of care' on female primary care-givers into the 1980s, in terms of privacy, family life, employment prospects and personal health. Female carers often felt guilty, helpless and exhausted, and suffered silently 'in the belief that care giving is their responsibility and theirs alone'.[14] It was expected that women would provide home care for the elderly at no cost to the state, as a labour of love, though at considerable emotional, physical and financial cost to themselves.[15]

Nettie's father became seriously ill in the 1920s and needed painful medical treatment. By the end of 1926 a good nurse had been

---

12 Jordan, *Nettie Palmer*, pp. 182-217.
13 Ibid., p. 14.
14 Valerie Braithwaite, 'Coming to Terms with Burden in Home Care', *Australian Journal on Ageing*, 6, 1 (1987), pp. 20-23. See also Valerie Braithwaite, *Bound to Care* (Sydney: Allen & Unwin, 1990).
15 Diane Gibson, *Aged Care: Old Policies, New Problems* (Cambridge: Cambridge University Press, 1998), pp. 24-26, 15, 71-76.

hired to relieve Katie.[16] Nettie would have liked to volunteer to help her mother for several months, but she was almost indispensable in her own home, and lived in the Dandenongs until 1925 and in Queensland until 1929. John Higgins died peacefully at Ardmore, the family home in Melbourne, in 1929 and Nettie reflected that 'he has returned to his friends and had little else to look forward to'.[17]

By 1933 Nettie's mother Katie Higgins' health was deteriorating, so Nettie sent her own daughters, Helen, aged sixteen, and Aileen, eighteen, to keep an eye on their grandmother at Ardmore in Melbourne. 'Will you and Helen in spite of difficulties, manage to take it in turns to be with Granny if and when Miss M. goes out? ... She's feeling pretty frail and "low" lately'.[18] By 1936 Nettie and her daughter Helen were taking turns to look after Katie at Ardmore as her memory started to deteriorate. Nettie joined Helen at Ardmore late in 1936 and reported to Vance: 'the situation's grimmish. Mother's often very frail and seems half drugged and remote, but then she has times of extreme clarity'.[19]

In January 1937 Vance Palmer was sympathetic to Nettie's difficulties in caring for her mother: 'It's not possible to believe she'll ever be very much stronger than she is now, and we'll have to adapt our lives to that'. Since Katie was unlikely to improve, 'it doesn't seem possible for you to leave her'.[20] So Nettie took care of her mother at

---

16 Nettie Palmer [hereafter Nettie] to mother Catherine Palmer [hereafter Catherine], 16 March 1926, 25 April, 3 July 1927, Papers of Vance and Nettie Palmer, 1889–1964, NLA MS 1174/1/2726, 2951-2, 2979.

17 Nettie to Catherine, 17 January, 12 March 1928, 31, 25 January 1929, NLA MS 1174/1/3067, 3087, 3301, 3308-9.

18 Nettie to daughter Aileen Palmer [hereafter Aileen], n.d. [1933?], NLA MS 1174/1/4345.

19 Nettie to husband Vance Palmer [hereafter Vance], n.d. [October 1936?], NLA MS 1174/1/5151.

20 Vance to Nettie, January 1937, 28 December 1936, NLA MS 1174/1/5185, 5188.

Ardmore for longer periods, leaving her own family to cope at home. Nettie told Vance, 'I only get ill if I have to spend too much time at Ardmore on the end of a string'. Her mother was manipulative, and 'some sort of attack' was a common outcome if her wishes were not respected.[21]

In 1941 Nettie Palmer herself had the first of a long series of minor strokes, which weakened her and limited her ability to write. Several undated letters to Vance suggest that she was not coping with the stress of caring for her demanding mother. This situation doubtless contributed to her own ill-health, as she usually returned home exhausted:

> This is the day-after-Ardmore, and as usual I'm rather shaky. I'm not a very skilled nurse and it's hard to be firm enough in an impersonal way: then I feel every inch of Mother's resentment, even if it's momentary and she forgets. Will I ever get back some real strength! ... Dear, it's as much for your sake that I hope to be normally strong and alert soon.

Nettie was sorry to saddle Vance with her 'feeling of inner collapse' and her sense of unfulfilled hopes. Her daughters kept reminding Nettie to ration her time at Ardmore: 'it was anxiety about Ardmore that made me crack up before'.[22]

By September 1943 Nettie had to spend every day with her mother, who now needed 'steady but not complicated nursing'. Nettie finally hired a full-time nurse to live at Ardmore, and paid the nurse out of her journalism income 'to save trouble'. By December 1943, 'Granny is weaker and not very happy: she has none of the serenity of old age'.

---

21 Nettie to Vance, 11 August 1941, NLA MS 1174/1/6001, 6007.
22 Nettie to Vance, n.d., NLA MS 1174/1/6008; Nettie to Aileen, 10 February, August 1943, NLA MS 1174/1/6292, 6294, 6396.

CHAPTER 11

Nettie regretted that 'I seem to have left every skerrick of my youth so far behind me ... I managed badly in being the sole Higgins woman in my generation'.[23] Nettie had a long history of being supportive – to her parents, to her younger brother Esmonde, and to her aunts Ina and Helen. Her remark reminds us that those who cared for the frail elderly in their last years were almost always the women in the family. Katie Higgins became unconscious on 28 September 1944 and died at Ardmore the next day. Nettie wrote to Miles Franklin that her mother was more peaceful towards the end and that it wasn't a sad or painful death. Even so, Nettie concluded that 'old age and illness are too much for mortals to bear' and 'death is always incredible'.[24]

Nettie Palmer and Family Death and Illness, 1944–64

Nettie was aged 59 on her mother's death in 1944. While caring for Katie, Nettie had suffered a minor stroke and began to feel that old age was approaching. Six months after her mother's death, Nettie confessed to her daughter Aileen that 'I've had this bit of a breakdown ... blood pressure and dizziness so that I've got to stay in bed and loaf'. Early in February 1945 she noted in her diary, 'Late in the afternoon rather cracked up – thrombosis. Had to ring for Dr Mackey'. Her daughter Helen was determined that they should have a housekeeper to run the house to allow Nettie to stay in bed in the mornings, to rest or to work, as health allowed.[25]

---

23 Nettie to Aileen, 30 October, 29 November, 5, 12 December 1943, 13 February 1944, NLA MS 1174/1/6432, 6445, 6457, 6459, 6502.
24 Nettie to Miles Franklin, 2 November 1944, State Library of NSW (Mitchell Library), Miles Franklin Papers, MS 364/24; Nettie's diary, [1944], NLA MS 1174, series 16.
25 Nettie to Aileen, 7 February 1945, NLA MS 1174/1/6699, series 16; Nettie's diaries, 5 February, 5 March 1945.

On 30 March 1945 Vance sadly explained the situation to Aileen, who was summoned back home from London, where she had been employed by Australia House:

> [Nettie] is better. Unfortunately, though, she'll have to consider herself mostly as an invalid, from now on. The trouble is with the arteries. Years of strain have made them less elastic: they can't distend sufficiently under a sudden pressure of blood: then comes a 'thrombosis', a minor stroke such as she had last year, or a 'spasm' (less serious) such as she had this [year]. There's no reason to worry, the doctor says, if she looks after herself, and we're doing our best to see that she has no responsibility from now on.

From this time on, Nettie made many references in her correspondence to her advancing years, occasionally signing off letters to her daughters as 'your old mother', and noting that 'I rest a lot and I'm very old'.[26] Her later years were improved by her inheritance of the family home, Ardmore, from her mother, along with nearly £30,000, which eased their earlier financial problems.

Despite serious family concerns about her own poor health, Nettie generously took considerable responsibility for two elderly aunts, Ina and Helen. Nettie had long been anxious about Aunt Ina's living arrangements at the age of 83, especially as she had become so frail. As Nettie put it to Aileen in 1944, Aunt Ina was 'so independent and yet needs help' because she would not look after herself properly. Ina was enterprising in supplementing her minimal income by taking in boarders, but she had no help and never lit a fire.[27] In February 1947 Aunt Helen had a stroke and was moved to Lancewood Nursing

---

26   Vance to Aileen, 30 March 1945, NLA MS 1174/1/6739; Nettie to Aileen, 17 September 1945, NLA MS 1174/1/6699.

27   Nettie to Aileen, 25 June 1944, Papers of Aileen Palmer, 1935–1979 [hereafter Aileen Palmer Papers], NLA MS 6759, 1/1/1.

CHAPTER 11

Home. Nettie visited both aunts at least weekly, finding Aunt Helen apparently contented up to her death in 1947. By 1948 Ina was so ill that Nettie's daughter Helen shared responsibility for Ina's care in her final year, with a nurse's assistance.[28]

The deaths of Nettie's mother and her aunts, coming so close to her own series of strokes, left her feeling vulnerable in her early sixties, especially as the strokes affected her writing arm. In October 1947 she noted that she had to take medication nearly every day to achieve any steady writing. Even so, Nettie still managed a relatively busy schedule, editing memoirs, short stories and translations. In 1948 Nettie also published *Fourteen Years: Extracts from a Private Journal 1925–1939*. Moreover, Nettie published studies of Henry Handel Richardson and, with Victor Kennedy, Bernard O'Dowd.[29]

In 1948 Professor E. Morris Miller, former vice-chancellor of the University of Tasmania, sent Nettie a sensitive letter of sympathy and encouragement on her declining health.

> May I express to you my regret at the distressing news of a transient palsy, which I trust will not increase in severity. The strains of life tell more and more as we begin our careers as sexagenarians ... A change of attitude becomes inevitable, mainly in the form of a slowing down process or complete avoidance of disturbing elements of whatever kind. We need to adopt a new outlook, preparing ourselves for the maturing of personality as an antidote to senility. Adjustments of this character are not easy, when family responsibilities increase in burden ... Still there are compensations in achievement, and you have a goodly store.[30]

---

28 Nettie's diary, NLA MS 1174/16/25-28.
29 Nettie's diary, NLA MS 1174/16/25-28; Jordan, 'Janet Gertrude (Nettie) Palmer'.
30 E. Morris Miller to Nettie, 26 October 1948, NLA MS 1174/1/7513.

The 'mental breakdown' of Nettie's daughter Aileen in 1948 was the most challenging blow so far. Aileen was a gifted writer and poet, and also an active member of the Communist Party. She had joined the British Medical Unit in the Spanish Civil War.[31] Aileen was diagnosed with manic-depression (now known as bipolar disease) and became a patient in a psychiatric clinic at the early age of 33. She spent the next ten years in and out of mental institutions and rehabilitation units as well as her family home.[32] Aileen's breakdown devastated her parents. Her treatment included electric shocks and insulin, and she had recurring mental problems for forty years until her death in a psychiatric institution in 1988.

More sorrow was to come to the Palmer family. From early 1949 Nettie noted in her diary that Vance was tired and unwell; in August he had a coronary occlusion and declared to the stretcher-bearers who drove him to hospital that 'I feel like going to my last resting place'. Nettie wrote sadly to a friend that it was 'terrible to have a companion and know that separation must come. This grief, to be heaped upon old age and probably on illness, makes the end of life an inevitably bad time.'[33] In 1953 Vance had another period in hospital with a heart attack and Nettie admitted, 'don't know about future'. This may have been the occasion of Vance's undated letter from St Andrews Hospital to his daughter Helen, in which he enclosed details of his will and his assets:

---

31 Sylvia Martin, 'Aileen Yvonne Palmer (1915–1988)', *Australian Dictionary of Biography*, vol. 18 (2012), pp. 254-55; Sylvia Martin, *Ink in Her Veins: The Troubled Life of Aileen Palmer* (Perth: UWA Publishing, 2016).

32 See Aileen to Kathleen Fitzpatrick, 26 April 1964, Aileen Palmer Papers, NLA MS 6759/1/9.

33 Nettie's diary, 28–29 August 1949; Nettie to Judah Waten, n.d. [1951?], Papers of Helen Palmer, 1918–1996 (hereafter Helen Palmer Papers), NLA MS 6083.

CHAPTER 11

> I left my affairs in a rather untidy state when I came in here ... I'm conscious that my enemy is a dirty fighter and may give me a stab in the back when I least expect it. So, do you mind if I go into some business details here in a down-to-earth way.[34]

In February 1954 Nettie had another 'spasm', leaving her 'rather shaky all day', her handwriting feeble and 'my foot rather dragging and my walk a bit crooked still'. In October 1954 Nettie required surgery on her feet, and acknowledged that 'In fact I'm very old' and could not manage 'steady free spells of work yet'.[35] Nettie suffered a more serious stroke in 1957 which affected her right arm, hand and side. Vance wrote to their friend Katharine Susannah Prichard that Nettie was now very dependent and he could not leave her again: 'Writing has become almost impossible to her now. A great frustration for her, since she really enjoyed keeping in touch with people ... It is a little death to her to be deprived of the use of her right hand.'[36]

Vance warned his daughter Helen in August 1957 that friends were shocked by Nettie's condition and the future would be tough. Nettie made 'heavy weather' of cooking, and felt humiliated when she broke dishes. Vance aimed to take over more of the housekeeping when his latest book was finished. His letter to Helen in 1958 was revealing about the family stress occasioned by the health challenges facing both Aileen and Nettie:

> I don't feel justified in leaving N. [Nettie] for any time in the present situation. No use pretending that it's happy. A. [Aileen] is considerate and kind when she's sober, but aggressive and devastating when she comes in to dinner after a couple of drinks.

---

34 Vance to Helen Palmer [hereafter Helen], n.d., Helen Palmer Papers.
35 Nettie's diary, 1954–55, NLA MS 1174/16/37.
36 Nettie's diary, 1954–55; Vance to K.S. Prichard, n.d. [1956–57?], NLA MS 1174/1/8847.

> Then occasionally there are outbursts that are hard to manage.
> While I'm here they can be smoothed over, but I don't feel it's
> fair to leave N. [Nettie] to cope with them alone.[37]

Evidently both Vance and Aileen made a determined effort to support Nettie as best they could between March 1958 and July 1959, despite Nettie's frailty and Vance's 'uneasy tension with my treacherous [heart]'.[38]

Vance Palmer died suddenly at home in Melbourne of another heart attack in July 1959. Aileen generously continued to live with her mother until Nettie's death in 1964, five years after Vance. Katharine Susannah Prichard understood well, in consoling her friend Nettie, that she was 'touching a wound almost too painful to bear'. She recognised that Nettie and Aileen had each lost in Vance a beloved person they could lean on: 'And the psychological problem may arise as to who is to be the leaned on now'. Katharine wisely advised the two women she loved to be as independent of each other as possible, sharing interests and obligations, but 'maintaining that separateness which is so essential to vital personalities'. Vance had left an estate worth about £11,000,[39] a vital consideration given the high costs of healthcare support at home and Nettie's fast diminishing capacity to live by her writing.

Aileen Palmer: 'the reluctantly rather dutiful daughter', 1960–64

When Vance Palmer died in 1959 Aileen was 44 and her mother thirty years older. In late July 1960 Aileen left the psychiatric clinic

---

37 Vance to Helen, 7 March 1958, Helen Palmer Papers.
38 Vance to Jack McKinney, 7 September 1958, Helen Palmer Papers; Nettie's diary, 12 May 1959.
39 K.S. Prichard to Nettie, 29 July 1959, Aileen Palmer Papers, NLA MS 6759/3/21, 1/9.

CHAPTER 11

and it soon became clear that she must stay with her widowed mother in Melbourne for the longer term during her illness, while Helen (1917–79) supported them all by teaching in a Sydney high school.[40] The sisters saw home care for Nettie as the only option, with no mention of a nursing home until the final months of Nettie's life.

However, Aileen did express legitimate concern about the realities of home care. Nettie was trying to dictate from her bed the hours Aileen should keep and the food she should eat: 'what's wrong with my mother's attitude is that it's a kind of hangover of my past breakdowns … of course you can't change old ladies nor expect them to adjust'. But Aileen's dedicated perseverance paid off. Aileen wrote to her sister in July 1962 that their mother was now more considerate of Aileen than in the past, so there had been no 'brawls' for a long time: 'Still I feel because of the past, she and I will always be strangers … We are polite, and on the whole, considerate strangers.'[41]

Meanwhile Aileen did all in her considerable power 'to give N. [Nettie] the feeling that her work is not at an end'. Aileen wrote to Helen of her difficulties in helping Nettie with work on Italian translation, especially as Nettie was now 'very lacking in critical powers about her own output'.[42] Aileen was well aware of her mother's diminishing capacity, and believed Nettie had never really recovered from the series of strokes since 1945. Helen wrote in January 1963 of Nettie's increasing frailty: 'In the past twelve months she has been steadily packing up. Not physically, particularly, though articulation and writing are getting to be such a struggle that she's virtually

---

40 Robin Gollan, 'Helen Gwynneth Palmer (1917–1979)', *Australian Dictionary of Biography*, vol. 15 (2000), pp. 562-63.
41 Aileen to Dr Bell, 14 September 1961; Aileen to Helen, 9 July 1962, Helen Palmer Papers, NLA MS 6083, Box 2.
42 Aileen to Helen, 21 July 1962, Helen Palmer Papers, NLA MS 6083, Box 2.

given up trying to communicate … Her span of concentration and its depth have much fallen away; they pursue their own subterranean channel.'[43]

While Aileen helped her mother, especially in 'protecting the image', she also had to share the house and create some sort of independent role for herself. A thoughtful letter from Helen to Nettie in September 1963 illuminated this dilemma:

> Aileen is 48, a legacy of fifteen years of uncertain ups and downs behind her, a first-rate brain, society saying she can only answer the phone and make tea, and then her family won't give her recognition for her poetry. She's the only person who could so well help you; and she recognises the importance of what you're doing. She can't always be on tap and have a job and have some time to herself; but she's anxious to give you allotted times. But when she's not, her life is her own, and it is her home. If she doesn't get in people's way, why not?[44]

Aileen subsequently told her sister how deeply she had appreciated Helen's letter to their mother. It explained clearly the challenges Aileen faced regarding her health, which Nettie had never really understood. Aileen said she had always felt 'terrifically protective' towards their mother, 'but if there was ever a creature in history or legend (Medea, was it?) who loved gobbling up her own children, that's her. The Puritan (though also poetic) mother.' Aileen apologised if this 'might sound a bit mad', and reassured Helen she still took all her pills.[45] Meanwhile Aileen's practical assistance to Nettie

---

43 Helen to Frank and Marie Davison, 13 January 1963, Papers of Frank Dalby Davison, 1859–1970 (hereafter Davison Papers), NLA MS 1945/1/1679, Series 1, Box 2.
44 Helen to Nettie, 8 September 1963, Aileen Palmer Papers, NLA MS 6759/1/1.
45 Aileen to Helen, 22 November, 11 December 1963, Aileen Palmer Papers, NLA MS 6759/1/9.

CHAPTER 11

continued, though she was fully aware she 'must keep all the wits I've got about me ... All in all, there's a terrific resilience in N [Nettie]'.[46]

In May 1963 Nettie Palmer had another stroke, causing her health to decline markedly in her final eighteen months. Helen wrote to Harold White at the National Library of Australia on 17 May 1963 about the future deposit of Nettie's papers there: '[Nettie] has deteriorated sharply in the last ten days and has only a little spark left; but it is a lively little spark, and as mercifully she has no specific or painful ailment, she is able to be aware of and react to familiar people'.[47] By the end of 1963 Aileen was finding the challenge of supporting her mother overwhelming. In addition to her other duties she was expected to undertake a substantial amount of Nettie's typing, leaving little time for Aileen's personal interests. Aileen observed, '[Nettie] has moments of too acute disillusionment about her present capacities, when I feel terribly sorry for her'. On other occasions Aileen was too exasperated to be sympathetic, especially when Nettie interrupted the little time available for her own independent work or personal life: 'If one could only remind her (tactfully enough, without spoiling her fun in life) what she used to say about when grannie did the same sort of thing to her.' Helen's response from Sydney was warm, deserved and reassuring:

> You've done a magnificent job in coping, and much better than I could ever do; I know how depressing, apart from just plain trying, it can be ... I think you're doing the best that can be done; it's not possible to do the impossible for which she longs, and that is to bring her back to health and strength and make

---

46   Aileen to Helen, 4 April 1962, 13 February 1963, Helen Palmer Papers, NLA MS 6759/1/2; Aileen to Helen, 13 February [1962?], Helen Palmer Papers, NLA MS 6083, Box 2.
47   Helen to Harold White, 17 May 1963, Helen Palmer Papers, NLA MS 6083, Box 2.

her able to write and think fluently as she has in the past. Nor will you help matters by making yourself her slave ... All I can suggest is you plug away at the line that you will give her so much time and that's it, when it mutually suits you; and that you have your own life to live.[48]

By mid-February 1964 Aileen was sure that year would be more challenging than the last, when she managed 'without major ructions, but didn't either meet the real demands of N. [Nettie] or my own conscience, to any degree'. She remained the 'reluctantly rather dutiful daughter', who only managed a few hours a day of her own writing. Aileen wanted Nettie 'to ease up on the buzzing and belling all round the 24 hours, as slaves must also get some rest to keep up their strength and sufficient good humour'.[49]

The Threat of a Nursing Home for Nettie Palmer

By March 1964 Mrs Ross the housekeeper was nearing the end of her contract. This led Jessie Macleod, a close friend of Helen's, to raise the challenging issue of a possible nursing home for Nettie, which the family had so far avoided: 'You should seriously consider a nursing home when Mrs R goes. Hard to find a nurse-housekeeper who could manage both Aileen and Nettie.' Jessie emphasised that Aileen was doing a good job, and expressed her considerable respect for the effort she was making.[50] This initiative led Aileen to consider the nursing home proposal more seriously but reluctantly, wondering

---

48   Aileen to Helen, 22 November, 11, 21–22 December 1963, Aileen Palmer Papers, NLA MS 6759/1/9; Helen to Aileen, 22 December 1963, Aileen Palmer Papers.
49   Aileen to Frank Davison, 15 February 1964, Davison Papers, NLA MS 1945/1/1782; Aileen to Jessie Macleod, 15 February 1964, Aileen Palmer Papers, NLA MS 6759/3/18.
50   Jessie Macleod to Helen, 3 March 1964, Helen Palmer Papers, NLA MS 6083, Box 3.

CHAPTER 11

whether Nettie had quite reached that stage. While feeling that her mother had in the past sometimes bullied her, Aileen 'couldn't bear her to be in a place where she might be bashed around'.[51]

This anxiety reflected Aileen's view of low prevailing standards in nursing homes in the 1960s. They must find a good nursing home recommended by their family doctor, but they needed to check carefully which nursing home costs they could afford. The family's sense of urgency increased in early April when Nettie talked a good deal about friends who had died: she was 'weak, vague and incoherent' and insisted she felt death was near. Jessie Macleod noted a 'big change for the worse in the last few weeks' and agreed with Helen that Nettie was preparing to die, refusing to eat and 'getting more difficult'.[52]

Fortunately the new housekeeper, Miss Kendall, was 'really good' with Nettie – they could not have hoped for better. Helen, Aileen and Jessie agreed on their joint policy of protecting Nettie's image: 'Nettie has a right to be remembered as she was and anything that blurs that should be concealed as far as possible. This is common justice not hiding of skeletons.' So they needed to censor Nettie's outgoing mail, 'with regard to what she communicates to the outside world'.[53] Aileen was especially concerned about Nettie's propensity to destroy or donate to friends precious papers and manuscripts collected so diligently over the years, as part of moving towards death. This led Aileen to take the drastic step of locking Nettie's filing cabinets to protect what Nettie would once have wanted as her literary

---

51   Aileen to Helen, 13 March 1964, Aileen Palmer Papers, NLA MS 6759/1/9. See Jalland, *Old Age in Australia*, pp. 215-34, on nursing homes from 1954 to 1972.
52   Jessie Macleod to Helen, [c. 4 April] 1964, Helen Palmer Papers, NLA MS 6083, Box 3.
53   Jessie Macleod to Helen, [c. 4 April] 1964.

heritage. Her papers were too rare and valuable to be lost or given away. At one point Aileen found Henry Handel Richardson's letters to Nettie scattered across Nettie's bed.[54]

Aileen felt that caring for her mother in her last years was like looking after a brilliant and precocious but difficult problem child. Nettie had become unsettled and unpredictable since the end of 1963, when 'the time of trouble' commenced, with extreme variations of behaviour. At times she was 'astonishingly physically capable' and hyperactive, pulling books off shelves and scattering them on the floor. At other times she was very low and depressed, either by the effect of a recent drug or an inevitable stage of physical decline. Nettie had nearly stopped reading or trying to express herself in writing and was so restless that it was difficult to keep her entertained; the sisters even considered hiring a television.[55]

During April 1964 the sisters and their advisors began to visit prospective nursing homes, though they agreed not to mention this to Nettie until a suitable home was found. They had several old friends with medical backgrounds willing to advise – Dr Keogh, Dr Dorothea Church and Dr Thompson. They quickly discovered that there was a generational difference in opinion among doctors and friends regarding nursing homes. The younger generation opted for nursing homes, whereas their elders strongly preferred home care where possible.[56] For Helen and Aileen the issue was complex as there was no agreement on the amount of time left to Nettie. Aileen still hoped life would settle down more smoothly now the excellent

---

54   Aileen to Helen, 21 April 1964, Aileen Palmer Papers, NLA MS 6759/1/2.
55   Aileen to Helen, 7, 12, 25 April 1964; Aileen to Kathleen Fitzpatrick, 26 April 1964, Aileen Palmer Papers, NLA MS 6759/1/2, 9.
56   Jessie Macleod to Helen, n.d., Helen Palmer Papers, NLA MS 6083, Box 3.

CHAPTER 11

Miss Kendall had become the new housekeeper.[57] Aileen was anxious about the high cost and the waiting lists of the two best nursing homes they visited, Lancewood and Glenwood. The latter seemed 'a very nice place, with air conditioning ... and a view from the patients' lounge over a pleasant garden'. The matron advised a three-bed ward would be appropriate for Nettie, costing £21 per week, with a government deduction of £7 for chronic patients in registered nursing homes. Their family doctor thought these expenses might be less 'than keeping her at home the way we live now', costing about £25 for the combined maintenance of the house, the housekeeper and Aileen.[58]

Eventually the sisters and their medical advisors settled on a compromise. An appointment was made for Nettie to go into the Geriatric Unit at the Mount Royal Hospital in Parkville, Melbourne, on 22 June 1964 for a geriatric assessment of her condition and needs, and to have crutches fitted.[59] Poetry had now become Nettie's chief intellectual sustenance, so friends read aloud to her the poems of Kath Walker, John Manifold and Nettie's daughter Aileen.[60] Aileen commented that Nettie only existed now on a 'poetic or fairly infantile level'. Dymphna Cusack wrote that 'I realised that life was far from easy for Aileen and this new move may give her some release. It can, alas, no longer distress Nettie'.[61] The social worker explained that the hospital was prepared to keep Nettie for only about a month,

---

57 Aileen to Kathleen Fitzpatrick, 26 April 1964, Aileen Palmer Papers, NLA MS 6759/1/9.
58 Aileen to Helen, 21 April 1964, Helen Palmer Papers, NLA MS 6759/1/2.
59 Aileen to Frank Davison, 10 July 1964, Davison Papers, NLA MS 1945/1/1820. See Jalland, *Old Age in Australia*, pp. 191-214, on geriatric medicine.
60 Aileen to Helen, 12 June 1964, Aileen Palmer Papers, NLA MS 6759/1/1/2.
61 Dymphna Cusack to Frank Davison, Davison Papers, NLA MS 1945/1/1815.

until a place became available at a suitable nursing home. The Mount Royal doctors were kind but said little. Clearly there was little a geriatric unit with an interest in rehabilitation could do for Nettie at this stage.[62]

The two sisters moved their mother to the expensive Harvey Memorial Home in Hawthorn in August 1964 where, as Aileen noted, 'she survives fairly comfortably, that's all'. But their new housekeeper was shocked to hear how much they paid to keep Nettie at Harvey Memorial. The sisters had been obliged to make a hasty decision about nursing homes at Mount Royal's insistence. But they still did not know how long she might live and worried that the costs could well be beyond them. Aileen felt obliged to ask the impossible question, 'How much should we sacrifice to our elders, to no purpose?' Aileen needed to contemplate her own future in a more positive way after the years of looking after their mother.[63]

By 16 September 1964 Nettie was in a 'fairly passive state, in which she is fairly comfortable and free of distress'. On some days she didn't even recognise her daughters, and they communicated by talking baby-talk and singing songs.[64] The sisters discussed the possibility of moving Nettie to a cheaper nursing home. They were currently paying £45 per week for the maintenance of the house, the housekeeper, and Aileen, as well as for the Harvey Memorial Home, which cut savagely into their limited capital. They agreed it felt dreadful to have to discuss these possibilities, 'but the approach of death is grim in any circumstances'.[65]

---

62 Aileen to Helen, 1 July 1964, Aileen Palmer Papers, NLA MS 6759/1/1/2.
63 Aileen to Matron, 3 September 1965, Helen Palmer Papers, NLA MS 6083, Box 2.
64 Aileen to Frank Davison, 16 September 1964, Davison Papers, NLA MS 1945/1/1825.
65 Helen to Aileen, 12 September 1964; Aileen to Helen, 6 September 1964, Helen Palmer Papers, NLA MS 6083, Box 2.

CHAPTER 11

The move to a cheaper nursing home was not necessary, as Nettie Palmer died at the age of 79 on 19 October 1964. Aileen was evidently well enough to take in three students as lodgers afterwards, and devote more time to her own poetry and writing, and making new friends. Not surprisingly, she was utterly exhausted after her mother's long illness, and busy with 'financial affairs, and reorganizing my domestic life'.[66] Aileen was also delighted that 'Nettie's fan-mail has been terrific'. Besides extolling the splendid achievements of Nettie's life and literary career, many condolence letters also recognised Aileen's substantial contribution in caring for her mother in frail old age. There was general agreement with Jessie Macleod's comment that 'Aileen is a wonder. She is coping in the most amazing fashion', at considerable cost to herself.[67]

* * *

In 1957 when Vance Palmer had less than two years to live, he had written to his friend, Katharine Susannah Prichard: 'Getting old is a tragedy: there is always the difficulty of keeping our personal selves intact'.[68] He left in his papers a typescript titled 'Death means this to me'. He noted that death often came gradually, 'filching away bit by bit the qualities that made him himself'. Failure of the body was far less important than 'narrowing in the mind, the tendency to restrict your interests and sympathies'.[69] In this respect Vance himself had been more fortunate than his wife.

---

66 Aileen to K.S. Pritchard, 15 July 1965, Helen Palmer Papers, NLA MS 6083, Box 2.
67 Jessie Macleod to Helen, n.d., ibid., NLA MS 6083, Box 3.
68 Vance to K.S. Prichard, 30 September 1957, NLA MS 1174/1/8912.
69 Vance, 'Death Means This to Me', NLA MS 1174.

The Palmer family had more choices about aged care between the 1920s and 1964 than many other families, and especially compared with the poor in earlier generations who were condemned to harsh institutions. The Palmers lived in Melbourne, close to hospitals and nursing homes. They had access to helpful medical information from several doctors they knew well, and had sufficient means to fund additional domestic and institutional help for elderly parents. They were able to visit and assess a range of nursing homes and the geriatric unit at Mount Royal Hospital. These institutions had serious deficiencies in the 1960s, but at least there was a modicum of choice available. The medical information and support the Palmer sisters received offered reassurance rather than any attempt at rehabilitation. This was consistent with the state of medical knowledge and the limitations of geriatric rehabilitation at Mount Royal in the early 1960s. However, the Palmer family's experiences of ageing clearly demonstrated that the vulnerability of old age was compounded by gender, and that wives and daughters were expected to care for frail elderly parents.

This essay illuminates the critical importance of gender in the historical experience of caring for older people. Women were presumed to be ready to sacrifice their needs and aspirations to the demands of family health. Further, the vulnerability of old age was compounded by gender since all women in the family, including older women, were expected to care for the disabled and infirm. A State or federal home care system didn't exist before the 1950s, and was limited thereafter. Valerie Braithwaite has noted that this 'burden of care' continued for primary carers in the 1970s and 1980s, with a heavy toll on women's privacy, employment prospects and personal health. Female carers often felt guilty, helpless and exhausted, but they

CHAPTER 11

suffered silently in the belief that it was their responsibility alone.[70] As Diane Gibson concluded in 1998, 'Women are the majority of the aged population, the majority of informal carers, the majority of service providers, and the majority of recipients of formal care'.[71]

This essay also acknowledges Geoffrey Bolton's pioneering interest in ageing in Australia, and his recognition of its importance in his biographies and wider studies. Biography in particular enabled Geoffrey to focus on the realities of later life, beyond the historical achievements of his largely male subjects. For example, this focus on ageing was illustrated in his biography of Dick Boyer in 1967, including Boyer's ongoing heart problems; and in his major biography of Edmund Barton in 2000, which dealt with Barton's poor health in his 70s and its effects on his career.[72] Gendered ageing could even be located at street level in *Daphne Street* in 1997, as part of 'The biography of an Australian community'.[73]

Geoffrey's final book in 2014 was characteristically a big biography of another international Western Australian, entitled *Paul Hasluck: A life*.[74] Both Geoffrey and Paul Hasluck lived life to the full for as long as they could. Both had impressive records of scholarly publication up to their deaths, writing prolifically when others might have slowed down. Like Geoffrey, Hasluck was 'still vigorous' past eighty. Hasluck drafted a paper for the Samuel Griffith Society shortly

---

70   Braithwaite, 'Coming to Terms', pp. 20-23.
71   Gibson, *Aged Care*, p. 24.
72   G.C. Bolton, *Dick Boyer: An Australian Humanist* (Canberra: Australian National University Press, 1967), pp. 61, 276, 279–281; Geoffrey Bolton, *Edmund Barton* (Sydney: Allen & Unwin, 2000), pp. 326–37.
73   Geoffrey Bolton, *Daphne Street* (Fremantle: Fremantle Arts Centre Press, 1997), pp. 73–74, 122. The cover page of *Daphne Street* included the sub-title 'The biography of an Australian community', but this sub-title wasn't on the title page.
74   Bolton, *Paul Hasluck*, pp. ii + 575 pp.

before his death in January 1993.⁷⁵ Geoffrey was similarly planning more projects in the months before his death, with contagious enthusiasm and energy. As historians we can all take encouragement in the model of older age which Geoffrey Bolton represented, as well as in his professional recognition and exploration of the importance of older age in his many biographies and other histories.

---

75   Ibid., p. 470.

   I am grateful to Karen Fox for her research assistance; and to John Hooper for his unfailing advice, encouragement and support over many years.

Chapter 12

WESTERN AUSTRALIAN ENTREPRENEURISM

The Life of Deborah Hackett

Lenore Layman

Western Australia is a *Land of Vision and Mirage*. This was Geoffrey Bolton's settled conclusion after a lifetime's reflection on the State's history. He had also long settled on his short history's cover image – one of Antony Gormley's gaunt metallic human figures set under a sunny sky in Lake Ballard's flat expanse of dry salt.[1] As Geoff's readers we are travellers in 'an antique land', seeing the impact of settlers' bold entrepreneurism on both fragile environments and dispossessed Aboriginal people. Environmental damage and human suffering reverberate through the history, each demanding redress if Western Australia is to be truly 'a good society'.[2] Has the entire Westralian project served only 'to pave the way for Alan Bond' and

---

1 *Antony Gormley: Inside Australia* (London: Thames & Hudson, 2005).
2 Bolton's last words in Geoffrey Bolton, *Land of Vision and Mirage: Western Australia since 1826* (Perth: University of Western Australia Press, 2008), p. 206.

fill prisons with Aboriginal people?[3] These questions remain unanswered and insistent at the close of the book.

Nevertheless, *Land of Vision and Mirage* is not predominantly bleak. A succession of visionaries who dream and develop without caution dominate its pages, all enterprising men. They provide the narrative's dynamic.

> Stirling with 'Hesperia', Hordern and the advocates of desert railways, Mitchell with his agricultural enthusiasms, de Garis and Chase the developers, Bond and Connell the bold riders of the 1980s – all allowed their dreams to outreach reality.[4]

And there are many others, more cautious entrepreneurs but still men (and they are all men) who bestride the history: merchant and pastoralist Walter Padbury, 'Monger of York', the Forrest brothers, timber king M.C. Davies, engineer C.Y. O'Connor, Fairbridge boys made good (Tom Ahern, Harry Hearn, Harry Howard), Wesfarmers' John Thomson, Winthrop Hackett, secessionist Keith Watson, Claude de Bernales, big farmer Eric Smart, Tom (the Cheap) Wardle, the most powerful of public servants Russell Dumas, and certainly not least Charles Court; nor should Lang Hancock be missed or Robert Holmes à Court or Brian Burke.

In Geoff's hands these men are enterprising rather than great and are set against others who seek a less developmentally oriented polity. Women are present on the margins, gradually increasing their public role in welfare and the arts but not at the narrative's core as drivers of development. All these West Australians who inhabit the *Land of Vision and Mirage* make it a human history and testify to Geoff's

---

3   Quote from poem by Sir Paul Hasluck; *Land of Vision and Mirage*, p. 186.
4   Bolton, *Land of Vision and Mirage*, p. 204.

CHAPTER 12

forty-year involvement with writing, editing and leading the State's contribution to the *Australian Dictionary of Biography*.

There is no gentry mythmaking in this history, no evidence of sanitising history to commemorate long-ago gentlefolk or honour stalwart pioneers. That has been a strong strand in Western Australian history making; Geoff pointed explicitly to Sir Hal Colebatch's 1929 centennial history and to the activities of the (Royal) Western Australian Historical Society, founded in 1926.[5] Subsequently the community's embrace of family and local history perpetuated the tendency. Geoff was never complicit. Tom Stannage, however, thought otherwise. Speaking to the Royal Western Australian Historical Society in 1976, Tom condemned the dominance of an 'authorised' version of WA's past which he labelled 'the gentry tradition'.[6] He elaborated the critique in 1985 in the context of national attention on the subject;[7] but his target had become 'the gentry or consensus tradition' with 'the pioneer' its central symbol.[8] This definitional expansion drew all previous historians of Western Australia (excluding W.B. Kimberly) into the net: Colebatch, J.S. Battye, Frank Crowley and Geoff himself. Yet from the commencement of his career Geoff explicitly distinguished between the gentry myth and a consensus view of WA history. He rejected the former, labelling it 'Cranford-on-the-Swan', while embracing the latter.[9] It seems a fair distinction

---

5   G.C. Bolton, 'Western Australia Reflects on its Past', in C.T. Stannage (ed.), *A New History of Western Australia* (Perth: University of Western Australia Press, 1981) pp. 682-83.
6   Tom Stannage, 'Uncovering Poverty in Australian History', *Early Days*, 7 (1976), pp. 90-106.
7   John Hirst, 'The Pioneer Legend', *Historical Studies*, 18, 71 (1978); as well as Judith Godden's and Marilyn Lake's articles in *Hecate*, 1979 and 1981.
8   C.T. Stannage, *Western Australia's Heritage: The Pioneer Myth* (Perth: University Extension, 1985), pp. 18.
9   G.C. Bolton, 'Review: Cranford-on-the-Swan?', *Labour History*, 4 (1963), pp. 52-54.

to make and for those of us who analyse Western Australian histories to maintain.

Geoff's consensus view began from a premise he never abandoned:

> We Sandgropers ... like to assume that our society was significantly different from Eastern Australia, especially before the gold-rushes of the nineties, but even to some extent until the Second World War.[10]

His inclination was always to see Australian history as 'a mosaic of diverse regional experience'.[11] The jurisdiction of Western Australia was one piece of the mosaic. And that piece, he insisted, was different from those of the eastern States. He concluded *A Fine Country to Starve In* (1972) with a summary of WA's distinctiveness: 'a relatively less stratified and possibly more mobile society' with 'opportunity to prosper by one's own honest efforts and to gain acceptance among the elite'; 'an undeveloped land of opportunity, open to all' with 'no strong sense of class antagonism' but rather a 'sense of common involvement'.[12] Assembling such a formulaic list risks over-simplification. It certainly obscures the subtlety of Geoff's position, which is well captured in the book's title – *A Fine Country to Starve In*. He savoured Edward Shann's words, using them again for the interwar chapter of his short history. Their irony conveyed so precisely both men's warm regard for the place juxtaposed with their awareness of its failings and the suffering these imposed.

---

10 Bolton, 'Cranford-on-the-Swan?', p. 54.
11 G.C. Bolton, 'The Belly and the Limbs', Augustus Wolskel Memorial Lecture delivered to the Royal Historical Society of Victoria, *Victorian Historical Journal*, 53, 1 (1982), p. 6.
12 G.C. Bolton, *A Fine Country tto Starve In* (Perth: University of Western Australia Press, 1972), pp. 268-69.

CHAPTER 12

A review essay in 1977 on Paul Hasluck's early-life autobiography *Mucking About* gave Geoff an opportunity to reiterate the importance of regional diversity at a time when national identity was a popular historical research topic. 'Western Australia was different', he insisted. Hasluck's view of the society in which he grew up and his understanding of his family's history coincided with Geoff's own: that WA was 'a secure, confident, and tolerant society, accessible to those who wished to improve themselves and their community'. Perhaps this 'self-concept' was an idealisation of the past, a community myth but nevertheless it was widely held, he stated.[13]

At this point 'the Bolton–Hasluck' thesis was created; in Geoff's view a straw man.[14] Attacks on the thesis climaxed in an issue of *Studies in Western Australian History* (1990) on the inter-war years, which assembled a series of articles by younger historians who argued that social conflict and exclusion were as much a part of the State's history as consensus and inclusion, that class mattered and a lively working-class culture existed, that conservative forces were adept at 'manufacturing consensus', and that overall WA was not different from the rest of the country.[15] There were necessary historical correctives in these articles, some of which Geoff acknowledged, although in his introduction to the new edition of *A Fine Country to Starve In* (1994) he expressed surprise (and apparent exasperation) that his history had been judged a 'conservative interpretation'. He

---

13 G.C. Bolton, 'A Local Identity: Paul Hasluck and Western Australian Self Concept', *Westerly*, 22, 4 (1977), pp. 71-77.

14 Tom Stannage, review of Stuart Macintyre, *Militant: The Life and Times of Paddy Troy*, in *Historical Studies*, 22, 86 (1986), pp. 154-55; G.C. Bolton, *A Fine Country to Starve In*, 2nd edn (Perth: University of Western Australia Press in association with Edith Cowan University, 1994), p. xvii.

15 Jenny Gregory (ed.), *Western Australia Between the Wars 1919–1939*, *Studies in Western Australian History*, 11 (1990).

acknowledged the new research but believed his interpretation had not been seriously undermined. 'On the whole I stick by my analysis of 1972.'[16]

And stick by it he continued to do. When he returned at the end of his career to distill the essence of Western Australia's past in *Land of Vision and Mirage*, his account of social relations until the middle of the twentieth century was unchanged: a 'clannish sense of fundamentally shared identity of interest seems to have formed an effective social cement'.[17] Even more central to his short history, however, was another Western Australian characteristic he had earlier identified and applauded – that opportunity was open to all men and boys of initiative and enterprise, no matter their humble birth or early poverty. 'Self-made men and their families who prospered more than their peers' formed Western Australia's elite but they did not found dynasties.[18] Merchants, farmers, pastoralists, land developers and businessmen – they all rose and fell in their time, leaving 'a residue of modest growth' and a relatively homogeneous society.[19] The history most sharply captures the opportunity afforded ambitious energetic individuals for significant influence in a small society.

So the *Land of Vision and Mirage* drawn by Geoff at the close of his career remained in large part a good society, although one weakened by the massive damage brought to both the First Peoples and the fragile natural environment of the place. For one reviewer who declared herself a t'othersider, however, Western Australia remained a puzzling and unattractive place. 'Dig it up, cut it down, sell it, carry it

---

16 Bolton, *A Fine Country to Starve In*, 2nd edn, pp. xvii-xxii.
17 Bolton, *Land of Vision and Mirage*, p. 3.
18 Bolton, *Land of Vision and Mirage*, pp. 53-55.
19 Bolton, *Land of Vision and Mirage*, p. 1.

CHAPTER 12

away and move on', how did this constitute a good society? Economic dependence on extractive industries was unappealing and the society it fostered perplexing.[20] The comment points to the major gap in Geoff's history making: an almost total inattention to that most important of WA industries – mining. The greatest of the gold booms, which began in the 1880s, is dealt with in six pages, when the eastern goldfields were second only to the Witwatersrand in international gold production and for a time the world's leader in metallurgical innovation; at the same time the largest and most cosmopolitan towns were located on the fields. The mine managers and metallurgists who shaped the boom are missing, chief among them George Ridgway, Charles Kaufman, George Klug, Ludwig Diehl, John Agnew and Bewick Moreing's managers.[21] Gold mining was an international industry: British companies and investment capital, managers drawn from overseas and the flow of wealth out of WA.

The mineral boom of the 1960s beginning with the big four Pilbara iron ore ventures (Hamersley Range, Mount Newman, Cleveland Cliffs and Mount Goldsworthy) is even more difficult to integrate fully into a short history of the State. These joint venture partners not only answered to boardrooms far away but their managers remained almost completely anonymous to Western Australians. Perhaps some even imagined Lang Hancock developed iron ore ventures! Only when Charles Copeman took on the Pilbara's 1980s industrial relations regime did a mining executive emerge to public prominence or, in many quarters, infamy.

---

20 Beverley Kingston, review of *Land of Vision and Mirage*, in *Studies in Western Australian History*, 27 (2011), p. 208.
21 Denis A. Cumming and Richard G. Hartley, *Westralian Founders of Twentieth Century Mining* (Perth: R.G. Hartley, 2014).

The mining industry ill-fitted Geoff's Western Australian history making, as it had the State's earlier general historians. Western Australia has been a society of small population where individuals and families became well known to one another, often across generations, and networks of kinship and friendship bonded people in at least an appearance of social agreement. The State's historians, no less than other Sandgropers, became part of the circle, only W.B. Kimberly passing through so swiftly as to remain an outsider-observer. The individuals and family groups who developed the farms, pastoral stations and urban businesses, Geoff's men of enterprise, all became prominent in the fabric of WA society, their personalities and behaviours a recognised part of the narrative. Mining capital and management did not live in this world and corporate structures masked individual decision-making. It is no wonder mining has been relatively invisible.

Geoff died with a large body of completed work to his name but also with a list of planned projects he was looking forward to tackling. One of these projects, perhaps surprisingly, was a biography of a woman who was categorised in her 1983 *Australian Dictionary of Biography* entry as, in part, a mining company director.[22] Regrettably we will never know what he would have made of the subject. My account below is intended to follow Geoff's biographical path to explore this lively and entrepreneurial woman who went by four names across her seventy-eight years of life – Deborah Drake-Brockman, Lady Hackett, Lady Moulden and Dr Buller Murphy. She figured in Geoff's talk entitled 'Vision & Mirage: Celebrating Entrepreneurial

---

22 'Who Are You? Geoffrey Bolton', 720 ABC radio interview, 18 September 2012. www.abc.net.au/local/audio/2012/09/18/3592467.htm, accessed 25 August 2016; Alexandra Hasluck, 'Deborah Vernon Hackett (1887–1965)', *Australian Dictionary of Biography*, vol. 9 (Melbourne: Melbourne University Press, 1983), pp. 149-50.

CHAPTER 12

Spirit in WA' at a 2011 fundraising function held among the treasures of the Kerry Stokes Art Gallery in support of the establishment of a Chair in Western Australian History at the University of Western Australia. On that occasion he sketched five pen portraits selected from the many energetic entrepreneurs who people his short history: Stirling, Padbury, Alex Forrest, de Bernales, Wardle and then one woman – Deborah Hackett.[23] As we shall see, she sits comfortably among this coterie of bold dreamers. Perhaps her ambitious energy and public achievement engaged Geoff's interest; but he might also have seen that her sharp individualism highlighted both the strongly gendered constraints of early twentieth-century elite society and the cultural colonialism within which she shaped her identity. It is in these contexts that I will explore her life.

* * *

Deborah Vernon Drake-Brockman was born on 18 June 1887 into the colonial elite, the fourth child of Frederick Slade Drake-Brockman and his wife Grace Vernon, née Bussell. The Bussell and Brockman/Drake-Brockman families were members of that 'handful' of families 'bound together by marriage, friendship and social intimacy' who dominated nineteenth century Western Australia. As Frank Crowley insisted, the colony was a sharply classed society from its birth with land ownership, social privilege and political influence accruing to this upper class.[24] Tom Stannage argued further that the colony's object was 'to let money make money'. He included the Brockmans

---

[23] 'Vision & Mirage: Celebrating Entrepreneurial Spirit in WA', University of Western Australia, event invitation, 29 November 2011; personal recall.
[24] F.K. Crowley, *Australia's Western Third: A History of Western Australia* (Melbourne: Heinemann, 1960), pp. 25-26.

and Bussells in his list of 'family dynasties' which prospered from their initial capital, indentured labour, familial and social connections, and official patronage.²⁵ A process of social control, he argued fiercely, secured these families' position in the colony into the twentieth century. The gold rushes, ongoing from the 1880s with their flood of t'othersiders and new radical voices, triggered the first public criticism of the power and privilege of these families. Newly arrived Irish lawyer John Horgan labelled them the 'Six Hungry Families', to the delight of Perth crowds.²⁶ He mocked their kin interconnections, saying that he had begun to sketch their genealogical tree but couldn't 'get a piece of canvas large enough'.²⁷ The cry was taken up and amplified around the goldfields where the 'Old Six-Fam'ly Gropers' became the regular butt of satire.²⁸ Sir John Kirwan described them as 'an oligarchy' whilst noting that there were more than six of them.²⁹

Geoff Bolton saw these families somewhat differently. He did not deny the existence of 'established ruling circles' but saw a 'ladder of opportunity' allowing entrée to talented young men of 'modest background'. Western Australia was not rich enough to have 'dynasties', he concluded, suggesting that notable families mostly retained intergenerational social status but not substantial wealth or power.³⁰ In one of his most influential publications concerning 'The Idea of

---

25   C.T. Stannage, *The People of Perth: A Social History of Western Australia's Capital City* (Perth: Perth City Council, 1979), pp. 12-25.
26   *Western Mail* (Perth), 12 June 1886, p. 43; Tom Stannage, 'John Horgan (1834–1907)', *Australian Dictionary of Biography*, vol. 9, p. 367.
27   Horgan speaking at election rally, *The West Australian*, 19 May 1888, p. 3.
28   See, for instance, the columns 'A Mingled Yarn' and 'Groperdom Gossip', *Sun* (Kalgoorlie).
29   Sir John Kirwan, *My Life's Adventure* (London: Eyre & Spottiswoode, 1936) ch. 3.
30   Bolton, *Land of Vision and Mirage*, pp. 31, 53.

a Colonial Gentry' across four centuries of imperial expansion, he identified a recurring characteristic of these gentry: they were 'just close enough to establishment in gentility to feel the pangs of deprivation most acutely'.[31] And so it was in Western Australia, with the Bussells and Brockmans and other similar families. They chose migration in order to preserve their social status and improve their material fortunes, forming a society that Geoff labelled 'shabby-genteel'. They were 'would-be gentry', not the real thing.[32]

The widow, five sons and three daughters of deceased Hampshire cleric, William Bussell, full of learning and social graces but unable to support themselves at home, migrated to maintain their social standing. They settled at the Vasse, where they struggled to make anything more than a modest living but were able to retain their social status for several generations. Edward Shann's account, published in 1926, of the Bussells' first colonising years uses their own words to record their view of themselves as rare 'gentle settlers' and to vividly picture their world. He concluded that the Busselton they created was 'an English Tory village' which 'dreamed on, aloof' as the nineteenth century progressed.[33] Sixth son of this family, Alfred Pickmore Bussell with his wife Ellen, grandparents of Deborah Drake-Brockman, worked hard at 'Broadwater', 'Ellensbrook' and 'Wallcliffe', to ensure a patrimony for their two surviving sons and good marriages for six of their seven daughters.[34] It was a continuing

---

31 G.C. Bolton, 'The Idea of a Colonial Gentry', *Historical Studies*, 13, 51 (1968), pp. 312, 319.
32 Bolton, *Land of Vision and Mirage*, ch. 1.
33 E.O.G. Shann, *Cattle Chosen: The Story of the First Group Settlement in Western Australia 1829 to 1841* (1st edn, London: Oxford University Press, 1926; facsimile edn, Perth: University of Western Australia Press, 1978), pp. 18, 142-43.
34 Wendy Birman, 'Alfred Pickmore Bussell (1816–1882)', *Australian Dictionary of Biography*, vol. 3 (1969), pp. 310-12.

struggle; and they were not alone, one observer recalling that many elite families were 'rather hard up, maintaining exalted social positions on inadequate incomes'.[35] Daughter Grace married well in 1882 when she wed Frederick Slade Brockman.[36] As a sixteen-year old, Grace had already won fame by riding into the surf at Margaret River on 2 December 1876 with Aboriginal stockman Sam Isaacs to rescue shipwrecked passengers from the *SS Georgette*. By the time the press had finished reporting the disaster she had become Western Australia's Grace Darling.[37] Whether such a title was warranted, Grace was clearly a person of initiative and courage.

Grace's husband and Deborah's father, Frederick (Fred) Slade Brockman (who resumed the family name of Drake-Brockman in later life), was a grandson of William Locke Brockman, who with wife and ten progeny founded the Brockman/Drake-Brockman family in Western Australia, together with his younger brother Robert James with his wife and eleven children. W.L. Brockman arrived in early 1830 as a young farmer with sufficient capital to claim a land grant of 20,160 acres in Upper Swan.[38] He was the fifth son and Robert the ninth son of a Kentish cleric's fourteen children. Migration enhanced the wealth and social standing of this junior branch of an old Kentish family of landowners, clerics, military and naval

---

35   H.V. Howe to A.F. Drake-Brockman, 30 June 1971, quoted in Alan Jackson (compiler), *Brockman & Drake-Brockman Family Tree: The Australian Branch 1830–1993* (Perth: Alan Jackson, 1994), p. 21.

36   *The West Australian*, 3 March 1882, p. 3.

37   *Argus* (Melbourne), 28 December 1876, p. 7; *Inquirer & Commercial News* (Perth), 31 January 1877, p. 3, 14 February 1877, p. 3, 23 January 1878, p. 1; *Western Australian Times* (Perth), 4 January 1878, p. 2; *Herald* (Fremantle), 9 February 1878, p. 3.

38   Rica Erickson (gen. ed.), *The Bicentennial Dictionary of Western Australians pre-1829–1888*, vol. 1 (Perth: University of Western Australia Press, 1987), pp. 321-25.

CHAPTER 12

officers, and colonial civil servants.[39] The family's economic successes (although there were as many failures) as well as official preferments, civic positions, advantageous marriages and complex kin interconnections are laid out well in numerous entries on the National Centre of Biography's biographical websites and in published family trees.[40] Frederick Slade Brockman, for instance, pursued a successful government career as a surveyor, explorer and board member, eventually becoming Western Australia's Surveyor General.[41]

Deborah Drake-Brockman was born into this large Brockman-Bussell kinship network. She was the middle child of seven, all born between 1882 and 1891: twins Enid and Fredericka (Rica), Edmund, Geoffrey, Deborah, Allan and Karl. According to brother Geoffrey, growing up at Guildford in the last decades of the nineteenth century was like living in 'a small country town' and theirs was a happy home, 'full of kids, kids' friends and family pets' with relatives and friends staying for long periods and a mother for whom 'growing things and making things was the order of life'. Both parents told their children stories of their own early lives and the children stayed for extended periods in 'Bussell country' at family homes 'Wallcliffe', 'Ellensbrook' and 'Burnside'. In old age Deborah described her youthful self as an adventurous child of the bush: 'revelling in an open air life, riding horseback and helping to drove cattle among tall timber, and exploring the caves that abound in that part of the country'.[42] This rural colonial persona and pride in her Bussell-Brockman heritage

---

39   David Henry Drake-Brockman, *Record of the Brockman and Drake-Brockman Family* (Lindfield, Sussex: D.H. Drake-Brockman, 1936), pp. 44-54.
40   Jackson, *Brockman & Drake-Brockman Family Tree: The Australian Branch 1830–1993*.
41   Wendy Birman, 'Frederick Slade Drake-Brockman (1857–1917)', *Australian Dictionary of Biography*, vol. 8 (1981), pp. 340-41.
42   Deborah Buller-Murphy, *An Attempt to Eat the Moon* (Melbourne: Georgian House, 1958), Foreword.

were central to her identity. Those who knew her as a young woman recalled her individualism, energy, beauty and charm. Brother Geoffrey remembered the young Deb as always 'an individualist' with 'temperament'.[43] One youthful admirer who ventured to advise her on how to handle a cow she was milking was showered with a bucket of milk.[44] She was destined for an elite marriage like her mother and older sisters rather than a professional career like her father and brothers.

In 1905, aged eighteen, Deborah 'disturbed' the family by choosing to marry Winthrop Hackett MLC, one of the most influential West Australians of his time, both wealthy and eminently respectable, but forty years her senior.[45] He was 'not good-looking' and 'something of a recluse', a bachelor and conservative urban gentleman in manner and lifestyle.[46] It proved an exceptionally wise choice. The couple's decision to wed at St Mary's Church, Busselton, followed the tradition of Deborah's mother and maternal grandmother, while the honeymoon at the newly built Caves House at Yallingup made them among the first to use what became an immensely popular destination for newlyweds.[47] Hackett was the main promoter and developer of the caves and Deborah had enjoyed them as a girl.[48] For him it

---

[43] Geoffrey Drake-Brockman, *The Turning Wheel* (Perth: Paterson Brokensha, 1960), ch. 1.

[44] H.V. Howe to A.F. Drake-Brockman, 30 June 1971, quoted in Jackson, *Brockman & Drake-Brockman Family Tree*, p. 21.

[45] Drake-Brockman, *The Turning Wheel*, pp. 36-37; Lyall Hunt, 'Sir John Winthrop Hackett (1848–1916)', *Australian Dictionary of Biography*, vol. 9 (1983), pp. 150-53.

[46] M.L. Skinner, *The Fifth Sparrow: An Autobiography* (Sydney: Sydney University Press, 1972), pp. 40-42.

[47] *Southern Times* (Bunbury), 5 August 1905, p. 5.

[48] Alexander Collins, '"A Veritable Augustus": The Life of John Winthrop Hackett, Newspaper Proprietor, Politician and Philanthropist (1848–1916)', Ph.D. thesis, Murdoch University, 2007, p. 363.

CHAPTER 12

was a 'marriage de convenience';[49] she was 'deeply in love' and those around them observed a 'blissfully happy' marriage.[50] Five children – Verna, Joan, Patricia, John and Deborah – were born between 1906 and 1913.

The family lived in St Georges Terrace on the corner of Milligan St in central Perth, where Hackett had built a splendid home for himself in the mid-1890s among what newspaperman Victor Courtney recalled as the 'dignity and affluence' of 'most of Perth's aristocracy'.[51] Demolished in 1958 at the beginning of the end of the Terrace's gracious colonial buildings, it was three-storeyed with twenty-five rooms and featured a marble staircase with carved mulga-wood balustrades.[52] Hackett was a keen supporter of the arts and covered the walls with his art collection. The house proved an ideal venue for many 'wonderful parties' and 'at homes', a whirl of social activity interrupted only by the children's births and the couple's frequent travels.[53] Deborah greatly enjoyed the role of society hostess, as her husband unhappily reported in a letter to a friend in 1907:

> We are having the usual round, an endless one, of entertainments, sometimes four in a day. It has become quite noxious to me, but my wife enjoys it with the whole-hearted delight of a young woman to whom everything is unfamiliar and delightful.[54]

---

49 Hackett to Walter James, 15 July 1905, quoted in Collins, 'The Life of John Winthrop Hackett', p. 310.
50 Skinner, *The Fifth Sparrow*, p. 42; Peter J. Boyce, 'The Hon. Sir J. Winthrop Hackett KCMG Hon LLD: His Life and Times', PR14514/HAC, item 3, p. 9, State Library of Western Australia (SLWA).
51 Victor Courtney, *Perth – and All This! A Story about a City* (Sydney: Halstead, 1962), pp. 278-79.
52 'Notes on the home of J.W. Hackett', RN 558, SLWA.
53 Drake-Brockman, *The Turning Wheel*, p. 37. Concert program, 'Dr and Mrs Hackett, At Home', 22 October 1909, PR14514/HAC, SLWA.
54 Hackett to Walter James; quoted in Collins, 'The Life of John Winthrop Hackett', p. 314.

Deborah's choices of frock, food, entertainment and floral decoration were regularly reported. A lively hostess, on one occasion she held a guessing competition where all the answers 'had to be given in the name of a fish'. She entertained lavishly, with an eye to visual beauty: 'every nook and corner of the house seemed filled with beautiful flowers and beautiful pictures'.[55] A dance (with progressive bridge for the non-dancers) christened the newly added ballroom in 1908: the ante-room 'full of art treasures and masses of violets and daffodils', the walls of the ballroom 'hung with beautiful paintings' and tables in the dining room and on the enclosed verandah covered with 'pale pink almond blossom in tall silver epergnes and the daintiest of refreshments'. The guests were an assemblage of the most successful of the gentry families.[56] Two years later the ballroom turned into a music room for son John's christening party, which included a concert with the baby in a cradle in an alcove at the end of the room in 'a perfect bower of lovely waterlilies and roses, intermingled with fern'.[57] Her children were generally present, beautifully dressed, well behaved and apparently much admired.

The Hackett home operated with a formality which Hackett had earlier instituted and was maintained by a staff of servants supervised by a housekeeper.[58] Service positions in the household were specialised – a nanny running the nursery, cook and kitchen staff, parlourmaids, housemaids, laundry maid, coachman and later chauffeur.[59]

---

55 *Western Mail*, 16 April 1910, p. 56, 30 October 1909, p. 41.
56 *The West Australian*, 4 August 1908, p. 7.
57 *Western Mail*, 17 December 1910, p. 19.
58 Skinner, *The Fifth Sparrow*, ch. 6.
59 'Situation Vacant', *The West Australian*, 19 March 1910, p. 16, 30 July 1910, 25 August 1914, p. 10, 23 October 1914, p. 10, 16 February 1917, p. 12, 5 March 1917, p. 10.

CHAPTER 12

The Hacketts' summer seaside residence at Mandurah also required staff. One young maid, fresh from Perth Girls' Orphanage in 1908, reported her pleasure at living and working there with two other maids.[60] The absence of most domestic responsibilities allowed the young wife and mother freedom to pursue her community interests.

Deborah did a surprisingly long and chatty interview for *The West Australian* following the family's return from the Imperial Press Conference in London in 1909. It revealed a vivacious young woman, supremely confident in her good looks, charm and social position. The *Truth* judged her 'a giddy gusher' whilst the *Sunday Times* mocked her naivety: 'Mrs Hackett had a perfectly ripping time, and we're so pleased, don't you know, to learn all about her little triumphs and to know that she met only the Very Best People'.[61] There was indeed a streak of snobbery and youthful insensitivity in the twenty-two-year-old. The Countess of Warwick was described as 'a big woman, and a Socialist' whose home had 'mauve blankets on the bed in the mauve room, and pink ones in the pink room. Fancy being a Socialist, and having mauve blankets.' Deborah was fascinated by the suffragettes but offended to have been thought one. She had empathy with a man who told her of his 'dream children', he and his wife so desperate for a family after ten years of marriage that they had together invented one; but, although his story moved her, that did not stop her repeating it publicly in detail. Yet there was also energy and quick intelligence in her observations. The naval review amazed her: 'travelling along 18 miles of battleships on one of those soft quiet grey days, when there is no colour anywhere on sea or sky'. She attended as

---

60 Leah Langoulant, 'My Letter Bag', *Daily News*, 5 December 1908, p. 10.
61 *Truth* (Perth), 25 September 1909, p. 4; *Sunday Times* (Perth), 26 September 1909, p. 6.

many concerts as she could and delighted in Luisa Tetrazzini's beautiful voice.[62] Deborah was maturing, blessed with a successful marriage, affluence and healthy children. The title of Lady was a happy addition when her husband was knighted in 1911.

An interest in fine arts was fostered by her husband's strong support for both the Art Gallery of Western Australia and the Society of Arts. Deborah instituted a prize for figure drawing at the Society of Arts in 1906 and annually presented prizes with her husband. Although she did not exhibit, she took up china painting, keeping some decorated bowls and plates among her personal possessions and eventually giving sixteen pieces to the Art Gallery of WA in 1962.[63] Her choice of wildflowers as decoration was a popular one among her circle of genteel ladies.[64] Singing was another accomplishment, her brother suggesting that she could have pursued a professional career.[65] In fact she confined her public singing to fundraising efforts among her coterie.

Deborah mirrored her husband in her conservative philanthropy. She became a fundraiser for chosen causes after her childbearing was completed. These causes were initially all children's charities: Perth Girls' Orphanage, the Child's Immigration Farm at Pinjarra, Lady Lawley Cottage by the Sea, the Charity Organisation Society, the Children's Protection Society and the Children's Hospital.[66] She worked her long list of social contacts to raise funds with stalls, at

---

62 'Adrienne', 'The Press Conference, from a Woman's Point Of View: An Interview with Mrs Hackett', *The West Australian*, 21 September 1909, p. 3.
63 Deborah Hackett, 12 Plates and 4 Bowls, 1962/00C1-00C16; registration list, Art Gallery of Western Australia; with thanks to Eileen Challis.
64 Des Cowley, 'Women's Work: Illustrating the Natural Wonders of the Colonies', *La Trobe Journal*, 69 (2002), pp. 15-18.
65 Drake-Brockman, *The Turning Wheel*, p. 24.
66 *The West Australian*, 9 October 1908, p. 2, 8 November 1912, p. 6.

CHAPTER 12

homes and concerts. On one occasion in 1913 she directed an 'Oriental play with Eastern music, with Eastern dancers', titled 'Dream Faces', at His Majesty's for a benefit concert.[67] In 1915, copying a successful British model, she introduced the street appeal as a fundraising strategy, establishing the Queen Alexandra Rose Club which was charged with holding an annual appeal in aid of the Children's Hospital.[68] She was also patroness of the Wattle Day League, which raised funds for the Children's Protection Society.[69] Along with many of her friends, she joined the King Edward Memorial Hospital for Women Committee, lobbied hard for the hospital's establishment and became a major fundraiser. When the hospital was finally opened in 1916 she was appointed president of the Official Visiting and Advisory Board (which took the place of a board of management because the government could not bring itself to give a committee of women the usual board power).[70] When war came, her fundraising widened to include the French Red Cross.[71] Paddy's Markets, food, flower and clothing stalls, at homes, concerts and balls – she was busy organising them all.

Deborah's embrace of the role of Lady Bountiful became a key component of her identity for the rest of her life. She crafted her philanthropy precisely – to focus on children and hospitals, to raise money rather than minister directly to those in need and to lead targeted fundraising projects rather than become enmeshed in the

---

67 *Western Mail*, 4 October 1913, p. 11, 24 October 1913, p. 44.
68 *The West Australian*, 25 March 1915, p. 8; *Western Mail*, 23 April 1915, p. 2.
69 *Daily News* (Perth), 1 December 1916, p. 5.
70 Jennie and Bevan Carter, *King Eddies: A History of Western Australia's Premier Women's Hospital 1916–2006* (Perth: King Edward Memorial Hospital Alumni, 2016), pp. 24-39.
71 *South Western Advertiser* (Perth), 22 December 1916, p. 3.

[ongoing] organisational life of any of the many women's charitable associations. Thus she remained free of routine administrative strictures and settled ways of doing things; she could exercise personal control of projects, try out her bright ideas, set targets and work hard towards them within limited timeframes. Her independence was therefore uncompromised and her inclination to the spectacular generally met.

Deborah's life changed dramatically on 19 February 1916 with the sudden death of her husband. Loss of the man who had been her guide through her transition to adulthood as well as her husband must have been a shock, although it was cushioned by the assurance of financial security. She was left with five children aged three to ten. A new arrival in Western Australia in 1882, Hackett had prospered greatly in both wealth and influence as editor and co-owner, then owner of *The West Australian* newspaper and as a politician. He was one of Geoff Bolton's men of enterprise who rose to join WA's 'ruling circles', in death leaving a family whose members had successful careers (beyond WA) but creating no family dynasty. Hackett's will left the family provided for, with Deborah bequeathed the two properties on St George's Terrace and the Mandurah house and their furnishings, £20,000 for investment and an annual income for life or until re-marriage. The children were also each left secure. Then, after a series of gratuities, the greater part of the residue of the estate was left to the University of Western Australia. This residue was not expected to be large but by 1926, when Hackett's newspapers were sold, its value had grown and the university received nearly half a million pounds.[72] In old age Professor Walter Murdoch indiscreetly

---

72 J.S Battye, 'Sir Winthrop Hackett and What We Owe Him', 30 October 1945, 6WF radio script, PR14514/HAC/2 SLWA.

CHAPTER 12

revealed that at this point widow Deborah wished to challenge the will but was dissuaded by her lawyers.[73]

Public life was resumed with the publication five months later of her edited book *The Australian Household Guide* which ran to 1,136 pages and covered every topic of household management from recipes, gardening and poultry-keeping to personal appearance, home nursing and 'what young people should know', with all its proceeds directed to charities.[74] It seems Deborah could do nothing by halves.[75] Although the publication did not become a popular cookery book (like the Golden Wattle or CWA cook books), it proved sufficiently profitable for her to revise and re-publish it in 1940 with the costs of production covered by the fifty-nine firms which paid to advertise in it. Profits were directed to the Red Cross.[76]

Deborah did not take long to re-marry. In October 1917 she became engaged to an Adelaide solicitor and civic figure, Frank Beaumont (Bay) Moulden, and, preparatory to moving to South Australia, sold her three WA properties with furnishings at year's end.[77] Moulden was a forty-one-year-old bachelor, a respected member of a prominent Adelaide legal family and partner in the family firm.[78] They married in April 1918 and Deborah became Lady Hackett-Moulden until her new husband was knighted in 1922, when she mostly

---

73 Walter Murdoch interview, *Pelican*, 18 April 1957; I am indebted to Gillian Lilleyman for this reference.
74 Lady Hackett (ed.), *The Australian Household Guide* (Perth: E.S. Wigg & Son, 1916); advertised for sale in *Western Mail*, 24 November 1916, p. 50.
75 Prue Joske, 'Lady Hackett's Household Guide', *Early Days*, 8, 2 (1978), pp. 68-83.
76 Deborah Buller Murphy, *Lady Hackett's Household Guide*, 2nd edn (Melbourne: Robertson & Mullens, 1940).
77 'For Sale', *Kalgoorlie Miner*, 17 November 1917, p. 7; *Sunday Times*, 10 February 1918, p. 11.
78 Elizabeth Kwan, 'Sir Frank Beaumont Moulden (1876–1932)', *Australian Dictionary of Biography*, vol. 10 (1986), pp. 600-1.

adopted the simpler title of Lady Moulden. In Adelaide she reprised her roles as wife and mother, hostess and charitable fundraiser. The zenith came as Lady Mayoress (1919–21) with the Prince of Wales' visit in 1920, when she organised two grand balls where the flowers, lighting and entertainments were a source of wonder. Supper included boar's head, sucking pigs, turkeys, chickens and hams; while decorated paper caps for dancers to don cascaded from six suspended giant bonbons onto the merrymakers. The second of the balls (with jazz orchestra) was for young people and was particularly enjoyed. Both balls were social triumphs.[79]

Philanthropic fundraising again engaged much of her energy. She took the presidency of several organisations – the National Council of Women, the Adelaide Hospital Women's Auxiliary and the Women's Charity Organisation – and coordinated a Carnival of Flowers at the Palais Royal in 1921,[80] as well as a succession of concerts, dances, fairs, fetes and street appeals – all for good causes: hospitals and maternity homes, sick children and invalid ex-servicemen.[81] Deborah had a talent for organising innovative and spectacular events, most visually beautiful and always entertaining. She could sell a fundraising idea, plan the occasion meticulously and coordinate multiple partners. She fully engaged in promoting each project and then worked hands-on at the event itself, proving herself a consummate fundraiser, organiser and, in that sphere, community leader.

This pattern of activity continued through the 1920s to the mid-1930s, although there were long absences as Deborah took her

---

79   *Mail* (Adelaide), 17 July 1920, p. 13; *Observer* (Adelaide), 24 July 1920, p. 39.
80   *Register* (Adelaide), 3 September 1921, p. 8.
81   *News* (Adelaide), 28 Sept 1928, p. 15.

CHAPTER 12

daughters to London for the season and maintained an establishment there.[82] In North Adelaide she re-created homes similar to the one she had enjoyed as a young wife in Perth. The last of them, in Brougham Place, contained twenty rooms, including a ballroom and staff quarters.[83] She named each house (and her subsequent residences in Melbourne) 'Lordello' after the Irish birthplace of her first husband. A retinue of servants was employed and 'At Lordello' became a regular item of Adelaide social news: children's parties, bridge parties, dances and concerts, morning and afternoon teas, luncheons and dinner parties, receptions, cocktail parties and debutant balls.[84] Entertaining was done in the same lavish style as Perth society had seen – a beautiful home full of rich furnishings, masses of flowers, the best of food and lively entertainment. Deborah's fame as a society hostess spread interstate.

After what seems to have been a second happy marriage, she was widowed again in April 1932. Sir Frank Moulden, who married only once and had no children, left her his entire estate valued at £37,000 to add to her previous investments. Aged 45 and an independently wealthy woman with children reaching adulthood, Deborah was free to pursue new ventures and did so with her usual imaginative verve, throwing herself into entrepreneurial mining activities in northern Australia. She also planned further book publishing, intending to interweave her family history with Aboriginal legends and language. Both these ventures brought the arc of her life back to its Western Australian colonial origins. The northern mining ventures expressed

---

82   *News*, 3 May 1927, p. 6.
83   'Auctions', *Advertiser* (Adelaide), 15 June 1936, p. 4.
84   See Adelaide newspapers – *Advertiser, Mail, News, Critic, Register, Chronicle* – all reporting these 'Lordello' occasions, 1919–36.

a colonial belief in bold northern development, which had underlain her father's surveying expedition to the 'unknown district' of the northwest Kimberley in 1901.[85] And her appropriation of stories of 'the Dordenup tribe' (the Wardandi dialect group of the Noongar people) from the Margaret River district (also Bussell country) reproduced those told by her Bussell mother, aunts and uncle. Both these activities in later life indicate the longevity and lingering afterlife of the colonialism in which Deborah had been raised and which she embraced as a valorising life narrative.

Deborah's third husband, Basil Buller Murphy, a Melbourne barrister (and later judge) whom she married in June 1936, provided insight into her self-identity in a booklet he wrote as 'BBM' – *A Lady of Rare Metal* (1949).[86] It was a paean of praise to his wife whom he presented as an exceptional creature intent on developing the resources of the outback in bold and adventurous spirit. She insisted, he wrote, that 'the pioneering days are by no means over'.[87] His biographical sketch positioned her as a woman of sturdy pioneering stock, equal to 'the rigours of the outback', cheerful in adversity and intrepid, someone pursuing the national interest with her enterprises. On the face of it, this move into the alluring but perilous field of northern resource development surprises; however, in shaping her life story, Deborah traced the beginnings of her interest in minerals to 'the pebbles and stones, gathered for me by my father' on his surveying expeditions.[88] His northern exploration stories surrounded

---

85   Fred. S. Brockman, *Report on Exploration of North-West Kimberley 1901*, WA Parliamentary Paper, no. 12 of 1902 (Perth: Government Printer, 1902); National Library of Australia digitised item Nf 994.65 B864.
86   BBM [Basil Buller Murphy], *A Lady of Rare Metal* (no publishing details, 1949).
87   BBM, *A Lady of Rare Metal*, p. 27.
88   D. Buller Murphy, draft introduction to planned book 'Meekadarriby', Deborah Buller-Murphy papers 1936–1955, Acc 1648/6/7/8, SLWA.

CHAPTER 12

the rocks with an aura of pioneering endeavour; now in her middle years, she was off pioneering herself.

Deborah had begun investing in northern mining in 1923–24 when she partnered with Adelaide mining engineer Frank Young to purchase prospectors' tantalite ore and to acquire mining leases at Wodgina in the Pilbara, the twentieth-century world's major source of the tantalite from which is produced the rare metal tantalum.[89] How the partners were initially attracted to this particular mineral is unclear; but in 1923–25 Mines Departments received requests[90] and newspapers carried appeals from US manufacturing firms for supply of the ore and it seems that some Wodgina leases might have been offered for sale in Adelaide in 1924.[91] By 1925 Young and Moulden had a ten-year contract for twelve tons per year from the Chicago electrical products firm Fansteel Metallurgical Corp.[92] In the 1920s it was Young who took the lead in visiting Wodgina and supervising production.[93] The partnership prospered as it acquired more leases at Wodgina and Strelley (working the latter on tribute), also advertising in both Western Australia and the Northern Territory for prospectors' high-grade ore.[94] By 1931, however, the partnership was over. In September of that year Deborah registered Tantalite Ltd with fellow directors Robert (Bob) J. Oswald and H. Thomson, with

---

89   E.S. Simpson, WA Government Geologist, 'Famous Mineral Localities: Wodgina, North West Australia', *American Mineralogist*, 13 (1928), pp. 457-68.
90   'Tantalite – General', Series 259 Cons 3712 Item 1905/084, State Records Office Western Australia (SROWA).
91   For instance, *Pilbarra Goldfield News* (Marble Bar), 6 February 1923, p. 2; and *Sunday Times*, 24 August 1924, p. 7; *The West Australian*, 19 May 1937, p. 7.
92   BBM, *A Lady of Rare Metal*, p. 31.
93   'Tantalum. Our Little Known Metals: Development at Wodgina', *Daily News*, 3 December 1926, p. 1; *Geraldton Guardian*, 22 November 1928, p. 4.
94   *Northern Times* (Carnarvon), 14 April 1928, p. 4; *Northern Territory Times*, 12 June 1928, p. 4.

capital of £50,000.⁹⁵ Four months later her new company acquired the Wodgina leases. As managing director, Deborah now took the lead role, although the Depression put paid to any plans for several years.⁹⁶ Mining and milling resumed in 1934 and in the following year Tantalite Ltd acquired tantalite and tin leases at Greenbushes in WA's southwest, giving the company close to monopoly control of the country's best tantalite deposits.⁹⁷

As the market recovered in 1935 and tantalite exports resumed,⁹⁸ Deborah set off by air to inspect her investments in the north. She had a pastoral interest as well as mining ones in the northwest, having purchased a £22,000 share in Minilya station in the Gascoyne in January 1933. One of the region's oldest, most improved sheep stations and mostly a profitable one, the land had been first leased to a relative, Charles Brockman, in 1873 and the lease sold to his brother Julius before being sold again to D.N. McLeod in 1901.⁹⁹ Don McLeod had married Charlotte Bussell, Deborah's aunt, and so Deborah's kin connections to this particular station were strong. Her share purchase made her joint director of Minilya Pastoral Co. Pty Ltd with her cousins D.G. and J.F. McLeod.¹⁰⁰ As a company director her travel and accommodation costs were met annually for the Minilya directors' meeting and she took the opportunity to visit the station as well as her mining interests.¹⁰¹ The press, ever attracted by

---

95   *Daily Commercial News and Shipping List* (Sydney), 24 September 1931 p. 5.
96   *Northern Times*, 10 May 1933, p. 2.
97   *The West Australian*, 24 September 1935, p. 12.
98   Annual Reports, Department of Mines Western Australia, 1925–39, reporting tantalite export tonnage and value.
99   Official settler names index, SROWA.
100 'Minilya Pastoral Co. Pty Ltd', D. Buller-Murphy papers, 1936–1955, Acc 1648A/4, SLWA.
101 Diaries, daybooks, ledgers showing visits and payments 1936–39, Minilya Station records, Acc 2766A/2, 16, SLWA.

CHAPTER 12

her flamboyance and not discouraged by her, presented these annual visits as outback camping adventures, around-Australia flights laced with hardship and danger that enabled her to visit and assess her far-flung enterprises – wolfram leases at Hatches Creek in central Australia, potential tantalite leases in the Northern Territory, as well as her Western Australian interests.[102] She had photographs of herself taken on the fields descending a mineshaft in a bosun's chair and inspecting the country, somewhat incongruous images given her apparel of frock and high-heeled shoes.[103] 'Let's call her the Tantalite Queen', the Sydney *Sun* declared with some admiration in 1938.[104] As managing director her views were now decisive in every part of her business and she enjoyed the company's success, altogether selling over 100 tons of tantalite profitably until overseas demand ceased in 1940 with wartime disruption to shipping and manufacturing.[105]

Deborah's entrepreneurial dream of building a mining empire is not in doubt. In addition to her ventures which proceeded to production with some success, there were others (in South Australia and NSW) which were tested and found wanting.[106] Developing Australia's tantalite resources became central to her dream. It was 'folly' simply to mine and export ore: to develop and prosper, she believed, Australia must process tantalum metal itself. Industrial and resource processing was where the nation's future wealth and greatness lay. Her drive to realise her vision places her among Geoff Bolton's Western Australian dreamers and visionaries and, as with

---

102 *News*, 9 June 1936, p. 10. *Sunday Times*, 16 May 1937, p. 4; *Northern Standard* (Darwin), 2 July 1937, p. 6.
103 BBM, *A Lady of Rare Metal, passim.*
104 *Sun* (Sydney), 2 January 1938, p. 2.
105 Series 164 Cons 961 Item 1948/2479, SROWA.
106 BBM, *A Lady of Rare Metal*, p. 7.

most of the others, reach exceeded grasp. Her time was increasingly devoted to convincing others to join in achieving her dream. In the late 1930s she took US and British businessmen and journalists on tours of her northern holdings[107] and visited Britain several times seeking to interest the British government or industry in establishing a tantalum refining company at the imperial centre.[108] William Makin has left a vivid picture of her in 1937 as she returned home from one of these unsuccessful trips: 'a large woman swathed in expensive Russian sables' who shared a luncheon basket (with champagne at her request) on the flight to Marseilles. She regretted that the British experts were 'not yet convinced'. Deborah was a memorable figure: 'that jovial but shrewd Australian business woman' who could discuss 'the secret war of metals'.[109] Reports of Tantalite Ltd's plans to establish an Australian metallurgical works to refine the ore made their first public appearance in 1937.[110]

Then the war interrupted her plans. Mining at Wodgina (and the company's other leases at Strelley, Tabba Tabba and Greenbushes) ceased until the Commonwealth used its wartime powers to resume the leases in 1943.[111] Tantalite mining and milling recommenced under the control of the Commonwealth Department of Supply and Shipping and the ore concentrates exported to the USA along with 1000 tons of beryl ore, which Tantalite Ltd had stockpiled on site at

---

107 BBM, *A Lady of Rare Metal*, pp. 5-9.
108 Tantalite Ltd to A.F Watts, Minister for Industrial Development, 24 March 1948, Item 1948/2479.
109 William J. Makin, *Brigade of Spies* (London: Robert Hale, 1937), pp. 270-73.
110 For instance, *The West Australian*, 11 September 1937, p. 15.
111 For an account of Wodgina's wartime mining by the Commonwealth Department of Supply and Shipping, see Bob Johnson, *Itchy Feet: The Life and Travels of 'Happy Bob'* (Perth: Hesperian Press, 2012), pp. 10-17.

CHAPTER 12

Wodgina, all sold under contract with the US War Department.[112] The leases were handed back in 1945 but the peacetime industry could not be re-established successfully: the US market had gone to Brazil, production costs had risen sharply and suitable labour could not be found. Equally importantly, Tantalite Ltd was totally focused on selling its proposal to process rare metals in WA. It developed a detailed prospectus for a new company – New Metals (Aust.) – and the State government agreed to set aside land in Perth's new industrial suburb of Welshpool. The plant was designed and publicised.[113]

While other governments kept their distance, the WA government became deeply embroiled in Deborah's plans.[114] As a successful local mining entrepreneur she had easy access to politicians and public servants, and her proposal of a small-scale mining and secondary processing project was exactly the development opportunity the State's Department of Industrial Development (under its influential director Norm Fernie) and the Mines Department were looking for.[115] The premier and ministers for Mines and Industrial Development, with their senior officers, attended her initial project presentation in January 1948.[116] 'You want to see this industry established. So do I', Deborah wrote encouragingly to Fernie in 1949.[117] She was a skilled and relentless lobbyer with the effective support of her lawyer

---

112 'Tantalite Mine Wodgina, Beryl Ore Shipments to USA', vols 1 and 2, Series 20 Cons 964 items 1943/0534, 0834, SROWA.

113 Editorial Staff, 'Smelting of Rarer Metals in Australia. Plant at Welshpool Planned to Produce Beryllium, Caesium, Tantalum, Columbium, Titanium and Zirconium Metal and Salts', *Chemical Engineering & Mining Review*, 10 March 1949, pp. 207-10.

114 See two large files – 'Dr Deborah Buller Murphy, Manufacturing of Tantalum from Tantalite etc (New Metals (Aust) Ltd. Co.) to be formed', vols 1 and 2, Series 164 Cons 961 Items 1948/0002, 2479, SROWA.

115 Lenore Layman, 'Development Ideology in Western Australia 1933–1965', *Historical Studies*, 20, 79 (1982), pp. 234-60.

116 Letter re 6 January 1948 meeting, Series 20 Cons 964, Item 1948/0111, SROWA.

117 Letter, 24 October 1949, Item 1948/2479.

husband. In fact his 1949 song of praise to her, *A Lady of Rare Metal*, was probably intended as a marketing tool.

For ten years after the war, in the face of repeated setbacks, Deborah struggled and failed to establish her new project. Tantalite Ltd paid no dividend after 1945 and Deborah drew on her own assets. Her dream was big: £100,000 from the WA government and the same amount again raised by public float together with Tantalite Ltd's resources to create New Metals (Aust.) as a public company.[118] She applied to the Capital Issues Board for permission for a public float but, when the delayed positive response came in January 1949, there was no investor interest in the project.[119] Competitors and disaffected former partners increasingly circled.[120] In 1948 she had sought a £50,000 loan from the WA government but could not meet its conditions. Instead in September of that year the company was lent £15,000 through the government's Rural and Industries (R&I) Bank. The loan was intended for use to prove ore reserves at Wodgina in order to show an adequate ore supply for a Perth processing plant but it was unwisely spent on plant restoration and upgrading, with very little developmental mine work done. Consequently, proved ore reserves remained very limited and the Mines Department withdrew its support for the project. A request in September 1949 for an additional £5000 loan failed;[121] thus in the following month, recognising its ongoing productivity problems, the company suspended production and placed its Wodgina and Strelley leases in caretaker mode.[122]

---

118   Item 1948/0002.
119   Tantalite Ltd Directors' Report, general meeting 14 December 1950, Item 1948/0002.
120   For instance, R.J. Oswald, Item 1948/0111.
121   D. Buller Murphy to N. Fernie, 21 September 1949, Item 1948/0111.
122   Series 164 Cons 961, Items 1948/0002, 1948/2479, SROWA.

CHAPTER 12

At the same time it took legal action against the Commonwealth for alleged failure to recompense for the caesium content in Wodgina's beryl ore sold during the war.[123] Then came protracted negotiations between the company and WA government over the interest repayments on the R&I's loan. Late in 1950 the government agreed to a once-off waiving of repayment but the company's request for further remission failed.[124] Finally and reluctantly in October 1951, the government gave up on the project and informed the company that the State could not assist and the R&I debt was to be repaid with interest.[125] Further attempts to persuade the government to forego interest repayments failed.

After another two long years 'a fairy godmother' came to the rescue.[126] Melbourne share broker and company director J.G. Donaldson purchased the Wodgina leases and plant for £52,740 through his newly formed company North West Tantalum NL in November 1953. Eventually, after the WA government refused Tantalite Ltd's request to transfer its debt of £12,264 to the new company, that debt was repaid and in 1954 Deborah ended her active involvement in mining.[127] Perhaps Donaldson's interest had been triggered by his directorship of Blue Spec Mining Co. NL down the road from Wodgina at Nullagine, but, whatever the motivation, Tantalite Ltd's assets proved a most unwise purchase. In 1955 his new company was liquidated. Tantalite demand did strengthen again eventually but not until 1978.[128]

---

123   Item 834/43.
124   Item 1948/0002.
125   A.F. Watts, Minister for Industrial Development to D. Buller Murphy, 31 October 1951, Item 1948/0001.
126   Basil Buller Murphy to his wife, 30 April 1955, Acc 1648A/2, SLWA.
127   Acc 1648A/3, SLWA.
128   Mark Jacobson, 'History of Mining the Main Tantalite Dyke: Wodgina Western Australia', *Mineral News*, 23, 6 (2007), pp. 1-8.

Deborah was an exceptional woman in her active participation in the pre-1970s mining industry; in a period of systemic gender exclusion she had few peers.[129] It was a wise choice on her part to mine rare pegmatite minerals where large-scale capital was unnecessary, value per ton of ore high and her competitors only prospectors; but it was unwise to think that short-term success in mining and exporting ore could be translated into an Australian-first metallurgical processing enterprise. The time was not propitious and she had neither the capital nor the professional knowledge and skill for success. Her initial success in an unlikely and challenging industry leading to an overly ambitious plan for a major resource processing development proved her a bold entrepreneur in the long Western Australian tradition.

The remainder of Deborah's life was based in Melbourne at Kilsyth, with energy unabated until her last years. She apparently enjoyed the titles her marriages brought her and, after her marriage to Basil Buller Murphy in 1936, named herself Dr Buller Murphy on the basis of an Honorary Doctor of Laws awarded her by the University of Western Australia in 1932. Her 'profuse, opulent' (her third husband's words) entertaining continued, Melbourne newspapers reporting on these occasions as Adelaide and Perth papers had previously done.[130] For instance, 'a real old English Christmas dinner' for two-hundred and seventy guests by candlelight in 1937 featured every extravagance.[131] Her grand Christmas parties were repeated annually. Melbourne's *Table Talk* wrote admiringly in 1939 of a hostess with originality 'who entertain[ed] differently'.[132] Her lunch party

---

129 Lenore Layman, 'Mining' in *The Encyclopedia of Women & Leadership in Twentieth Century Australia*, www.womenaustralia.info/leaders/biogs/WLE0382b.htm
130 BBM, *A Lady of Rare Metal*, pp. 12-21.
131 *Argus*, 23 December 1937, p. 7.
132 *Table Talk* (Melbourne), 20 April 1939, p. 9.

CHAPTER 12

for two hundred Olympic Games guests in 1956 was 'fabulous', according to the *Argus* Women's Page.[133] As ever, her parties catered for large numbers of guests in her beautiful home and garden with copious quantities of food flown in from around Australia, elaborate decorations and organisational precision. And her fundraising also continued. During the war, as well as publishing a new edition of her Household Guide to benefit the Red Cross, Deborah opened the United Services Café in Melbourne's Block Arcade in 1940 to raise money for the British War Orphans Fund. Heading a staff of volunteers, she attended daily, providing homemade jams and preserves. Profit totalled £2000 when the café closed in 1942.[134] In those same years she claimed to have made two tons of jams and preserves to raise funds for Heidelberg Military Hospital.[135] Her efforts continued post-war, when she undertook most of the catering for the 'Australia Makes It' exhibition in 1947 to raise funds for Queen Victoria Hospital. As a philanthropic fundraiser and social hostess she remained exceptional.

As she grew older Deborah was drawn back to her Western Australian colonial identity – the proud daughter of 'pioneering stock' who believed she was doing her own pioneering through her northern mining enterprises. To that achievement she intended to add a publication in two volumes concerning Western Australian colonisation – recording the 'Language, Art, Legends and Customs of the Aboriginals of the South-West and North-West of Western Australia' alongside an account of colonial endeavour. Advertised as 'In Preparation' in 1940, it was titled 'Meekadarriby', after one of

---

133 *Argus*, 19 November 1956, p. 8.
134 BBM, *A Lady of Rare Metal*, p. 7; *Argus*, 28 August 1942, p. 5.
135 *News*, 26 May 1942, p. 5.

the Margaret River places in Wardandi Noongar legend as told by the Bussell family.[136] She intended interweaving nineteenth-century Aboriginal and settler pasts – fifteen Dordenup/Wardandi legends together with a dictionary of the language (as recorded by her uncle A.J. Bussell); Bussell and Brockman histories, in particular her father's 1901 Kimberley exploration report with its extended account of local Aboriginal culture; the poetry of her Brockman grandmother, Elizabeth Deborah Slade; and extracts from W.B. Kimberly's 1897 history of the colony and C.G. Nicolay's 1880 Handbook.[137] Such a collation appropriated Aboriginal culture and people into a narrative of colonisation. Deborah saw the Dordenup people as 'a departed race' but believed herself able to speak for them because of her childhood contact and that of the whole Bussell family: 'As a child I had read or told to me by my mother and father, and by my uncles and aunts, many of the legends of the Dordenup people, as other children have had read or told to them the fairy tales of Andersen and Grimm'. Guarantee that the stories were genuine and authoritative came from personal communications: 'From the authentic lips of her [Jinny's] son Indeal I first heard some of the legends of this childlike but laughing and lovable people'.[138] The planned publication would recognise what she believed to be the sad loss of a people while eliding the bitter facts of dispossession and suffering. Such an approach created an elegiac sense of honouring a people whose time had passed

---

136 Advertisement in *Lady Hackett's Household Guide*, p. 991; Brad Goode & Associates Pty Ltd, *An Aboriginal Cultural Heritage Management Assessment for the Ellensbrook Catchment: A Report Prepared for the National Trust of Australia and the Department of Environment and Conservation*, August 2010.

137 Substantial manuscript materials testify to the long gestation and varied inputs into this planned publication; Buller-Murphy papers 1648A/5-8.

138 D. Buller-Murphy, *An Attempt to Eat the Moon: And Other Stories Recounted from the Aborigines by Deborah Buller-Murphy* (Melbourne: Georgian House, 1958), pp. ix-x.

CHAPTER 12

in the same way that 'the wild tracts of country in which he made his home' no longer existed because of the coloniser's cultivation of the land.[139] Implicitly it was a moral defence of colonisation.

Publishers who were offered the manuscript, however, recommended publishing only the Aboriginal legends and, after considerable delay, Deborah accepted the advice.[140] *An Attempt to Eat the Moon: And Other Stories Recounted from the Aborigines by Deborah Buller-Murphy* appeared in 1958 consisting of just fifteen Wardandi legends. It is difficult to see this as a children's book (as Marcus notes of other similar texts)[141] in this instance because so many of the legends concerned young girls in love with young boys but already given to lustful and often cruel old men. Nevertheless, the Book Council recommended it as 'suitable for all age groups'.[142] Similarities with Mary and Elizabeth Durack's children's books are striking, made more so by Elizabeth Durack's familiar line drawings which enhance the pages of Deborah's text.

This last major public project of her life brought Deborah back to her colonial beginnings. She dedicated the book to her mother and father, and identified her Bussell and Brockman kin with achievements in Western Australia's development. The book's cultural framework demonstrated her faithfulness to the colonial values in which she was raised and the resilience of those values into the second half of the twentieth century. She died on 16 April 1965, aged 77, predeceased in 1963 by her third husband. He left her almost all his estate valued at £29,382.[143] Her own death was headlined in *The Sydney*

---

139   Buller-Murphy papers, 1648A/6.
140   Buller-Murphy papers, 1648A/6.
141   Julie Marcus, 'Children's Books', *Olive Pink Society Bulletin*, 6, 2 (1994), p. 20.
142   'Book Council Reviews of Australian Books', *Canberra Times*, 14 June 1958, p. 11.
143   *Age*, 7 June 1963, p. 4.

Morning Herald: 'Richest Woman in Australia Dies'.[144] While the claim seems unlikely, she certainly died a rich woman with an estate valued at £87,922, comprised mostly of her Melbourne residence and personal effects together with stocks and shares in South Australia and Western Australia.[145]

Deborah had lived to the full the life of an early twentieth-century elite woman and in middle age transcended it. She could not pursue the public career which undoubtedly could have been hers (like her father, brothers and son) had she been born male. Her sex constrained her choices but she made the most of the opportunities it also provided. Her series of wise spousal choices delivered her personal happiness, children, material comfort and continuing high status. As Lady Bountiful she fulfilled a desire to assist the good causes of which she approved and at the same time satisfied her passion for spectacle and entertainment. Philanthropic service provided her with fulfilling leadership roles. The charitable model was a conservative one that suited her and, although the good ladies were frequently mocked, current feminist scholarship recognises the social benefits they delivered.[146]

Then, in Bussell-Brockman pioneering mode, Deborah ventured into the hyper-masculine mining world, not as a lady investor but as managing director of her own company. Her wise decision to concentrate on rare metals brought her initial success before her entrepreneurial ambition outgrew her means and skills. And so she came

---

144 *The Sydney Morning Herald*, 18 April 1965, p. 15.
145 I am indebted to the *Australian Dictionary of Biography* for probate details. Also Supreme Court of WA Probate Jurisdiction, Affidavit of Assets and Liabilities, 24 July 1965. Series 1915 Cons 5398 Item 7620/1, SROWA.
146 Melanie Oppenheimer, 'Voluntary Work', *The Encyclopedia of Women and Leadership in Twentieth-Century Australia*, www.womenaustralia.info/leaders/biogs/WLE0623b.htm

CHAPTER 12

to join the long list of bold entrepreneurs nurtured in Geoff Bolton's *Land of Vision and Mirage*. Consensus on the need for economic and social development strongly united most Western Australians across the divides of class and status. These divides, however, remained sharp. While Deborah's philanthropic and mining enterprises were widely admired and valued, the privileged life her birth and marriages furnished was well recognised with equal parts of admiration, amusement and resentment. The *Sunday Times* exaggerated in 1900 when it declared that 'anything is possible for a first family groper', yet the inter-generational benefits were there for all to see.[147] Geoff was right, however, in insisting that it took individual enterprise to seize the opportunities offered. Deborah Drake-Brockman, Hackett, Moulden, Buller Murphy was nothing if not enterprising.

---

147   *Sunday Times*, 22 July 1900, p. 12.

Works by Geoffrey Bolton

Books

Alexander Forrest: His Life and Times (Melbourne: Melbourne University Press in association with the University of Western Australia Press, 1958).
(with Ann Mozley) *The Western Australian Legislature, 1870–1930* (Canberra: Australian National University, 1961).
A Thousand Miles Away: A History of North Queensland to 1920 (Brisbane: Jacaranda in association with the Australian National University, 1963).
Richard Daintree: A Photographic Memoir (Brisbane: Jacaranda Press, 1965).
The Passing of the Irish Act of Union: A Study in Parliamentary Politics (London: Oxford University Press, 1966).
Dick Boyer: An Australian Humanist (Canberra: Australian National University Press, 1967).
A Fine Country to Starve In (Perth: University of Western Australia Press, 1972; 2nd edn, 1994).
Britain's Legacy Overseas (London: Oxford University Press, 1973).
Spoils and Spoilers: Australians Make Their Environment 1788–1980 (Sydney: Allen & Unwin, 1981; 2nd edn, 1992).
(with Prue Joske) *History of Royal Perth Hospital* (Perth: Royal Perth Hospital, 1982).
It Had Better Be a Good One: Murdoch University's First Ten Years (Perth: Murdoch University, 1985).
(with David Black, assisted by Ann Mozley and Patricia Simpson) *Biographical Register of Members of the Parliament of Western Australia*, vol. 1, 1870–1930; vol. 2, 1930–2010 (Perth: Western Australian Parliamentary History Project, 1990; rev. edn, 2011).
The Oxford History of Australia. Volume 5, 1942–1988: The Middle Way (Melbourne: Oxford University Press, 1990; 2nd edn, 1996).
A View from the Edge: An Australian Stocktaking, Boyer Lectures (Sydney: ABC Books, 1992).
Daphne Street (Fremantle: Fremantle Arts Centre Press, 1997).
(with Jenny Gregory) *Claremont: A History* (Perth: University of Western Australia Press, 1999).
Edmund Barton: The One Man for the Job (Sydney: Allen & Unwin, 2000).
(with Geraldine Byrne) *The Campus That Never Stood Still: Edith Cowan University, 1902–2002* (Perth: Edith Cowan University, 2002).
(with Geraldine Byrne) *May it Please Your Honour: A History of the Supreme Court of Western Australia 1861–2005* (Perth: Supreme Court of Western Australia, 2005).

Land of Vision and Mirage: Western Australia since 1826 (Perth: University of
  Western Australia Press, 2008).
Paul Hasluck: A Life (Perth: UWA Publishing, 2014).

Edited Books

Everyman in Australia, Octagon Lectures 1970 (Perth: University of Western
  Australia Press, 1972).
(with Heath Vose and Genelle Jones) *The Wollaston Journals*, vol. 1, 1840–42
  (Perth: University of Western Australia Press, 1991).
(with Heather Vose, Allan Watson and Suzanne Lewis) *The Wollaston Journals*, vol.
  2, 1842–44 (Perth: University of Western Australia Press, 1992).
(with Wayne Hudson) *Creating Australia: Changing Australian History* (Sydney:
  Allen & Unwin, 1997).
(with Richard Rossiter and Jan Ryan) *Farewell Cinderella: Creating Arts and
  Identity in Western Australia* (Perth: University of Western Australia Press,
  2003).
(with Deborah Gare, Stuart Macintyre and Tom Stannage) *The Fuss That Never
  Ended: Essays on the Life and Work of Geoffrey Blainey* (Melbourne: Melbourne
  University Press, 2003).
(with Paul Longley Arthur) *Voices from the West End: Stories, People and Events that
  Shaped Fremantle* (Perth: Western Australian Museum, 2012).

Occasional Publications

History of the OUCC [Oxford University Cricket Club] (Oxford: Holywell Press,
  1962).
Planters and Pacific Islanders (Melbourne: Longmans, 1968).
(with Wendy Birman) *Augustus Charles Gregory* (Melbourne: Oxford University
  Press, 1972).
(with David Williamson) *The Australian Image*, Counterpoint Forum (Perth:
  Murdoch University, 1982).
John Ramsden Wollaston: The Making of a Pioneer Priest (York, W.A.: Holy Trinity
  Church York Society, 1985).
(with Keith J. Solomon and Rob Watkins) *Story of Australia* (Tunbridge Wells:
  World Book, 1987).
Who Owns Australia's Past? Inaugural lecture delivered at The University of
  Queensland, 18 March 1992 (Brisbane, University of Queensland Press,
  1993).
The Muses in Quest of a Patron (Perth: School of Music, University of Western
  Australia, 1996).
Crossroads: The Murdoch Lecture for 2000 (Perth: Murdoch University, 2000).
Why Is Robert Philp Worth Remembering? Who Was Robert Philp? Sir Robert Philp
  Lecture Series, Number 1 (Townsville: Townsville City Council, 2008).

Independent Committee Constituted by The Hon. Robert Nicholson AO, Emeritus Professor Geoffrey Bolton AO and retired Associate Professor David Standen AM, *Report on the Written Submissions of Invited Experts on Difficulties in the Perth City Waterfront Development (Elizabeth Quay)* (Perth: CityVision, 2013).

Book Chapters, Journal Articles and Reference Works

'Alexander Forrest', *University Studies in History and Economics*, 2, 1 (1953), pp. 21-78.

'The Kimberley Pastoral Industry', *University Studies in History and Economics*, 2, 2 (1954), pp. 7-53.

'The Founding of Cairns', *Journal of the Royal Australian Historical Society*, 45, 1 (1959), pp. 28-37.

'The Exploration of North Queensland: Some Problems', *Journal of the Royal Australian Historical Society*, 46, 6 (1960), pp. 352-59.

'Labour Comes to Charters Towers', *Labour History*, 1 (1962), pp. 25-34. Republished in K.H. Kennedy (ed.), *Readings in North Queensland Mining History*, vol. 1 (Townsville: Department of History, James Cook University, 1980), pp. 145-60.

'The Choice of Speaker in Australian Parliaments', *Parliamentary Affairs*, 1, 3 (1962), pp. 355-64. Republished in C.A. Hughes (ed.), *Readings in Australian Government* (Brisbane: University of Queensland Press, 1968), pp 155-62.

'Australian Country Towns', *Hemisphere*, 7, 3 (1963), pp. 13-18.

'The Valley of Lagoons: A Study in Exile', *Business Archives and History*, 4 (1963), pp. 99-116.

'Some British Reactions to the Irish Act of Union', *Economic History Review*, 18, 2 (1965), pp. 367-75.

'The Founding of the Second British Empire', *Economic History Review*, 19, 1 (1966), pp. 195-200.

'The Rise of Burns, Philp, 1873–1893', in Alan Birch and David S. Macmillan (eds), *Wealth and Progress: Studies in Australian Business History* (Sydney: Angus & Robertson Sydney, 1967), pp. 111-27.

'The Idea of a Colonial Gentry', *Historical Studies*, 13, 51 (1968), pp. 307-28.

'The Hollow Conqueror: Flax and the Foundation of Australia', *Australian Economic History Review*, 8, 1 (1968), pp. 3-16. Republished in Ged Martin (ed.), *The Founding of Australia: The Argument about Australia's Origins* (Sydney: Hale & Iremonger, 1978), pp. 91-104.

'Broken Reeds and Smoking Flax', *Australian Economic History Review*, 9, 1 (1969), pp. 64-70. Republished in Martin (ed.), *The Founding of Australia*, pp. 115-21.

'Unemployment and Politics in Western Australia', *Labour History*, 17 (1969), pp. 80-96.

'The Development of the North', in Richard Preston (ed.), *Contemporary Australia: Studies in History, Politics, and Economics* (Durham, NC: Duke University Press, 1969), pp. 120–52.

'Australian Historians in Quest of a Theme', *Teaching History*, 3, 2 (1969), pp. 5-20.

WORKS BY GEOFFREY BOLTON

'1939–1970', in James Griffin (ed.), *Essays in the Economic History of Australia* (Brisbane: Jacaranda Press, 1970), pp. 283-313.

'Louis Hartz', *Australian Economic History Review*, 13, 2 (1973), pp. 168-76.

(with B.E. Kennedy) 'William Eden and the Treaty of Mauritius, 1786–87', *The Historical Journal*, 16, 4 (1973), pp. 681-96.

(with David Hutchison) 'European Man in Southwestern Australia', *Journal of the Royal Society of Western Australia*, 56, 1–2 (1973), pp. 56-64.

'1939–51', in F.K. Crowley (ed.), *A New History of Australia* (Melbourne: William Heinemann, 1974), pp. 458-503.

'The Surveyor in a Developing Community: A Historian's Approach', *Australian Surveyor*, 27, 3 (1975), pp. 124-31.

'The Historian as Artist and Interpreter of the Environment', in George Seddon and Mari Davis (eds), *Man and Landscape in Australia: Towards an Ecological Vision* (Canberra: Australian Government Publishing Service, 1976), pp. 113-24.

'Attempting History at Murdoch', *Australian Historical Association Bulletin*, 13 (December 1977), pp. 6-13.

'A Local Identity: Paul Hasluck and the Western Australian Self-Concept', *Westerly*, 22, 4 (1977), pp. 71-77.

'History: 150 Years of Rapid Growth', in Richard Woldendorp, *Looking West* (Perth: Day Dawn Press, 1977), pp. 14-22.

'Robert Philp: Capitalist as Politician', in D.J. Murphy and R.B. Joyce (eds), *Queensland Political Portraits 1859–1952* (Brisbane: University of Queensland Press, 1978), pp. 193-220.

(with Su-Jane Hunt) 'Cleansing the Dunghill: Water Supply and Sanitation in Perth 1878–1912', *Studies in Western Australian History*, 2 (1978), pp. 1-17.

'Regional History in Australia', in John A. Moses (ed.), *Historical Disciplines and Culture in Australasia: An Assessment* (Brisbane: University of Queensland Press, 1979), pp. 215-27.

'A Whig Utopia in Northern Australia, 1835', *Push from the Bush*, 5 (1979), pp. 120-28.

'Sir James Mitchell the Optimist', in Lyall Hunt (ed.), *Westralian Portraits* (Perth: University of Western Australia Press, 1979), pp. 159-67.

(with David E. Hutchison) 'The Beginning', in Brian J. O'Brien (ed.), *Environment and Science* (Perth: University of Western Australia Press, 1979), pp. 1-21.

'William Eden and the Convicts, 1771–1787', *Australian Journal of Politics and History*, 26, 1 (1980), pp. 30-44.

(with Howard Petersen) 'The Emanuels of Noonkanbah and GoGo', *Early Days*, 8, 4 (1980), pp. 5-21.

'Black and White after 1897', in C.T. Stannage (ed.), *A New History of Western Australia* (Perth: University of Western Australia Press, 1981), pp. 124-78.

'Western Australia Reflects on its Past', in C.T. Stannage (ed.), *A New History of Western Australia* (Perth: University of Western Australia Press, 1981), pp. 676-91.

'The Fenians Are Coming, the Fenians Are Coming!', *Studies in Western Australian History*, 4 (1981), pp. 62-67.

'Who were the Pensioners?', *Studies in Western Australian History*, 4 (1981), pp. 84-89.
'The Historical Context of Aborigines in Western Australia', *Anthropology News*, 18 (1981), pp. 57-66.
'Western Australia', in *The Heritage of Australia: The Illustrated Register of the National Estate* (Melbourne: Macmillan of Australia in association with the Australian Heritage Commission, 1981), part 6.1.
(with Horst G. Ruthrof) 'In Reply to Half a Case For (Or Against) Small Universities', *Vestes*, 24, 2 (1981), pp. 26-27.
'Cranking the Parish Pump: Recent Local Histories of Western Australia', *Studies in Western Australian History*, 5 (1982), pp. 86-91.
'The Belly and the Limbs', Augustus Wolskel Memorial Lecture delivered to the Royal Historical Society of Victoria, *Victorian Historical Journal*, 53, 1 (1982), pp. 5-23.
'Aborigines in Social History: An Overview', in Ronald M. Berndt (ed.), *Aboriginal Sites, Rights and Resource Development* (Perth: University of Western Australia Press for the Academy of the Social Sciences in Australia, 1982), pp. 59-68.
'Sir Charles (I): The Rising Politician', *Westerly*, 27, 2 (1982), pp. 67-72.
'Court in Power', *Westerly*, 27, 3 (1982), pp. 57-64.
'Maritime Archeology and Australian History', in Joost Daalder and Michelle Fryer (eds), *Aspects of Australian Culture* (Adelaide: Abel Tasman Press, 1982), pp. 8-14.
'The Anglo-Irish and the Historians, 1830–1980', in Oliver MacDonagh, W.F. Mandle and Pauric Travers (eds), *Irish Culture and Nationalism 1750–1950* (London: Macmillan, 1983), pp. 239-57.
'Legends of Australian Identity', *Meridian*, 2, 1 (1983), pp. 47-51.
'The Strange Career of William Beresford', *Early Days*, 9, 2 (1984), pp. 5-16. Republished in Bob Reece (ed.), *Exiles from Erin: Convict Lives in Ireland and Australia* (Basingstoke: Macmillan, 1991), pp. 284-303.
'The Image of Australia in Europe', *Journal of the Royal Society of Arts*, 132 (1984), pp. 171-83.
'The Gold Discovery of 1851–1880 and Ireland', in Colm Kiernan (ed.), *Ireland and Australia* (Sydney: Angus & Robertson, 1984), pp. 34-46.
'The Empire Strikes Back at Russell Square', *Australian Historical Association Bulletin*, 39 (1984), pp. 6-8.
'Australian Studies in the United Kingdom: The Prospect before Us', in Patricia McLaren-Turner (ed.), *Australian and New Zealand Studies: Papers Presented at a Colloquium at the British Library, 7–9 February 1984* (London: The British Library, 1985), pp. 14-21.
'The Irish in Australian Historiography', in Colm Kiernan (ed.), *Australia and Ireland, 1788–1988: Bicentenary Essays* (Dublin: Gill & Macmillan, 1986), pp. 5-19.
'Cultural Aspects of Australia's Maritime Tradition', in *Maritime Australia 86: Putting It Together* (Canberra: Australian Centre for Maritime Studies, 1986), pp. 64-70.
'The Opportunities of Distance', The 1985 Knud Broady lecture to the International Council for Distance Education, *Distance Education*, 7, 1 (1986), pp. 5-22.

WORKS BY GEOFFREY BOLTON

'Newspapers for a Depression Child', *Westerly*, 31, 4 (1986), pp. 76-83.
'Writing Home', *History Today*, 36, 5 (1986), pp. 58-59.
'Hartigan's Syndrome', the 50th George Adlington Syme Oration, *Australian and New Zealand Journal of Surgery*, 57, 11 (1986), pp. 809-12.
'Tommy Dower and the Perth Newspapers', *Aboriginal History*, 12, 1–2 (1988), pp. 79-83.
'Introduction' to reissue of *Australia. Cambridge History of the British Empire*, vol. 7, part 1 (Cambridge: Cambridge University Press, 1988), pp. xiv-xxi.
'Historians and Technological Change', in Pam Matthews (ed.), *The National and International Environment: Proceedings of the 6th Biennial Conference of the Australian Society of Archivists, Perth, 21–25 April 1987* (Perth: Society of Archivists, 1988), pp. 60-64.
'Who Are the Australians?', *The Unesco Courier*, 12 (1988), pp. 4-11.
'Perth: A Foundling City', in Pamela Statham (ed.), *The Origins of Australia's Capital Cities* (Cambridge: Cambridge University Press, 1989), pp. 141-55.
'The Spread of Colonization', in John Hardy and Alan Frost (eds), *Studies from Terra Australis to Australia* (Canberra: Australian Academy of the Humanities, 1989), pp. 183-93.
'Too Many Historical Journals?', *Australian Historical Association Bulletin*, 58 (1989), pp. 7-10.
'WAY 1979: Whose Celebration?', *Studies in Western Australian History*, 10 (1989), pp. 14-20.
'Transcontinental Railways: Why So Few and Far Between?', *Queensland Geographical Journal*, 4th series, 4 (1989), pp. 1-12.
'The History of the Historian' (1975) and 'Questioning the Past – and Future', in Rae Frances and Bruce Scates (eds), *The Murdoch Ethos: Essays in Australian History in Honour of Foundation Professor Geoffrey Bolton* (Perth: Murdoch University, 1989), pp. 270-74.
'The Good Name of Parliament, 1890–1990', in David Black (ed.), *The House on the Hill: A History of the Parliament of Western Australia 1832–1990* (Perth: Parliament of Western Australia, 1991), pp. 471-93.
'Samuel Griffith: The Great Provincial', in *Papers on Parliament*, 13 (1991), pp. 19-33; also presented as Clem Lack Memorial Oration, *Journal of the Royal Historical Society of Queensland*, 14, 9 (1991), pp. 350-63.
(with Kay Saunders) 'Girdled for War: Women's Mobilisations in World War Two', in Kay Saunders and Ray Evans (eds), *Gender Relations in Australia: Domination and Negotiation* (Sydney: Harcourt Brace Jovanovich, 1992), pp. 376-97.
(with Helen Gregory) 'The 1891 Shearers Strike Leaders: Railroaded?', *Labour History*, 62 (1992), pp. 116-26.
'Hypocrisy', in Ross Fitzgerald (ed.), *The Eleven Deadly Sins* (Melbourne: William Heinemann, 1993), pp. 39-54.
'Beating Up Keating: British Media and the Republic', in Don Grant and Graham Seal (eds), *Australia in the World: Perceptions and Possibilities* (Perth: Black Swan Press, 1994), pp. 148-51.
'Businessmen in Politics: A Comment', *Business Council Bulletin*, 107 (1994), pp. 102-4.

'The Price of Protest: Press and Judiciary in 1870', *Studies in Western Australian History*, 15 (1994), pp. 14-22.

'The Civil War We Never Had: Western Australian Secessionism', *Proceedings of the 3rd conference of the Samuel Griffith Society, Fremantle, 5–6 November 1993* (Melbourne: Samuel Griffith Society, 1994), pp. 83-96. http://samuelgriffith.org.au/docs/vol3/v3chap5.pdf

'Portrait of the Historian as a Young Learner', in Duncan Graham (ed.), *Being Whitefella* (Fremantle: Fremantle Arts Centre Press, 1994), pp. 119-25.

'History in Australia: The Prospect in 1995', *Australian Historical Association Bulletin*, 78–79 (1994/1995), pp. 8-11. Reprinted in *Academy of Social Sciences in Australia Newsletter*, 14, 1 (1995), pp. 16-20.

'A.C.V. Melbourne: Prophet Without Honour', in Stuart Macintyre and Julian Thomas (eds), *The Discovery of Australian History 1890–1939* (Melbourne: Melbourne University Press, 1995), pp. 111-24.

'Two Pauline Versions', in Scott Prasser, J.R. Nethercote and John Warhurst (eds), *The Menzies Era: A Reappraisal of Government, Politics and Policy* (Sydney: Hale & Iremonger, 1995), pp. 33-55.

'The Art of Consensus: Edmund Barton and the 1897 Federal Convention', *Papers on Parliament* 30 (1997), pp. 33-48.

(with Wayne Hudson] 'Creating Australia', in Wayne Hudson and Geoffrey Bolton (eds), *Creating Australia: Changing Australian History* (Sydney: Allen & Unwin, 1997), pp. 1-11.

'Paul Hasluck', in Graeme Davison, John Hirst and Stuart Macintyre (eds), *The Oxford Companion to Australian History* (Melbourne: Oxford University Press, 1998), p. 302.

'Henry Parkes', in Graeme Davison, John Hirst and Stuart Macintyre (eds), *The Oxford Companion to Australian History* (Melbourne: Oxford University Press, 1998), pp. 493-94.

'The Western Australians: A Silent Majority', *New Federalist*, 1 (1998), pp. 57-62.

'The Making of "Australia's Noblest Son"', *New Federalist*, 2 (1998), pp. 4-9.

'Who Should Be in Parliament?' *Legislative Studies*, 12, 2 (1998), pp. 76-79.

Deborah Gare, 'Images from a Life in Australian History: An Interview with Geoffrey Bolton', *Limina*, 4 (1998), pp. 90-95.

(with Duncan Waterson), 'The Colonies' Paths to Federation: Queensland', in Helen Irving (ed.), *The Centenary Companion to Australian Federation* (Cambridge: Cambridge University Press, 1999), pp. 93-128.

'How Uneasy Lies the Head? The Health of Australian Prime Ministers', *Health and History*, 1, 2–3 (1999), pp. 169-81.

'Rediscovering Australia: Hancock and the Wool Seminar', *Journal of Australian Studies*, 23, 62 (1999), pp. 159-70. Reprinted in D.A. Low (ed.), *Keith Hancock: The Legacies of an Historian* (Melbourne: Melbourne University Press, 2001), pp. 180-200.

'The Valley of Lagoons: A Rehearsal for Canberra?', *New Federalist*, 3 (1999), pp. 22-25.

'Sir Samuel Griffith: Behind the Scenes Operator', *New Federalist*, 4 (1999), pp. 45-48.

WORKS BY GEOFFREY BOLTON

'A Provincial Viewpoint', in Bruce Bennett (ed.), *Australia In Between Cultures: Specialist Session Papers from the 1998 Australian Academy of the Humanities Symposium* (Canberra: Australian Academy of Humanities, 1999), pp. 79-85.

'Richard Buzacott', in Ann Millar, (ed.), *The Biographical Dictionary of the Australian Senate*, vol. 1 (Melbourne: Melbourne University Press, 2000), pp. 365-67.

'Norman Kirkwood Ewing', in Ann Millar (ed.), *The Biographical Dictionary of the Australian Senate*, vol. 1 (Melbourne: Melbourne University Press, 2000), pp. 336-39.

'The Greatest Miracle of All: Western Australia Joins the Federation', *Early Days*, 11, 6 (2000), pp. 713-44.

'William Morris Hughes', in Michelle Grattan (ed.), *Australian Prime Ministers* (Sydney: New Holland Press, 2000), pp. 100-25.

'A Trinity Man Abroad: Sir Winthrop Hackett', in Bob Reece (ed.), *The Irish in Western Australia: Studies in Western Australian History*, 20 (2000), pp. 67-80.

'Duncan Waterson: A Lapidary Historian', in *From the Frontier: Essays in Honour of Duncan Waterson, Special Joint Issue of Journal of Australian Studies*, 25, 69 (2001) and *Australian Cultural History*, 20 (2001), pp. 9-16.

(with John Williams) 'Edmund Barton' in Tony Blackshield, Michael Coper and George Williams (eds), *The Oxford Companion to the High Court* (Melbourne: Oxford University Press, 2001), pp. 53-56.

'Confessions of a Library User', *LASIE: Library Automated Systems Information Exchange*, 33, 1 (2002), pp. 7-16.

'Between the Wars', in Peter Beilharz and Trevor Hogan (eds), *Sociology: Place, Time and Division* (Melbourne: Oxford University Press, 2003), pp. 174-80.

'Reflections on Comparative Frontier History', in Bain Attwood and S.G. Foster (eds), *Frontier Conflict: The Australian Experience* (Canberra: National Museum of Australia, 2003), pp. 169-84.

'*The Tyranny of Distance* Revisited', in Deborah Gare, Geoffrey Bolton, Stuart Macintyre and Tom Stannage (eds), *The Fuss that Never Ended: The Life and Work of Geoffrey Blainey* (Melbourne: Melbourne University Press, 2003), pp. 28-38.

'Richard Daintree, 1832–1878, in *The Oxford Dictionary of National Biography*, vol. 14 (Oxford: Oxford University Press, 2004), pp. 918-919.

'Sir Hal Colebatch', in Harry Evans and Ann Millar (eds), *The Biographical Dictionary of the Australian Senate*, vol. 2 (Melbourne: Melbourne University Press, 2004) pp. 33-36.

'Edward Bertram Johnston', in Harry Evans and Ann Millar (eds), *The Biographical Dictionary of the Australian Senate*, vol. 2 (Melbourne: Melbourne University Press, 2004), pp. 37-40.

'The Shoals of Celebrity', *Meanjin*, 63, 3 (2004), pp. 144-48.

'Harry Marshall: A Fremantle Larrikin in Politics', *Fremantle Studies*, 4 (2005), pp. 1-7.

'Thoughts of an Elitist Republican', *Sydney Papers*, 17, 1 (2005), pp. 105-9.

'Western Australian History: The Next Assignments', Address to the History Council of Western Australia', *History Australia*, 2, 2 (2005), pp. 48.1-7.

(with M. Calver, H. Bigler-Cole, J. Dargavel, A. Gaynor, P. Horwitz, J. Mills and G. Wardell-Johnson) 'Why "A Forest Consciencesness"?', in *A Forest Consciousness: Proceedings of the 6th National conference of the Australian Forest History Society* (Rotterdam: Millpress Science Publishers, 2005), pp. 729-39.
'Parkes, Henry (later Sir Henry)', in David Clune and Ken Turner (eds), *The Premiers of New South Wales 1856–2005* (Sydney: Federation Press, 2006), pp. 121-38.
'The Art of Australian Political Biography', in Tracey Arklay, John Nethercote and John Wanna (eds), *Australian Political Lives: Chronicling Political Careers and Administrative Histories* (Canberra: ANU E Press, 2006), pp. 1-13.
'Sir Paul Hasluck: The Opportunities of His Career', *Early Days*, 12, 6 (2006), pp. 732-51.
'Custodians of the National Memory', in *Memory of a Nation* (Canberra: National Archives of Australia, 2007), pp. 7-15.
'Money: Trade, Investment and Australian Nationalism', in Deryck M. Schreuder and Stuart Ward (eds), *Australia's Empire* (Oxford: Oxford University Press, 2008) pp. 211-31.
'Charles Robert, Baron Carrington', in David Clune and Ken Turner (eds), *The Governors of New South Wales 1788–2010.* (Sydney: The Federation Press, 2009), pp. 332-51.
'Sir Augustus William Frederick Spencer Loftus', in David Clune and Ken Turner (eds), *The Governors of New South Wales 1788–2010* (Sydney: Federation Press, 2009), pp. 317-31.
'Victor Albert George Child-Villiers, Earl of Jersey', in David Clune and Ken Turner (eds), *The Governors of New South Wales 1788–2010* (Sydney: Federation Press, 2009), pp. 352-61.
'Reflections on Oombulgurri', *Studies in Western Australian History*, 26 (2010), pp. 176-90.
'John Peter Sim', in Ann Millar (ed.), *The Biographical Dictionary of the Australian Senate*, vol. 3 (Sydney: University of New South Wales Press, 2010), pp. 510-14.
'Andrew Murray Thomas', in Ann Millar (ed.), *The Biographical Dictionary of the Australian Senate*, vol. 3 (Sydney: New South Wales University Press, 2010), pp. 535-38.
'Environmental History in Western Australia before 1980', *Studies in Western Australian History*, 27 (2011), pp. 1-12.
'Alexander Forrest's Expedition 1879 and Early Development of the Cattle Industry', in Cathie Clement, Jeffrey Gresham and Hamish McGlashon (eds), *Kimberley History: People, Exploration and Development* (Perth: Kimberley Society, 2012), pp. 101-12.
'Australia and the Occupation of Japan' in Ian Nish (ed.), *The British Commonwealth and the Allied Occupation of Japan, 1945–1952: Personal Encounters and Government Assessments* (Leiden, The Netherlands: Koninklijke Brill NV, 2013), pp. 55-62.
'John Ritchie: Consolidating a Tradition, 1987–2002', in Melanie Nolan and Christine Fernon (eds), *The ADB's Story* (Canberra: ANU E Press, 2013), pp. 153-71.

'The Making of Australian Foreign Policy 1960–1972: An Overview', in Melissa Conley Tyler, John Robbins and Adrian March (eds), *Ministers for Foreign Affairs 1960–1972* (Canberra: Australian Institute of International Affairs, 2014), pp. 23-67.

'The Making of a Historian: The Early Life of Tom Stannage', in Deborah Gare and Jenny Gregory (eds), *Tom Stannage: History from the Other Side. Studies in Western Australian History*, 29 (2015), pp. 15-26.

'Australian Historians Networking', in Doug Munro and John G. Reid (eds), *Clio's Lives: Biographies and Autobiographies of Historians* (Canberra: ANU Press, forthcoming).

Entries in *Australian Dictionary of Biography*

Volume 1 (1966)

Bateman, John (1789–1855) merchant
Clark, William Nairne (1804–1854) lawyer and publicist
Holt, Joseph (1756–1826) Irish rebel and farmer

Volume 2 (1967)

Morrill, James (1824–1865) sailor
Stokes, John Lort (1812–1885) explorer and hydrographer
Wollaston, John Ramsden (1791–1856) Anglican archdeacon

Volume 3 (1969)

Allingham, Christopher (1829–1876) explorer and pastoralist
Black, Maurice Hume (1835–1899) sugar-planter and politician
Chester, Henry Marjoribanks (1832–1914) public servant

Volume 4 (1972)

Daintree, Richard (1832–1878) geologist and photographer
Fitzgerald, Thomas Henry (1824–1888) sugar-grower and politician
Hamilton, John (1841–1916) politician
Hann, Frank Hugh (1846–1921) explorer and pastoralist
Hann, William (1837–1889) explorer and pastoralist

Volume 5 (1974)

(with Kathryn Cronin) Leon, Andrew (1841–1920) businessman
Mosman, Hugh (1843–1909) mine owner
Normanby, second Marquess of (1819–1890) governor
Palmerston, Christie (1850–1897) explorer and prospector
Pearse, William Silas (1838–1908) merchant

Volume 6 (1976)

Randell, George (1830–1915) businessman and politician
Scott, Walter Jervoise (1835–1890) pastoralist
Sellheim, Philip Frederic (1832–1899) pastoralist and mining official
Swallow, Thomas (1823–1890) manufacturer
Whish, Claudius Buchanan (1827–1890) sugar-planter and civil servant

Volume 7 (1979)

Anderson, Peter Corsair (1871–1955) educationist
Angelo, Edward Houghton (1870–1948) politician
Barron, Sir Harry (1847–1921) soldier and governor
Bedford, Sir Frederick George Denham (1838–1913) governor
(with H.J. Gibbney) Bennett, Mary Montgomerie (1881–1961) teacher and advocate of Aboriginal rights
Boyle, Ignatius George (1882–1960) publican and politician
Campion, Sir William Robert (1870–1951) governor

Volume 8 (1981)

Connolly, Sir James Daniel (1869–1962) politician
Crowder, Frederick Thomas (1856–1902) businessman and politician
(with Pat Simpson) Draper, Thomas Percy (1864–1946) politician and judge
Durack, Michael Patrick (1865–1950) pastoralist
Ellis, Henry Augustus (1861–1939) physician and politician
Emanuel, Isidore Samuel (1860–1954) pastoralist
Forrest, Alexander (1849–1901) explorer, politician and investor
(with B.K. De Garis) Fowler, James Mackinnon (1863–1940) politician

Volume 9 (1983)

Green, Albert Ernest (1869–1940) politician
Illingworth, Frederick (1844–1908) speculator and politician
Johnston, Edward Bertram (1880–1942) politician
Johnston, Harry Frederick (1853–1915) surveyor
Keenan, Sir Norbert Michael (1864–1954) lawyer and politician
Kingsmill, Sir Walter (1864–1935) politician

Volume 10 (1986)

Mitchell, Sir James (1866–1951) premier and governor
Moran, Charles John (1868–1936) politician and farmer
Morgans, Alfred Edward (1850–1933) mining investor and politician

Volume 11 (1988)

(with Wendy Birman) Parker, Hubert Stanley Wyborn (1883–1966) solicitor and politician

(with Wendy Birman) Parker, Sir Stephen Henry (1846–1927) politician and chief
    justice
Rason, Sir Cornthwaite Hector (1858–1927) premier
Scholl, Horatio William (1852–1927) grazier and politician
Scholl, Richard Adolphus (1847–1919) public servant
Scholl, Robert Frederick (1848–1909) pearler and investor
(with Jenny Mills) Smith, Henry Teesdale (1858–1921) timber-miller and contractor

Volume 12 (1990)

Steere, Sir James George Lee (1830–1903) politician
Strange, Benjamin Edward (Ben) (1868–1930) cartoonist
Venn, Henry Whittall (1844–1908) pastoralist and politician
(with Wendy Birman) Wittenoom, Sir Edward Charles (Horne) (1854–1936)
    pastoralist, politician and company director
(with Wendy Birman) Wittenoom, Frederick Francis (Frank) (1855–1939)
    pastoralist, mine and business manager

Volume 13 (1993)

Boyer, Sir Richard James Fildes (1891–1961) grazier, publicist and broadcasting
    chief
Burke, Thomas Patrick (Tom) (1910–1973) politician
Button, Percy Archibald (1892–1954) acrobat and itinerant
Collins, Harold Henry (1887–1962) farmer and politician
Courtney, Victor Desmond (1894–1970) journalist
Davidson, David Lomas, (1893–1952) town planner

Volume 14 (1996)

Durack, Kimberley Michael (Kim) (1917–1968) agricultural scientist
Evatt, Herbert Vere (Bert) (1894–1965) politician and judge
Hughes, Thomas John (1892–1980) politician
(with Alex Cohen) Hunt, Bruce Atlee (1899–1964) medical practitioner
Johnson, Herbert Victor (1889–1962) trade unionist and politician

Volume 15 (2000)

(with Tresna Shorter) McDonald, Sir Robert Ross (1888–1964) lawyer and politician
Moseley, Henry Doyle (1884–1956) magistrate

Volume 16 (2002)

Pilpel, Joshua (1891–1978) master printer
Pollak, Hans (1885–1976) philologist
Prescott, Sir Stanley Lewis (1910–1978) university vice-chancellor
Tomlinson, Ernest William (1871–1947) engineer
Uren, Malcolm John Leggoe (1900–1973) journalist

Supplementary volume (2005)

(with Geraldine Byrne) Grave, James (1848–1906) investor
Cameron, Robert George (1886–1960) educationist
Hughes, Thomas (Tom) (1866–1944) outlaw
Marshall, Thomas Henry (Harry) (1862–1909) publican and politician
(with R.J.S. Barrett-Lennard) McClemans, William Joseph (1874–1960) clergyman and educationist

Volume 17 (2007)

(with Andrew Morant) Baker, Harry Frederick (1904–1986) speedway motorcycle rider and aviator
Birman, John (1913–1989) adult educationist
Blythe, Lindsay Gordon (1908–1986) pastoralist and businessman

Volume 18 (2012)

Robinson, Ellis Alfred ('Alan' or 'Allan') (1927–1983) underwater explorer
(with Geraldine Byrne) Ruston, Gertrude Winifred (1897–1985) community worker
(with Andrew Morant) Wigmore, Alice Ivy (1895–1982) violinist and philanthropist
(with Lynn M. Fisher) Wilson, Norma Linley (1898–1990) dancing entrepreneur
Wise, Frank Joseph Scott (1897–1986) agricultural adviser, premier and administrator

Dissertations

'A Survey of the Kimberley Pastoral Industry from 1885 to the Present', M.A thesis, University of Western Australia, 1953.
'The Parliamentary Background of the Irish Act of Union of 1800', D.Phil. thesis, University of Oxford, 1960.

Interviews, Radio and Television Presentations

'Worm's Eye View: A User among the Western Australian Archives', Talk to the Friends of the Battye Library, 1982, Sound Recording, State Library of Western Australia OH1093.
'Happy Families; Human Relationships in Australia 1900–1960', ABC, Adelaide, Study Guide for a Six Part Radio Series Produced and Presented by Gillian Berry, ABC Adelaide, 1986, State Library of Western Australia PR12921.
Interviewed by Neville Meaney, 11 September 1986, Sound Recording, National Library of Australia TRC 2053/6.
'Discovering Daphne Street', Talk to Oral History Association (WA) Conference, 1988, Sound Recording, State Library of Western Australia OH1254.

WORKS BY GEOFFREY BOLTON

Interviewed by Stuart Reid for the Battye Library collection, 1994–95, Sound Recording, State Library of Western Australia OH2618.
Interviewed by Chris Cunneen, 1998, Sound Recording, National Library of Australia TRC 3754.
Cover to Cover: Interviews Discussing Book Covers with Authors, Interviewed by Stuart Reid, 1998, Sound Recording, State Library of Western Australia OH2858.
Interviewed by Bill Bunbury for ABC Hindsight, 29 April 2001, CD.
Interviewed by Nikki Henningham for the Academy of the Social Sciences in Australia, 2006, Sound Recording: National Library of Australia TRC 5722. http://catalogue.nla.gov.au/Record/3797567.
'The Secular State', 2011, Sound Recording, ABC National.
(with Geoffrey Blainey & Geraldine Doogue) 'Is Australia Going West?' 2012, ABC Television.
'Who Are You? Geoffrey Bolton', 720 ABC radio interview, 18 September 2012, www.abc.net.au/local/audio/2012/09/18/3592467.htm.
Interviewed by Rob Linn for the Australian Academy of the Humanities, 2015, Sound Recording, National Library of Australia TRC 6540/6.

Papers

Papers of Geoffrey Bolton, circa 1950–2002, are held in the National Library of Australia in four accessions.
MS Acc05/53 comprises subject files, including files on Bolton's publications (5 boxes).
Acc05/139 consists of papers relating to Bolton's academic career and research (5 boxes).
Acc06/118 comprises files of correspondence, notes, research material, drafts of writings, cuttings and other printed material (4 boxes).
Acc07/6 includes research material and drafts for Bolton's biography of Edmund Barton.
Also included are research notes for other projects, correspondence, and the work of students and other authors (11 boxes). National Library of Australia.
Further papers, 1939–1995, are held by the State Library of Western Australia.
MN 3010, ACC 2378A, 8585A, 8670A, 8671A comprise research papers relating to *A Fine Country to Starve In*, Dutch and other shipwrecks, and *Alexander Forrest: His Life and Times*.